An Introduction to the Life and Works of Richard Wagner

Chappell White
Emory University

Prentice-Hall, Inc., Englewood Cliffs, New Jersey

This book is dedicated to the memory of my brother,
Goodrich C. White, Jr. (1918-1944)

Current printing (last digit):
10 9 8 7 6 5 4 3 2 1
C

Library of Congress Catalog Card Number: 67-12591
Printed in the United States of America

Prentice-Hall International, Inc., London
Prentice-Hall of Australia, Pty. Ltd., Sydney
Prentice-Hall of Canada, Ltd., Toronto
Prentice-Hall of India (Private) Ltd., New Delhi
Prentice-Hall of Japan, Inc., Tokyo

Preface

Richard Wagner's life, his personality, and his works have called forth an astonishing flood of words. Controversy was the element in which he lived, and controversy continued around his accomplishments after his death. No musician has ever been so worshipped and so reviled.

This book makes no pretense at removing Wagner from controversy, but it does assume that the battles of the "Wagnerites" and the "anti-Wagnerites" have faded into the past. There remain works of extraordinary, lasting power and a life of significance to our cultural history; both demand our continued attention.

Despite the deserved popularity of Wagner's music in the symphonic repertory, his works are dramas. I have approached them as such and have included interpretation of his ocasionally obscure dramatic meaning.

An introduction, after all, is only a beginning. I have tried to suggest something of the special nature of each of the ten great operas and to indicate specific points that will help the reader. The experienced student of Wagner, however, may find that his favorite work is given less space than another, that the motives he considers most important are not quoted, that his own approach to these varied works is not emphasized. My hope is that the reader will be encouraged by what he finds here to seek out his own approach and to find those ideas that are for him most significant. This he can accomplish only by the musical experience of the works themselves.

For the convenience of those who are not acquainted with the stories of the operas, brief summaries are included. These should not be considered to be complete prose versions of the texts.

Unless otherwise noted, the translations from Wagner's essays are by Ashton Ellis (*The Prose Works of Richard Wagner* [London: Kegan, Paul, Trench, Trübner and Co., Ltd., 1892-99]). Those from *Mein Leben* are based on the "authorized translation" (London: Constable and Co., 1911), but in most cases I have made some changes in the wording. Since there was no need to consider declamation in the present context, I have made my own rather literal translations of the excerpts from the opera poems.

The genesis of this book was in the undergraduate classroom. To the students who have unwittingly furnished the inspiration for the work, I give my thanks. For valuable suggestions and sympathetic interest, I am grateful to Robert Mann, Associate Conductor of the Atlanta Symphony; to my father, Dr. Goodrich C. White; and to Prof. Gregor Sebba of the Institute of Liberal Arts at Emory University. My thanks also go to the Research Committee of Emory University for a grant in support of this work. The editors and staff of Prentice-Hall, Inc. have been courteous beyond the call of duty. Above all, my gratitude goes to my wife, whose contributions to this book are much more than she knows.

Chappell White

Contents

A Note About Money

Wagner's money transactions were reported in a variety of coinage. While it would be futile to try to translate each in exact terms of modern equivalents, this summary may be of some help.

The thaler equals between three and four francs. Two thalers equal three gulden. A little more than five thalers equal a louis d'or. One thaler equals three marks.

A gulden and a florin are the same thing. Eight gulden equal one louis d'or.

Very roughly, the reader may think in the following scale relative to the dollar. These values are not, of course, in terms of today's buying power.

1 thaler	about	$ .75
1 franc	"	.20
1 gulden (florin)	"	.50
1 mark	"	.25
1 louis d'or	"	4.00

1

Early Years, 1813-1833

The family into which Richard Wilhelm Wagner was born on May 22, 1813 was respectable, undistinguished, and not especially artistic. Karl Friedrich Wagner, the father, held a modest position as a Police Actuary in Leipzig, but he was a man of some education and literary taste. His greatest interest in life was the theater. He lived close to it, attended regularly, and was, in Richard's later phrase, "not altogether free from a gallant interest in actresses."

Through his passion for the theater, Karl Friedrich became a close friend of Ludwig Geyer, a young actor of unusually versatile artistic ability. Geyer was a member of a dramatic company that played in Leipzig and Dresden, and he was in addition both a portrait painter and a playwright.

In October, 1813, Karl Friedrich fell victim to typhus and died exactly six months after Richard's birth. His widow, Johanna, was left in desperate financial straits. Richard was the ninth child, the seventh surviving, and none was old enough to contribute to the family income. As a friend of the family, Geyer was a frequent visitor in the stricken home. On August 28, 1814, he and Johanna Wagner were married and settled in Dresden. Less than six months later (February 26, 1815) a daughter, Cäcilie, was born.

There is a distinct possibility that Geyer was also Richard Wagner's natural father. Without question, Wagner himself thought so in later years, and it is tempting to see in Geyer's talents a foreshadowing of Wagner's versatile genius. Exhaustive investigation has furnished no conclusive proof, however, and the truth will probably never be known.[1] The matter was once thought to have

---

[1] For a full discussion of the questions in Wagner's ancestry, see Ernest Newman, *The Life of Richard Wagner*, 4 vols. (New York: Alfred A. Knopf, Inc., 1933-1947), II, 608-619.

peculiar irony as well as psychological interest in that the anti-Semitic Wagner might have been the son of a Jew. But it has now been proven that Geyer's forebears were thoroughly German for at least five generations and that some were in fact Protestant church musicians.

On his mother's side also Richard Wagner's ancestry is in doubt. Evidence is strong that Johanna, ostensibly the daughter of a baker in Weissenfels, was the natural child of Prince Constantin of Weimar. "An exalted fatherly friend" (to use Wagner's phrase) placed her in an exclusive girls' school in Leipzig, but her education and her literary tastes were evidently limited. She was a vital, eccentric little person and Richard was devoted to her. Her influence on him intellectually, however, was probably small.

Richard was a small, energetic child with intensely blue eyes and blond hair. From earliest childhood he was abnormally sensitive and imaginative. He had frequent nightmares, in which he was beset by ghosts that were very real to his boyish fancy. When left alone he would often stare at the furniture in a room until it seemed to come to life, and he would scream in terror.

The theater was naturally a constant force in the Geyer household, and Richard was attracted to it at an early age. The scenery and costumes sometimes frightened him, but he was fascinated by every aspect. Neither Geyer nor Johanna was anxious to have the children enter the theatrical profession. The girls were finally allowed to study acting, but Geyer, who was apparently a devoted and responsible father, wanted something else for Richard.

At age six Richard was sent to the nearby village of Possendorf, where the local pastor maintained a small school. A little more than a year later, in September, 1821, Geyer was taken seriously ill, and Richard was brought home. Johanna, hoping to ease her husband's mind, asked Richard to show what he could play on the piano. When he had finished two small pieces, Geyer turned to his wife and asked, "Is it possible he has a musical talent?"

As dawn was breaking the next day, Johanna came into the nursery in tears, and waking each child she told them their father was dead. To Richard she gave a last message: "He hoped to make something of you."

After Geyer's death, Johanna was hard-pressed but scarcely destitute. The oldest son, Albert, was already supporting himself as an actor and singer in Breslau. Rosalie, nineteen, was a member of the Royal Court Theater in Dresden. Luise, sixteen, also went on the stage, joining Albert at Breslau. Julius had been apprenticed to

Geyer's brother, a goldsmith in Eisleben. Klara was fourteen and already studying to be a singer. Ottilie was ten, Richard, eight, and Cäcilie, six. After a year at a private school in the small town of Eisleben, Richard returned to Dresden and entered the Kreuzschule in December, 1822. He was not a good student, and he refused to work on subjects that did not interest him. Even when his curiosity was aroused, as it was by Greek drama, he grew impatient with the normal routine of learning.

In 1826 his family moved to Prague, where Rosalie had a good position in the theater, and Richard was left, rather casually it seems, with the family of a friend in Dresden. By the end of the following summer, Johanna Wagner had moved her family to Leipzig. Discontented in Dresden, Richard left school, and in December made his way home, where he was enrolled in St. Nicholas School. But the school authorities offended his young vanity by placing him in the third form instead of the second, and he worked even less than before.

In Leipzig, Richard fell under the beneficial influence of his Uncle Adolph. Adolph Wagner was the most distinguished member of the family, a respected scholar whose culture was broad and genuine. He was happy to open his library to Richard, to talk with him, and to read Greek drama to him.

Richard was now at work on a project he had started in Dresden, a drama called *Leubald und Adelaïde*, in which violence and bloodshed mingled with the supernatural in a manner he fancied reminiscent of Shakespeare. His sister Ottilie was his only confidante, and she was terrified by the gruesome story. But she found, as did many others in later years, that it was not easy to stop Richard Wagner from reading his own works. Sensing an inevitable family crisis over his school work, Richard planned to present his "masterpiece" to Uncle Adolph, who was to transmit to the family the good news that Richard's vocation had been found. Thus would the shock of his failure at school be eased.

The plan was ingenious and, in an immature fashion, characteristically Wagnerian. It failed because neither Adolph nor Richard's immediate family thought the news indicated by *Leubald und Adelaïde* was good. It merely confirmed the suspicion that he was wasting his time and again aroused his mother's fears that he might choose a career in the theater. But the fifteen-year-old boy took his scolding calmly, for he had made a startling discovery: his drama could be properly judged only when he set it to music.

Richard Wagner had very little musical training as a small child, but his contact with the theater brought important musical impressions. Carl Maria von Weber, who had come to Dresden in 1817 to found the new German Opera, visited the Wagner home occasionally, and his epoch-making *Freischütz* had created a sensation in Dresden in 1822, a year after its premiere in Berlin. Richard was fascinated by the mysterious elements in the opera, and he admired Weber personally, contrasting him with another visitor, an Italian castrato singer, whose corpulence and high voice horrified him. On this basis did the impressionable child prefer German opera to Italian.

When Richard was about twelve, his mother had reluctantly engaged a piano teacher for him, but the lessons did not continue very long. Richard felt that he had attained his goal as soon as he could struggle through the *Freischütz* overture.

Once he had decided to set his drama to music, however, he realized that he needed some knowledge of composition. He borrowed a book on thorough-bass, and without the knowledge of his family began to take lessons from a musician named Müller. The scholarly, pedantic approach helped him little, but in other ways his musical horizons were widening. Through the concerts of the Leipzig Gewandhaus Orchestra he began his acquaintance with the instrumental works of Mozart and Beethoven, who were quickly enthroned in his mind beside Weber.

He was now composing constantly. A piano sonata, a string quartet, and music for a pastoral play flowed from his facile but inexperienced pen. Much of this work was done while his family was away during the summer of 1829. When the family returned, they discovered that Richard had not attended school for six months. A council was held and a trade agreed upon: if Richard would go back to school, he could study music. To the suggestion that he go to Weimar and study piano with Hummel, Richard objected strenuously; he wanted to be a composer, not a performer. In the end the situation remained about the same. He went back to school but avoided his lessons assiduously, and the music teacher selected was the same Müller from whom he had learned little a short time before.

As he continued his education in his own way, Richard's childish curiosity about the theater developed into passionate interest. His sister Rosalie was now a member of the Leipzig company, so he was able to get into all performances including operas. Marschner's romantic German *Vampyr* impressed him deeply, and when the

Dresden company visited Leipzig, he began to enjoy Italian opera.

But his great experience, one of the turning points of his life, came when he saw Wilhelmine Schröder-Devrient in Beethoven's *Fidelio*. "If I look back on my life as a whole, I can find no event that produced so profound an impression upon me," he wrote years later. Richard rushed home and wrote the soprano a note, telling her that his life had now acquired its true significance and that she would be responsible for the great things he would accomplish in the world of art. What had impressed young Wagner about Schröder-Devrient was the quality of her acting. She revealed to him, with a suddenness that shook him to the depths of his spirit, the dramatic potential of opera.

One of Richard's methods of study was to copy works that appealed to him. In this manner he became acquainted with Beethoven's Ninth Symphony, and at once it became for him "the mystical goal of all my strange thoughts and desires about music." The inspiration lasted until he heard it performed by the Gewandhaus Orchestra on April 14, 1830; the result resembled so little the sounds he had heard in his imagination that he was thoroughly confused.

The Gewandhaus Orchestra, although not yet in its great days under Mendelssohn, was regarded as one of Germany's finest. Why should its performance of Beethoven disappoint a sensitive listener? The answer lies in the musical situation in Germany. From the vantage point of the twentieth century, Beethoven appears as the heir of an already long and distinguished German tradition. Bach and Handel, Haydn and Mozart, Beethoven and Schubert—these are, in our view, the greatest composers of their eras, and their eminence seems to assure the Germany of 1830 a position of unquestioned leadership. Such was not the view of Wagner's contemporaries. Wide interest in Bach was just beginning, and the general recognition of his transcendent powers was still at least a generation away. Haydn and Mozart were viewed (with some justification) as partially Italianate composers. And Beethoven, while widely regarded as a man of genius, was thought to have been at least half mad by the end of his life. Even the works of his "middle period" were often misunderstood or neglected, while his late works were in many cases unknown or considered incomprehensible.

There was a strong element of provincialism in much of Germany's musical life. Although Weber's *Freischütz* had created a wave of excitement, French and Italian taste still dominated German opera houses. On his first trip to Vienna in 1832, Wagner was disappointed that he gained no new insight into Beethoven or even Haydn or Mozart; Hérold's *Zampa* was sweeping the city.

Performance standards in Germany were extremely low. Concerts were for the most part second-class adjuncts of the opera house. The conductor usually did not even possess a full score of the work being played, and Pohlenz, who conducted at Leipzig in 1830, took his place at the desk only for the fourth movement of the Ninth Symphony—he directed only vocal works. It is by no means a coincidence that Wagner's first clear view of both Beethoven's symphonies and his late quartets came from performances in Paris, where a higher economic standard supported higher technical competence. The peace that followed the collapse of Napoleon's empire had re-established the reactionary rule of German princes; wretched pay for musicians and limited musical taste were imposed in Germany from above.

The inadequate Ninth Symphony performance that young Wagner heard was no doubt typical, and it reflected limitations of understanding and practice that were widely characteristic. After brooding for a while, Wagner allowed himself to become absorbed in other matters.

In early February, 1831, Wagner succeeded, after months of effort, in entering the University of Leipzig. He had no interest in studying, but student life seemed free, romantic, and dissipated to him. Enthusiastically he plunged into typical student excesses. He joined a club, hastily practiced swordsmanship, and was quickly challenged to three duels. Fortunately none of his opponents was able to meet him. One was killed in another duel, a second badly hurt, and a third more ingloriously injured while drunk in a brothel.

Richard was almost as reckless at the gambling table as he was in dueling. He lost all his own money and began to gamble with his mother's pension. When he had staked the last thaler, his luck finally turned. He emerged with considerable profit, had the satisfaction of an emotional confession to his mother, and found himself cured of the gambling fever.

In the fall of 1830, Richard had presented an overture in B-flat to Heinrich Dorn, a young music director of the Leipzig Theater, and in December Dorn performed it. A repeated and apparently irrelevant crash on the kettle drum soon began to amuse the audience, but amusement turned to astonishment as the overture ceased without warning. Wagner had scorned a conventional ending.

He was disappointed but not discouraged by the effect of his work, and he continued to compose a little throughout his experiments in "student life." As he turned back to serious musical thought, however, he realized that he needed help. Fortunately, he found the right man in Theodor Weinlig, cantor of the Church of St. Thomas—the position J. S. Bach had occupied a century earlier.

Weinlig was a contrapuntist of some reputation, and a gentle, persuasive man whom Richard admired. He set his pupil to work first at harmony and counterpoint and then at fugue; finally he allowed him to manipulate themes in sonata style. For the first time Wagner began to understand the reasons for "rules." He worked under Weinlig for six months. Then the old man abruptly dismissed him and refused a fee for his work. "Probably you will never write fugues or canons," he told Wagner; "but what you have achieved is independence. You can now stand alone."

Weinlig's instruction immediately bore fruit in composition. Wagner's opus 1, a piano sonata, and opus 2, a polonaise for four hands, were issued by Breitkopf and Härtel in the spring of 1832. Three of his overtures were performed in the course of the Leipzig season.

During the summer, despite a pleasant trip to Vienna and an unhappy infatuation for an aristocratic girl named Jenny Pachta, Richard still found time for work. He wrote a song cycle to verses of his friend, Theodor Apel. It is unfortunate that the work is lost, as he later spoke more favorably of this than of most of his youthful efforts. He also sketched the libretto of an opera called *Die Hochzeit (The Wedding)*, a gruesome, fantastic tale showing the influence of the German romantic, E. T. A. Hoffman. He composed the first four numbers of *Die Hochzeit* and won Weinlig's approval for the clarity of the style. When his sister Rosalie disapproved of the drama, however, he unhesitatingly destroyed it.

By the end of 1832, Wagner had completed a symphony in C, his most ambitious effort to date, and it was performed by the Gewandhaus Orchestra on January 10, 1833. The work is energetic, imitative, and a little crude, but it was favorably received. Wagner was especially gratified by the approval of Heinrich Laube, the influential editor of the *Zeitung für die elegante Welt*. But when Laube offered an opera libretto, Wagner refused it.

He thought Laube's libretto too conventional. When he inquired as to the meaning—what Wagner called the "real action" of the story—Laube expressed surprise that he should look for anything beyond an exciting tale rich in incident. Even at this early stage in his development, Wagner found it impossible to consider "setting a text" in the usual meaning of the phrase; music and words were to grow from the same creative force. Already he was at work on another libretto of his own.

2

The Provincial Conductor, 1833-1839

Immediately after the performance of his symphony in the spring of 1833, Wagner accepted a temporary position training the chorus in the theater at Würzburg, where his brother Albert was manager. Since he was not quite twenty and had had virtually no experience in the operation of a musical theater, it is scarcely surprising that Wagner felt a rare attack of diffidence. However, his vigorous interest quickly dispelled any feeling of inadequacy, and he soon felt so sure of himself that he tried to reform the time-honored convention of allowing the singer a free cadenza at the end of an aria, brashly driving his point home by singing the aria "correctly" himself.

Apparently Wagner was not re-engaged, but remained in Würzburg until January of the following year, not only to continue work on his opera *Die Feen* (*The Fairies*), but also because he was enjoying himself. This was his first acquaintance with the free atmosphere of a provincial theatrical company, and he found relief from work in two rather callow love affairs. He began to suspect that he had unusual power with women.

Having finished *Die Feen* by January 6, 1834, he returned to Leipzig with the hope that Rosalie, always his most understanding supporter in the family circle, could be of help to him through her position in the Leipzig theater. But Wagner found himself confronted by his first experience with the evasive tactics of theater management. He met it with more tact than he usually showed later in life, and he was still persisting courteously when circumstances took him away from Leipzig. Without the presence of the composer, the opera was soon forgotten. Wagner himself, moreover, was undergoing important changes that caused him to lose interest in *Die Feen*. In early summer he began sketches for his next opera, *Das Liebesverbot* (*The Ban on Love*), which was based on Shakespeare's *Measure for Measure* and called for a different musical style. Aside from excerpts given in Würzburg and a few performances of the overture, *Die Feen* was not presented in his lifetime.

Although it contains little or nothing to foreshadow the powerful works that eventually followed, *Die Feen* is skilfully written for a young man of twenty, and there are features of significance for the student of Wagner's development. The libretto, based on one of Gozzi's fables, contains the intimate blend of the supernatural with real life that is an essential feature of German Romantic opera. Fairy stories were popular in the simple late-eighteenth-century *singspiel*, but the relationship between the natural and the supernatural established by Weber in *Der Freischütz* (1821) created a new world of fantasy in opera. The whole mood and atmosphere of German Romantic opera were dependent on this integration of fantastic elements into the everyday world. Such was Wagner's starting point, and it may well be regarded as the prelude to his search for universal meaning in legend and his later skill in creating a specific mood for each opera.

The music of *Die Feen* conveys little more than the impressions made by Weber and Marschner, while the text provides for the conventional recitatives, arias, and ensembles; yet it is not difficult to understand from this early work the sympathetic interest of a number of good musicians, for there is a facility that proceeds only from genuine talent. Wagner was in no sense a child prodigy, but his first works are the creations of a mind born to musical expression.

By mid-summer, 1834 a significant change had taken place in Wagner's frame of mind. He was filled with a zest for living that called for action and experience rather than speculation. He had been reading the literature of the "Young German" movement, and Laube had influenced him toward the philosophy of "frank sensualism" that was sweeping the youth of Wagner's generation.

Shortly after his return to Leipzig, he had heard Schröder-Devrient in one of Bellini's operas, *I Montecchi ed i Capuletti*, and in her performance he saw for the first time the dramatic possibilities in the melodic Italian style. The learned German style seemed in comparison cold and pedantic. Despite his discovery of strength in the long Italian tradition and his dissatisfaction with conditions in Germany, Wagner never ceased to be aware of the weaknesses in the Italian conventions. The ideal, he decided, would be a blending of the two styles, a German composer writing Italian melody.

While Wagner was on an uninhibited pleasure trip through Bo-

hemia with his wealthy friend, Theodor Apel, an offer came to him
to join the theatrical company of Magdeburg as musical director.
He went immediately to look the situation over, and found that
the management was artistically slack and financially insecure. But
now a chance encounter changed the course of his life: he met
Minna Planer. Wagner was immediately so smitten that he notified
the director of his acceptance and agreed to conduct *Don Giovanni*
the following Sunday.

Christine Wilhelmine Planer was a leading actress of the Magdeburg company. More than three years older than Wagner, she came
from a respectable lower-middle-class family that had fallen on hard
times when she was a child. When she was not quite seventeen, she
was seduced and gave birth to a daughter, who was called Natalie.
The affair was kept strictly secret, and Natalie was reared as Minna's
sister. Wagner knew the truth early in his relationship with Minna,
but kept the secret scrupulously.[1]

Minna's professional stage career was modestly successful, but
she had none of Wagner's passion for the theater. She was coolly
practical toward the entire theatrical world, and this attitude extended also to her relationships with men. Her conduct was reserved
and discreet, but she allowed familiarities and flirtations—"conde-
scensions," Wagner later called them—which she deemed necessary
to her continued success as an actress.

She had, in short, arranged her life in a well-controlled pattern.
She managed her affairs in a businesslike, resourceful way; she regarded the world serenely but without a trace of idealism. Her
attitude could scarcely have been in stronger contrast to that of the
passionate, idealistic, sometimes irresponsible, young Wagner.

Wagner's musical facility and his personal magnetism soon won
him the support of the singers and orchestra, and he made some
progress in the quality of the productions. Despite a busy schedule,
he found time to work on *Das Liebesverbot* and to compose both a
successful New Year's cantata and an overture to his friend Apel's
drama *Columbus*. The high point of the musical season came with
guest appearances in April, 1835 by Schröder-Devrient. Collaboration with the artist whom he revered above all others was highly
inspiring to Wagner, and she was so impressed by his work that
she agreed to return to Magdeburg to take part in his benefit concert.

---

[1] Except, of course, in his autobiography, *Mein Leben,* which was to be made
public only after the death of those involved.

Wagner had been living beyond his means, and now his optimism soared. He planned a gala evening and raised the price of tickets. Unfortunately, the wary Magdeburgers refused to believe that the great Schröder-Devrient would appear for the benefit of their unknown young conductor, and they stayed away in large numbers. By the end of the concert, even the few who attended were gone. As the final number, Wagner had programmed Beethoven's "Wellington's Victory," complete with cannon and muskets, and the sound in the small hotel salon was so overwhelming that the audience fled in panic, led by the faithful but frightened Schröder-Devrient.

An accounting the next morning showed that the concert had left Wagner even further in debt, and only with the greatest difficulty did he put off his many creditors. In early May, the opera season over, he left for Leipzig, accompanied only by the inevitable dog, a brown poodle which he considered extraordinarily intelligent.

Wagner's relations with Minna, meanwhile, had progressed to the point of an open, serious love affair. When Minna's caution cooled their initial friendship, he played with unerring intuition on her sympathy: he adopted the role of a heart-broken young man deliberately choosing the path to dissolute ruin. After friendly relations were again established, Wagner broke through the wall of her discretion by the simple expedient of arriving at her room one evening drunk and rowdy. When Minna saw that his condition was such that he could not go home without creating a disturbance, she "gave up her bed to me without hesitation . . . . We breakfasted quietly and decorously together . . . , and from then on, as acknowledged lovers, we freely and without timidity pursued our tender interests."

In large part because of Minna, Wagner accepted re-engagement at Magdeburg, and he rashly advanced from his own pocket (which meant from his own borrowings) the funds for a journey to recruit singers. The results were an improvement in the Magdeburg company and a worsening of Wagner's already critical financial state. Despite these worries, he worked hard and happily. Affairs in the opera house went well, and the composition of *Das Liebesverbot* proceeded rapidly. Professional problems soon arose for Minna, however, and she began to fear for her own security. Early on the morning of November 4th, without a word to Wagner, she departed by coach for Berlin. Wagner was distraught, and he allowed his frustration to overcome his judgment. Although he had not considered marriage, he now formally proposed, and he bombarded Minna with a series of passionate, sad letters. With overpowering fluency, for page after page and day after day, he poured out his reproaches and his misery.

Poor Minna never had a chance. Her practical mind must have known that it was time to break with this impetuous young man whose future was so uncertain. Faced with the full force of Wagner's personality, she was overwhelmed. In scarcely more than two weeks she left a promising career in Berlin and returned to Magdeburg.

As a result of his recruiting trip in the late summer, Wagner had been promised a benefit performance, and he determined to present *Das Liebesverbot*. By the time he had completed the opera in March of 1835, however, the Magdeburg company was bankrupt, and it was only because of their respect for Wagner that the singers consented to remain at all. At the first performance the audience was completely ignorant of what was going on. The director had failed to have the libretto printed, and the singers, with little chance of being paid, had not bothered to learn their parts.

For the second performance, only a handful of people appeared. Just before the curtain was to go up, the husband of the leading soprano attacked one of the tenors, of whom he had reason to be jealous. The lady tried to intervene, and the affair ended with the tenor nursing a bloody nose in the dressing room, the soprano in hysterics, and the rest of the company taking sides in a general uproar. The performance was canceled.

For a few weeks, Wagner kept up his spirits. He wrote an article for Schumann's *Neue Zeitung für Musik* and hopefully sent his C-Major Symphony to Mendelssohn in Leipzig, but appeals to his friends and family for financial help were in vain, and he finally became immersed in gloomy thoughts. Only Minna was a comfort to him. As always in their early years together, she meant the most to Wagner when his practical affairs were at their worst.

Early in May Minna departed for the Prussian city of Königsberg, where she had a contract with the theater. There was some chance for Richard in the same city, and Minna hoped to pave the way. Leaving his creditors still unsatisfied, Wagner went soon after to Berlin, in the hope of arranging a performance of *Das Liebesverbot*. Prospects seemed good, and once more his spirits rose. But he found that the road between a promise and a performance in the theater is long and hazardous, and he was finally forced to admit that no one had any intention of producing his work.

He had one fruitful experience in Berlin, however: he heard a performance of Spontini's *Fernand Cortez*. Although Wagner had reservations about some aspects, he was tremendously impressed by the precise organization of the whole production. "I gained," he wrote, "a fresh insight into the peculiar dignity of big theatrical representations."

His failure in Berlin and the vision gained from *Fernand Cortez* spelled the end of Wagner's real interest in *Das Liebesverbot,* although he did try to secure a performance in Paris later. It was, of all his early works, the one from which he felt most decisively separated in later years, because it reflected a frivolity that he regarded as an aberration of his youth. Both the musical style and story are Italianate, with perhaps some influence of French comedy. *Das Liebesverbot* thus acts in Wagner's development as a foil to the thoroughly German *Feen;* it is less the aberration that Wagner thought it than it is a rounding out of his early experience.

Wagner proceeded to Königsberg in July. He found Minna already well established but his own situation far from satisfactory. The temporary conductor, who was on leave from Riga, was loath to return to his regular post because he preferred the company of Königsberg's leading lady to that of his wife. The director Hübsch, anxious not to lose Minna, put Wagner on a small retaining fee and finally, in September, promised him the conductorship not later than Easter. As an added inducement, he offered a benefit performance for Wagner's marriage to Minna.

On November 24, 1836, Richard Wagner and Minna Planer were married in the small Tragsheim church in Königsberg. Wagner later testified that he was in the grip of a strong conflict. There can be no doubt that he was deeply in love with Minna, but already part of his mind knew with remorseless clarity that the marriage could bring only suffering to both of them. Minna admired his talent, but she was incapable of understanding his dreams. He realized early in their relationship that he could not discuss his work with Minna, and part of him knew that in the end this would be fatal to their union. His impetuosity and his inability to do without anything he wanted had driven him to persuade Minna against her better judgment. The bonds between them were now too strong to be easily broken.

Wagner noted sadly that there were no friends at the wedding. His mind wandered through most of the service, but when the minister spoke of a friend to whom they could turn in time of need, Wagner, always sensitive to possible financial aid, looked up hopefully. He was disappointed when he found that the name of the unknown patron was Jesus.

Wagner's months in Königsberg were unhappy and artistically fruitless. The day after his wedding he had to appear in court to answer creditors from Magdeburg, who were put off temporarily by a legal maneuver. The temporary conductor intrigued against him and made his relations in the theater difficult. In April Wagner at last became conductor, but scarcely a month later the theater went into bankruptcy.

Worst of all, things were not going well at home. Apparently Richard and Minna had always had quarrels, generally stemming from Richard's jealousy. After their marriage Minna continued to receive such masculine attentions as she thought necessary to her position, and Wagner's jealousy increased. Domestic strain, added to financial worries that she had always avoided for herself, soon began to change Minna's equable personality, and the quarrels became bitter on both sides. Finally Minna could stand it no longer. On May 31, without a word of warning, she fled.

At first Wagner tried to follow, but his funds were insufficient, and he returned in complete misery. There was now nothing to keep him in Königsberg; he somehow found the money to go to Dresden, where he stayed with his sister Ottilie and her husband, the noted philologist Hermann Brockhaus.

For a short while, he seems to have contemplated divorce. Then he found Minna, who was with her parents in Dresden, and her obviously disturbed condition filled him with remorse. He began to talk of new prospects for their life together, and she was finally persuaded to live with him. In a few weeks, however, she fled again, and this time Wagner did not try to follow. A wealthy man by the name of Dietrich, who had already aroused Wagner's jealousy in Königsberg, had journeyed to Dresden at the very time of Minna's disappearance. To Wagner the circumstances seemed all too clear.

It is wholly characteristic of the man that, in this time of deepest suffering, Wagner began to develop new interests that marked the end of a creatively barren year and the beginning of his return to the ideals he had partially abandoned three years before. He found comfort and creative stimulus in the company of Ottilie and her kindly, learned husband. He went to the Dresden opera and heard the works of Halévy and Spontini, and he began to sketch an opera based on Bulwer Lytton's historical novel *Rienzi*. Years later Wagner recognized the importance of this brief period of renewal. "Though obliged for the present to return to the limitations of a small theater," he wrote, "I tried from this time onwards to aim at enlarging my sphere of action."

In early September Wagner made the long journey to Riga, where he had been engaged as conductor. Finding the company without a leading soprano, he persuaded the director to hire Minna's sister, Amalie Planer, and he soon learned from her that Minna had returned home to her parents in pitiable condition. By now, however, Wagner knew that Minna had been living with Dietrich, and he refused to take any interest in her plight. Then Minna herself wrote to him, confessing her infidelity and describing the physical and moral state to which her conduct had brought her. She assured him that never before had she been so fully aware of her love.

Wagner was deeply moved. In later years poor Minna suffered grievously from Wagner's absorption in his own point of view, but on rare occasions he could see himself and others with objective clarity. He forgave Minna completely, took the blame on himself, and never mentioned the affair again. Thus in October of 1837 the Wagners set up their household again. They agreed that Minna should end her career, and she appeared on the stage only at the very end of their Riga residence, when money was vitally necessary for their flight.

The German theater in Riga was small, and the conditions under which Wagner worked were certainly no better than in Magdeburg or Königsberg. But Riga was important to Wagner for internal development rather than external events. It was here, he wrote later to his friend, Apel, that "it became ever clearer to me that I am not built to earn my bread in this way."[2] The change that had begun in the last unhappy days in Dresden now became manifest in a bold plan: he would finish *Rienzi*, and with it make an assault on Paris.

Wagner was by now thoroughly disillusioned with the prospects of accomplishing anything in the small theaters of Germany, and he knew that the surest entrance to the larger German theaters was a success in Paris. In Paris the quality of the productions would surely give greater scope for his imagination, and in Paris success would bring fortune and relief from intolerable financial conditions. To anyone except Wagner the plan would have looked foolhardy. In Paris one needed either a reputation or powerful friends; Wagner had neither. Only a man sublimely ignorant or sublimely confident in his destiny could have imagined that he would conquer Paris under such conditions.

[2] Quoted in Newman, *Life of Wagner*, I, 242.

It is a reflection of the importance of finances in Wagner's career that this bold, artistically-motivated plan was set in motion by money difficulties. Minna's retirement from the stage had reduced the Wagners to living on one small income. Debts once more began to pile up, and the town committee, foreseeing serious difficulties, informed Wagner in March, 1839 that his services would not be required after the summer. He was in effect given two months' salary and plenty of time in which to plan his escape.

To leave by ordinary means was out of the question, for Wagner's passport had already been impounded by his creditors. With the help of friends, he carefully plotted a secret dash across the heavily guarded Prussian border and arranged to board a small ship for London outside of Königsberg.

The journey turned out to be a mixture of high adventure, comedy, and sheer nightmare. Everything was complicated by the presence of a large Newfoundland dog with the English name of Robber, whose devotion was such that Wagner steadfastly refused to leave him behind. Their small ship, the *Thetis*, was buffeted by violent storms, and once took refuge in a Norwegian fiord, where Wagner absorbed impressions that later bore fruit in *The Flying Dutchman*. Minna and Richard were seasick much of the time, and Richard became convinced that they were regarded as "Jonahs" by the crew and feared that they would be thrown overboard.

When the little vessel finally limped up the Thames, however, Wagner was in highest spirits. His debts seldom worried him when he was out of reach of creditors, and he felt that he was entering a new phase of his career. A week of rest for Minna in London, and they crossed the channel to Boulogne, armed only with two acts of *Rienzi* and Richard's unquenchable hope.

Behind were five years of frustration and disillusionment in the confining atmosphere of the German provincial theater. In these years Wagner had become an excellent conductor and had learned the practical work of the theater well; otherwise, he had little to show for his experience. He had entered into an unwise marriage, and he had established a disastrous financial pattern that was to plague him through most of his life; but what he had learned as a creative artist was still buried in his imagination.

3

Paris, 1839-1842:
Rienzi and *The Flying Dutchman*

The man to whom Wagner was looking for help in Paris was his compatriot, Giacomo Meyerbeer, whose *Robert le Diable* (1831) and *Les Huguenots* (1836) had established him as the undisputed master of French grand opera. Wagner therefore lost no time when, on arriving in Boulogne, he found Meyerbeer vacationing nearby. Meyerbeer received him graciously and submitted to a reading of *Rienzi*, promising to look over the two completed acts at his leisure. Probably he was impressed with his young compatriot's work, although it has been suggested that he was merely following a lifelong policy of offending no one needlessly. For whatever reason, Meyerbeer treated Wagner with real kindness; he promised him a letter to Duponchel, director of the Paris Opera, and introduced Wagner to a few well-known musicians who were in the area. For the first time Wagner felt that he was gaining an entrance into the lofty world of celebrated artists.

In very little time after his arrival in Paris on September 17, the feeling was dispelled. Having established himself and Minna in a drab, furnished hotel room in the market quarter, Wagner hopefully began his campaign by calling on Duponchel. As he watched the director read Meyerbeer's letter without any sign of interest, he was suddenly aware that Duponchel must have seen many such letters before.

Still using Meyerbeer's help, Wagner persuaded Habeneck, conductor of the Opera and director of the Paris Conservatory Orchestra, to play his *Columbus* Overture in rehearsal. A public performance, however, was out of the question, and the *Columbus* Overture made little impression.

Like every other contact established in Paris, the one with Habeneck brought no public success, but it resulted in a positive influence on Wagner's state of mind. The Paris Conservatory Orchestra was one of Europe's finest, and Habeneck had made the concerts a showcase for the finest symphonic music, including the German repertory. Wagner was able to listen to repeated rehearsals of Beethoven's Ninth Symphony, and finally he heard it emerge as the profound, coherent expression he had first felt it to be.

All his doubts as to the direction of his artistic development had begun with the miserable Beethoven performance in Leipzig. The road back to certainty ended now where it had begun, with Beethoven's Ninth. Years later Wagner wrote: "The whole period of the deterioration of my taste . . . now sank down before me as if into an abyss of shame and remorse." The path before him was to be long, but from this time forward it was undeviating. Wagner never again suffered doubts as to his artistic mission.

The immediate result of his experience with the Ninth Symphony was the sketching, in January, 1840, of an overture to *Faust,* which he projected as the first movement of a symphony. When the Conservatory Orchestra refused to give the work a hearing, he laid it aside; but some fifteen years later, at Liszt's urging, he rewrote some parts. Although it does not compare favorably with the best of his later operatic overtures, the *Faust* Overture has a seriousness of purpose and a depth of poetic expression lacking in his earlier orchestral works and even in *Rienzi.*

As soon as he realized that Duponchel had no intention of doing anything for him at the Opera, Wagner began to cast about for other roads to success. Feeling that perhaps *Das Liebesverbot* would be suitable for French taste, he had a friend translate three arias, and Meyerbeer's agent arranged an audition at the Théâtre de la Renaissance, the third and least desirable of the lyric theaters in Paris. As usual, Wagner anticipated success, and in April, 1840, he and Minna moved to a larger and more expensive apartment. They were hardly settled, obligated to remain for a full year, when their first visitor arrived bringing news that the Théâtre de la Renaissance was bankrupt.

Wagner's position was now desperate. In the first six months in Paris he had seemingly exhausted every financial resource. The only person he had known when he arrived was Edward Avenarius, the fiancé of his sister Cäcilie. Avenarius had helped all he could, but his position was a modest one, and he finally had to let Wagner know that he could do no more. Wagner's old friend Heinrich Laube, now married to a wealthy widow, had arrived in Paris in

January. He also contributed to Wagner's support, as well as arranging for periodic small contributions from Wagner's sister Luise.

But there was never enough money, even for necessities, and Wagner was not one to get along on necessities. The last of the wedding presents, the remainder of Minna's theatrical wardrobe, finally even the wedding rings, went to the pawn shop, and then the pawn tickets were sold.

Another small source of income was found when Wagner began in the summer of 1840 to write occasional articles for the *Gazette Musicale*. In all, he contributed ten essays to the *Gazette*, and about a dozen more appeared in German journals. Most of the essays reflect his homesickness and his growing idealization of conditions in Germany. A few, especially "A Pilgrimage to Beethoven," contain important basic ideas which he elaborated at greater length later. Wagner always enjoyed expressing his opinions, but journalism at this time was only pot-boiling to him. Ironically, it brought him a small reputation that his musical efforts failed to achieve.

In October, 1840, Wagner's financial state became so critical that he was sent to prison for several weeks. Although this is one of the few events in his life about which we know little, it is evident that some creditor brought charges against him. In September he had written an urgent letter to his friend, Theodor Apel, the first communication between the two in more than four years. The unhappy Minna wrote again in November, and it was presumably Apel's second response that secured Wagner's release.

The fear of losing his freedom again was probably responsible for Wagner's ready acceptance of a wretched offer made him by Maurice Schlesinger, proprietor of the *Gazette Musicale*. For a fee of 1,100 francs, Wagner made no less than six different arrangements of an entire opera, Donizetti's *La Favorita*. This is an appalling amount of musical hack work, and it must have been a bitter blow to Wagner's pride as an artist.

He did, however, meet all of his troubles with determination, and his high spirits in the face of repeated disappointments amazed his friends. His closest companions in Paris were three Germans, whom he humorously referred to as his "board of advisors": Anders, a destitute aristocrat who held a minor post at the Bibliothèque Royale; Samuel Lehrs, a fine scholar who eked out a precarious living making translations of Greek classics; and Ernst Kietz, a painter who, according to Wagner, never finished a portrait. All three were poor, and all three were in one way or another failures. Devoted to both Richard and Minna, they possessed that indispensable attribute for lasting friendship with Wagner, a whole-hearted interest in his plans and progress. Since Minna spoke almost no French and Richard's French remained poor even after two years in Paris, the warm friendship of these cultured Germans, who knew from bitter experience what the Wagners were facing, did something at least to alleviate their loneliness.

Wagner kept up an intermittent correspondence with Kietz for the rest of his life. It was Lehrs, however, already in his final illness before Wagner left Paris, who significantly influenced his thought by stirring his interest in philosophy and introducing him to medieval poetry.

Minna probably meant more to Richard Wagner at this period than at any other time of his life. She gave him full, unstinting support without reproaching him for their plight. Even in later years when they had grown far apart, Richard never forgot the trials she had suffered for his sake in Paris.

At no time was Wagner taken into the inner circle of musical celebrities in Paris. He met Liszt twice, but the circumstances were not yet right for the friendship which later developed between these two giants of the Romantic age. Liszt had no time to take the measure of an insignificant German opera composer, and Wagner saw in Liszt only the sensational virtuoso.

Wagner felt a special desire to know Berlioz, having understood at once that he alone among Parisian composers had something to offer him. But Berlioz was absorbed in his own battles and could have given little help even had he understood the extent of Wagner's gifts. Berlioz's music, however, made a deep impression. Wagner recognized the daring imagination and was excited by the poetic expression, but something in the French master also puzzled and repelled him. This reaction was typical of the entire relationship between the two. In later years they watched each other's development, sometimes with admiration but always with a certain distrust born of strikingly different temperaments.

During the winter and summer of 1840, Wagner found time to work on *Rienzi*, completing it except for the overture by the middle of September. By then, he knew it had no chance in Paris, and after his release from prison he sent the score to the intendant of the Dresden Theater.

He did not give up all hope at the Paris Opera so quickly, however. He succeeded in arranging an audition of *Das Liebesverbot* before the director and the influential librettist, Scribe. Both men professed to be charmed by the music, but nothing at all was offered. Wagner knew he was being politely brushed aside, and he was a little ashamed of having presented himself as the composer of a work with which he was now entirely out of sympathy.

He then turned to a plan which was eventually to be of great significance. The legend of the "Flying Dutchman"—a sea-captain doomed to sail eternally without rest—had haunted his imagination for some time, and he conceived the idea of molding it into a one-act opera that could serve as a curtain-raiser to an evening of ballet. He presented the sketch to Pillet, new director of the Opera, and after considerable delay received word that Pillet wanted to buy it for another composer.[1]

Wagner was naturally outraged. He soon realized, however, that there was nothing to prevent him from going on with his own plans for *The Flying Dutchman,* so he swallowed his pride and accepted.

The rather generous fee of 500 francs arrived at a most opportune time. Richard and Minna had finally rid themselves of their expensive apartment and moved to the suburb of Meudon for the summer of 1841. Although Wagner had managed to finish the libretto of *The Flying Dutchman,* his work for Schlesinger had prevented composition since completing *Rienzi* the preceding fall. On receipt of the 500 francs in July, he immediately rented a piano and plunged into the composition so enthusiastically that the entire work (exclusive of the overture and orchestration) was finished in seven weeks.

In the meantime, good news came from Dresden: *Rienzi* had been accepted, and production was optimistically set for early fall. Despite Wagner's steady stream of letters to his Dresden friends, however, one postponement followed another, and he soon began to feel that the work might be permanently pushed aside unless he himself could go to Dresden. In the fall of 1841, therefore, Wagner began to make plans to leave Paris. He wrote a few more articles, but it was more important to him financially that he was again able to call on his family and friends for help. With the acceptance of *Rienzi* at Dresden, his career seemed worthy of their interest once more.

In March, 1842, the Berlin Opera accepted *The Flying Dutchman,* and Wagner felt fully justified in returning to Germany whatever

---

[1] Whether the offer was made by Pillet himself or by the librettist Foucher is not clear. A French version, called *Le Vaisseau fantôme,* was composed by Philippe Dietch.

the cost. On April 7, with Paris looking its bright spring best, the faithful "advisory board" escorted Minna and Richard to the coach. The ever-thoughtful Kietz pressed a last five-franc piece into Richard's hand, and the Wagners were off, their eyes filled with tears from the mixed emotions of sorrow at parting and joy at their deliverance from the most difficult months of their lives.

Wagner's attempt to conquer Paris had been doomed from the beginning, but it was not only lack of success that disillusioned him. He had sought more than fame and fortune. In Paris he had hoped to find freedom from the conditions that made his life miserable in the small theaters of Germany; instead he found the conditions intensified. There was wealth, brilliance, and technical competence; but these things hid a morass of intrigue and cynicism that was all the more repellent to him for being superficially covered by social graces. Idealism had no place in Europe's greatest opera house. Although circumstances were soon to throw him once more into an official theatrical position, he knew, deep in his essential artistic being, that his ideals could never be realized in the theater as it then existed. Paris laid the foundations of dissatisfaction on which Richard Wagner built the greatest of operatic reforms.

Paris also made Wagner a German. His disillusion with French and Italian opera and with the taste of the French public created in him the feeling that only in Germany could his artistic work be understood. During the last months in Paris, he had delved into German history and legend. Lonely, homesick, hating his surroundings, he began to sense a deep, almost mystical sympathy with the traditions of his fatherland.

The bitter lessons of Paris were of great importance to Wagner's development; it is no coincidence that the two works he completed there mark a turning point in his career. The differences between *Rienzi* and *The Flying Dutchman* are not merely a matter of competence; they reflect an essential difference in viewpoint. *Rienzi* is the end of his apprenticeship as a conventional opera composer seeking conventional success; *The Flying Dutchman* sets him squarely on the road to the *music drama*.[2]

---

[2] The term *music drama* is normally applied to Wagner's works after *Lohengrin*. While it is a convenient distinction, the broader term *opera* still rightfully includes the late works. Wagner himself did not entirely approve of *music drama*, but he never found a completely satisfactory substitute.

Rienzi

Despite its importance as Wagner's first successful opera, *Rienzi*'s place in the present-day repertory is limited to occasional European performances. The most admiring Wagnerian scholars are, indeed, likely to find it more unsatisfactory than the two earlier operas. Ernest Newman summarized this feeling:

> One can forgive the eager young-mannishness of these very youthful works: but one expects a composer to show more indubitable signs of originality at twenty-six or twenty-seven. The commonplace of *Rienzi* is different from that of the preceding operas: it is almost an offensive commonplace. . . . The obvious faults of the work are due not so much to technical inexperience or limitations of vocabulary as to a sheer failure of the imagination. . . .[3]

The somewhat baffled irritation reflected in these lines is caused, not by Wagner's failure, but by his success. In *Rienzi* he accomplished perhaps the most un-Wagnerian act of his life: he wrote an almost perfect example of a wholly conventional opera. The work is seldom presented because the conventions of French grand opera are, of all nineteenth-century operatic conventions, the most distasteful to our time.

The nature of *Rienzi* as a representative of French grand opera can be explained by the description of one scene, the finale of Act III.

The setting is Rome in the fourteenth century. Rienzi has led a successful revolt against the ruling patricians. He spares his opponents but is forced by their treachery to prepare for battle against them. In the scene preceding the finale of Act III, the young patrician Adriano has sung of his agony in being torn between family loyalty and his love for Rienzi's sister, Irene.

The finale opens with sounds of battle. Armed men, accompanied by brass instruments, march on stage, followed by a procession of priests and monks with banners, women and children, high clergy, more armed men, senators on horseback, and finally Rienzi himself, mounted and in full armor, with Irene at his side. The entire en-

---

[3] *Wagner as Man and Artist* (New York: Vintage Books, 1960; reprint of rev. ed., 1924; 1st ed., 1914), p. 311.

semble, accompanied by orchestra and the stage band, sing the "Hymn of War" while the soldiers beat their swords against their shields. Adriano tries to dissuade Rienzi from waging war against the nobles, but Rienzi is resolute. All of the men except Adriano march off, singing the second verse of the "Hymn of War." Adriano and Irene discuss the difficulties of their position, and then join the women and children in a prayer, sung against the background of battle noises, the sound of the wind, and an off-stage band. The entire procession of soldiers, priests, high clergy, and senators returns, climaxed by the entrance of the victorious Rienzi on horseback. To the accompaniment of muted trumpets and muffled drums, the bodies of the patrician leaders are brought in, and Adriano collapses on the corpse of his father, while more dead and wounded are carried across the stage. Adriano rouses himself to deliver a curse against Rienzi. Rienzi dismounts and enters a triumphal chariot brought in by the Messengers of Peace, while the entire crowd joins in a chorus of victory and more soldiers march by displaying the trophies of war . . . Curtain.

There are, of course, dramatic moments and chances for individual brilliance in this scene and elsewhere in the opera, but the emphasis is obviously on spectacular effects. The poignancy of Adriano's dilemma, the tragedy of civil war, the heroism of Rienzi —everything is lost in the incredible welter of costumes, processions, choruses, corpses, and bizarre stage properties. Wagner tried in later years to claim that the subject matter had guided him in the treatment of details, but he was much closer to the truth when he admitted that the conception of the subject was constantly ruled by the grand opera form.

The handling of the conventions, however, is skillful. The story is not overly complicated, and Rienzi himself is impressive, even if he never emerges as more than a figure. Certainly the libretto is dramatically more compact than Meyerbeer's influential *Robert le Diable* and its characters are intrinsically more interesting. There is a grain of truth in Hans von Bülow's ironic remark that *Rienzi* is Meyerbeer's best opera.

As the overture shows, a great deal of energy flows from the music of *Rienzi*, but much is tasteless and vulgar (the trombone countermelody, for example, in the final break-neck rush of the overture), and very little is strikingly original. The remarkable thing that *Rienzi* illustrates about Wagner is the unconscious intuition that prevented him from going too far too soon. However clearly his rational mind rebelled against operatic conventions, his creative mind used them for as long as was necessary to his development. Wagner started late in life for a composer; it is extremely fortunate that he took the time to master convention before beginning the process of change.

Specifically, *Rienzi* gave him experience in handling large scenes and a large orchestra. Wagner had written one German Romantic opera and one Italianate opera; being a grand opera of the French type, *Rienzi* completed his early experience as a composer in strikingly logical fashion.

Der Fliegende Holländer (*The Flying Dutchman*)

In *The Flying Dutchman* Wagner seized for the first time upon a story whose substance is contained in one basic idea, redemption through love. It is a theme to which he returned again and again, and his absorption in it is doubtless responsible for the intensity of the opera.

The story as Wagner tells it is simple:

A Dutch sea captain attempts to round the Cape of Good Hope, vowing to succeed if it takes eternity. Taken at his word by the devil, he is condemned to sail the seas forever, but an angel intervenes with the possibility of redemption. The Dutchman is allowed one day every seven years on land; if he can find a woman who will follow him to death, he will be released.

As the opera opens two ships take refuge in a cove on the coast of Norway, one commanded by Daland, the other by the Dutchman. Impressed by the Dutchman's wealth, Daland offers hospitality and promises the hand of his daughter Senta to the Dutchman.

Senta is waiting with the other maidens for the return of her father's ship. She reveals that she is strangely moved by the story of the Flying Dutchman's suffering and has a strong desire to save him. Erik, her lover, tries to persuade her to abandon her wild dreams. Daland and the Dutchman arrive together, and Senta agrees to marry the Dutchman.

Outside Daland's house, the ships lie at anchor. The Dutchman hears Erik accusing Senta of breaking a past promise to him. Assuming her incapable of fidelity, he puts out to sea. Senta calls that she is faithful till death and throws herself from the rocky cliff into the sea. At once the Dutchman's ship sinks beneath the waves, and Senta and the Dutchman are seen rising toward heaven.

The final form of the libretto is not quite so economical as a bare outline indicates. Wagner has added static scenes at three points: the song of the helmsman in Act I; the chorus of the spinning girls which opens Act II; and the prolonged chorus of the sailors and the maidens at the beginning of Act III. The first of these is dramatically plausible and serves as relief between the opening storm and the entrance of the Dutchman. The second is perhaps less well integrated into the drama, but it is effective as an introduction to Senta's all-important ballad, in which she reveals her desire for sacrifice. The choruses of Act III, however, are pure operatic padding, and they are no doubt the result of expanding the original one-act sketch into three acts.

Wagner was also mindful of operatic conventions in Erik's cavatina and in the repetitious finales of Act I and Act II. None of the conventionalities is very disturbing, however. The spinning song is deservedly popular, while the helmsman's song is truly an inspiration. The sailors in Act III behave more like juveniles on a picnic than seamen home from a long voyage, but opera audiences are notoriously tolerant as long as the music is pleasant.

The serious student, however, will find the essence of *The Flying Dutchman*—and with it the first unleashing of Wagner's powerful imagination—in three elements: the character of the Dutchman, the character of Senta, and the presence of the sea.

Although it is important to note Senta's central position in the plot, Wagner himself realized that the entire dramatic situation hinges on the Dutchman. Senta's motivation will seem weak unless his suffering and desperate longing are experienced. In the Dutchman's first monologue (*"Die Frist ist um"*), Wagner articulates these feelings strongly, and in doing so he places a heavy load on the dramatic ability of the singer.

The monologue is cast in the form of a recitative followed by an aria in three sections, but it is treated as one dramatic progression of feeling. There are passages more declamatory than melodic, and the technique is more flexible than that of the ordinary aria. The emotion moves from exhaustion through violent memories of his voyages and the hope of the angel's promise, to final, agonized despair. The music imparts an utter conviction which Wagner had never achieved before and which, indeed, he did not surpass until *Tristan*.

Senta's ballad was the first part of *The Flying Dutchman* Wagner composed, and its central position supports its dramatic importance. Musically, it contains the most important elements of the work—

the motives associated with the Dutchman (Ex. 1), the sea (Ex. 2), and Senta's redeeming sacrifice (Ex. 3).

Example 1

Example 2

Example 3

All three motives are used throughout the opera (the listener hears them first in the overture). Wagner and others had used recurring motives before, but the importance of these three mark an important step toward the elaborate leitmotive technique of the later music dramas. Perhaps more significant for the future than the simple association of musical motives with elements of the drama, however, is the manner in which the motives are occasionally transformed. Two examples of the "redemption" motive will suffice. At the end of the ballad, when Senta gives way to her sudden inspirational vision, the motive reflects her excitement and resolution (Ex. 4). In another form it takes its place in the ecstatic close of the duet occurring at the first meeting of Senta and the Dutchman (Ex. 5).

In such simple transformations lies the germ of an important factor in the flexible relationship Wagner later achieved between music and drama.

Neither the Dutchman nor Senta is drawn as a well-rounded personality in the realistic sense. Each is concentrated in a single feeling, the Dutchman in tortured longing, Senta in the desire for complete self-sacrifice. Even romantic love between them has no place.

As the personification of emotions that are universal in scope and heroic in intensity, they are made convincing by Wagner's music.

Example 4

Example 5

Finally, there is the sea. It is not, as has been claimed, in every page of the score, but it is certainly in the best pages; and it is much more than a mere backdrop to the action. Pictorial music is at its best when it has musical and emotional significance. The sea in *The Flying Dutchman* gives the work its individual stylistic unity and its peculiar emotional mood. The listener is never far removed from the Dutchman's curse and the awful act of sacrifice it demands for redemption.

Wagner was critical of *The Flying Dutchman* in later years. He was dissatisfied with the poetry, with the continuity of the scenes, and with the square, four-bar construction of the musical phrases. But he never lost interest in the work as he did in his three earlier operas. He re-orchestrated some parts, eliminating bombastic effects, and he added a masterful touch at the end by allowing Senta's "redemption motive" to have the last word. (He also changed the end of the overture in the same way.) He still intended, late in life, to re-cast the work in one-act form.

Despite faults more obvious to him than anyone else, Wagner recognized the significance of *The Flying Dutchman*: his musical imagination had finally been freed by a dramatic idea. That this was primarily a development of Wagner, the musician, is one of the paradoxes in this most complex of artists; the more the musician deferred to the poet, the more the music molded the poetic form.

4

Dresden, 1842-1849:
Tannhäuser and *Lohengrin*

In 1842, Dresden, the capital of Saxony, was a city of about 70,000. Despite the presence of the King and his court, it was a quiet city, and it ranked second to Leipzig as the commercial and cultural center of the country.

The history of Italian opera in Dresden went back well into the eighteenth century. In 1817 a German Opera had been founded under the leadership of Carl Maria von Weber, and the city was still revered by his admirers as an early center of German Romantic opera. In 1832 the German Opera had absorbed the older institution, but the Italian repertory maintained its strength in the combined organization.

As in most German opera houses of the time, the affairs of the Dresden Opera were directed by a political appointee of noble rank, whose qualifications were neither musical nor artistic. Baron von Lüttichau had assumed the duties of General Intendant in 1824 after ill health forced him to give up his position as the King's forester. He was an efficient, responsible administrator, with no more limitations than might have been expected of one of his background.

The musical direction of the Opera was in the hands of two conductors, each of whom had the title of Kapellmeister. Karl Gottlieb Reissiger, the younger of the two, was assigned the German works. A man in his middle forties, he was regarded as competent, but his reputation was neither wide nor distinguished.

The Dresden Orchestra was a good one for its day and its situation, but by modern standards discipline was quite slack. The concertmaster exercised at least equal authority with the conductors, who were expected to concern themselves with the singers. Although the pay was poor, the players had more security than was good for the musical standards. A policy of tenure made it impossible to force retirement, and Berlioz reported in 1843 that he found one of the Dresden bass players so feeble he could scarcely support his instrument.

Excepting the presence in its company of two internationally famous singers, the soprano Schröder-Devrient and the tenor Joseph Tichatschek, the Dresden Opera probably differed only in detail from other German opera houses of similar status.[1] The management was content to amuse its public with reasonable efficiency and let Berlin and Paris set the fashion. Complacency reigned quietly throughout the organization.

This was the situation into which Richard Wagner came on April 12, 1842. Despite his elation over his escape from Paris, an ominous feeling descended on him as he crossed the German frontier. Faced with the realities of Dresden, much of his idealistic picture of his homeland faded.

There was little time for brooding, however. Wagner found cheap lodgings and, leaving Minna to rest, set out at once for Leipzig to visit his relatives. Doubtless the visit was in the nature of the return of the prodigal son; the wild youth who had caused his family such uneasiness was apparently on the verge of success. But in one way he was still the prodigal: he needed money, and his patient family provided a small amount that was supposed to last until the production of *Rienzi*.

After a brief and futile trip to Berlin on behalf of *The Flying Dutchman*, Wagner went to work to push the production of *Rienzi*. Letters written at the time report to his friends that both Lüttichau and Reissiger received him warmly, but he probably told the truth years later when he said that they were frankly amazed to see him. Wagner had not been invited, and both men must have seen at once that this aggressive young composer might become a nuisance.

Wagner soon found it impossible to accomplish much, because the two leading singers were away. On June 9, he and Minna went to Töplitz for a vacation, where they were joined by his mother; but Wagner was in no mood to rest, and he sought relief from the frustrations of the moment in creation. Leaving the two ladies together, he set out on a hiking tour in the mountains. There, in the solitude

[1] Newman describes its position as "a high place in the second [rank]." *Life of Wagner*, I, 358.

of scenery that always inspired him, he made a detailed prose sketch of what was to become his next opera, *Tannhäuser.*

On July 18, he was back in Dresden, and finally in early August rehearsals for *Rienzi* began. As was his invariable custom, Wagner threw himself into the work with energy that was almost irresistible. Wilhelm Fischer, choral director, and Ferdinand Heine, an old friend of Geyer's who was in charge of costumes, were his ardent supporters from the beginning; and Reissiger, although hardly an asset, caused no trouble.

But it was the tenor Tichatschek whose enthusiasm infected the whole company. He was delighted with his role, and he took almost as much pleasure in the costumes as in the music. His genial nature and his admiration for Wagner led to a cordial relation between the two, but Wagner soon found that working with him was a waste of time. Vocally, Tichatschek was ideal, as fine a tenor as Wagner ever found; dramatically, he was incapable of understanding anything beyond the ordinary operatic conventions of the day.

Schröder-Devrient caused difficulty of a different kind. Her temperament, always unpredictable, was not improved by her dissatisfaction with the role of Adriano, which was not the feminine lead. Although she far surpassed Tichatschek in dramatic talent, she lacked his musical facility, and once during a rehearsal she threw the score at the composer's feet and stormed from the stage. But Wagner admired her too deeply to be seriously affected by such incidents. He professed to be shocked by her language, but he handled her with tact.

The first performance of *Rienzi* took place on October 20, 1842, and its success was immediate. The Dresden Opera had never presented a new work of such importance before, nor had it ever had such a popular hit with the public. Even the Leipzigers came to see *Rienzi,* and Wagner became the man of the hour. He was flooded with social invitations, but perhaps more significant of his triumph was the envy he felt turned on him by other artists.

The Dresden management was now anxious to follow *Rienzi* with an immediate production of *The Flying Dutchman,* and Wagner wasted no time in peremptorily demanding the return of the score from Berlin, where the management was still hesitating. There was no part in the *Dutchman* for Tichatschek, but Wagner was happy that he could pacify Schröder-Devrient with the leading role of Senta. Mutal admiration had created a close relation between them. She had fallen into the habit of confiding in him about her complex love affairs, and she loaned him one thousand thalers, most of which went to pay old debts. Twice she took him on concert trips with her, the second to Berlin, where Wagner again met Liszt and received a much more favorable impression than in Paris.

After *The Flying Dutchman* went into rehearsal, however, Wagner realized that he had relied too heavily on Schröder-Devrient alone. At the first performance on January 2, 1843, Wächter demonstrated his complete inability to realize Wagner's conception of the Dutchman, and the first act became, as Wagner put it, "nothing but a dull conversation between Herr Wächter and Herr Risse" (as Daland). The audience was distinctly disappointed. Expecting the brilliance and pomp of *Rienzi* to be repeated, they found the *Dutchman* gloomy and boring. After four performances before diminishing audiences, the departure of Schröder-Devrient on an extended leave-of-absence gave the management a welcome excuse to drop the opera from the repertory. It was not presented in Dresden again until 1865.

The comparative failure of *The Flying Dutchman* was by no means fatal to Wagner's prestige, but it set him to thinking deeply about the nature of his success. He was too clear-sighted in the practical affairs of the theater to place the whole blame on Wächter's failure in a key role. *Rienzi*, he knew, had been Tichatschek's triumph as much as his own, and the public had cheered most vociferously those parts which Wagner felt were least worthy. "I thus had my doubts," he wrote, "as to the intrinsic divergence between my inner aims and my outward success."

In less than a month following the premiere of *Rienzi*, the Dresden Opera lost by death its senior Kapellmeister and one of its two assistant Music Directors. At first Wagner was considered for the lesser position, but he let it be known that it did not interest him. As the success of *Rienzi* continued, news came to him that the King might consider appointing him Kapellmeister. The difference between the two posts was substantial. As a royal appointee, the Kapellmeister had tenure for life, and the social prestige was difficult for a young man to resist. Still Wagner hesitated, fearful of entering once more the routine of the theater. But finally, under pressure from his friends and his wife, he gave in. On February 2, 1843, Wagner became Royal Kapellmeister at an annual salary of 1500 thalers.

The change in his situation had been nothing short of sensational. Two of his operas had been presented in less than three months; his name was now known in operatic circles all over Germany; he had received a coveted appointment in a substantial opera house. In the eyes of his wife, his relatives, and his friends, he had achieved at the age of thirty a position that assured him life-long security and continued success. But Wagner himself knew better. In accepting the post of Kapellmeister he had not satisfied his doubts; he had merely stifled his vague forebodings in order to follow the only practical course at the moment.

One result of his sudden rise to fame was the appearance of old creditors, and the 1000 thalers generously loaned him by Schröder-Devrient in January did not meet the demands. As usual, Wagner complicated matters by living in a manner that would have put a strain on his income in any event. He was partially justified, perhaps, in feeling that his position demanded a certain style, but Wagner was already incapable of denying himself the luxuries of life if there were means of securing them short of compromising his art. Physical comfort and even sensuous self-indulgence became an increasing necessity to him. It was a characteristic that caused him untold difficulty and exposed him on numerous occasions to bitter criticism.

Wagner, as well as his friends and family, had expected that his success would result in immediate income from productions of his works in other cities, but their hopes proved too optimistic. *Rienzi* was considered expensive to produce, and many managers felt that it would fail without Tichatschek. *The Flying Dutchman* was somewhat easier, but its relative failure in Dresden did not commend it to other theaters.

The opposition of the press also contributed to the slow spread of Wagner's works. Both of the leading critics in Dresden were men of limited talents and narrow vision. Unfortunately, under the prevailing system in Germany, they also served as correspondents for newspapers in other cities, and they thus achieved the dubious distinction of filling the first rank in the phalanx of critical opposition that attacked Wagner throughout his life.

Potentially the most important of the few performances that took place outside Dresden in the two years after Wagner's appointment was the Berlin production of *The Flying Dutchman* in January, 1844. Wagner himself conducted, and the public responded satisfactorily if not entirely enthusiastically. The critics were, however, unanimous in their condemnation, and the opera quickly disappeared from the Berlin repertory. Wagner began to feel keenly the disparity between the friendly response of the public and the hostility of the professionals.

Before accepting his post as Kapellmeister, Wagner had made it clear that he expected to make some changes. He had, in fact, already laid the foundations in his own work for the conception of conducting which was finally to dominate the musical world. To apply it fully in 1843, however, meant inevitable conflict with those who were comfortable in the old way of doing things.

The first battle came with the orchestra. Wagner had celebrated his appointment by conducting a successful performance of Gluck's *Armide,* which was new to the Dresden repertory. With the familiar operas, however, his conception clashed with that of the orchestra, and even his friends were disappointed in the results. Finally matters came to an open quarrel, probably brought about by Wagner's attempt to bypass the usual system of promotions through seniority, and a meeting was held on May 1, 1843, in which both parties aired their grievances before Lüttichau. Wagner evidently lost his temper, as he usually did in an argument, for the next day he apologized to Lüttichau. Without withdrawing his criticisms, he promised to move more gradually toward his goals.

During his first two years in Dresden, Wagner was actively involved in the musical life of the city outside the theater. He became conductor of the Dresden *Liedertafel,* an amateur choral society of men, and wrote for them a chorus with orchestra called "The Love-Feast of the Apostles"—not one of his finer efforts. Another chorus for male voices occupied him briefly when he furnished a "Festival Song" for the dedication of a memorial to Friedrich August I, and in the summer of 1844 he organized and vigorously directed a musical tribute to King Friedrich August II.

The public occasion which meant most to Wagner personally in his early Dresden years was the return of Carl Maria von Weber's body from London in December, 1844. Wagner played a leading role in making the arrangements, which faced opposition from both the King and Lüttichau. He arranged a funeral march from Weber's themes, delivered the funeral oration, and composed a chorus to his own text. Wagner was deeply gratified by his part in the tribute to one of his musical heroes.

The productions of *Rienzi* and *The Flying Dutchman* kept Wagner away from his creative work for several months, but by May, 1843 he had managed to complete the poem of *Tannhäuser.* Thereafter the composition of the music proceeded steadily, despite his official duties and the extent of his other activities, and by the middle of April, 1845 the score was complete.

Tannhäuser

Although *The Flying Dutchman* is justifiably considered Wagner's first opera on a legendary subject, *Tannhäuser* is the first fruit of his studies in German legend and mythology. The story is a combination of two separate legends, that of Tannhäuser and Venus and that of the Song Contest at Wartburg. Wagner found both in Grimm's *Deutsche Sagen*, but for both he had older sources as well as more modern literary treatments.

Essentially what he did was to integrate the Song Contest itself into the Venusberg story, combining the characters of the two heroes, Tannhäuser and Heinrich von Ofterdingen. The most fundamental changes are the granting of salvation to Tannhäuser and the creation of Elisabeth as the instrument of his salvation.

> *Act I:* The knight Tannhäuser is living in the mountain of Venus. Longing for the simple joys of the human world, he asks Venus for his release, but she tries to dissuade him. At last he invokes the aid of the Virgin Mary. Venus at once disappears, and Tannhäuser finds himself in the valley before the Wartburg. A procession of pilgrims crosses the valley, and Tannhäuser drops to his knees in prayer. Here he is discovered by a hunting party made up of his old friends. Wolfram reminds him of Elisabeth, who still loves him, and persuades him to rejoin them at the court of Landgrave Hermann of Thuringia.
>
> *Act II:* In the Hall of Song in the Wartburg, Tannhäuser and Elisabeth greet each other, both deeply moved by the meeting. There is to be a song contest, in which Elisabeth's uncle, the Landgrave, has given her the privilege of awarding the prize. The theme of the contest is the nature of love. When the nobles have gathered, Wolfram and other minstrels praise the purity of love, but Tannhäuser disputes them. Finally losing control of himself, he sings the praises of Venus. The knights advance on Tannhäuser with drawn swords, but Elisabeth protects him, pleading that he be given a chance to seek his salvation. Tannhäuser agrees to join the pilgrims seeking the absolution in Rome.
>
> *Act III:* It is autumn in the valley before the Wartburg. Elisabeth is praying as she awaits Tannhäuser's return. As Wolfram watches from afar, the song of pilgrims is heard, but Tann-

> häuser is not among them. Elisabeth now prays to the Virgin Mary to take her life that she might intercede for Tannhäuser's redemption. After she departs, Tannhäuser appears. The Pope has declared that the dead staff in his hand will put forth leaves before Tannhäuser can be absolved. In despair Tannhäuser has determined to seek Venus again. As Wolfram tries to dissuade him, the figure of Venus appears, beckoning and calling. For the second time, Wolfram says the name of Elisabeth. Tannhäuser repeats the name, and Venus disappears, as a torch-lit procession comes from the Wartburg bearing the body of Elisabeth. Tannhäuser sinks down on her bier and dies. More pilgrims enter, bearing the blooming staff that is the sign of Tannhäuser's salvation.

Obviously the story is not so compact as that of the *Dutchman,* and it contains more conventional grand opera scenes; the libretto, in a word, is closer to *Rienzi.* But the fundamental dramatic situation in *Tannhäuser,* the conflict between the sensuous and the spiritual, was one that had a deep appeal for Wagner, and his resolution of it embodies the basic theme of the *Dutchman:* redemption by a love that is completely self-sacrificing.

In *Tannhäuser,* however, the issue is clouded by conventional religion. It is not Tannhäuser's penitence, nor his pilgrimage to Rome, nor even his initial faith in the Virgin Mary which saves him; it is the love and death of Elisabeth. The repeated emphasis on the pilgrims is dramatically unnecessary, and Wagner's attitude toward them in relation to his hero remains a puzzle.

The ambiguity of the place of orthodox religion might not have been a serious factor had Wagner found the musical means for clarifying it emotionally; there are examples of ambiguous and cloudy meanings in Wagner's later works where just such a clarification takes place. But here there is a definite weakening of the drama as a whole. The pilgrims, one suspects, may be an excuse for a popular operatic convention, the religious procession. The emphasis on orthodox religion, moreover, is one factor in the failure of Elisabeth's characterization to convince us of the final redemption. In effect, Wagner divided the spiritual forces between the pilgrims, representing formal Christianity, and Elisabeth. He did not see that in so doing he was risking a distinct advantage for the goddess Venus.

Nevertheless, it must be emphasized that if Tannhäuser's final redemption fails to be convincing, it is a musical failure. The dangers of the libretto might have been overcome had not the sensuous pleasures of Venus inspired Wagner to create the most memorable music in the opera. To Wagner, the Goddess of Love exercised a power of fundamental significance; he did not portray Tannhäuser's passion as sentimental nor as a conventional, ugly evil. Venus is not a temptation to be resisted, but an area of life that must be renounced, and the renunciation can be fully understood only if that area has been experienced. Wagner's music convinces us that Tannhäuser knows more about life and love than do Wolfram and his chivalrous companions.

Significantly, the Venusberg motives (Ex. 6a and 6b) embody

Example 6a

Example 6b

the strongest use of the chromaticism that is the most striking expressive advance of *Tannhäuser* musical style. It is the Venusberg —not the Court of Landgrave Hermann, nor the religion of the pilgrims, nor even the sacrifice of Elisabeth—that has touched the depths of Wagner's originality.

Although Wagner gave more attention to Elisabeth as a personality than to Venus, few listeners find in her the single-minded intensity of Senta. Her first appearance, with the aria, *"Dich, teure Halle,"* is brilliant and effective enough, but it reflects only joyous excitement, and gives no hint of spirituality or the whole-hearted obsession necessary for the sacrifice that lies ahead. Her quiet prayer in the last act is attractive in itself but surprisingly sensuous, and in the final scene, as the pilgrims' voices swell, Wagner makes no attempt to shift the musical attention to Elisabeth's sacrifice. His interest, despite himself, was more on the side of Venus, and it has been rightly pointed out that in its most impressive moments the music for the pilgrims and for Elisabeth tends perilously close to the Venusberg style (Ex. 7, associated with the pilgrims).

Example 7

Andante maestoso

There are other flaws as well in *Tannhäuser*. Much of Wolfram's music is commonplace, and his famous cavatina to the evening star seems a gratuitous, sentimental interruption. The most disturbing feature, however, aside from the final dramatic failure, is Wagner's inability to resist repetitious, conventional climaxes in the first two acts and to a lesser extent in the duet between Tannhäuser and Elisabeth. The two finales have been greatly admired, and they are without question impressively written, but they stop the action when every dramatic force demands that it move on. The effect is to bring us painfully back into the world of operatic convention.

It would be a mistake, however, to regard all of the obvious conventionalities in *Tannhäuser* as flaws. If, as some critics have found, the famous march and the songs of the pilgrims bring disturbing memories of *Rienzi*, the earlier work is in every instance triumphantly surpassed.

Although arias, recitatives, and ensembles are still recognizable, they are joined together in a nearly continuous flow. Even in the song contest, Wagner took care to avoid a stereotyped series of arias. Recitative has become something like declamatory song, and one of Wagner's most difficult tasks in preparing the performance was persuading the singers to abandon the free, rhythmic recitation of the old style.

Nowhere is Wagner's increased skill seen more clearly than in his mastery of dramatic transition. The most intense example is found at the change of scene in Act I, when the Venusberg disappears in a crashing orchestral climax and gives way to the peaceful valley before the Wartburg, with the lone shepherd piping his simple tune. Others less violent but no less impressive occur when Wolfram twice effects a change in Tannhäuser by speaking the name of Elisabeth.

The most important advance in Wagner's control of dramatic and musical continuity is found in the increased use of recurring motives and themes. Generally the themes that recur are fully developed melodies, such as the pilgrims' chorus, Elisabeth's plea for Tannhäuser, and various melodies from the Venusberg music. The initial association is clear, and the return, directly suggested by the text, is usually outstanding; but in a few instances the quotation is short, and the meaning, subtler. An excellent example occurs in the song contest. Tannhäuser's hymn to Venus (Ex. 8), heard three times in

Example 8

the first act, climaxes his reckless excitement, but other fragments of the Venusberg music precede it. Hardly have the lords and ladies expressed their approval of Wolfram's song than the orchestra gives us a hint of Tannhäuser's reaction with Ex. 6a. After Walther's response the motive is stated more decisively, as Tannhäuser's reaction becomes stronger.

Recurring motives are used most flexibly and effectively in Act III. The prelude contains a complex of motives in short alternating periods, a structure that contrasts with the large sections of the overture, but the most advanced motivic treatment is in Tannhäuser's narrative, in which he tells Wolfram of his pilgrimage. Here the musical continuity is preserved almost entirely in the expressive motives of the orchestra, leaving the voice free to declaim in a song-like style that is somewhere between recitative and fully developed melody (Ex. 9). The procession of motives in the orchestra reminds us of Tannhäuser's agonized penance, contrasts his misery with the joy of the other pilgrims, and finally leads naturally and gradually into the essentially symphonic texture of the Venusberg music that accompanies his despairing decision to return to Venus. The narrative is hardly designed to bring joy to the heart of an ambitious tenor, but it is dramatically one of the most effective points of the opera; and it is, in a sense, a small preview of Wagner's later technique.

If the conflict of the drama is to be meaningful, it must be reflected in the personality of Tannhäuser. Wagner knew this, and the detailed instructions for performance which he wrote in 1852 give emphasis to the importance of the role. Tannhäuser, Wagner wrote, never feels nor does anything by halves; the passion that leads to his outburst at the song contest must be matched by the intensity of his remorse. The contrasts in emotion, plus the difficulty of the music, make Tannhäuser one of the most demanding roles Wagner ever wrote. Unfortunately for the effect of this brilliant, yet uneven, opera, tenors capable of meeting all demands convincingly are almost as rare today as in Wagner's time.

Example 9

Fifteen years after completing *Tannhäuser,* Wagner made extensive revisions in preparation for its presentation in Paris.[2] To some critics, it appears that he revised exactly that portion which was most successful, the Venusberg music. This was evidently still the part of the drama that interested him most, and, with *Tristan* completed, Wagner felt that he could at last deal adequately with Venus. The first scene, therefore, was greatly expanded. A long ballet, the famous bacchanale, precedes the conversation between Tannhäuser and Venus, and the latter's role is enlarged.

There is no question that Wagner intensified the music; the Venusberg music of the Paris version fairly blazes with a passionate sensuality that was beyond Wagner's powers—or anyone else's—in 1845. But critical opinion is divided concerning the value of the revision to the opera as a whole. Some feel that the Paris version is

[2] There were also a few changes made soon after the first performance. In the original, Venus did not appear in the last act, nor did Elisabeth's funeral procession. The early changes are included in the score of the Dresden version.

the authoritative one, Wagner's last word on *Tannhäuser*; others find that the expanded first scene overbalances the rest of the work, destroying the unity and accentuating the unevenness that is, in any event, the opera's worst flaw.

The Paris Venusberg music is well known in the concert hall as the *Overture and Bacchanale*. This arrangement, which Wagner made for a performance in Vienna in 1872, consists of a shortened version of the original overture dovetailed with the Paris ballet music.

The audience at the first performance of *Tannhäuser* on October 19, 1845 received it apathetically. The role of Elisabeth was sung by Wagner's niece Johanna, who had been engaged as soprano the previous year. The girl was talented and her voice was fresh, but she was only eighteen at the time and could not bring to the role the psychological insight that Wagner wanted.[3] Schröder-Devrient was as always successful dramatically, but she was no longer suited vocally to the role of Venus and her figure was decidedly matronly.

The greatest failure was Tichatschek. He was effective in the brilliant passages, but the expression of remorse was beyond his powers. Knowing that any effort to change him was futile, Wagner accepted the blame for the failure himself and cut several passages. In later years these cuts were a great annoyance to him, for other theaters accepted them as authorized by the composer.

At the second performance the audience was small, but it was so enthusiastic that the word spread, and the third and fourth nights were sold out. *Tannhäuser* had not triumphed as had *Rienzi*, but it achieved a solid success.

Although Wagner felt that the enthusiasm did not reflect an understanding of the drama, *Tannhäuser* attracted a number of intellectuals, some of whom did not patronize the opera house regularly. They sensed a new seriousness and a new power in Wagner's conception. *Tannhäuser* was a factor in solidifying the support of a small group fanatically dedicated to Wagner and his cause.

In the opera house, Fischer and Heine had been joined in their support of Wagner by August Röckel, a young man serving as the

---

[3] Johanna was the step-daughter of Wagner's brother, Albert. Wagner hoped to make her the first "Wagnerian" soprano, but she followed the road to quick success by singing all the popular roles. Wagner quarreled with her and her father about the matter.

music director who assisted Wagner. He possessed no extraordinary musical talent, but he was well educated and intelligent. From the beginning of rehearsals Röckel was absolutely convinced of *Tannhäuser's* coming success, and he helped after the first performance by anonymously answering adverse criticisms in the Dresden press.

One whose admiration was slower to develop but with whom the friendship became warmer was Theodor Uhlig, a violinist who had joined the Royal Orchestra in 1841 at the age of nineteen. Uhlig was not only an excellent musician but a man of culture and sensitivity, and he became Wagner's closest friend in Dresden.

In the audience at an early performance of *Tannhäuser* was a boy of fifteen who had already worshipped Wagner from afar for three years. His name was Hans von Bülow, and his life was destined to be inextricably bound to Wagner's. Brilliant, sensitive, frail in health, Bülow was already showing the qualities that were to be dominant in him as a man. When in 1846 he finally introduced himself to Wagner, there began that attachment to a stronger nature which seemed essential to his personality.

There were many others: Karl Ritter, a young friend of Bülow's whose mother, Frau Julie Ritter, later played a very practical role in Wagner's support; Alwine Frommann, a mature and cultured woman whose memories of *The Flying Dutchman* were so vivid that she traveled from Berlin to Dresden to see the premiere of *Tannhäuser*; and Anton Pusinelli, Minna's physician, whose friendship survived the ultimate test of being Wagner's creditor.

Among composers it is perhaps understandable that Wagner had few close friends or supporters. After Schumann gave up the editorship of the *Neue Zeitung für Musik* and moved to Dresden in 1846, the two men met frequently, but no real friendship developed. Despite his support of new causes, Schumann had an academic turn of mind that formed a gulf between him and Wagner. He never wrote a review of Wagner's work, but his reactions to *Tannhäuser,* expressed in letters to Mendelssohn, reveal much. At first, when he had only seen the score, he criticized Wagner as "one of those people who have not learned their harmony lessons, or learned how to write four-part chorales." After seeing the performance, he added, "I have to take back some of the things I wrote to you after reading the score: from the stage everything strikes one very differently. I was quite moved by many parts of it." [4] Schumann was as always sincere and fair, but he was clearly puzzled.

[4] Robert Schumann, *On Music and Musicians,* ed. by Konrad Wolff, trans. by Paul Rosenfeld (New York: Pantheon Books, 1946), p. 251.

Wagner continued to cultivate Meyerbeer, and the latter's behavior was always courteous. There was nothing whatsoever to justify Wagner's later antagonism and suspicion. Their relationship, however, was never more than politely cordial. Wagner had long since turned against Meyerbeer's music, even to the unpleasant extent of writing an anonymous article denouncing it. When his disapproval became personal and open in later years, Meyerbeer was understandably bitter.

The great exception among musicians was Liszt. When Liszt came to Dresden to see *Rienzi*, a true friendship began, and the foundations were laid for the great services Liszt was later to perform for Wagner. Wagner visited Liszt in Weimar in 1848, and it was Liszt who gave the first *Tannhäuser* performances outside Dresden. Liszt did not always escape the unpleasantness that Wagner inflicted on his friends by his egocentric desire to dominate, but the bond between them was one of mutual love and respect.

In the summer of 1845, between the completion of *Tannhäuser* and its first performance, Wagner had gone with Minna to Marienbad for an extended cure. Minna was probably already suffering from the chronic heart condition that became manifest a few years later, and his own health was far from satisfactory. Wagner possessed, in truth, a strong constitution, but his continually excited emotional state affected his day-to-day health and left him subject to minor disorders. He was seldom very sick yet he seldom felt really well, and his nervous energy constantly drove him beyond the capacity of his physical powers.

As reading material he took with him the poems of Wolfram von Eschenbach and the anonymous epic of Lohengrin, thinking that contemplation of this faraway world of idealism would relax him. But soon he was seized with a longing to write down his own version of the Lohengrin story, which had been more or less on his mind since Paris days. Deliberately he turned his thoughts to another subject, that of the Mastersingers and the shoemaker-poet Hans Sachs. Suddenly the outline of yet another opera took shape in his mind. Feeling that a pleasant comedy would not excite him, he wrote out a complete sketch. But *Meistersinger* was not yet ready, and *Lohengrin* was not to be so easily exorcised. One morning, while trying to relax for the prescribed hour in the waters, the urge to create became irresistible. Wagner leaped from the bath and hurried to his room to begin working out a detailed prose sketch for *Lohengrin*. At this point the doctors understandably informed Wagner that he was completely unfit for such a cure. He returned to Dresden after five weeks, his health perhaps no better, but carrying sketches for two more operas.[5]

Lohengrin continued to haunt Wagner throughout the rehearsals and first performances of *Tannhäuser*, and somehow he managed to find time to complete the poem in early November. A month later he made a futile trip to Berlin with the two-fold purpose of arranging a performance of *Tannhäuser* and interesting King Friedrich Wilhelm IV of Prussia in *Lohengrin*. He attained neither goal, and returned home resigned to writing *Lohengrin* for Dresden.

Wagner never really liked Berlin nor did he have a very high opinion of performances there, but it offered the only possible hope for improving his situation. *Tannhäuser* was receiving even less attention from other theaters than *Rienzi* and the *Dutchman*. Berlin would open the door to other performances, and Berlin would mean royalties. At Dresden Wagner was paid for the first performance; thereafter, only the management profited from his success.

His hopes rose, therefore, when he finally received word that *Rienzi* was scheduled in Berlin in early fall, 1847. Once again, despite the friendly public, an inadequate tenor and a hostile press spelled disaster. After eight performances *Rienzi* was withdrawn. The final bitter blow was delivered by Küstner, the director, who refused to pay an additional fee for Wagner's conducting. Wagner was welcome, he said, but he had not been invited.

Although Wagner had determined after his first conflict with the Dresden orchestra to leave reform for a later date, he was incapable of allowing any part of his artistic work to slip into conventional habits, and the years 1846 and 1847 are marked by his two most significant efforts as a conductor of works other than his own.

For the orchestra's pension fund concert on Palm Sunday, 1846, he overcame considerable opposition and presented Beethoven's Ninth Symphony. It was an unprecedented success. His careful preparations included the instruction of the audience as well as the performers, and he succeeded, perhaps for the first time in Germany, in making the Ninth Symphony accessible to the public.

The following winter he triumphed again with Gluck's *Iphigenia*

---

[5] The seed of *Parsifal* also took root in Wagner's fertile mind during this brief "vacation."

in Aulis, presented in a revised version that, in Wagner's opinion, eliminated clumsy conventionalities. The public had never before taken so much interest in Gluck, and the management was so delighted that Wagner's name was added to the program as "reviser."

Wagner knew, however, that he could not accomplish his reforms by such isolated successes. Even while involved in the preparations for the Ninth Symphony, he was working on a long report proposing the complete reorganization of the Royal Orchestra, which he sent to Lüttichau on March 1, 1846. Point by point Wagner analyzed the difficulties and proposed rational solutions. Many of the improvements, he argued, could be instituted at once without cost; and to cover the needed increase in salaries, he suggested a series of winter concerts that would also allow the public to hear the masterpieces of German instrumental music.

Wagner's *Report on the Royal Orchestra* is the work of one who knew the organization of the orchestra and the theater intimately and who viewed it from a thoroughly practical but still idealistic standpoint. Two things only were wrong with the *Report*: it was proposed by the junior Kapellmeister, and to put it into effect would shake the whole institution out of its complacency. After a year with no response at all, the *Report* was curtly rejected.

Although he tried once more, when political conditions seemed ripe for a change, to push sweeping reforms on the Dresden Theater, Wagner must have been aware that the rejection of his *Report on the Royal Orchestra* marked the end of his hopes. During the summer of 1846, he had taken a vacation in his beloved mountains of Bohemia, where he made a complete musical sketch of *Lohengrin*; and now he plunged almost desperately into the task of completing it, identifying himself more and more with his hero who lived in the world of men without becoming a part of it. By March, 1848, *Lohengrin* was complete.

Almost immediately Wagner began to consider his next great creative project. In the summer he wrote a long essay in which he tried, not too successfully, to clarify his thoughts about the Nibelungen myths. Then in the fall he began sketches for an opera, and in November finished the poem entitled *Siegfrieds Tod* (*Siegfried's Death*).

About Wagner's relations with Minna during the entire Dresden period we know very little that is specific, but there is no doubt they were drifting apart. Minna was three years older than Wagner.

She had none of his youthful resilience of spirit, and her health was already declining. In short, she was aging more rapidly than her husband in every way. More important, however, was Wagner's steady retreat into the ideal world of his imagination. Minna could never follow him there, and he knew it. His sense of loneliness was constant and often acute.

Even in the world of reality, there was ample ground for misunderstanding. Minna had looked on Wagner's court appointment as the beginning of peace and security. It was too much to ask that she accept without complaint or question continuing financial harassment.

While Wagner's artistic development was making it difficult for him to work in a conventional theater, his financial problems were growing to such magnitude that they made it almost impossible for him to live in a conventional society. His old debts were by no means cleared up when in 1844 he made an agreement with the court printer in Dresden, whereby Wagner himself would pay the cost of publishing his operas and the printer would receive ten per cent of the sales. *Rienzi, The Flying Dutchman,* and finally *Tannhäuser* were issued under the agreement. Wagner was forced to go to other friends and even to professional money lenders to raise the needed funds. It is hardly necessary to add that his estimate of the sales was far too optimistic.

By 1846 Wagner's financial plight was becoming desperate. In March he tried to defend himself from the rising criticism by writing his friend and creditor Dr. Pusinelli, deploring the idle and exaggerated talk about his private affairs. At Wagner's suggestion Pusinelli published the letter; a few days later Wagner asked him for a further loan of 500 thalers.

Wagner's enemies made the most of his misfortune through the press and through gossip, but it was Schröder-Devrient who delivered the decisive blow. Now nearing the end of her career, jealous of the beautiful young Johanna Wagner, she became suspicious of Wagner himself and instigated legal action for payment of the 1000 thalers she had loaned him three years earlier. Wagner had no choice but to ask the court for help.

Lüttichau was evidently anxious not to lose the services of his brilliant and troublesome young Kapellmeister, for he arranged a loan of 5000 thalers from the theater pension fund. Wagner was required to list his debts, but even now he did not dare let the court know the true extent of his trouble: he omitted from the report personal debts to his friends.

Early in 1848 Wagner petitioned the King for a raise of 500 thalers a year, the amount withheld from his salary for repayment of the debt. Although the request was refused, he was given an emergency payment. But this time the answer to his petition was accompanied by a stinging reprimand, which accused Wagner of vanity and ingratitude, and stated clearly that he must mend his ways or face dismissal.

Wagner made a few more efforts to find a way out of his most pressing problems, but all were doomed to failure. When he finally fled from Dresden, his total debts may have been as much as 20,000 thalers. While it would be an oversimplification to imply that Wagner became a revolutionary because of his debts, a man who owes more than ten times his annual salary is likely to be receptive to ideas of radical change.

In February, 1848, revolution broke out in Paris. Certain factions in the German states, already restive and eager for liberal reform, were quick to follow, and unsuccessful uprisings took place in both Berlin and Vienna. In Dresden, one of the leading advocates of reform—by revolution if need be—was Wagner's friend and assistant, August Röckel. The extent of his influence on Wagner is open to some question, for Wagner was certainly exposed to Röckel's ideas from other quarters. But the two men talked together frequently, and it is almost certain that Wagner was stimulated to see connections between his dreams of theatrical reform and Röckel's dreams of political reform.

In the spring of 1848, Wagner joined the *Vaterslandverein,* an organization devoted to the arming of the people as a National Guard. In May, at one of the meetings, he read a poem commending the uprising in Vienna and urging Saxons to draw their swords. The following month he read a paper in which he attempted to fit his idealized conception of the German prince into a republican system.

At first the authorities took a lenient view of Wagner's political activities, but late in 1848 Lüttichau suddenly cancelled the projected performance of *Lohengrin.* The effect on Wagner was to increase his open criticism. On January 16, 1849, he published an article on "Theater Reform" which was a violent condemnation of control by royally-appointed courtiers. In February he advised the Royal Orchestra that, since his own plan for reorganization had been rejected, they should take the initiative themselves. The speech was reported to Lüttichau, who reprimanded Wagner and threatened him with dismissal. Wagner in turn threatened to go to the

King, and the personal break between the two men was complete.

By the spring of 1849, Wagner was openly consorting with revolutionary leaders; he was publicly advocating policies that were revolutionary; and he had forfeited all personal support from the court. Furthermore, his artistic and financial affairs were in such condition that the future looked hopeless without some cataclysmic change.

This was the situation when revolution broke out in Dresden on May 3, 1849. Wagner lost no time in demonstrating where his sympathies lay. For the next week he was in almost constant association with the revolutionary leaders, among them the famous anarchist Bakunin. Although he was not armed, he was frequently seen at the barricades. For nearly 24 hours, he was posted in the 300-foot tower of the Kreuzkirche, observing the fighting and dropping messages to the revolutionary troops.

By the fifth day of fighting, the King's forces, aided by troops from Prussia, were gaining control of the city, and Wagner sent Minna, their pets, and as many belongings as possible to his sister Klara in Chemnitz. Then he joined his friends for the retreat, still hoping to establish a provisional government outside Dresden. In the confusion, however, he was separated from them, and he made his way alone to his sister's, arriving on the morning of May 10.

Only later did he learn that companions he had sought had been captured while resting at an inn in Chemnitz. Bakunin, Röckel and several others were subsequently tried and condemned to death. Although the sentences were later commuted, they all served long prison terms. Only by the narrowest of margins had Richard Wagner escaped an imprisonment that might have brought his creative career to an early end.

Wagner was not yet safe, however, and on the night of May 12, 1849, his brother-in-law Wolfram hid him in a carriage and smuggled him to Weimar, where Liszt was now Kapellmeister. Under the spell of his great friend's welcome, Wagner began to feel secure once again and even to consider returning to Dresden.

His sense of security was dispelled rudely on May 19 by the issue in Dresden of a warrant for his arrest. No German state could now provide a haven. Minna arrived in Weimar on the 22nd, and with Liszt's advice it was decided that Wagner should go to Paris by way of Zurich. Supplied with a false passport and name, he departed on the 25th and arrived without incident in Switzerland on the 28th.

Wagner was now a political refugee and an exile, penniless and without prospects. Probably he was not yet fully aware of his position. The truth was that he would not see Germany again for twelve years, and for the next fifteen years he would experience scarcely a moment of real security. It would have surprised him even more, however, had he known that nearly five years would pass before he would compose again; for, just as the revolution ended for all time his connection with the conventional theater, *Lohengrin* ended his connection with conventional opera.

Lohengrin

The story of Lohengrin, like that of *Tannhäuser*, is based on medieval legend. There is a brief version at the end of Wolfram von Eschenbach's *Parzival*, and Wagner found more useful material in the anonymous epic which he took with him on his futile attempt to "take the waters" in the summer of 1845. His final story seems to include an amalgamation of several variants.

> *Act I:* Elsa, daughter of the late duke of Brabant, has been accused by Friedrich of Telramund of killing her young brother, Gottfried, so that she may rule. Henry of Saxony orders that the dispute be settled by holy combat. Elsa tells of a dream in which a strange knight defends her honor. Lohengrin now appears in a small boat drawn by a swan. He declares that he is Elsa's defender and asks for her hand in marriage if victorious, but he lays down one condition: she must never ask his name nor whence he came. Lohengrin defeats Telramund but spares his life.
>
> *Act II:* Ortrud, the wife of Telramund, now emerges as the evil force behind him. She persuades him to plan an attempt on Lohengrin's life, and she plants seeds of doubt about Lohengrin in Elsa's mind. The King appoints Lohengrin Protector of Brabant, and preparations are made for the wedding of Lohengrin and Elsa.
>
> *Act III:* Immediately following the wedding, Lohengrin and Elsa are conducted to the bridal chamber. Their tender love scene is gradually clouded by Elsa's anxiety, and finally she asks the forbidden question. Before Lohengrin can respond, Telramund bursts in and attacks him. Lohengrin kills him with one blow. Then he solemnly promises Elsa an answer the next day and departs.
>
> Before King Henry and the noblemen, Lohengrin gives his answer: he is a knight of the Holy Grail and the son of Parzival.

He can remain no longer, for the Grail demands that its knights return if they are recognized. The swan appears, and Ortrud reveals that the swan is Gottfried, whom she placed under a magic spell. With Lohengrin's departure the spell will remain. As Lohengrin sinks to his knees in prayer, the dove of the Holy Grail appears. The swan disappears into the water, and Gottfried arises in its place. Lohengrin steps into the boat and is drawn slowly away by the dove, as Elsa, with a last cry, sinks lifeless into the arms of her brother.

One of Wagner's friends and supporters objected to the ending of the story when Wagner sent him the poem in 1845, and surprisingly Wagner experimented briefly with a less tragic denouement. Today it appears that the dissatisfaction was a failure to appreciate the fundamental symbolism of the story, while Wagner's indecision was the result of difficulty in adapting a drama to a symbolic idea.

The listener who approaches the opera without any attempt to understand its symbolism may find the forbidden question arbitrary, Elsa's curiosity justified, and the punishment harsh out of all proportion. Order and meaning emerge only when one sees the story in terms of universal needs and conflicts: Lohengrin as the love of God which can remain among men only so long as faith is unquestioning, and Elsa as the individual who desperately needs this love but whose faith is too weak to withstand the evil personified in Ortrud.

As with any symbol, it is dangerous to state its meaning so baldly, and it must always be remembered that Wagner's works are dramas, not religious rites. Nevertheless, it is well for the matter-of-fact twentieth-century student of Wagner to bear in mind that all of his operas—and most especially those from *Lohengrin* on—imply a meaning beyond the simple facts of the story.

Although some critics find *Lohengrin* a less imaginative work than *Tannhäuser*, almost all agree that the quality of its inspiration is more even. Despite its length, *Lohengrin* is more concentrated, and the music—the most consistently lyrical Wagner ever wrote—can focus on creating the otherworldly atmosphere that is the essence of the story's meaning.

The impressive difference in mood between *Tannhäuser* and *Lohengrin* is the measure of Wagner's remarkable ability to adapt his expression to the needs of the drama. The extremes of pomp and passion in *Tannhäuser* called forth a brilliant kaleidoscope of styles, dominated by the chromaticism of the Venusberg. Lohengrin has moments of brilliance, too—the famous Act III Prelude, for example—but the serious calm of Lohengrin himself and the aura of the Grail are expressed in a predominantly diatonic style of crystalline clarity. Although both *The Flying Dutchman* and *Tannhäuser* have their own individual atmosphere, Wagner's genius for grasping and sustaining a dominant mood through a long work comes to its first full strength in *Lohengrin*.

From the structural standpoint, the use of recurrent motives is carried a step further in *Lohengrin* than in *Tannhäuser*, and the motives begin to have more psychological significance. The most striking one is that associated with the "Forbidden Question" (Ex. 10). Here is a ready-made situation for a "reminiscence" motive:

Example 10

each time the question is mentioned or the mystery of Lohengrin's origin touched on, the motive to which Lohengrin sang his initial warning is repeated. Perhaps its most effective use involves no dialogue, but combines a gesture with a statement in the orchestra. At the end of Act II, Elsa has with effort overcome her fear; as she is entering the cathedral with the King and Lohengrin, she turns momentarily and sees Ortrud, "who raises her arm against her as if in triumph." At that point the first phrase of the motive sounds in the orchestra, striking ominously across the joyous ceremonial atmosphere.

There are also important recurring motives associated with the Grail (Ex. 11, heard first in the prelude), with Ortrud's evil (Ex. 12 and Ex. 13, the second particularly with Ortrud's influence on Elsa), with Lohengrin (Ex. 14), and with the love of Lohengrin and Elsa (Ex. 15), as well as a few other lesser motives. None, however, undergoes real development such as occurs in the later music dramas; these motives are simply quoted as effective reminders.

Wagner also moves a step closer to continuous opera in *Lohengrin*. Recitative and aria styles are still sometimes discernible, but a

Example 11

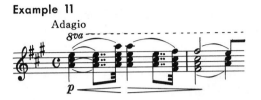

Example 12

Example 13

Example 14

Example 15

free, declamatory arioso is prevalent. The outlines of a set number are only occasionally clear, as in Elsa's prayer in Act I, while the ease and variety with which the scenes are joined in a continuous dramatic flow show further advance in Wagner's craftsmanship. Aside from the preludes, only the wedding chorus clearly stands out from the context as an effective individual number.

The chorus in *Lohengrin* has a less active part than in *Tannhäuser*, but the choral passages are quite extended, especially in the second act. Usually these are shortened in performance, and it must be admitted that, despite the skillful writing they contain, few even among Wagnerian purists can object.

Lohengrin is the only opera Wagner wrote in reverse order. Perhaps because of his doubts about the ending, he began the music with Act III, and followed with Acts I and II. Last of all he created the prelude, and it is the crowning glory of the opera. For both *The Flying Dutchman* and *Tannhäuser*, Wagner wrote overtures that summarize the drama by use of the contrasting themes associated with the most important elements. Both are excellent and effective compositions; both have been accused of being too self-contained and of leaving too little to be said by the opera. The *Lohengrin* prelude aims to present the essence of the idea that motivates the drama. It depicts, not the story of the opera, but the descent of the Holy Grail to man.

The prelude consists of a masterful expansion of the orchestral part of Lohengrin's narrative from Act III, which is itself based on the "Grail" motive (Ex. 11). Four solo violins in a high register create an ethereal atmosphere, and then all violins, divided into four parts, begin the unfolding of the motive. As it winds downward, the violins are joined first by the woodwinds, then by the violas, cellos and horns, then by the trombones, trumpets and timpani in a gradual, controlled crescendo. At the highest climax the strings cease, and the woodwinds, brass, and percussion ring forth in a richness of sound that had never been heard before. In Wagner's own description of the prelude (characteristically, it is a poetic interpretation rather than a musical analysis), this climax represents the parting of the mists and the unveiling of the Grail to the sight of man. One can only say that the sound itself seems to open with dazzling brightness. The following diminuendo is accomplished quickly, with the violins extending the Grail motive and mounting again into the ethereal regions of the beginning.

The *Lohengrin* prelude is comparable in Wagner's works only to a few later achievements, such as the prelude to *Tristan* and the prelude to Act III of *Die Meistersinger*. For Wagner it represents a new control of emotions through the perfection of musical structure. Orchestration, harmony, and the tonal progression combine to produce the effect of the climax. The free-flowing counterpoint, bridging over cadences and delaying resolutions, supports the feeling of continuous expansion; the instrumental color and register are essential parts of the musical idea; and the proportions of the build-ups and the relaxations are beyond criticism.

To some critics the entire opera is perfection. Ernest Newman called it "the old opera transformed" and wrote: "As one watches that diaphanous and finely spun melodic web unfold itself, one is almost tempted for the moment to regret that the daemon within him drove him on so relentlessly to another style." [6] But to others Wagner has gone too far in his transformation and has depended too heavily on the unifying force of repeated motives without a compensating control of large musical form.

Whether because of its perfection or because of the special nature of its failings, it is certain that *Lohengrin* marks the end of a period in Wagner's creative development. He became aware of the crisis in his growth only gradually, and for five years he grappled tenaciously with the problems before he felt ready to begin composition again. In the *Lohengrin* prelude, we see a superb foreshadowing of his ultimate solution.

[6] Newman, *Wagner as Man and Artist*, p. 317.

5

First Years of Exile, 1849-1857:
The Beginning of the *Ring*

On his arrival in Zurich, Wagner was surprised to find that he was already well known, and a cordial welcome from a few friends there pleased him. He stayed just long enough to obtain a Swiss passport, and on May 30, 1849, set out for Paris. He had no desire to go, knowing that Paris represented everything that he was committed to fight against, but he was eager to please Liszt and to demonstrate his chances to Minna. So he whipped up his hopes and tried Paris once more.

Before he had done much more than renew old friendships, his power of decision began to return. When Liszt urged that he try to produce *Rienzi* at once, he answered that he had outgrown the work. By June 26 he was back in Zurich with plans to begin a new opera. His hope for a livelihood now rested on the slim chance of Liszt's securing a pension from the Duke of Weimar.

Such was the dubious future that Wagner could offer his wife. He had tried to raise her hopes by exaggerating prospects and minimizing difficulties, but Minna was not to be deluded. She had no comprehension of the inner forces that had driven him into the revolution, and she was furious with him for destroying their security and social position. Her health was poor; she felt unable to face again the hardships she had endured without complaint ten years earlier.

That Minna understood Wagner superficially is clear enough, for at one point she wrote: "You never adapt yourself to the world as it really is but demand that the whole world adapt and form itself according to your ideas." [1] This was no less than the truth, and

[1] This letter and others that passed between Richard and Minna at this period are found in *Letters of Richard Wagner. The Burrell Collection*, ed. by John Burk (New York: The MacMillan Co., 1950), pp. 225-260.

Wagner knew it himself. But to Minna it was a cardinal sin; adapting to "the world as it is" was the cornerstone of her life. To Wagner, Minna's "reality" was hateful and false; his mission was to bring to light the true reality, the world of his imagination.

Poor Minna suffered a personal tragedy from which she never recovered when she ceased being "Frau Kapellmeisterin," but her deeper tragedy was her failure to see her husband as anything more than a conventional conductor-composer, like Reissiger, or, if luck were very good, perhaps like Meyerbeer.

Only reluctantly, after considerable recrimination and delay, did Minna finally agree to rejoin Wagner, and in early September they settled in inexpensive but comfortable rooms in Zurich. The practical problem was now well formulated in Wagner's mind, and he had a characteristic answer. On November 19, he wrote a long letter to his Dresden friend, Ferdinand Heine:

> Unhappily, I am no artisan to earn my daily bread; it must be offered to me as things stand now, so that I may remain an artist. Who is to do this? Only those who love me. . . . They should see in me not a person in need of help, but an artist and an art trend which they want to preserve for the future and not allow to perish.[2]

Heine had to refuse Wagner's request that he form a committee of those willing to contribute, and for once Wagner understood and apologized for causing his old friend trouble. But his state of mind as well as his finances were becoming desperate, as no road seemed open that would give him the needed freedom and security.

Finally he could no longer withstand the pressure of Liszt's advice and Minna's nagging. On January 20, 1850, he started again for Paris, carrying the prose sketch of another opera called *Wieland der Schmied*. As he expected, nothing went well. He was ill, disheartened, and miserable. On February 24, he wrote to Uhlig in Dresden that he had decided on a treatment for his illness: he would never write an opera for Paris; he would return to Zurich, write a German *Wieland* and *Siegfried's Death*, and bequeath them to posterity.

Perhaps a factor in the decision was word received from Frau Julie Ritter, mother of his young Dresden friend Karl, that she was prepared to join another admirer, Mme. Eugène Laussot of Bordeaux, in guaranteeing him 3,000 francs a year. Almost equally

[2] *The Burrell Collection,* p. 264.

welcome was an invitation to recover his health by visiting the Laussots in Bordeaux.

Wagner stayed in Bordeaux less than three weeks, but it was long enough. Jessie Laussot was an attractive young Englishwoman who had met Wagner briefly in Dresden and had come under the spell of his music. Refined, sensitive, an excellent pianist, she had an ardent and romantic nature. Apparently her own marriage was not entirely happy. Wagner read *Siegfried's Death* and *Wieland* to her. She was enraptured and identified herself with the bride of Wieland, who inspired him to break his bonds and create the wings by which he escaped from his tormentors. For the unhappy Wagner her warmth and sympathy were like water in the desert. Quickly the two fell in love, and together they discussed a bizarre plan. In Europe there was no hope of understanding. Could they not flee together, first to Greece, then to Asia Minor, and leave the whole sordid, materialistic society behind?

Whether there was a definite understanding between them when Wagner left Bordeaux on April 3 is uncertain, but by April 15, back in Paris, he had reached a decision. He first wrote to Uhlig of his hopes when Minna returned to him in Zurich, of her misunderstanding, of her threats to separate from him. Then he wrote Minna asking for a final separation. Considering Wagner's infinite capacity for self-pity, it was a kind letter, and his judgment of the situation seems clear-sighted. It was, however, hardly a frank letter; he did not mention Jessie Laussot nor an elopement to the East.

Minna, who had been suspicious of the Bordeaux trip from the beginning, went to Paris on April 21, but Wagner avoided her. By early May she was back in Zurich, and Wagner was hiding at Villeneuve on Lake Geneva, expecting to join Jessie in Marseilles shortly and embark for Greece.

As he was about to leave, a letter came from Jessie. She had told her mother of their plans, and her mother had immediately passed the news on to Jessie's husband, who reacted in the approved fashion by threatening to shoot Wagner on sight. Desperately in need now of understanding, Wagner first wrote to Frau Ritter, begging her to come to him. Then he started for Bordeaux to see, not Jessie, but Eugène Laussot. It is perhaps fortunate, in view of Laussot's threat, that the two did not meet, although one would have liked to hear Wagner explain to the irate husband the error of his ways. Laussot had removed his family from Bordeaux and notified the police, who promptly expelled Wagner from the city.

He returned to the sympathy of Frau Ritter, who had answered his plea, still believing that the affair might end happily. On June 15 word came from Jessie: she had come to see him in a new light and would hereafter refuse all communication from him. Two and a half weeks later, having received assurances from Minna and written a lengthy, somewhat devious explanation to her, Wagner returned to his wife in Zurich.

Wagner's conduct had been indefensible from the conventional viewpoint, but it would be a mistake to accept this as complete. In common with most artists of the time, Wagner felt no sympathy with bourgeois morality; the bonds of love he considered beyond conventional restrictions. But he was no libertine, and he was far too sensitive and serious a person to trifle callously with the feelings of others. Throughout the Laussot affair he acted, according to his own view, honorably and with kindness.

Without a doubt Wagner was highly sexed, but feminine companionship and understanding were necessary to him in a deeper sense than the merely physical. Each of his serious affairs was intimately connected with his development as an artist. In 1850 he was at the most critical stage of his creative life, battling with problems so fundamental that he could not even begin their solution without years of struggle. His domestic situation had become an intolerable hindrance, and European society showed no signs of providing him with the conditions necessary to his art. In the depths of his despair, he planned flight from both.

Minna cannot be blamed, of course, for her failure to understand. To a large extent, her view was held by almost everyone, for the music that would eventually change the judgment was not yet written. Faith and intuition were needed to see what Richard Wagner might become and to sympathize with his struggles toward his goal.

Wagner felt that his actions throughout the Jessie Laussot affair were fully justified and tried to convince himself that Minna understood, while Minna felt that virtue had triumphed and credited herself with great powers of forgiveness. Nevertheless, the two settled down together with reasonable good will, and Wagner was probably as happy in Zurich as he could have been anywhere in his state of mind. He soon became the center of a group of intellectual and artistic refugees, some of whom remained lifelong personal friends and supporters. Their interest and their willingness to listen to his ideas were a much needed solace to him, and some were called upon for help of a more material nature as well.

Although he stubbornly refused an official position, Wagner was inevitably drawn into the musical life of Zurich. As early as January, 1850, he began to conduct occasional large works, usually Beethoven symphonies, at the Concert Society, and in the spring of 1852 he produced *The Flying Dutchman* at the Zurich Opera. The following year the Concert Society paid him the tribute of organizing the first Wagner Festival. Players were imported to create an orchestra of seventy, Wagner himself conducted, and the success of the three programs attracted favorable comment even in Germany.

Early in 1855 Wagner was persuaded to produce *Tannhäuser* and to conduct one performance, but Zurich, he found, despite the honors it might bestow upon him, resisted his efforts to reform its artistic life just as stubbornly as Dresden had earlier. Wagner quietly withdrew from further activities in the town.

Jessie Laussot had preferred *Wieland* to *Siegfried* but Wagner knew better, and once back in Zurich he cast *Wieland* aside for good. Early in August of 1850, he sketched a few pages of music for *Siegfried's Death*, but evidently he was dissatisfied and unable to capture the mood for composing. The truth was that the long germination process was still far from complete. There is no more remarkable facet of this always remarkable artist than the apparently unconscious control exercised over his creative process. At this time he was not critical of his poem for *Siegfried's Death*, and he certainly had no doubts of his ability to compose. But he knew that the proper inspiration did not come upon him, and he was wise enough not to force it. While his conscious mind dealt with related generalities, his subconscious struggled with the poetic and musical form of his great drama.

The "related generalities" took the form of prose essays. Shortly after leaving Dresden, he had written *Art and Revolution, The Art Work of the Future*, and *Art and Climate*. On August 24, less than two weeks after the *Siegfried* sketch, he finished the essay which is, of all his prose writings, the least defensible and the most potentially dangerous—*Judaism in Music*.

A trend toward anti-Semitism was gaining among German intellectuals and nationalists in the mid-nineteenth century, and Wagner simply picked up the notion, as he did in a number of other instances, and adapted it to his own problem. The basis of principle on which his anti-Semitism rested was his strong belief in the importance of *das Volk*[3] in the development of art. Despite much that is uncomplimentary, he did not insist on the inferiority of the Jewish race, but he considered the Jewish people a foreign element. When he looked for the internal enemies of true German art, he thought he found them in the watered-down Beethoven and Handel styles of Mendelssohn and the commercialized French-Italian style of Meyerbeer.

Certainly another impulse toward anti-Semitism sprang from his treatment by the press. The Jewish element was strong in German journalism, and Wagner convinced himself that it was dominant. The Jews became for him a scapegoat, an explanation for the plight of German music and for opposition to his own work. As Liszt once wrote with ironic humor, "With him,['the Jews' is] a generic term of very wide meaning."

Perhaps the best that can be said for Wagner's anti-Semitism is that it seldom extended to his personal relations and that a number of Jewish artists and musicians were able to overlook it. Nevertheless, anti-Semitism remains the most distasteful and damaging aspect of what became known as Wagnerism, and no rationalization can excuse him for lending his name and prestige to a movement that culminated in the horrors of National Socialism.

Judaism in Music was published in the *Neue Zeitung für Musik* in September, 1850. Although it appeared under a pseudonym, the authorship was not in doubt, and it caused bitter opposition to Wagner in some quarters. Meyerbeer, of course, was from now on an open enemy; some admirers of Mendelssohn and much of the press never forgave Wagner.

Still, as an event in Wagner's development, *Judaism in Music* is little more than an indication of the gradual hardening of some of the less pleasant aspects of his personality. Much more important for the progress of his thinking was his next prose essay, *Opera and Drama*, written between October, 1850, and February, 1851. To consider it, we need to turn first to two of the earlier essays, *Art and Revolution* and *The Art Work of the Future*.

Let it be said to begin with that there is much in all three of these works that is of little interest except to the specialist; Wagner was unquestionably long-winded. It is also well to remember, as

[3] There seems no way to handle this word except to translate it literally as "the folk." The word *people*, which seems more natural in English, carries a different connotation.

many of his followers did not, that Wagner was an amateur philosopher. He was trying to express ideas that arose from his problems as a musical dramatist, rather than from abstract speculation or objective observation, and he was discussing music that had not yet been written. Although his literary talent was considerable, he was by no means the master of words that he was of sounds. Frequently he had difficulty in expressing himself clearly, and his style is often dense and laden with symbolism.

Above all, one must avoid the trap of considering that Wagner's purpose can be wholly discovered in his prose writings, and that the great music dramas that followed are to be judged by their adherence to the principles enunciated. The prose essays are an offshoot of the art works, an excess of creative energy, and most of all a necessary intellectual catharsis.

Art and Revolution is Wagner's theoretical justification for his participation in the Dresden uprising. Wagner places the theater squarely at the center of national culture, and then relates this central position to the need for social revolution. The highest art is public art, the creation of a free and healthy folk such as (Wagner thought) existed in ancient Greece. The commercialization of society destroyed the proper condition. On the one hand we worship gold; on the other hand Christianity (distinct in Wagner's mind from the teachings of Christ) preaches renunciation and acceptance of the world. The true artist might even now create the art work of the future, but not until social revolution trains men to seek beauty and strength will the conditions for it be right.

The Art Work of the Future, which followed two months later, seizes upon a phrase from *Art and Revolution* and undertakes to explain it in detail. Again Wagner emphasizes the communal nature of true art and the need for a free, revitalized society. But now he rationalizes the history of music. Beethoven in his symphonies had brought absolute music to the highest possible point; in the Ninth Symphony he added the word.

> This *last symphony* of Beethoven's is the redemption of music out of its own element as a *universal art*. Beyond it there can be no *progress*, for there can follow on it immediately only the completed art work of the future, *the universal drama*, to which Beethoven has forged us the artistic key. . . . The art of tone, by being wholly *itself* and by moving within its own primeval element, attained strength for the most tremendous and most

generous of all self-sacrifices—that of self-control, indeed of self-denial—thus to offer to its sister arts a redeeming hand.[4]

The art work of the future, then, is to be a universal drama, a collective art work (Wagner's famous word is *Gesamtkunstwerk*) embracing all of the arts and aiming at "the glorification *in art of mankind in general.*" In the collective art work the art of tone will reach its highest fulfillment primarily through the means developed in its isolation—the orchestra.

Wagner thought he had finished with theoretical speculation at this point, but *Opera and Drama* is his most exhaustive treatment of his theories. It resulted in the widespread belief that Wagner had created a rigid system of composition. It might have been better had he left things with the generalities of the first two essays.

Yet *Opera and Drama* makes its unique contribution by attacking the problem squarely from the standpoint of opera: "The error in the art-genre of opera consists herein: that a Means of Expression (Music) has been made the object, while the object of expression (the Drama) has been made a means." At great length, Wagner supports his thesis historically and then proceeds to define what the new relationship of music and drama should be. He develops an elaborate theory of the origin of speech, goes into detail as to the relation of melody and harmony to words, and elaborates one of his favorite metaphors, that of music as woman and poetry as man.

The core of his argument is this: Music, the most powerful organ of expression, cannot specify the feelings it expresses; Poetry, on the other hand, addresses itself to the understanding. The two must be unified to serve the higher drama of feeling. The potential of each will be raised in combination. The result will be, not opera in the old sense, but complete drama. The proper subject matter is myth, because it embodies truth in terms of feeling.

The other arts also must come into this complete drama, for sight and gesture are important. The bond between the elements is the orchestra, which can express the unspeakable, allying itself with gesture and suggesting emotions past and future. Everything, however, must be at the service of the drama; the melodies that recall or predict are not used for *purely* musical reasons. There will be no chorus (characters included merely to create more tone), and there will be no set numbers for the sake of abstract musical form. The form of the drama will be molded by the poetic idea.

[4] *Source Readings in Music History*, selected and annotated by Oliver Strunk (New York: W. W. Norton and Co., Inc., 1950), pp. 874-903.

Wagner's rationalization for the time spent in writing prose essays (Minna as well as others thought he was wasting his time) was that his views must be understood by thinking men before his operas could flourish. He learned quickly, however, that his theorizing was of value primarily to himself and that his effort to explain works not yet written was largely futile. In May, 1852, he wrote to Uhlig, "I can only look back to [my literary activity] with pleasure in so far as I feel that by its means I have become quite clear in my own mind." [5]

In April, 1850, while still involved in the Laussot affair, Wagner had sent an urgent appeal to Liszt, asking that he produce *Lohengrin*. As so often in these difficult years, Liszt responded, and on August 26, 1850, the first performance of *Lohengrin* took place at Weimar. It proved to be one of the greatest services Liszt ever rendered Wagner. *Lohengrin* was an immediate success, and it marked the beginning of a period of prosperity for Wagner's works.

The excellent impression made by the opera itself was not alone responsible. Weimar was a small theater, and its success removed to some extent the stigma of impossible difficulty from Wagner's works. The patronage of the Grand Duke of Weimar also helped, for now others were emboldened to take up works by the "revolutionary Kapellmeister."

Not that participation in the revolution had been entirely bad for Wagner's reputation. Many liberal intellectuals had looked favorably on his political activities, while among advocates of the *status quo* even bad publicity was still publicity. Wagner's writings added fuel to the fire. They were perhaps more discussed than read and more reviled than understood, but they forced people to reckon with his name.

In Dresden Uhlig wrote a number of excellent essays supporting Wagner's musical views and works. In Berlin, in 1849-50, Bülow had fought violently to bring Wagner's essays to the attention of the conservative press, and he continued his work from Weimar, where he had gone to study with Liszt. The *Neue Zeitschrift für Musik*, Schumann's old journal, announced: "This paper will henceforth have for its task the emphatic advocacy, from every point of view, of the transformation upon which the art of music is now entering."

[5] *Wagner's Letters to his Dresden Friends*, trans. by J. S. Shedlock (London: H. Grevel and Co., 1890), p. 223.

The young Wagnerians were forming battle lines, and *Lohengrin's* success furnished them with a valuable weapon. In the early 1850's Wagner became the most talked-of composer in Germany.

All of the circumstances after the Weimar *Lohengrin* indicated that Wagner should write another work as soon as possible, and it seemed logical that it should go to Liszt. By May, 1851, therefore, Liszt had negotiated a contract with his court offering Wagner 500 thalers for *Siegfried's Death*, the score to be completed no later than July, 1852. Wagner accepted but with a proviso: he would deliver, not *Siegfried's Death*, but *Young Siegfried* (*Der junge Siegfried*). In a characteristic flash of inspiration, the result of long brooding and unconscious struggle, he had realized that he must prepare the audience for *Siegfried's Death* by writing a preliminary drama.

The poem for *Young Siegfried* was finished on June 24, 1851, but again Wagner delayed beginning composition. In July he went on a walking tour in the mountains with Uhlig. In August he wrote a long autobiographical essay called *A Communication to My Friends*. The following month, still hardly knowing why he was avoiding his essential work, he went to a mountain resort called Albisbrunn to try one of the "water cures" that were then popular. It was here in the midst of a torturous regime of diet and cold baths that Wagner conceived the final design for *The Ring of the Nibelung*.

His new plan called for writing another drama (*Die Walküre*) to precede the two Siegfried dramas, and still another (*Das Rheingold*) to serve as a prelude to the trilogy. (*Young Siegfried* became *Siegfried; Siegfried's Death* became *Götterdämmerung*.) Wagner wrote to Uhlig on November 12 that he had been led to make the expansion by the wealth of dramatic material. But he added:

> One other thing determined me to develop this plan—that is the impossibility which I felt of producing *Young Siegfried* in anything like a suitable manner either at Weimar—or anywhere else. I cannot and will not endure anymore the martyrdom of things done *by halves*. . . . I shall erect a theatre on the banks of the Rhine, and issue invitations to a great dramatic festival. . . . However extravagant this plan may be, it is nevertheless the only one to which I can devote my life and labours.[6]

Wagner's plan, magnificent in its scope under any circumstance,

[6] *Wagner's Letters to his Dresden Friends*, p. 140.

was all the more audacious for a man in his position, for of course the contract with Weimar had to be broken. Wagner had in effect severed his last link with the hope of security and embarked on a profitless project that would take, by his most optimistic estimate, at least three years to complete.

Secretly, he held hopes of practical success at an earlier date than seemed possible to his friends. For more than a year he had clung almost obsessively to a belief that the French elections of 1852 would initiate a drastic change in the political and social order. It was a heavy blow to him when Louis Napoleon's *coup d'état* of December, 1851 destroyed this hope beyond all question.

This was the end of Wagner's expectation of rapid social and political reform. His philosophical speculations, however, were not entirely or even primarily directed by outside events. A change had already begun as early as spring, 1851, if we can accept the evidence afforded by the development of the *Ring*. *Siegfried's Death* ends triumphantly with Siegfried entering Walhalla led by Brünnhilde. Apparently while writing *Young Siegfried* in May, 1851, Wagner decided to destroy the Gods, as is familiar now in *Götterdämmerung*. The final form of the ending was still to cause him considerable trouble, but it is obvious that the change from an optimistic ending to the present veiled and mystic tragedy did not derive from political events in December, 1851.

When he wrote his most important theoretical essays, Wagner's favorite philosopher was Ludwig Feuerbach, whose doctrine of "healthy sensuality" and opposition to orthodox Christianity had made him a hero to the younger German intellectuals. After *Opera and Drama*, however, Wagner gradually turned to a less active, more pessimistic view. He was amply ready to embrace the gloomy philosophy of Schopenhauer when introduced to it in 1854, and not long thereafter he immersed himself in the meditations of Eastern philosophy.

Wagner continued to work slowly at the poem of the *Ring* throughout 1852. The text of *Walküre* was finished on July 1, 1853, *Rheingold* on November 3, and a month later the necessary revisions were made in the two Siegfried dramas. Hardly was his work done than Wagner gathered his friends and read it to them.

Although he was an excellent actor, Wagner's passion for reading to his friends was more than capricious vanity; it was an impelling need to communicate, part of his complex desire to dominate and to be understood. Already he had read *Siegfried's Death* in public and had devoted twelve evenings to reading *Opera and Drama*. Now, in addition to the reading of the *Ring*, he had fifty copies printed at his own expense for circulation among his friends.

He soon realized that his zeal had once again led him into error. No one was able to fathom the meaning of the *Ring* nor to conceive how it could be made into an opera. There were no arias, no ensembles, no finales. The lines were short, concise, and frequently alliterative, a far cry from the long, measured lines of *Lohengrin*. Today, for those familiar with the music, there can be no doubt that Wagner had a definite, if largely unformed, conception of what the music was to be at the time the text was written. He did not compose a text and then set it to music; he created a text that was already intimately bound with the as-yet-unwritten music and which was incomplete without it. Occasional rhythmic notations on the poetic manuscript are only one proof of this. He was, as always, first and foremost a musician. It is little wonder that his friends, forced to contemplate only the incomplete poet portion of the musician-poet were left in confusion. Wagner saw the difficulty clearly, but he was profoundly depressed that even his closest friends could not see the nature of what was in his imagination.

The death of his beloved friend, Theodor Uhlig, perhaps the one person to whom he could have explained the *Ring* at this time, added to his sadness at the beginning of 1853. He found the Zurich winter difficult, and his health was still poor. But his outward circumstances were not actually calculated to evoke such waves of self-pity as his letters reflect. He lived comfortably, he had a modest regular income, and his works were in constant demand throughout the small theaters of Germany. Moreover, he had not yet exhausted the generosity of his Zurich friends. The basic cause of his depression, and probably of his poor health as well, was his inability to begin the composition of *Das Rheingold*.

In answer to a desperate plea, Liszt arrived on July 1. Wagner was in a frenzy of joy. He talked incessantly, he read his poems, and he listened to some of Liszt's recently completed symphonic poems, the harmonic daring of which impressed him strongly; but when Liszt departed, Wagner's gloom was deeper than ever.

Still restless and unwell, he tried a "cure" at St. Moritz and then started out for Italy. On September 3 he came to Spezia, spent a sleepless night, and the following afternoon, after a long walk, stretched himself on the bed to rest.

I fell into a kind of somnolent state [he wrote in *Mein Leben*] in which I suddenly felt as though I were sinking in swiftly flowing water. The rushing sound formed itself in my brain into a musical sound, the chord of E-flat major, which continually re-echoed in broken forms; these broken chords seemed to be melodic passages of increasing motion, yet the pure triad of E-flat major never changed, but seemed by its continuance to impart infinite significance to the element in which I was sinking. I awoke in sudden terror from my doze, feeling as though the waves were rushing high above my head. I at once recognized that the orchestral overture to *Das Rheingold,* which must long have been unable to find definite form, had at last been revealed to me.

He had finally found the cure that no waters could bring.

Wagner began the composition of *Das Rheingold* on November 1, 1853, and he completed everything except the orchestration on January 14, 1854. That he could have composed it in little more than ten weeks is clear proof of how fully the work had developed in his subconscious. So far as the world could see, he had devoted his energies between 1848 and 1853 to politics, aesthetic speculation, and poetry. The truth is that his musical imagination had never been more active.

Once he was successfully launched on the composition of the *Ring,* his health improved. He finished the orchestration of *Das Rheingold* on May 28, and plunged into *Die Walküre.* By the fall of 1854, however, he was tired of Zurich and suffering from home-sickness. Although he continued to work on the *Ring,* his mood was changing. Just before the completion of the composition sketch of *Die Walküre* in December, 1854, he wrote Liszt that he had worked out a drama based on the legend of Tristan and Isolde.

Because his finances were as usual in a critical state, Wagner interrupted his work in the spring of 1855 to conduct a series of concerts in London. The press was hostile, partly because of genuine conservatism, partly because the admiration for Mendelssohn in London amounted almost to a cult; but the concerts were successful, and at the last one both audience and orchestra gave Wagner a standing ovation. He made a number of new friends, and his relations with Berlioz, who was in London at the time, became momentarily warm, as each felt for perhaps the only time an intuitive sympathy for the other's problems.

Nevertheless, Wagner's letters from London are a rising crescendo of misery. Like all tourists in England, he was cold. The programs were too long, reminding him, he said, of the English coachman's cry, "Full inside!" The performers were not as good as he had hoped, and work on the scoring of *Die Walküre* went slowly. English taste and English reserve were incomprehensible to Wagner, but his real trouble in London was deeper. Any position in which he was expected to compromise with convention, to cater to critics, to compete with a Meyerbeer or even a Berlioz, was now agony for him. It was only salt in his wounds to find that expenses had left him a profit of only 1,000 francs for four months work.

Back in Zurich he began to work again on the orchestration of *Die Walküre*, but he was tired, and his spirit suffered another blow when his beloved little dog Peps died on July 10. During the summer he began to be plagued with erysipelas, a malady that had frequently afflicted him as a young man. He suffered thirteen attacks in the next year, each of which interrupted his work and left him exhausted.

Not until March 13, 1856, did he complete the scoring of *Walküre*, which he had hoped to finish in London a year earlier. The following summer he found, at long last, a sensible physician, who diagnosed his difficulty as largely nervous and prescribed rest and moderation. Wagner was not troubled with erysipelas again for years.

No doctor could cure the sickness in his soul, however; its causes were multiple and interrelated.

Conditions in his home were worse than ever. Minna was now quite ill, and the drugs prescribed for her chronic heart condition increased her emotional difficulties. She was nervous, suspicious, and jealous. The bitter scenes between Minna and poor Natalie were a continuous trial to Wagner.[7]

His imagination was overcrowded. While the *Ring* was still in the forefront of his thoughts, the Tristan idea developed rapidly, and his study of Buddhism led to the formulation of still another drama, which he called *Die Sieger* (*The Victors*). Even while working on *Siegfried,* he was suffering the usual pangs that accompanied the development of a new creation.

Furthermore, something else was now contributing to his disturbed state of mind. In 1851 a wealthy young merchant named

[7] The worst side of Minna's character seems constantly displayed in her relation with her daughter. Apparently she nagged, scolded, and berated the poor girl unmercifully. There is evidence that Wagner treated her with more kindness than did Minna.

Otto Wesendonk had settled in Zurich with his beautiful wife Mathilde. The couple soon became friends of Wagner's, and inevitably Otto was among those called on for substantial financial help. Just when Wagner fell in love with Mathilde Wesendonk we do not know, but by 1856 the relationship had certainly advanced beyond the usual affection for the wife of a friend and benefactor. As the conception of *Tristan* grew, Wagner's secret longing for Mathilde grew also. He began the composition of *Siegfried* on September 22, 1856, and he worked at it diligently. But his state of mind was changing rapidly; the "*Tristan* mood" was almost upon him.

Although the larger theaters were now presenting Wagner's works—Munich gave *Tannhäuser* in 1855 and Berlin finally capitulated in early 1856—the wide demand had passed its peak of the early 1850's. The fees were never enough to provide more than temporary financial relief. Wagner was therefore delighted to accept a proposal of help from Otto Wesendonk. Wesendonk had purchased an estate outside Zurich, on which he was erecting a mansion. In February, 1857, he suggested that Wagner lease a small house on the property for the quite reasonable sum of 1,000 francs a year.

The Wagners moved into their new home, which Wagner called the Asyl, in late April. Here at last was Wagner's retreat in the country, where he could work without disturbance, soothed by a garden and a magnificent view of Lake Geneva—and inspired by the proximity of Mathilde Wesendonk. He continued to work on *Siegfried*, even while his soul became more absorbed in *Tristan*. Then, as so often happened in Wagner's life, finances entered to force a decision that his artistic progress made necessary.

In January, 1857, his last hope of securing help from the Grand Duke of Weimar had come to an end. In early June, Breitkopf and Härtel, with whom he had been carrying on negotiations for some time, refused his suggestion of advance payments against the delivery of the *Ring*.

When he stopped work on June 27 in the midst of the second act of *Siegfried*, Wagner wrote across the score, "When shall we see each other again?" The following day he wrote to Liszt: "I have led my young Siegfried into the beautiful forest solitude; there I have left him under a linden tree, and, with tears from the depths of my heart, said farewell to him." [8] But he could not cut the

---

[8] Quoted in Newman, *Life of Wagner*, II, 512.

thread of his thought so abruptly. He returned two weeks later, and on August 9 finished the orchestral sketch of Act II. This time, when he started work again, it was to begin the poem of *Tristan und Isolde*.

Ostensibly, Wagner had dropped *The Ring of the Nibelung* for practical reasons: he needed a new work to follow the success of *Tannhäuser* and *Lohengrin*, and the *Ring* was not suitable for conventional theaters. Actually, his artistic sense was in control, as it usually was. In one way or another the *Ring* had occupied most of Wagner's thought and working time for nine years, and in plain language he was tired of it. A fresh conception, peculiarly in tune with his present mood, had arisen in *Tristan*.

The decisions of an artist must be judged in terms of result. When one considers the final, brilliant completion of the *Ring* and the towering strength of the two creations (*Tristan* and *Die Meistersinger*) which interrupted it, Wagner's decision to stop work when he did must be regarded as the bravest, the boldest, and the wisest of his life.

The First "Music Dramas"

Wagner's progress from *Lohengrin* to *Rheingold* brought about the greatest and most fundamental reform in the history of opera. Although both *Rheingold* and *Die Walküre* will be discussed in their proper place as part of the *Ring*, it is necessary at this point to look into the nature of this reform as seen in the works themselves. (For the story of the *Ring*, see Appendix, p. 174).

Wagner's basic objection to conventional opera was its undramatic nature; yet the persistence of weak, irrational drama was not only the result of capricious singers, cynical intendants, and composers bent on material success. Opera presents as part of its inherent nature the problem of combining two independent and self-sufficient arts.

Only two aspects of this complex problem need concern us here: first, the limitation of the expressive or articulative power of music; and, second, the conflict between dramatic structure and musical structure. The two problems of course are interrelated. It is conventionally admitted that music can articulate emotions but that it does not deal effectively with specific details of action. While dealing with emotion, music may follow the logic of its own internal structure, which traditionally falls into some type of closed form

In other cases the transformations reflect a broadening and deepening of the motive's associations. The first clearly defined motive in the *Rheingold* prelude (Ex. 19a) seems to be associated with the Rhine River; but it soon becomes evident that this motive has to do with the Rhine only insofar as the river itself is a symbol. In a slightly different form (Ex. 19b), it accompanies Erda's warning to Wotan in the last scene of *Das Rheingold* and continues as Wotan meditates on her words. In inversion (Ex. 19c), it is associated with Erda's prediction of the downfall of the Gods in the same scene. Further, it is closely related to Ex. 19d, consistently associated with the acceptance of fate. In still another form it appears connected with Wotan's frustration after bowing to Fricka's will in Act II of *Die Walküre* (Ex. 19e). Surely the mere labeling of this motive

Example 19a

Example 19b

Example 19c

Example 19d

Example 19e

in any of its forms is insufficient, and it can be dangerous unless treated with great care; but just as surely the motive and its near relatives have to do with the immutable aspect of destiny and the individual's powerlessness before it.

"Family likenesses" often exist between motives that clearly refer to different things.[10] Ex. 20a is the "Ring" motive on its first ap-

Example 20a

Example 20b

pearance. After Alberich steals the gold, a transformation occurs, and the next scene opens with Ex. 20b representing Walhalla—recognizably the same motive, now harmonically stable. The transformation occurs between Scene 1 and Scene 2; the orchestra thus tells the perceptive listener of a relationship that will emerge later in the drama.

For the listener, the question of what to do about the leitmotives is crucial: should he memorize the motive and its label and carefully identify each entry as he listens, or should he ignore them, leaving associations to his subconscious? There is no categorical answer. Ideally, the listener should learn the motives in context, making his own associations as his perception sharpens. The complex meaning of the motives should be gradually revealed, not labeled and memorized; but since ideal situations seldom exist for opera, some study of the motives and the generally accepted meanings can be of value, provided the ideal is kept in view.

There is, however, a greater danger than rigid, literal interpretation of the meaning. Too much concentration on detail may prevent

---

[10] The similarity of motives ranges from the obvious and obviously intentional to the obscure and probably unconscious. The search for derivatives can be carried to almost any extreme the analyst wishes.

the comprehension of larger matters of fundamental importance. Just as one does not come to an understanding of a Beethoven symphony merely by identifying the themes of each movement, so the knowledge of leitmotives is no guarantee that one understands the dramatic value in Wagner's works. The leitmotives are, of course, one factor in the unity of the works and in the articulation of the drama, but they are by no means the only factor. Of equal and perhaps greater importance are the musical elements of tension and relaxation, of the hierarchic building of climaxes, of transition, and of the relationship of large sections—in a word, musical form over long time spans. This is an aspect of Wagner's works that has received much attention and caused much disagreement. To his opponents his music is formless; to some fanatical supporters it is as tightly organized as a Beethoven symphony. The truth lies somewhere between. Dramatic progression is always a factor in the coherence of Wagner's works, and some passages are inexplicable without the text; but his control of musical proportion is nevertheless phenomenal, given the time spans he covers continuously.

It is by this control of the larger musical shape, in which the motives are unifying details, that Wagner defines the emotional progress of the drama and carries the emotions of the listener along with it. The wise listener, therefore, guards against concentrating exclusively on the identification of motives. He listens for larger relationships as well.

In *Das Rheingold* the long-range control is not so striking: here, if anywhere, one might suspect the "system." In *Die Walküre* the "Master" has arrived. The skillful interweaving of the motives is never pursued in a fashion so rigid as to hamper expansive lyricism. This lyricism is most marked in the first act, with its glowing expression of tragic love between Siegmund and Sieglinde. As a revelation of complex and progressing emotions, however, Act III is even more masterful.

Scene 3 of Act III typifies Wagner's characteristic structure: the gradual building to an emotional climax that is expressed in soaring symphonic lyricism. On the long, slow build-up, smaller climaxes are attained, in which the lyricism is cut off before reaching the full potential of its expansiveness. Thus, over a long span the structure builds through irregular cycles, and the emotional rhythm is one of tension alternating with relaxation that does not bring full release, until finally the resolution is achieved.

Scene 3 opens quietly, the tense hush contrasting with the confused excitement of the fleeing Valkyries in the preceding passage.

The first cycle is carried largely by Brünnhilde, with Wotan checking the lyrical tendency occasionally with sharp, dry interjections; her justification has not yet touched him. The first climax begins with her words, *"Der diese Liebe mir in's Herz gehaucht . . ."* ("He who this love into my heart had breathed"), and the dominant motive, which may be called "Wotan's love for the Wälsungs" or "Brünnhilde's justification," is the one with which the scene began (Ex. 21a). Its expansion is carried on largely in the orchestra, with

Example 21a

Example 21b

the voice in a thoroughly characteristic relation (Ex. 21b). But the expansion is suddenly halted, first by the brief intrusion of another vocal style and then decisively by a deceptive cadence.

Now Wotan has been affected; his answer is of considerable length and rises to a pitch of real agony before returning to his grim, curt style. The second cycle, longer and more complex, again begins with Brünnhilde, her mood quiet but more confident. As her plea disturbs Wotan's decision, he answers more violently. Finally the forward movement almost stops as Brünnhilde, her pleas seemingly exhausted, asks her fate. He replies with the soft chromatic motive of the "Magic Sleep" (Ex. 22) and from this point on, there is no break in the gradually mounting momentum. Brünnhilde's passionate protest and her rising inspiration generate a sweeping lyricism that flows over Wotan's single objection. With her last words

Example 22

the orchestra thunders forth the "Valkyrie" motive, which leads to a magnificent ornamentation of the "slumber" motive (Ex. 23a and b). Wotan joins in, and most impressively, with the words *"Leb'*

Example 23a

Example 23b

wohl, du kühnes, herrliches Kind!" ("Farewell, thou bold, glorious child!") But there is already no doubt that Wotan's decision has given way before his devotion to Brünnhilde. The emotional resolution of the conflict is in the orchestra.

This climax is too great to be choked off abruptly, as was the last, but it subsides rather quickly, for the greatest expansion is yet to come. Wotan continues his farewell, leading from subdued passion through the mounting excitement of the "fire" motive to a clear statement of the "Siegfried-as-hero" motive (Ex. 24) at the signifi-

Example 24

cant words, *"Denn Einer nur freie die Braut, der freier als ich, der Gott"* ("But one may wed the bride, one freer than I, the God").

This time the climax is purely orchestral, and it provides in full the expansion of Ex. 21b promised in the first climax, as well as something close to harmonic resolution.[11] The climax is thematically related to the beginning of the scene, the expansive potential is exploited, and the tension gradually developed over the entire scene is at last released.

The remainder of Wotan's moving and beautiful farewell serves in the structure as the necessary soft reflection of the strong emotion, the calm that follows the release. Loge's "fire music" and Siegfried's prophetic motive are, musically speaking, a coda—for this is, after all, the end of a long act and a long opera; it demands an ending of size and power.

The scene has been criticized for its length. Aside from the dramatic significance, such a view is difficult to justify. The scene is not an abstract structure, like the movement of a symphony; but neither is it formless. Its own individual form and its proportions amplify and bring to life the emotional progress of the drama.

With *Tannhäuser*, Wagner had become an adept, imaginative orchestrator in the most advanced style of the day; he had learned well from both Meyerbeer and Berlioz and added his own sensitivity. With *Lohengrin*, he began developing that close association between emotional mood and instrumental color which distinguishes his orchestration from that of composers interested in color for its own sake.

In the *Ring*, having cut himself off from the conventional theater, he felt free to create an orchestra commensurate with his mighty drama. He specified no less than 32 violins, 12 violas, 12 cellos, and 8 basses. He added a fourth part to the usual three in the flute, clarinet, and oboe families, and a third bassoon to the usual two. He called for two pairs of timpani, plus other assorted percussion instruments, and he wrote six separate harp parts. But his most important additions came in the brasses. *Tannhäuser* requires as many as 16 horns, but 12 are on stage. (It was easy for a court opera house to borrow brasses from the military band.) The *Ring* requires eight horns in the orchestra. Four of the players alternate on high tubas, instruments not yet in existence except in Wagner's imagination. Wagner also demanded the construction of a new bass tuba

[11] The key is the same, and the deceptive cadence is replaced by a prolongation of the tonic chord in its cadential second inversion, which then slips quietly into a closely related key.

and a new bass trumpet, and he wrote a bass trombone part along with the usual three tenor trombones.

The great richness and power in the lower and middle brasses is characteristic of the sound of Wagner's orchestra; no other composer makes such continuous use of his horns. At the massive climaxes, such as the entrance of the Gods into Walhalla at the end of *Rheingold* or the "fire music" in *Walküre*, the melodic weight usually lies in the brasses and woodwinds, while the strings weave complex, extremely difficult figuration in the background. But Wagner's orchestral palette is as versatile as it is powerful. In Act I of *Walküre*, the important expansion of the love motives, which takes place as Siegmund drinks the mead brought him by Sieglinde, is a superb sample of the delicacy and variety with which Wagner can mix his instrumental colors.

Although he did not use quite so large an orchestra in the works that interrupted and followed the *Ring*, Wagner continued throughout his life to develop his technique of orchestration along with other aspects of his craft. With the first dramas of the *Ring*, however, he became the master of the great instrument he helped create. The future brought only a growing refinement and an increased sensitivity to the role of color in emotional mood.

6

Continued Exile,
Amnesty, and Rescue, 1857-1864:
Tristan

Wagner had entered the Asyl in the firm hope that it would be a retreat for life, and for a few months all went smoothly. His sadness at abandoning the *Ring* was overcome by joy in the creation of *Tristan*. With more than two operas in his mature style now completed, he was at the height of his powers; never had his ideas poured forth more facilely or more powerfully.

Wagner finished the poem of *Tristan* on September 18, and shortly thereafter he read it to a group of friends gathered at the mansion on the Green Hill, into which the Wesendonks had moved on August 22. Again he made a mistake; only Mathilde was not puzzled. The prelude was completed on October 1, and by the beginning of the new year (1858) Wagner had prepared the sketch of the entire first act.

On the strength of this progress, Breitkopf and Härtel agreed to undertake the publication. Wagner was to receive 200 louis d'or, half of which was advanced in March, and he expected to deliver the completed work by September, 1858. He also composed during the winter of 1857-58 five songs with text by Mathilde. Two of these, "Träume" and "Treibhaus," are studies for *Tristan* and contain material that eventually found its way into the second and third acts.

Sensible critics have long since disposed of the notion that Mathilde Wesendonk "inspired" the music of *Tristan*, but in Wagner's mind she was now his Muse. He did not contemplate leaving Minna nor breaking up the Wesendonk home, however. He respected Otto, despite the shabby treatment he gave him later in *Mein Leben*.

Besides, Mathilde's marriage was happy, her relation with her husband was frank, and she had children. Apparently Wagner saw no reason why he could not have Mathilde as his beloved Muse and Otto as his financial helper, while his old comrade Minna provided him with the comforts of a home. That he could ever have seriously considered such a situation as a lasting solution is an indication of how completely he was absorbed in the world of his imagination.

By the first of the year (1858) something had already occurred to disturb the tranquility of this unlikely paradise. On January 11 Wagner wrote to Liszt: "I am at the end of a conflict in which everything that can be holy to a man is involved. I must come to a decision, and every choice that lies open to me is so cruel that when I do decide I must have by my side the one friend heaven has given me." [1] Liszt could not come, however, and Wagner retreated for the moment on a brief business trip to Paris. He was back by February 5, and driven by the need for an advance from Breitkopf he finished the first act of *Tristan* on April 3.

On the 7th the impending storm broke. Wagner sent Mathilde his pencil sketch of the *Tristan* prelude, and with it he sent an eight-page letter. Minna, who had watched the daily visits between the two houses with increasing jealousy, intercepted the servant carrying the package and read the letter.

To Minna the letter was evidence of Wagner's infidelity, of a sordid and ordinary affair with Mathilde. To anyone whose mind is not poisoned by illness and jealousy, it shows nothing of the sort. A large part of it is devoted to explanation of some points that had arisen earlier about Goethe. Wagner speaks of the joy and comfort of Mathilde's visit two days earlier, and complains that she is so much occupied with another visitor. But that part of the letter referring to love is anything but ordinary. It is couched in mystical, literary terms that, for all their depth of feeling, hardly pass as evidence of a commonplace affair.

> What nonsense I am talking! [he wrote in reference to the Goethe explanations]. Is it the pleasure of speaking alone, or the joy of speaking to you? Yes, to you! But when I look into your eyes, then I simply cannot speak any more; then everything I might have to say simply becomes void! Look, then everything becomes so indisputably true to me, then I am so sure of myself, when this wonderful, holy glance rests upon me, and I submerge

[1] Newman, *Life of Wagner,* II, 533.

myself within it! Then there is no longer any object or any subject; then everything is one united, deep infinite harmony! Lo, that is peace, and in that peace the highest, the perfect life! O fool who would seek to win the world and peace from without! How blind the one who would not recognize your glance and find his soul there! Only inside, within, only deep down does salvation dwell! It is only when I do not see you—when I may not see you—that I can speak and explain myself—[2]

In Ernest Newman's word, Wagner is "Tristanizing."

Minna immediately confronted Wagner with the letter and launched her attack along classic lines: she would leave, but she would not tolerate the deception of Otto. Wagner tried to explain, but mystical "Tristanizing" had no meaning for her; it was merely more of his *"vortreffliche Suade"* (his "gift of gab").

The next morning, with Minna exhausted and Wagner in despair, it was arranged that she should go to Brestenberg, a resort noted for the treatment of heart disease. Once she had restored her health, she would return, and perhaps things could resume their finely balanced calm. But before she went, and despite a promise to the contrary, Minna talked to Mathilde and threatened to go to Otto.

Mathilde, highly insulted, went to Otto herself immediately. Apparently Otto was already aware of the situation and had determined to put up with it for the sake of his wife, his home, and his children—and perhaps as well in admiration for Wagner's genius. The Wesendonks blamed Wagner for not being as frank with Minna as Mathilde had been with Otto. In their eyes, a delicate situation calling for restraint and understanding had suddenly become sordid.

When Minna returned on July 15, Wagner was optimistic. But now the two incompatible natures that were Richard and Minna Wagner could no longer exist together; inevitably the bitter recriminations began again. In despair Wagner saw that the situation was hopeless, and he made his decision quickly. They must give up the Asyl for good; Minna should go to her relatives in Dresden, while he sought some retreat where he might finish *Tristan*.

On the 17th of August, under a brilliant early-morning sky, Wagner said farewell to his unhappy refuge. Minna accompanied him to town, but he did not look at her and they rode in silence. At the station Minna's emotions overcame her. As always, despite her repeated threats, she could not face final separation from him. Wagner

[2] *The Burrell Collection,* pp. 369-372.

was beyond tears. It was only on the train that the release from intolerable tension brought a flood of relief to him. For the first time in months he felt at peace, and the second act of *Tristan* was before him.

There is much that will probably never be known about Wagner's relations with the Wesendonks. His own mood, exceptional even for him, and Minna's neurotic state of mind have left us with accounts so diametrically opposed that they seem to be about different events. Minna's viewpoint was the only one possible for her. While Wagner could understand her in a way she could never understand him, his own view of this affair was romanticized and dramatized until the facts become obscure.

He never denied his love for Mathilde, but he insisted to the end that his relations with her did not violate morality. A factor in his decision to break up the Asyl establishment may very well have been the increasing feeling that he could not live indefinitely in close proximity to Mathilde without possessing her fully.

Whether Mathilde was intellectually or spiritually worthy of the devotion Wagner fixed upon her is questionable, and it is of little importance.[3] His development and state of mind are what concern us. The relationship with Mathilde—if not Mathilde herself—played an important part in the creation of *Tristan* and a somewhat lesser part in *Die Walküre* and *Die Meistersinger*. Wagner was absorbed at this time in the Schopenhauerian conception of the "negation of the will" and in the Buddhistic doctrine of a bodiless state of Nirvana free from desire. Throughout his life he was haunted by the concept of renunciation as the entrance to higher spiritual realms. It is a part of almost every work he wrote, but in none is it so central as in *Tristan*, where the final revelation is achieved only by renunciation of life, and death is a transcendental entrance into joyous oblivion. Regardless of what we believe concerning details of the relationship, the affair with Mathilde Wesendonk was to Wagner the living experience of the doctrine of renunciation. When it threatened to become something either more or less, he fled. As Ernest Newman has so aptly stated, "It was *Tristan*, rather than

---

[3] Not much is known about Mathilde's background. She evidently felt considerable urge toward creative art without having much talent. After her relations with Wagner became distant, she developed an interest in Brahms, but he never responded very warmly.

Minna and Mathilde, that drove him from the Asyl." [4] As always, the creative artist in Wagner was in control at the time of crisis.

The next year of Wagner's life was exceptionally quiet. Accompanied by Karl Ritter, he went to Venice and rented two large rooms in one of the old palaces on the Grand Canal. He knew few people other than Karl (who was away from November to January), and he took part in no activities. He was susceptible to the beauties of Venice, but he referred to it as "the exquisite ruin of this wonderful city." It suited his mood to perfection; his detachment was almost complete.

Because gossip was rampant, the Wesendonks returned his letters unopened, but both Wagner and Mathilde kept diaries for each other. His love for her continued, but he was more than normally peaceful, more absorbed in his own contemplations. He felt a vast sympathy for the suffering of mankind and for animals as well, but he felt no call to action, no special bond with any individual. Here, in the midst of *Tristan*, his imagination for a moment seemed to project itself more than twenty years into the future, and he spoke of the Good Friday scene in *Parsifal* which he would someday write.

By early spring Venice had served its purpose for Wagner; he finished Act II of *Tristan* on March 9. Wishing to avoid the Venetian summer, he journeyed on March 23 to Lucerne, where he was again fortunate in renting quiet, spacious quarters. Wagner had wanted to visit the Wesendonks at Christmas, but had been warned away from the gossip. Once he was settled in Lucerne, however, Otto, who evidently handled the entire matter with strength and good sense, invited Wagner to the Green Hill for a few days. Wagner described the meeting as "melancholy but in no way embarrassed." Other visits followed, and the basis for a new, calm relationship was established. The effects were to remain with Wagner for some time to come; but he was almost through with *Tristan*, and his ardor for Mathilde was cooling.

While in Venice, Wagner had written to Minna regularly, urging her to recover her health that they might eventually re-establish a home together. Now she saw in his visits with the Wesendonks only vulgar intrigue and another insult to herself. A few visitors

[4] Newman, *Life of Wagner*, II, 556.

came and went during the summer, but in the main Wagner worked undisturbed. By early August *Tristan* was completed.

Tristan und Isolde

The legend of Tristan and Isolde is one of the most artistically developed of all medieval tales. As always Wagner sought out a universal meaning, discarded many incidents, and molded the story to his own purposes; but there are more psychological and moral implications, as well as a firmer structure, in the Tristan legend than in any other with which he dealt. His main source was Gottfried von Strassburg's version, written in the twelfth century when the legend was already old.

The story as Wagner tells it contains a minimum of outward dramatic detail:

> *Act I:* The scene is on a ship. The knight Tristan is escorting the Irish princess Isolde to Cornwall where she is to marry his liege-lord and uncle, King Marke. Isolde discloses to her serving lady Brangäne that Tristan had killed her fiancé in combat. Wounded himself, Tristan later came unknown to Ireland, where Isolde healed his wounds. She planned to kill him, but found herself unable to when he looked into her eyes. Isolde now orders Brangäne to prepare a death potion, with which she will kill both Tristan and herself. The terrified Brangäne substitutes a love potion instead, and the already smoldering attraction between Tristan and Isolde becomes irresistible.

> *Act II:* In Cornwall, a garden outside Isolde's chambers. Tristan and Isolde have agreed to meet secretly while King Marke and the rest of the court are on a night hunt. Brangäne tries to warn Isolde, but Isolde refuses the cautious advice. The long scene between Tristan and Isolde is interrupted by the unexpected return of Marke and the hunting party, including the knight Melot, who has aroused the King's suspicions against the lovers. Marke sadly questions Tristan but receives no answer. Tristan fights with the treacherous Melot and is badly wounded.

> *Act III:* Tristan has been taken by his squire Kurwenal to his castle in Brittany. A shepherd, piping a mournful tune, is watching for the promised arrival of Isolde. In semi-delirium Tristan recalls the events of the past and longs for Isolde. Finally the shepherd's joyful tune is heard, indicating that Isolde is coming. In his excitement Tristan tears the bandage from his wound and dies in her arms. A second ship arrives with Marke, Melot, and

others. Kurwenal kills Melot and is himself killed. Marke forgives the lovers, but it is too late. Isolde follows Tristan in death.

The poem, of course, is not nearly so simple as a bare outline of the story would indicate. The richness of detail is confined to inward progress and to symbolism. Once this is understood, one perceives that *Tristan* is worked out with a rigorous consistency exhibited by no other Wagnerian drama.

The story of *Tristan und Isolde* is a gradual revelation. The lovers find that their love is not merely a strong attraction that one may yield to or resist, according to one's morals and character. It is the whole of life; honor, fidelity, and finally existence itself sink into meaningless insignificance. But in the world of ordinary existence this all-embracing love can find no place, and it is therefore the most intense, unsatisfied longing. It leads inevitably to death, which becomes a mystic transformation of the two individuals into one unknowing unity. The consummation of love and the cessation of longing are found only in the transfigured happiness of unconsciousness.

This is nothing less than a view of life, and to most people it is both unacceptable and unattractive. For some, the nature of the philosophy behind the drama stands as a barrier to the appreciation of the work of art, but it need not. Wagner's means is the music drama, his end a work of art. In art one does not accept or reject on the basis of philosophical truth; one needs only to understand and experience.

Audiences and even knowledgeable critics have sometimes tended to look on Isolde as the dominating figure of the drama. Actually, the center of the drama moves steadily to the hero. The first act belongs largely to Isolde, ending with action by both. The second is shared equally, but ends with action by Tristan. And the third is Tristan's, despite the final interpretation of his experience by Isolde.

Even in Act I, Tristan is more perceptive than is Isolde. He tells her cryptically, "The mistress of silence [Isolde] bids me be silent. I grasp what she conceals; but what I conceal, she does not grasp." He understands the love that drives her to hatred, he is telling her, but she does not understand that his love is held in check by honor.

Tristan also knows that she means to kill him. Both are attempting suicide when they drink the potion, but his state of mind is closer to that which they come to later. "Endless sorrow's only solace, forgetfulness' kind potion—thee I drink without flinching!" he cries.

In Act II Isolde, absolving Brangäne from responsibility, makes doubly clear the role of the love potion: it is not the cause but only one element in bringing about their submission. The potion, then, is the primary symbol of inevitable destiny.

The lovers' long conversation in Act II is dominated by another symbol, that of "Day" versus "Night"—the day representing the world of conventional reality and values, the night the inner world in which their love exists. Again it is Tristan who takes the lead, gradually bringing Isolde to the understanding that only in death can their union be complete. *Tr.:* "Let me die! Never to awaken!" *Is.:* "But must not the day waken Tristan?" *Tr.:* "Let the day be overcome by death!" Gradually she grasps his meaning and joins him in the words, "So should we die, undivided, always one, without end, without awaking, without fear, nameless in love surrounded . . ."

Later the lines are switched to reflect her complete comprehension. *Tr.:* "Must the day still waken Tristan?" *Is.:* "Let the day be overcome by death!"

At the end of Act II, when Isolde promises to follow Tristan, she is promising to join him in death. He then draws his sword and attacks Melot, but purposely lowers his weapon. Once again he has sought death.

However, Tristan does not die; his revelation is not yet complete. In Act III, through two great characteristic Wagnerian cycles, Tristan painfully dredges up his memories and seeks the meaning of his fate. Finally the blinding truth is revealed to him. His whole life, the destiny of which he is a part, created the potion; he himself is responsible.[5] "The fearful potion . . . , I myself brewed it! In father's need, in mother's woe, in love's tears for ever and ever, in laughter and weeping, rapture and wounds, I found the potion's poison . . . Cursed be the fearful drink! Cursed be he who brewed it!" Only now is he ready for Isolde and for death.

The final articulation is left to her in the famous *"Liebestod."* But that word, taken from the second act, was not applied here by Wagner; he called the final monologue *"Verklärung"* ("transfiguration"). Her words are virtually impossible to translate literally into intelligible English, but it is clear that death for her is an absorption into universal, unconscious being—not a tragedy but a fulfillment.

---

[5] Tristan's responsibility does not involve freedom of choice. But he himself is a part of his fate, if not its master; he cannot curse one without cursing the other. The situation reflects one of Wagner's favorite ideas, the need of the individual to "will necessity." Compare with Wotan's position in the *Ring, infra.* p. 146.

Of the minor characters, King Marke has the most significance for the central meaning, although both Brangäne and Kurwenal are perhaps more vivid. Brangäne is unswervingly faithful to Isolde, but she continually voices conventional fears. Kurwenal's motivation and morals do not go beyond his complete devotion to Tristan; he is widely regarded as the prototype of Wagner's perfect friend.

Marke, like the other two, lives in the world of "day," but he has a much deeper sense of its values. Insofar as he is characterized, he is the drama's tragic figure, a man of nobility whose ideals are destroyed by a fate he does not understand. His monologue in Act II has importance in its representation of the suffering of one who clings to the false values of "day." To the end, Marke questions in vain. His last speech, echoing his words to Tristan in Act II, begins, "Why, Isolde, why this to me?"

The consistent concentration of the dramatic ideas in *Tristan* is matched and intensified by the music. The recitative-like passages of *Das Rheingold* and *Die Walküre,* punctuated by leitmotives, have almost disappeared. The symphonic texture—sometimes loose, sometimes tightly developmental, occasionally primarily lyrical—is in one form or another virtually continuous.

Identification and labeling of motives is more difficult and even more dangerous in *Tristan* than in the *Ring,* precisely because the concentration of the drama results in concentration of musical material. A brief consideration of the first three motives of the prelude will illustrate. Example 25 embraces two motives. Example 25b,

Example 25

perhaps the most basic motive of the entire work, is frequently called "Isolde's magic," because of its association at its first appearance, but the use is so wide that Ernest Newman finds it best to call it "desire." Example 25a is essentially a melodic inversion of 25b, shortened and with an up-beat added. Newman calls it "grief," although it has also been called "confession of love," because the first outstanding statement occurs as Isolde drinks the potion. Examples 25a and b together have also been labeled the "love potion," as well as being identified separately with "Tristan" and "Isolde."

Example 26a, which is a rhythmic variation and extension of "25b," is most commonly called "Tristan's suffering." It is closely related, however, to the second part of the motive associated with the ecstasy of love and the final transfiguration (Ex. 26b, motive x).

Example 26a

Example 26b

The dramatic elements—grief, Isolde's magic, desire, the love potion, suffering, ecstasy—are so closely related that they merge, one into another. The same close relationship, the same merging together, is heard in the motives. There is no other work of Wagner's in which the labeling of motives is so futile, but none in which a thorough knowledge of the material and its relation to the text is more rewarding.

The harmonic as well as the melodic idiom of *Tristan* is highly chromatic; and the deceptive cadence, an increasingly important tool of Wagner's style since *The Flying Dutchman,* becomes in *Tristan* the characteristic progression. Chromaticism combines with the lack of decisive, satisfying harmonic resolution to articulate most strongly the fundamental emotional mood, longing that cannot be satisfied. Here, certainly, is the clearest illustration of Wagner's expression of a fundamental dramatic idea by a fundamental feature of musical style.

There are a few passages in which the unresolved chromaticism gives way momentarily for obviously dramatic reasons—the music that escorts Brangäne through the sailors on the deck of the ship in Act I, for example, and some of Kurwenal's music in Act III. These are brief passages, and could not in themselves save Wagner from the problems of a style that is both concentrated and specialized. That he overcame the dangers is a tribute in part to his subtle manipulation of details, in part to his control of long-range structure, and in part to an intensity of feeling that makes monotony impossible.

The prelude to *Tristan und Isolde* was the first part of the opera written, and it contains only themes that occur in the first act. It is in no sense a dramatic exposition of the story, but, like the *Lohengrin* prelude, a musical distillation of the basic dramatic conception. In style it foreshadows the mood and texture of the whole opera. The chromatic harmony moves continuously from dissonance to dissonance without firm resolution, and harmonic color is supported by instrumental color. Melodic lines interweave and accompanying lines acquire thematic significance. The intensity builds, relaxes without resolution, begins again and again, and finally subsides after a violent, dissonant climax. It subsides, not to the satisfaction of a stable chord, but to the chromatic motives of "desire" and "grief," and the tense, unstable harmony of the famous "Tristan" chord (the first beat of the second measure, Ex. 25).

After a prelude of such emotional importance, the opening of the first scene might have been a problem. Wagner solved it easily and swiftly with the strange, unaccompanied song of the unseen sailor on the mast. From then until the entrance of Tristan before the drinking of the potion, the mood is dominated by Isolde's rage. Her long narrative, with its climactic curse on Tristan, brings together a number of expressive motives, and it succeeds in throwing some light on Tristan's character as well as Isolde's.

The essential drama at the drinking of the love potion consists of the sudden change in feeling, and it is confined exclusively to the orchestra. The singers stand in silence as the music reflects the first powerful reaction, the stunned confusion, and the growth of tenderness and passion. It is, of course, a difficult histrionic problem (what one would give to see Wagner demonstrate!), but it is not undramatic, as has been charged. The progression of emotion can be drama, and it is exactly that progression that is here so admirably portrayed. In objecting to the love potion, the anti-Wagnerian critic

Hanslick commented, "In the theater we believe only what we see." [6] Nevertheless, in opera we believe what we hear, and the sensitive listener hears the change in Tristan and Isolde.

The second act prelude, after an initial statement of the motive to be associated with the symbolic "day" (Ex. 27a), is constructed of material from the immediately succeeding scene depicting Isolde's impatience. The opening conversation between Isolde and Brangäne is not among the more interesting parts of the opera, either musically or dramatically; it underscores what we already know about the love potion and foreshadows Melot's treachery. Perhaps its primary function in the musico-dramatic structure is that of a "lull before the storm." Once Isolde throws down the torch as the signal to Tristan (another symbol, by the way), the excitement grows to such proportions at his entrance that a relatively inactive section of some length is needed to prepare it.

Tristan's entrance is not one of Wagner's beautifully moving lyrical climaxes; it is sheer, unbridled excitement, with an element of ferocity and certainly of hysteria in its intensity. The gradual progress downward from the climax (it is not, of course, a continuous descent) is correspondingly long and covers much of the conversation about "day" and "night." Again it is less interesting than what went before and what comes after.

The completion of the relaxation, which has dramatically brought about increased understanding on the part of the two lovers, leads to a long duet (this is the only possible term, despite Wagner's objections) which begins in tender sensuality with the words, *"O sink' hernieder, Nacht der Liebe"* ("O descend, night of love") (Ex. 28).

The remainder of the scene, as far as the entrance of the hunting party, expresses in the most passionate lyrical terms the love between the two. Except for the now-transformed "day" motive (27b), the melodic material is new, though closely related; the lovers, after all, have reached a new understanding. Again it follows Wagner's favorite structural plan of building to a climax, dropping to a quieter level, and beginning once more. Twice, as the lovers reach the point at which no further expression is possible, the voice of Brangäne floats down from the watch tower in lonely warning. The final ascent, which will be used again with utmost effect at the end of the opera,

[6] Eduard Hanslick, *Vienna's Golden Years, 1850-1900,* trans. and ed. by Henry Pleasants III (New York: Simon and Schuster, 1950), p. 249.

Example 27a

Example 27b

Example 28

is built primarily on Ex. 29, which we may call the *"Liebestod"* motive since its first statement (Ex. 29a) accompanies the words *"So
stürben wir"* ("So should we die"). At the very height of the climax,
with the listener's every nerve demanding resolution, a shatteringly

Example 29a

Is: So stur - ben wir, um un - ge - treunt,

Trem:
Bass: E♭ D♮

Example 29b

Tris: Wie es fas - sen, wie sie las - sen, die - se Won - ne

Bass: F♯ E D♮

dissonant deceptive cadence interrupts with the power of a physical blow. Brangäne screams, and Kurwenal rushes in to warn his master, followed quickly by Melot, Marke, and the hunting party. All stand for a moment in stunned silence as the orchestra sings the *"Liebestod"* motive quietly. Then Tristan says softly, to the accompaniment of the "day" motive, *"Der öde Tag zum letzten Mal!"* ("The bleak day for the last time!").

Marke's monologue, which occupies much of the remainder of the act, is another of those passages whose length can be justified only by the strength of the emotions that preceded it. At the end he asks the reason for his suffering, and Tristan replies, "O King, that I cannot tell you; and what you ask, that you can never learn." But the orchestra has the answer; it softly gives forth the combined motives of "grief" and "desire."

The wounding of Tristan at the end of Act II is symbolic, as is virtually every active incident in the opera, and most of Act III is taken up with clarifying the psychological nature of the wound and with the gradual illumination that comes to Tristan. Both are masterfully exposed. The short prelude is one of Wagner's finest mood pictures. The low register and thick texture in the strings; the repeated use of the open G-string in the violins; the manner in which the two violins detach themselves from the heavy opening and wind upward into nothingness; the sweet, hopeless melancholy of the motive first heard in the horns (Ex. 30)—all combine to produce an

Example 30

Mässig langsam

oppressive sense of loneliness and space. Once more, as in Acts I and II, the curtain rises to music on stage—this time the mournful English horn tones of the shepherd's *alte Weise* ("old tune"), which is to be of importance in the scene that follows.

The long scene familiarly known as "Tristan's delirium" usually undergoes some cuts in performance. This is especially unfortunate not only because of the dramatic importance of every detail, but also because the scene is cast in a great double cycle, the marked balance of which is used to register the progress made by Tristan from his own self-willed unconsciousness. In an exceptionally perceptive essay dealing centrally with Act III, Joseph Kerman has outlined the progression of each cycle through *recollection—curse—relapse —anticipation.*[7] As Tristan regains consciousness—his return from "night" to "day"—he can recall only the terrible suffering of his love for Isolde, and he curses "day." His recollection in the second cycle, however, embraces his whole life. The shepherd's melancholy tune recalls the death of his father and the day he learned that his mother had died giving him life. Gradually, searching for a meaning, his memory traces the events culminating in the drinking of the love potion. Up to this point, the familiar leitmotives, masterfully transformed, have matched Tristan's recollections. Never before and never again did Wagner succeed in endowing with such significance the dramatic device of recounting past action; but when the truth is revealed to Tristan, Wagner introduces a new and powerful motive that articulates with convincing force the newness of Tristan's revelation (Ex. 31).

After the violent curse on the potion and on himself, Tristan's suffering has been purged. His vision of Isolde is one of calm, ineffable beauty; the transformed and somehow transfigured motives of the second act (Ex. 32) create a feeling of almost unbearable poignancy. It is perhaps the rarest, most moving moment in this most moving of operas.

[7] Joseph Kerman, *Opera as Drama* (New York: Vintage Books, 1959; 1st ed., 1952), pp. 192-216.

Example 31

Example 32a (Act II)

Example 32b (Act III)

The musical treatment of Isolde's entrance subtly suggests Tristan's Act II entrance, but the excitement, though equally frenzied, is less physically powerful. The fever is almost over. Tristan sinks into Isolde's arms and raises his eyes to her face. Slowly and softly the orchestra sings the motive associated with the look whereby the wounded and helpless Tristan first touched Isolde's heart (Ex. 33). It fades into silence, and Tristan is dead. Isolde tries to revive

Example 33

him so that they might die together, while the orchestra hints at the beginning of the "*Liebestod*." But she sinks down in despair as the shepherd brings the news of the second ship.

The fight, Kurwenal's death (in itself quite moving), and Marke's explanation are handled with relative brevity. Then Isolde, "unaware of everything around, fixes her eyes with growing inspiration on Tristan's body."

The so-called "*Liebestod*" is one of the most famous concert selections from Wagner's works. Its full emotional effect, however, comes only from the perception of its relation to the whole, for the "*Liebestod*" is a repetition of the end of the love duet in Act II. The tempo is slower, the orchestral texture less active, and the voice part re-arranged. But the music is, in the symphonic sense, a recapitulation up to the point of that great deceptive cadence. This time the release can be granted, and the resolution takes place. Not abruptly, to be sure, for not until the final measures does the harmony settle on the tonic chord. The prolongation of the resolution merely serves to intensify the sense of emotional release; it is the final consummation of Isolde's mystic transfiguration.

The "*Liebestod*" is a much longer repetition than one usually encounters in Wagner, but it typifies one of the major problems posed for the listener. To experience the full effect of the recapitulation in the first movement of Beethoven's Ninth Symphony, for example, one must remember the statement in the exposition for some fifteen minutes. To experience the full effect of the resolution in the "*Lie-*

bestod," one must remember the deceptive cadence of Act II for more than an hour. The unconscious memory will contribute, and the total emotional result of four-and-a-half hours of unresolved chromaticism plays a major role. The full experience comes, however, only to one who is aware of the relationship with Act II— aware of the changes that have purified the driving excitement of the ascent, and aware, above all, of the terrible dissonance that shattered the earlier climax. Only then does one feel the significance when the dissonance is replaced by an ecstatically prolonged resolution.

In *Tristan* the sustained intensity of Wagner's imagination has transcended many dangers and limitations. Here as nowhere else he has created his ideal: the indissoluble unity of music and drama, which can be understood only in terms of the total work itself. For there can be no mistake, the drama that Wagner has brought so powerfully to life could be experienced only through music.

For the historian and the analyst, *Tristan* is an unavoidable work. More than the *Ring*, much more than *Parsifal* or *Die Meistersinger*, it is the primary focal point of Wagner's creative life, and it is by the same token a focal point in the cultural history of the era. Not by mere coincidence does Jacques Barzun place *Tristan und Isolde* beside Darwin's *Origin of Species* and Marx's *Critique of Political Economy*.[8]

The chromaticism that is the most marked feature of the "Tristan style" was not of course new. It had been an increasingly important device in Romanticism for more than a generation, and virtually every advanced composition from the songs of Schubert to the symphonic poems of Liszt made some use of it, if highly charged emotional expression was required. Wagner himself had made what was for the time very strong application of chromaticism in *Tannhäuser*. Now, in complete technical control and driven by the intensity of what he had to say, Wagner applied it with such consistency that he brought a new dimension to emotion in music, and in doing so he carried a fundamental stylistic trend to its ultimate limits. Among his own later works, only *Parsifal* has chromatic passages of such extremes as *Tristan*, and in *Parsifal* the style is not so consistent.

This continuous chromaticism, combined with the avoidance of harmonic resolution, became for other composers a fundamental problem; the style is so saturated that it points no way to the future.

---

[8] Jacques Barzun, *Darwin, Marx, Wagner*, 2nd rev. ed. (Garden City, New York: Doubleday Anchor Books, 1958; 1st ed., 1941).

They could hardly ignore it, so they retreated, or sought other paths, or finally pushed on beyond its limits into atonality—a move so fundamentally different from the music of the past as to seem a complete break with tradition. The most radical of important innovators in the early twentieth century began with post-*Tristan* chromaticism.

For the listener, the range of experience in *Tristan* is so wide and so intense that reactions are bound to be various. Those who cannot or will not follow the experience to its conclusion may see it as no more than the longest, most elaborate hymn to erotic love, for this element is certainly present, in the music if not in the text. Those who find its unrestrained emotion exhausting, tedious, or even unpleasant understandably react against it with some vehemence. Those who can willingly submit to its spell, who can follow its development both intellectually and emotionally, often find in *Tristan* as rich an experience as the world of art has to offer.

Once *Tristan* was completed, Wagner again faced difficult practical decisions. An early production of his new work was essential to his material fortunes, but he was reluctant to turn it over to someone else. After considering various possibilities, he agreed to give *Tristan* to Karlsruhe, in the hope that the Grand Duke of Baden might obtain partial amnesty for him by Christmas. In the meantime, he longed to be at the center of things, as he usually did after finishing a large composition. He wanted no more Zurichs, and his choice was distinctly limited. In Paris there were always intriguing possibilities, and besides he might be able to see Liszt, for whose friendship he still felt a need despite some recent misunderstandings.

For the moment Wagner had funds: Otto Wesendonk had consented to buy the publishing rights of the *Ring* at 6,000 francs for each score. Toward the middle of September, therefore, with 12,000 francs for *Rheingold* and *Walküre* in his pockets, Wagner was off to Paris once more.

Things started badly. Minna joined him in November and immediately added to the difficulties of his work. Ill both mentally and physically, poor Minna was the last person Wagner should have had to live with at this time; his was not a temperament to deal easily with the broken and pitiable woman she had become.

From Karlsruhe rumors had begun about *Tristan* almost at once, and finally word came that it had been abandoned because of unprecedented difficulties. Wagner could scarcely have been surprised covering a relatively limited time span; but if it attempts to deal with action, the demands of its own structure (in terms of repetition, balance, and form) will conflict with the need of the action to move forward.

For most of the eighteenth century, the dominant type of opera recognized these problems in the construction of the libretto. Each scene consisted of two sections, the first carrying *action* (or more likely the recounting of action through conversation), the second being the *reaction* (emotion, feeling) of a character. From the musical standpoint, the first part was set in recitative, which made almost no structural demands and in which the text dominated. The second part was an aria, a fixed musical form, in which the music was free to make the necessary expansions and repetitions according to its own needs.

This system is beautifully rational, and it was finely tailored to the musical conventions and aesthetics of its time; but the dangers are obvious. The dramatic interest tends to follow the musical interest, thus emphasizing the dramatically static area. Reaction becomes more important than action. It then becomes fatally easy to feel little concern with the motivation of the reaction. Effect becomes everything; cause, nothing. The drama, then, as Wagner saw quite clearly, becomes a meaningless scaffold on which individually effective musical numbers are hung.

Nevertheless, the eighteenth-century system, stylized and rigid though it became, was an efficacious method of constructing an opera, and it was remarkably persistent. The first break toward greater dramatic continuity came through the ensembles of Italian comedy. In the hands of Mozart, the ensemble became an unsurpassed means for integrating conversation and dramatic progress with coherent musical structure. However, the delicate balance of the Mozart ensemble was not only beyond the capacity of his successors, but was frequently outside their realm of interest. The Romantic era demanded larger, more massively brilliant effects; it demanded heroism and melodrama, and the technique of fast-moving comedy and subtle characterization was of little use.

Neither the ensembles of Mozart nor the more self-conscious reform of Gluck, which dealt primarily with specific abuses, could solve the nineteenth century's operatic problems. The movement toward continuous opera took the form of a gradual relaxing of the rigorous stylistic division between recitative and aria, but the old system of set numbers, of recitative alternating with aria, remained discernible in less rigid fashion. This was, briefly, the situation in

Tannhäuser and *Lohengrin,* with the continuous tendency carried in the latter to an extreme beyond which it was impossible to go without the development of a different technique.

Wagner's problem was complex. In order to realize his ideal, he needed a type of drama that could be continuously articulated by music, but first he must conceive a technique that would be flexible enough to mold itself to dramatic form without the complete loss of musical coherence. Although the text must of course be written before the music, the musical problem was both central and primary. Wagner was convinced that the poetic idea germinated the music; perhaps he was right, but the musician necessarily controlled the actual construction of the poem.

Wagner's answer was a music drama in which the orchestra, spinning a nearly continuous symphonic texture, became the major articulating force and the primary means of carrying the musical continuity, while the voice projected a new kind of melodic declamation within that texture. The word "nearly" in the preceding sentence covers a great deal of ground. In both *Rheingold* and *Walküre* some passages are difficult to call anything but recitative, although admittedly it is scarcely a conventional type. Even in later operas, when Wagner mastered more fully the integration of narrative and exposition into the musical texture, one can discern passages of high emotional lyricism alternating with passages that are dramatically active and less expansive musically.

Wagner was far too practical to tie himself rigidly to a system; he was writing dramas, not proving the feasibility of symphonic opera, but the essence of the technique by which he implemented his reform is symphonic. The short motives, the frequent modulation, the flexible and often contrapuntal texture—all clearly derive from the development section of the symphony and, more specifically, the symphony of Beethoven.

Beethoven was not only Wagner's greatest inspiration, he was also the "patron saint" of the Romantic movement in music. Although he was claimed by widely divergent groups, there were primarily two aspects of his works that interested the advanced Romantics: first, the poetic content, and second, the inner organic unity. It is beyond the scope of this study to discuss whether or not Beethoven's successors viewed his works accurately on either count. The important point here is that there was a strong movement toward the use of the orchestra for poetic purposes, toward the unification of a large composition by means of recurring thematic relationships, and toward the imbuing of each detail of the composition with demonstrable inner significance. Berlioz's program symphonies and Liszt's symphonic poems are only the two most obvious of many examples illustrating this trend.

When Wagner carried these ideals into opera, he did so with characteristic thoroughness and intense individuality. Despite his originality, he was drawing together and bringing into sharp focus the strongest forces of the Romantic era.

The most widely known technical feature of Wagner's reform is the leitmotive.[9] By simplest definition it is a recurring musical idea that is associated with some element in the drama, and thus it has its predecessors not only in Wagner's earlier works but in the operas of other composers and in the *idée fixe* of Berlioz's program symphonies. In actual practice, Wagner's use of the leitmotive warrants the special term to distinguish it from earlier examples.

The characteristics of the leitmotive may be briefly summarized: it is short, usually not more than two measures, sometimes even less; it is flexible, frequently harmonic in character, and suited to transformation and sequential development; and it is "open at both ends," being easily joined to other motives or to repetitions of itself.

Sometimes the dramatic association of the motive is clear and consistent, and the motive itself consistently the same. Such a case is the "sword" motive (Ex. 16). It is a pictorial figure, and it flashes

Example 16

forth in the orchestra every time the sword Nothung is mentioned or thought of. Only in Act I of *Die Walküre,* when Siegmund is meditating on his need for a weapon, and later as Sieglinde tells the story of Wälse's visit, does the treatment approach transformation or sequential development. Such a motive poses no problem for the listener, and such a use could never serve all Wagner's complex purposes.

Occasionally the dramatic meaning of a motive seems to change from the specific to the general or vice versa. The motive associated with Fafner in the form of a dragon is first heard in Scene 3 of

[9] The German word is *Leitmotiv,* meaning "leading motive." It is common now to anglicize it rather than use the awkward translation.

Rheingold, when Alberich demonstrates the power of the Tarnhelm by turning himself into a great serpent. The listener who insists on a strict application of meaning will wonder whether the motive refers to Fafner or to dragons and serpents in general.

But this problem is minor and usually occurs only in connection with motives of minor importance. Of much more significance is the question of motives whose meaning seems to expand and acquire various different relationships. For example, the motive that is first associated with Alberich's curse on love (Ex. 17) in Scene 1 of *Das*

Example 17

Rheingold reappears when Siegmund declares his love for Sieglinde and again as Wotan takes leave of Brünnhilde at the end of *Die Walküre.* It is not, then, simply a "renunciation-of-love" motive, as it is frequently called; it is associated with the suffering of love—with "longing," according to one analyst, with "acceptance" according to another. In retrospect the later associations throw new light on Alberich's renunciation.

The situation becomes more complex and more important for the drama when a motive undergoes various transformations that add to its significance. Sometimes the transformation and its relation to the dramatic situation is simple. Thus a transformed motive (Ex. 18a) from the group associated with the love of Siegmund and Sieglinde in Act I of *Walküre* becomes the basis for the symphonic passage accompanying their flight in Act II (Ex. 18b).

Example 18a (Act I)

Example 18b (Act II)

Bewegter

and he may even have felt relief, for he longed to supervise the production himself.

To interest Paris in *Tristan* at this time was patently impossible, however. Although Meyerbeer had passed the peak of his popularity, his prestige and power were still enormous, and his faction understandably disliked Wagner. *Tannhäuser* offered the best possibility of paving the way for *Tristan,* but even in this case Wagner needed to make some preparation. So he planned a series of three concerts for the winter, hoping to follow them quickly with a season of German opera, including *Tannhäuser* and *Lohengrin* and culminating with *Tristan* in June.

He found backing easily, and the concerts took place on January 25, February 1, and February 8, 1860. The faithful Hans von Bülow had left his duties in Berlin to help with the preparations, the orchestra was excellent, and Wagner himself conducted. Musically the results left nothing to be desired, and virtually every important musician, including Meyerbeer and Berlioz, attended. The opposition of the press, most of it controlled by Meyerbeer's party, was balanced by support from some of the finest minds in Paris. Berlioz was uncertain—he apparently could not fathom the prelude to *Tristan*—but Gounod and the brilliant young Saint-Saëns became confirmed Wagnerians, at least for a time. Baudelaire was also won over by the concert, and he wrote Wagner a fine letter in which he apologized for the conduct of the press.

While the concerts were indecisive in their effect on Wagner's musical fortune, there was no doubt of the financial result. The deficit was 11,000 francs. The backers were naturally discouraged, and plans for a season of German opera were abandoned. About the middle of March, however, when no further prospects seemed open, Emperor Napoleon III suddenly ordered that *Tannhäuser* be given at the Opera.

His motivation was political, rather than artistic. His regime less stable than it appeared, Louis Napoleon wanted to ingratiate himself with the German faction, and he was using all means of diplomacy.

One indirect result of the *Tannhäuser* order was the granting of partial amnesty to Wagner. The German princes, whose lack of interest in Wagner had been notoriously marked, were now embarrassed by this favor from the French emperor. In July, 1860, King Johann of Saxony agreed to let Wagner enter any part of Germany except his own realm. Wagner received the news apathetically; he was now committed to the long and exhausting business of producing *Tannhäuser* in a foreign capital and in a foreign tongue.

When rehearsals began in September, no expense was spared, and Wagner was given complete control. Working ceaselessly, he won over most of the company. Even those who were unsympathetic did their tasks competently, for the Paris Opera was nothing if not efficient. In late October, however, Wagner was taken seriously ill and missed several weeks of rehearsals. It was during this time that most of the revisions that he was making in the score, imposing new difficulties on some of the singers, were delivered. When he returned, weak and exhausted, he found a different atmosphere.

Troubles increased in February, 1861, when the regular conductor, Philippe Dietch, took over for full rehearsals.[9] In agony Wagner watched while the precision, the perfection of nuance, and the feeling for tempo, on which the entire company had labored for months, disappeared in a matter of minutes. Morale fell to a new low.

Although Wagner could never have been satisfied with a performance under the incompetent Dietch, more serious problems soon arose. The most important supporters of the Paris Opera were a group of young aristocrats known as the Jockey Club. Their main interest was ballet—or, to be more accurate, ballerinas. They dined late and invariably missed the first act. They were accustomed to seeing their mistresses dance in the second act, and they insisted that Wagner not disappoint them.

Wagner agreed to include a ballet in his revision of the Venusberg scene in the first act, but he could not countenance such a thing in the second act. He refused, and continued to refuse under every conceivable type of pressure. It soon became apparent that a full-fledged battle was at hand. The political forces that had worked in Wagner's favor a year earlier now proved a handicap, as the Jockey Club and the press saw an opportunity to discredit the entire German faction in Paris. Even the presence of the Emperor would not deter them. At the first performance, whistles and jeers began in the second scene and brought rejoinders from the majority who wished to hear the opera. The performance went on, and the Wagner forces felt they had won a victory. On the second night the Jockeys held their fire until well into Act II; this time they made sure that the opera was disrupted.

In a last desperate effort, the management scheduled the third

[9] The same Dietch who composed the French version of *The Flying Dutchman*.

performance for Sunday, when the Jockey Club did not normally attend; but by now it was too late. The press had happily reported a fiasco, and "Wagner whistles" were being sold in the street. Now the young aristocrats, those "ruffians in white gloves," moved in for the kill. The uproar was such that the performance was sometimes delayed as much as fifteen minutes at a time, and the travesty was complete.

This time Wagner had wisely stayed at home. A few old friends who came to offer him sympathy after the performance found him calm and even able to joke a little. But his hand was trembling. The following day, with quiet dignity, he requested that *Tannhäuser* be withdrawn.

The *Tannhäuser* scandal had some unexpected results. In Germany, it unquestionably helped Wagner. The honor bestowed on him in Paris had embarrassed the Germans; this insult now made him a hero.

A number of the finer young Parisians were deeply mortified, and they rallied to Wagner's cause. There was even talk of starting a Wagner theater in Paris. The Jockey Club was clearly a minority, whose power was symptomatic of an unhealthy, corrupt government. As Baudelaire put it, "A handful of rowdies has disgraced us *en masse.*"

Wagner's wife had another explanation: it was all Richard's fault, she wrote to Natalie; he had been stubborn again.

A number of Parisian friends had come to Wagner's rescue after the financial disaster of his concerts. Otto Wesendonk had advanced another 6,000 francs for the incomplete *Siegfried*. When Wagner sold *Das Rheingold* to B. Schott's Sons in Mainz, he should, of course, have paid back Otto's previous advance. Instead, Otto accepted a receipt for the 6,000 francs that would eventually be due Wagner for *Götterdämmerung* as payment for the debt on *Das Rheingold*; it was a peculiarly Wagnerian arrangement.

All in all, Wagner received from various sources enough money to live well, although not in undue luxury, during his time in Paris, but the future of his works was mortgaged and his new debts were heavy; everything had depended on the success of *Tannhäuser*. For the production of *Tannhäuser*—for seven months of prodigious labor and the privilege of being insulted—he received the munificent sum of 750 francs. For singing the title role, the tenor Albert Niemann received 54,000 francs.

In the last decade certain unpleasant aspects of Wagner's personality had become more dominant. His egocentric tendency to use people for his own purposes had increased, and he was more un-reasonably bitter toward those who did not help him as much as he thought they should. In the main, however, his character had weathered the disappointments of his exile and the moral crisis of the Wesendonk affair well enough. In the three years following the *Tannhäuser* fiasco, a grievous decline set in which threatened to ruin the man and the artist.

Money was as usual at the root of his trouble. Throughout his life, Wagner's handling of his personal affairs was unwise and frequently reckless; he was curiously insensitive to the feelings and rights of others where money was concerned. It should be recognized, how-ever, that after the success of *Rienzi*, Wagner would never have been in financial difficulty had he worked under a system even remotely fair to the creative artist. In Germany many people made money from Wagner's works, but the composer was at the bottom of the operatic totem pole. Even Paris was miserly with composers compared to the amount spent on singers and productions. Meyer-beer himself achieved riches only through carefully calculated pop-ular success and skillful manipulation of the power he acquired.

Such calculation and manipulation were not for Wagner; he would not have been the artist he was if compromise had been possible for him. Had he been completely ruined, as very nearly happened, his last works would have remained unwritten, and the blame would have rested primarily on society rather than on the flaws in his character.

Wagner's French friends and his supporters in the embassies joined forces to help him out of his immediate financial trouble, and in the middle of April he journeyed to Karlsruhe to try to arrange a performance of *Tristan*. He easily persuaded the Grand Duke of Baden that the difficulties could be overcome, and in early May he proceeded to Vienna to look for the right singers. His works were by now doing well at the Vienna Opera, and the management in-vited him to a special rehearsal of *Lohengrin*.

Wagner was impressed by this cordial welcome, and by the qual-ity of two singers, the tenor Aloys Ander and the soprano Luise Meyer-Dustmann. It occurred to him that he would be in a much better position to present *Tristan* in Vienna, rather than Karlsruhe, and he made the arrangements before returning to end his affairs in Paris.

The future was too unsettled to allow the establishment of a home, so it was decided that Minna should settle in Dresden, while Wagner followed his fortune where it might lead him. He promised to send her 3,000 marks a year, and somehow he seems to have kept his promise. Back in Vienna he settled in the home of a new friend and supporter, Dr. Joseph Standhartner. The doctor was away on vacation, but he left as housekeeper his attractive young cousin Stephanie Mauro. Wagner was enchanted and apparently carried on a rather lighthearted affair with her.

At the theater things went badly. The management, which had been so eager in the spring to soothe the insults of Paris, now began to make excuses. The tenor Ander had trouble with his role, lost his voice temporarily, and became convinced that Tristan would kill him. Also, as always, Wagner had powerful enemies.

Just why he decided to visit the Wesendonks in November is not known, but it seems likely that he was more interested by now in Otto's purse than in Otto's wife. The couple was in Venice, and Wagner found them happy and perfectly friendly. But the results of the visit were negative; it marked the final cooling of his relation with Mathilde, and he received no money from Otto.

Apparently he talked over a new scheme with Mathilde, however. Since *Tristan* had turned out to be difficult, he would revise his early sketch of *Die Meistersinger* and write a happy, easily playable comedy, suitable for either large or small theaters. This plan he had outlined to Franz Schott (of B. Schott's Sons, Mainz) at the end of October. In early December, Schott succumbed to Wagner's persuasion and paid him 10,000 francs in advance. Wagner expected to have the work in the theaters in a year.

By now it was apparent that *Tristan* would not be produced very soon, and Wagner began to search for a place where he might live cheaply and work on *Die Meistersinger* in comfort. He went to Paris for a few weeks, and there finished the poem, which he promptly read to his friends. Having exhausted all the possibilities of finding a hospitable friend to shelter him without cost, he finally picked out Biebrich, a small, quiet town on the Rhine, which was centrally located and accessible to his publisher in Mainz.

He was scarcely settled, toward the end of February, when Minna arrived unexpectedly. Wagner was moved but hardly overjoyed. Almost at once she began to nag again. Unfortunately, an innocent package, a slight Christmas gift delayed in delivery, arrived from Mathilde Wesendonk, and Minna began the old scenes: "The old madhouse opening out in front of me again!" Wagner wrote to a friend.

After "ten atrocious days," Minna departed, but her letters continued to worry and accuse, destroying the calm he sought for his work. In the early summer Wagner wrote to Dr. Pusinelli for advice: Would it be desirable, from the standpoint of Minna's health, to settle on a permanent separation? The doctor's answer was to suggest divorce to Minna. Wagner, he knew, was desperate, and as Minna's physician he felt that a final acceptance of the situation would be beneficial to her. Although Minna refused to consider the advice, it probably had the desired effect, for her letters became calmer. She had asked Wagner to settle with her in Dresden, clearly not because she wanted him but only to vindicate herself. To please her, he applied on May 28, 1862, for complete amnesty. This time, given the excuse of Minna's poor health, the Saxon authorities granted his request. He did not go to Dresden until the following November, however, and then only for a few days; it was his last meeting with Minna. The break between them was now complete.

Meanwhile, consoled by a number of friends, Wagner made progress on *Die Meistersinger*. August Röckel appeared in the spring, having been released from prison after thirteen years. Hans von Bülow, who was now married to Liszt's youngest daughter Cosima, visited during the summer, and he was sent into rhapsodies of joy by his first view of *Die Meistersinger*. "To have Wagner as a neighbor," he wrote to a friend, "means that everything else shrivels into insignificance, becomes utterly childish, null and void."

Nor was feminine companionship lacking. Mathilde Maier, an intelligent and exceptionally sweet-spirited young woman who lived in Mainz, extended the intellectual sympathy so necessary for him, and there is some evidence that he considered marrying her when divorce from Minna seemed possible. With Friedericke Meyer, an actress and sister of the Viennese soprano Luise Meyer-Dustmann, Wagner probably had a conventional affair; that was, at any rate, the interpretation put on the relationship by her sister.

Considering the advance from Schott and various gifts and loans, Wagner's income since the Paris *Tannhäuser* should have been sufficient, but he was now spending with reckless disregard for the future. When an infected hand stopped his work for two months in July and August, he fell behind in the composition of *Die Meistersinger*, and thus could not ask Schott for another advance. Autumn found him again without funds.

By the middle of November he was back in Vienna to push the production of *Tristan*, which was supposedly in rehearsal again, but the situation quickly became more hopeless than ever. Ander remained a problem, and Frau Meyer-Dustmann became an enemy because of the affair between Wagner and her sister, who now had an engagement in Vienna. Most serious of all was the opposition of Eduard Hanslick.

Hanslick, the most powerful critic in Vienna, had been an early admirer of Wagner in the Dresden days, but had not followed him past *Tannhäuser*. He had acquired a reputation as a thinker with the publication in 1854 of *The Beautiful in Music*, a tightly argued but strictly limited exposition of the anti-Wagnerian aesthetic of absolute music. As a critic, he was conscientious, and he wrote in a lucid, impressive style. There is little indication, however, that his musical perception was keen, and certainly his taste was narrow. He succeeded in misjudging Verdi almost as thoroughly as he misjudged Wagner. Bizet, Berlioz, Hugo Wolf, Bruckner—all came under his stern disapproval. Brahms alone among contemporaries of great talent won his praise without serious qualification.

While Hanslick's opposition to Wagner was based on principle, he may have been ready to be more friendly in response to several efforts made to bring the two together. But Wagner thought Hanslick a pedant and a fool, and he treated him with utmost coldness. Any chance of amicable relations disappeared for good when Dr. Standhartner unwisely invited Hanslick to a reading of the poem of *Die Meistersinger*. It was widely assumed in Wagner's circle that the ridiculous Beckmesser was a caricature of Hanslick; indeed, Wagner had at one time given him the name "Veit Hanslich." Wagner assumed complete innocence, but he could not have been surprised when Hanslick became pale and tense during the reading and left quickly at its end.

As the chances for *Tristan* faded, Wagner turned to concerts as a means of raising money and presenting his music to the public. Three concerts in Vienna were enthusiastically received (except, of course, by Hanslick), but the only profit Wagner made was a gift of 1,000 gulden from the Empress. Doubtless much of this was spent on a recklessly extravagant dinner for the performers.

In February, 1863, Wagner made a tour in Russia, where his success was triumphant and his profit substantial. His reaction was typical: he rented an expensive house in the Viennese suburb of Penzing, furnished it richly, hired servants, and stocked the wine cellar. By summer, it was necessary to give more concerts.

In July he gave two in Pesth, in November two in Prague and two in Karlsruhe, in December one in Breslau. By the middle of December, he was back in his house in Penzing, full of honors, surrounded by his friends, and living well. It was all a desperate front; he was deeply in debt, and there was still no prospect for the production of *Tristan.*

During the preceding year, Wagner had exhausted the resources of his friends, and finally he resorted to professional money lenders. When plans for a second Russian tour failed to materialize, his last hope was gone. It was still possible in Vienna to go to prison for debts. On March 24, 1864, Wagner fled. He went for refuge to an old friend and supporter, Frau Eliza Wille, who lived in a suburb of Zurich. She received him warmly and with understanding, but even feminine sympathy could not now lighten his dark and bitter depression.

Wagner was at the low point of his entire life. He had in his portfolio three completed operas, two-thirds of a fourth, and a substantial beginning of a fifth, none of which had the remotest prospect for performance. The friends who had supported him so generously for so long understandably felt unable to continue giving money for a lost cause. His debts were widespread and heavy, his reputation such that further financial help from normal sources seemed highly unlikely. His career appeared to have come to a ruinous end—his strength and his courage dissipated by hardship and folly, his great works unfinished or unperformed, a large part of his magnificent talent wasted.

Exactly at this point came the most dramatic event of his life, the stroke of good fortune of which he had dreamed and which he had prophesied.

In 1863 Wagner had written a preface for the public edition of the *Ring* poem. Here he had outlined his plans for a festival performance and suggested that it could be accomplished only with the support of a German prince who felt a sympathy for his work. "Will this prince be found?" he concluded. "In the beginning was the Deed!"

Among those who read these words was the Crown Prince of Bavaria. In March, 1864, this young man became Ludwig II. A month later he issued an order to Franz von Pfistermeister, his Cabinet Secretary: "Find Richard Wagner and bring him to me."

After three weeks Wagner had left Zurich and gone to Stuttgart, where a friend agreed to help him find a retreat in the mountains. In Stuttgart Pfistermeister caught up with him and delivered the King's message on May 2, 1864. Wagner was to come to Munich at once, where everything needed to continue his work would be given him.

Before departing the next evening, Wagner sent the King a brief note:

> These tears of the heavenliest emotion I send to you, to tell you that now the marvels of poetry have come as a divine reality into my poor, love-lacking life. And that life, its last poetry, its last tones, belong henceforth to you, my gracious young King: dispose of them as your own property.[10]

At long last the miracle had occurred.

[10] Newman, *Life of Wagner,* III, 220.

7

Munich and Triebschen, 1864-1871:
Die Meistersinger

King Ludwig II of Bavaria was less than nineteen years old when he came to the throne. An education that pampered in some ways and over-disciplined in others had limited his fine natural abilities and turned him within himself. No one was close to him, and his love of solitude was almost an obsession. Although he had little technical knowledge of music, Ludwig's response to beauty was evidently abnormally intense; it was only in the world of beauty, of his imagination, that he could exist. The legends and myths of the Middle Ages became for him a substantial ideal, and he found them realized in the works of Wagner.

To say that he was neurotic explains nothing. He was a highly complex personality, whose strength lay in his intelligence and his nobility of spirit and whose weaknesses were almost incredible inexperience and emotional immaturity. In the spring of 1864 he was a handsome and appealing boy, but anyone with knowledge of the world might have guessed he was marked for tragedy.

Wagner's first meeting with King Ludwig took place on May 4, 1864, and for both it was a moving experience. Before they could discuss plans at length, however, there were practical matters to be taken care of. Armed with 4,000 gulden from the King, Wagner went to Vienna to clear up his affairs there. As far as he could, he concealed from his far-flung creditors the extent of his good fortune, but even so the money did not go far toward meeting his pressing debts. It was shortly arranged that he should receive 4,000 gulden annually, and a little while later the King made a second outright gift of 16,000. Wagner had estimated that this would be enough to rid him of all debts; it was not the end of that story, however, by any means.

Bringing with him from Vienna his servants and his old dog, Wagner proceeded on May 14 to Starnberg Lake, where the King provided a villa for him. Each day he spent an hour or more with Ludwig discussing their great plans for the future, and a feeling of mutual warmth developed between them.

While Ludwig was content with solitude when not with his beloved friend, Wagner craved more company than an hour a day with a youth of nineteen. The Bülows were planning a visit in July. When Ludwig left on state business in mid-June, Wagner sent a plea that they come at once. Bülow himself was ill and could not change his plans, but he sent Cosima and the two children ahead.

There is a haze of mystery over the relationship between Wagner and Cosima Liszt von Bülow in the years before she came to him at Starnberg. That there was a strong attraction, admitted by both, is evident from veiled hints in *Mein Leben*. From the time she arrived at Starnberg on June 29, 1864, however, until the day of her death, Cosima was dedicated to Wagner and to no one else. When Hans arrived ten days later, he found himself part of a complex and painful triangle. In April, 1865, Cosima gave birth to a daughter, who was named Isolde; there is no doubt that Wagner was the father.

Cosima Liszt was born in 1837, the second illegitimate child of Liszt and the Countess Marie d'Agoult. From her seventh year onward, she saw her parents only occasionally, but apparently she adored her father. Her education, supervised by an elderly Russian governess, was strictly disciplined, and the normal emotional outlets of family life must have been largely lacking.

When she was eighteen, Cosima was sent to Berlin to study music with Bülow. It is probable that her attachment to Hans began as a deep sympathy rather than as romantic love. She was already a formidable personality, poised, intelligent, and highly serious. Bülow's poor health and his constant struggles for his ideals may have aroused in her something of that desire to dedicate herself to an artist—which eventually bound her to Wagner.

The marriage was not a happy one. Bülow was a difficult person to get along with, irritable, nervous, and impatient. Although he was not a great creator, he was one of the finest musicians of his generation and an artist of distinction in his own right, yet there was something in his personality that called for self-abasement; he needed to lean on some stronger spirit, such as Wagner or Liszt, and to realize his own inferiority while doing so. It has been suggested that he married Cosima from some obscure desire to legitimize the daughter of Liszt. Whatever truth there is in such a notion, it is certain that Bülow felt himself Cosima's inferior; she had all the strong traits of character that he lacked. He was devoted to her; he depended on her and drew heavily from her strength, but he knew that he was not making her happy, and he frequently asked forgiveness for his failure as a husband.

Cosima's background was French; she brought social grace to Wagner's life, as well as a diplomatic skill that was foreign to him. Both her cool manipulation of his affairs and the *salon* atmosphere she later created around him alienated some of his German friends from her. If her manner of living and her technique of handling problems were French, her thinking and feeling were German. She was more strongly anti-Semitic than Wagner, and she was less inclined in her devotion to German culture to see redeeming features in other nations. She was, in brief, more inflexible and more coldly calculating than he.

There is strong evidence that Cosima was frank with Bülow concerning the relation between Wagner and herself,[1] yet all three of them seem to have felt that no open break could be contemplated. Cosima was to remain Bülow's wife before the world, to keep his home, to support him as much as she could under the circumstances; but she was to belong to Wagner.

This situation demanded that the Bülows settle in Munich, which fitted in well with other of Wagner's plans, for he had need of Hans as a conductor and teacher. In September, therefore, King Ludwig appointed Bülow court pianist at a salary of 2,000 florins a year. He was the first of an influx of young Wagnerians into Munich.

In the middle of October, Wagner rented a fashionable house, which included a garden and a guest cottage for the Bülows, and he proceeded to decorate it in the most luxurious fashion. Pfistermeister, the King's Cabinet Secretary, warned that the whole establishment was too lavish, but Wagner was confident and in no mood to deny himself. The rental on the house, which was 3,000 florins a year, as well as 15,000 florins for furnishing and for more debts, was paid by Ludwig as part of a contract calling for Wagner to complete the *Ring* in three years. Included also was an additional 2,000 florins a year, added to Wagner's regular stipend of 4,000.

---

[1] Ernest Newman's evidence against the belief that Bülow was deceived for nearly two years is quite convincing (see *Life of Wagner*, III, 520-537). See Julius Kapp, *The Loves of Richard Wagner* (London: W. H. Allen, 1951), pp. 273-275, for a contrary view.

The *Ring* was to be the King's property, to be disposed of as he wished.[2]

In addition to plans for completing the *Ring*, Wagner had outlined for the King a whole program of productions which still included *Die Sieger* and ended with *Parsifal* in 1872. The first step was to be a production of *Tristan* in the spring of 1865, and for this Wagner now knew that only one tenor was possible, Ludwig Schnorr von Carolsfeld. Schnorr, who was 29 years old in 1865, was the son of a famous painter. Both his education and his intelligence were beyond that of the average singer, and his dramatic talents were unusual. Wagner was delighted with him, and he was scarcely less enthusiastic about Schnorr's wife, Malvina Garrigues, as a potential Isolde.

The Schnorrs arrived in Munich in February, and preparations went on through the winter. As the performance date approached, friends and supporters began to gather from all over Europe. Liszt, who had taken minor orders in the Catholic church, did not choose to leave his retreat in Rome. It is likely that he knew by this time of the triangle in which his two friends and his daughter were involved.

On the 11th of May, 600 people attended a full dress rehearsal. The morning of the 15th, the performance date, Schnorr arrived at Wagner's house in tears: Malvina was hoarse; the performance would have to be postponed.

Many of the guests who had traveled considerable distance were unable to wait for her recovery, and the hostile press was delighted. *Tristan* was obviously unperformable, as had been contended all along. Not until June 10 was the first public performance finally given. The journalists understood nothing as usual. How much the audience understood is questionable, but the general reaction was good. Even today one's first hearing of *Tristan* is frequently an experience too powerful to be grasped fully; it is hardly surprising that the audience in 1865 was overwhelmed but somewhat confused. The performance itself must have been outstanding. The orchestra under Bülow was excellent, Mme. Schnorr more than satisfactory, and Schnorr himself incomparable.

Three more performances were given, the last at the request of the King, and the guest singers prepared to depart, Schnorr filled

[2] Of course the publication rights to the *Ring* really belonged to Otto Wesendonk, until such time as Wagner paid back the advances. Otto generously renounced his claims at Wagner's request, and Wagner never paid him anything.

with gloomy thoughts at returning to a repertory that now seemed insignificant. Back at his post in the Dresden opera house, the exhausted Schnorr was taken ill. On July 21 Wagner received the news that Ludwig Schnorr was dead.

In his delirium Schnorr had sung to his own notes passages from *Siegfried* that were not yet composed. His last moments were calm, and his thoughts turned to Wagner. His final words were: "Farewell, Siegfried! Console my Richard!"

At once the contemptible rumor began: *Tristan* had killed Ludwig Schnorr. In his more emotional moments even Wagner was inclined to look on Schnorr's death as a sacrifice to him, and it is of course likely that intense strain left him subject to illness. But Schnorr had proven the role of Tristan possible. Wagner never found another tenor of such ability and understanding.

Throughout the fall and winter of 1864–65, plans had gone forward for realizing Wagner's dreams, but progress was difficult. As a royal favorite, Wagner was looked on with suspicion by politicians, and in musical circles there were institutions—a court theater and a conservatory—which were threatened by his plans. In November, 1864, the King announced to Wagner that he was determined to build a great Festival Theater for the production of the *Ring* in 1867, and the following month Wagner's old friend, the architect Gottfried Semper, came to Munich to discuss the design. This was exactly the type of project calculated to arouse the most stubborn opposition of the politicians. As long as expenses were personal and involved only Wagner, the matter was recognized as the King's affair. A Festival Theater, however, would make heavy demands on the public treasury, and every means known to bureaucracy—including feeding lies to the press—were used to delay and postpone.

As early as February, 1865, someone in the inner circle of the court managed to arouse the King's irritation against Wagner, and the newspapers seized the opportunity to launch a massive and distorted attack. Bülow answered briefly and violently. Wagner had until now exercised considerable caution, but he also answered at length. The whole affair was trivial, but it had one unfortunate effect on Wagner's attitude. In his relations with Ludwig, he had concerned himself almost entirely with art. He now began to feel a responsibility to protect the King from his advisers. His attempts to instruct Ludwig in matters of state increased the determination of his enemies and undermined the strength of his position as an artist.

After the strain of *Tristan* and the shock of Schnorr's death, Wagner took stock of his position and found it wanting. On August 4 he complained that he did not get to see the King enough. Four days later he asked for more money—a great deal more, totaling 200,000 florins. Apparently Wagner had managed to run up debts in Munich and new ones in Vienna despite his ample income. And he could never, it seemed, be entirely clear of his old debts. In addition he was seeking security. He had no fear that Ludwig would desert him, but there was a real possibility that the King, who detested politics, might abdicate. And of course in the event of Ludwig's death Wagner's pension would almost certainly end.

The King's cabinet was strongly opposed to Wagner's request, and in the course of the negotiations Pfistermeister, insulted by the tone of Wagner's letters, demanded that he be relieved of any responsibility where Wagner was concerned. After more than two months, the King relented, and Wagner got what he wanted; but his fate in Munich was now sealed, for the Cabinet was henceforth committed to all-out war against him.

For once in his life Wagner was overmatched; he was battling against masters of court intrigue who were not hampered by sensitive scruples. On November 25 there appeared in the Munich *Volksbote* a cleverly twisted attack on Wagner which contained an outright misrepresentation of the money paid him. Wagner rose to the bait, lost his temper, and committed a disastrous indiscretion.

First he wrote to the King, strongly urging the dismissal of Pfistermeister and Pfordten, leader of the Cabinet. Then he published a long, violent article in which he presumed to use the King's name freely. Once this article had appeared, Ludwig, who had previously simply refused Wagner's advice, could no longer protect him from his enemies. Pfordten warned the King that if Wagner did not leave the country a Cabinet crisis would be provoked. Sadly, and with a moving protestation of his fidelity, the King bowed to the pressure and ordered Wagner out of Bavaria.

Without question the attack on Wagner had been unscrupulous, and much of it was motivated by selfishness. It is equally certain that Wagner's own folly had caused his downfall this time. Ludwig's support would have been ample to protect him had he stayed out of politics and lived with restraint.

Wagner left Munich on December 10, 1865 and went to Switzerland, where he rented a country house outside Geneva. Ludwig hoped to arrange his return to Munich in a few months, but Wagner was already considering the change as permanent. For one thing, he was anxious now to devote his time to composition again. For another, the arrangement with the Bülows had been predictably unsatisfactory, although of the three Wagner was certainly in the least difficult position. He longed now to do away with "half-way measures."

On January 25, 1866, a telegram arrived from Pusinelli saying that Minna had died during the night. Wagner was saddened, but he was honest enough not to pretend grief. He and Minna had hardly corresponded since their last meeting in 1862, and she had continued to be bitter against him.

In Munich Wagner had scored the second act of *Siegfried*, but now that a performance of the *Ring* seemed distant, he turned happily to *Die Meistersinger*; by March 23, the orchestration of the first act was complete. Cosima came to him in early March and stayed three weeks. During the months in Munich she had remained close to him, handling as much of his business and social life as her position allowed. He had become more and more dependent upon her.

While returning from a trip to Bern, they discovered a house that seemed to offer the perfect haven for Wagner. It was called "Triebschen," and it was beautifully situated among the poplar trees on the lake a short distance from Lucerne. A few days later Wagner asked for an advance of 5,000 francs to pay one year's rent; the King replied by sending the money as a gift.

For now, however, one thing was wrong with Triebschen: Cosima could not remain permanently with Wagner. She returned again in early May, and when Bülow arrived in June, there must have been discussion of their situation. Despite his intensely painful position, Bülow wanted to continue his work in Munich. It was essential to Wagner that he do so, and neither of them wanted an open breach at this time; yet the triangle was common knowledge in Munich, and Wagner's enemies took full advantage of it. To preserve the *status quo* in the strange tragi-comedy, the support of the King was needed.

Wagner, aided by Cosima, and almost certainly by Bülow, proceeded to play on Ludwig's trust to deceive him publicly. Pressed by a desperate appeal from Cosima and a scarcely veiled threat by Wagner to withdraw from Munich entirely, the King agreed to send a letter to Bülow, expressing outrage at the attacks on his honor and the good name of his wife. Bülow of course published the letter.

The attacks in the press did not stop, but the conspirators now had royal vindication.

Wagner never acted more despicably than in his deception of the high-minded and devoted young King who idolized him, and both Cosima and Bülow must share the blame.

During the fall and winter of 1866–1867, Wagner worked in relative tranquility. Cosima was with him, and the domestic happiness was something he had never experienced before. In the spring of 1867, when Bülow was appointed regular Kapellmeister, Cosima had to return to Munich.

In the fall, the new "Wagnerian" music school opened with Bülow as director, but other plans for making Munich into Wagner's cultural kingdom ran into continuous trouble. The theater project was gradually abandoned in a maze of subterfuge, evasion, and deceit. A journal, the *Süddeutsche Presse*, was founded under the editorship of Julius Fröbel, a Wagner supporter, and in the fall of 1867 Wagner wrote a series of articles called "German Art and German Politics." The contents were typically nationalistic German. France, the leader of European civilization, is spiritually decadent; the objectionable elements in Germany are foreign; the Germans are akin to the ancient Greeks; the spirit of the German folk will regenerate the culture of all Europe. And so on and on. The only significant development for Wagner's thought was an increasing admiration for Prussia. Prussia's victory over Austria in 1866 had seemingly opened his eyes to some possibilities.

At first the King was pleased with the articles, but when Wagner indulged more specifically in criticisms of the state and the church and gave advice to rulers, Ludwig forbade the continuation of the series. After a little more than a year, the Government withdrew its support of the *Süddeutsche Presse*.

These difficulties were symptomatic of the serious deterioration in Wagner's relation with the King. Ludwig continuously lamented his lack of contact with Wagner, but he made little effort to see him. Even when Wagner answered an urgent appeal and spent several days at Starnberg in late May, 1867, Ludwig saw him only once. It is likely that Ludwig was suppressing his suspicions of the real situation between Wagner and Cosima, and Wagner's political advice, which he recognized as amateurish, was now annoying him. The King's complex nature was quite capable of ardently longing for contact with his beloved friend and then shrinking from it.

It is a foreshadowing of Ludwig's later relationship with Wagner that in the midst of difficulties between them he refused to reduce

Wagner's pension, as should rightfully have happened according to the contract calling for the *Ring* to be delivered in the fall of 1867. In place of the *Ring*, Wagner sent as a Christmas gift the completed score of *Die Meistersinger*.

Die Meistersinger von Nürnberg

The story

Veit Pogner has offered the hand of his daughter Eva as the the choice, but she must choose a Mastersinger.
prize at a song contest on St. John's Day. Eva herself will make

Act I: Walther von Stolzing, a knight visiting Nürnberg, falls in love with Eva at church. David, who is apprenticed in both craft and song to the shoemaker Master Hans Sachs, instructs Walther in the art of the Mastersingers, but the time is much too short. The Masters grant Walther a trial, but his song provokes the ridicule of Beckmesser, the town clerk and "marker" of the Mastersingers Guild. (The marker counts the mistakes of the candidate.) Only Hans Sachs is impressed by the knight's unconventional song.

Act II: Eva gently chides her old friend Sachs for not entering the contest for her hand. Sachs, knowing he is too old for her, discovers her feelings for Walther by criticizing him and provoking her anger. Furious with the Masters for refusing him, Walther suggests an elopement to Eva, who agrees. Eva exchanges clothes with her nurse Magdalene; but as she and Walther start to flee, Sachs blocks their way by shining a light into the alley. As Sachs begins to work in the doorway of his shop, Beckmesser arrives to serenade Eva, whose place is taken at the window by Magdalene. Sachs interrupts the song continually by pounding on the shoes he is making—one strike for each mistake, as if he were a marker. As Sachs triumphantly holds up the completed shoes, David, having observed the serenade, attacks Beckmesser in jealousy over Magdalene. The neighbors are aroused and rush into the street, taking sides in the fight. Sachs quickly pushes Eva into her own house and draws Walther into his shop, as the Night Watchman's horn sounds. The crowd disappears, and the Watchman comes upon a quiet empty street.

Act III: Sachs, brooding in his workshop the next morning, finally casts aside his sadness and decides to help Eva and Walther despite his own love for her. Gently and wisely, he instructs the knight in the art of controlling his inspiration, and writes from dictation the first verses of Walther's Master-song (known as the Prize Song). Beckmesser finds the song, and thinking it by Sachs, takes it for his own use. When Eva enters, Sachs apprises her of the situation by suggesting that Walther sing a third verse. After Eva expresses her gratitude, Sachs calls David in and promotes him from apprentice to journeyman. Magdalene joins the other four in a quintet, and all depart for the contest and festivities.

On the banks of the River Pegnitz, the various craft guilds march in singing their songs, followed by the apprentices and finally by the Masters. Beckmesser is the first contestant. Confused by the new style of the song he has stolen, he makes nonsense of it and leaves in a rage. Then Walther sings the song and is awarded the prize by Eva. When Walther at first refuses the rank of Master, Sachs urges him to honor his German tradition. Walther accepts, and the people sing in praise of Sachs as Eva takes the laurel wreath from Walther and places it on Sachs' head.

There are a number of basic points of difference between *Die Meistersinger* and Wagner's other mature music dramas. Its subject matter, first of all, is neither legendary nor mythological. The Mastersinger guilds, successors to the aristocratic Minnesingers, flourished in the fifteenth and sixteenth centuries, and they were organized around the strong craft guilds of a new German "middle class." Wagner's sources were Gervinus' *History of National German Literature*, Jakob Grimm's *Concerning the Old German Master-Song*, and Wagenseil's *Nürnberg Chronicle*, the last published in 1697.

The characters are ordinary, everyday people—not gods and goddesses, not heroes, but a cobbler, a goldsmith, a town clerk, and so on. The problems they deal with are everyone's problems, and they are neither helped nor hindered by "fate" or self-interested immortals. They are under no curse and subject to no magic potion.

The story is devoid of symbolism. Part of the opera's intended meaning for contemporaries was nationalistic, but this turns out to be the least convincing, and thus the least important, element. What "message" *Die Meistersinger* actually carries is neither philosophical nor doctrinaire; it portrays the essentially human values of love, common sense, work, freedom, and the wisdom of experience. Narrowness, hot-headedness, ignorance, and pedantry are the vices against which these contend.

Die Meistersinger is a comedy. It ends happily and triumphantly for all the major characters except "the villain" Beckmesser, who is more ridiculous than villainous. In a number of scenes and many small touches Wagner gave full rein to his sense of humor. This side of his personality, an important part of his high spirits in private life, had been totally absent from his artistic creations since the early and ill-fated *Liebesverbot*.

Die Meistersinger, then, is Wagner's most human music drama, and Wagner's admirers will always feel a special gratitude for it. Without it there would be a lingering doubt as to whether Wagner could deal with emotions or situations on any but an epic, heroic level. *Die Meistersinger* is the living proof of Wagner's universality.

A human drama is dependent on the ability of the dramatist to create believable characters. One of the major criticisms of Wagner's other works is that he lacked either the ability or the interest to make his characters life-like. It is not wholly justified; Siegmund and Sieglinde, Brünnhilde and Wotan, Tristan and Isolde, even minor characters such as Kurwenal—all are endowed with the dramatist's spark of life. However, the individuality of the personalities created by Wagner is sometimes overwhelmed by the force of the emotion they are projecting, and they tend on occasion to become personifications rather than persons. The emotional appeal of *Meistersinger* is great; it can be, indeed, as moving, if not as emotionally exhausting, as any of Wagner's other works, but the emotions spring from within the characters, not from elemental forces that use them.

It is in *Meistersinger* that we find the most complex, the most appealing, the most believably human of all Wagnerian characters, Master Hans Sachs, shoemaker and poet. He is the dominating figure of the drama, and his spirit creates the particular mellow glow that characterizes the entire opera. His sadness and his wisdom add the depth that is a necessary serious counterpart to all truly great comedy.

Like the skillful dramatist he was, Wagner did not establish Sachs' central position at once. The two lovers, Walther and Eva, are presented first, and with them the subsidiary couple, David and Magdalene. Although we learn a little about Sachs from David's explanation to Walther, he is not really differentiated from the other Masters until he suggests that Pogner allow the people a part in judging the contest for Eva's hand. He is further characterized by his defense of Walther's Trial Song and by his firm good-humor in the face of Beckmesser's shrill unpleasantness. The picture of Sachs that is drawn in the Trial scene is brought into clear focus musically, without a word being said. He alone stands quietly in the tumult and confusion. As the last of the other Masters disappears, the orchestra suddenly softens and outlines his thought by bringing forth a motive from Walther's song, now more expressively stated (Ex. 34). Then shrugging his shoulders with a gesture of humorous indignation, Sachs follows the others.

Example 34

This motive dominates Sachs' Act II monologue, and it undergoes some symphonic expansion there. It belongs more to Sachs now than to Walther; in its transformation it expresses more of his nostalgia than of the young man's ardor. And in this monologue we begin to see into Sachs' soul and mind, to feel the poetic aspiration of the simple shoemaker.

The following conversation with Eva establishes their relationship in remarkable fashion; much more is understood than is said. The music underscores the tender, warm feeling between them, yet there is a reserve, especially on Sachs' part. Wagner handles a potentially tasteless and sentimental situation with great delicacy and clarity.

Already, in provoking Eva's anger in order to be sure of her love for Walther, Sachs has displayed cleverness. For the rest of Act II, throughout the wild comedy of Beckmesser's serenade, he is the man of action, playing the part he has chosen with gusto and humor, always keeping his wits about him for the serious end in view.

With the prelude to Act III Sachs' domination is complete. This prelude is a picture of his state of mind, which will be made specifically clear in the action and the great monologue that follow. The first motive (really two motives joined; Ex. 35a and b) is associated throughout Act III with Sachs' sadness, his renunciation of his own love for Eva, and his resignation. The second (Ex. 36), which receives a statement of magnificent richness from horns and bassoons aided occasionally by trombones, is the "Reformation" chorale

Example 35

Example 36

with which the people greet Sachs in the final scene. The third is from Sachs' cobbling song of Act II, now beautifully transformed into a soft, pensive mood (Ex. 37). A long development seems draw-

Example 37a (Act III)

Sei-nem En-gel rief er zu: da mach' der ar men Sünd'rin Schuh'

Example 37b (Act III)

ing to a quiet close when a dramatic deceptive cadence brings back the "resignation" motive like the stab of a sudden painful memory. Finally the sadness dissipates, and David's motive accompanies the opening of the curtain.

This superb mood-picture introduces Sachs' state of mind for the scene with David, in which he is quiet and obviously preoccupied. The great monologue beginning *"Wahn! Wahn! Überall Wahn!"* ("Illusion! Illusion! Everywhere illusion!") defines it precisely and articulates the progress that leads to action.[3] The development of

---

[3] The word *Wahn* has no exact English equivalent. For performance it is usually translated "craze."

the motives is in no sense rigorously symphonic, but never has Wagner's gift for catching an emotion and mood in a short phrase shown to better advantage. And never has his declamation been stronger or more expressive. The sequence of the motives is as follows: the "resignation" motive (first 35a, then 35b); the "Nürnberg" motive (Ex. 38) as Sachs thinks of the peaceful ways of his beloved

Example 38

city; two of the motives associated with the riot the night before, rising to a pitch of some violence; the melting strains of the "midsummer's night" motive (Ex. 39), as Sachs' calm wisdom asserts

Example 39

itself; the second of the two "riot" motives, now quieter and not nearly so serious; and finally the "St. John's Day" motive (Ex. 40) as

Example 40

Sachs puts his sadness and doubts from him in a flood of confident decision.

In the following scene Sachs explains, often in homely terms, the poet's art to Walther—and in doing so, of course, he speaks in part for Richard Wagner. "My friend, just that is the poet's work, that he perceive and explain his dreams!" And later: "Now take the poet's art in hand: many have found through it what has been lost.

[Dreams and poetry] are friends; they stand together gladly. . . .
You make [the rules] yourself and then follow them. Think of the
beauty of your dream this morning; for the rest, let Hans Sachs
take care."

In the scene with Beckmesser, Sachs simply maintains a quiet,
dignified and friendly attitude, while standing aside to let the other
trap himself.

The entire conversation with Eva has a double meaning; ostensibly about her shoes, it is actually about Walther. His entrance
and the third verse of the "Prize Song" bring a lyrical climax in
which Sachs' feelings are deeply involved. This is the moment at
which the two lovers, especially Eva, realize what Sachs has done.
But it would be out of keeping with the role he is playing and with
his character for Sachs to express his true emotions. He gently
shifts Eva into Walther's arms, steps aside, and begins to grumble—
about the lot of a shoemaker, a poet, and a widower. There is no
touch of sadness in the words, and the music mentions it only
briefly by referring to Ex. 35. Yet what is not expressed is much
more important here than what is expressed. It is a subtle and telling
psychological stroke on Wagner's part; unfortunately, it is frequently cut in performance.

In Wagner's works it is usually the woman who interprets the
experience, and Eva does so here. In a burst of gratitude, she tells
Sachs that, were her will free, she would choose him. Still keeping
the depth of his feeling hidden, he answers by reminding her of
King Marke's position; and the orchestra softly quotes from *Tristan*.

Sachs' part in the great quintet is a meditation unheard by the
others. It is his only admission of his love for Eva, his "beautiful
morning dream," that he hardly dares explain. He consoles himself
with the thought that only through poetry is the prize won. If the
listener knows the words and applies the emotional mood to Sachs
as well as to the younger people, the quintet completes the revelation of his personality. He shares the beauty of the moment, but
colors it with his sadness. It only remains in the second half of Act
III to see him honored, to see how humbly he accepts the honors,
how skillfully he brings about the acceptance of Walther—and
especially to hear occasionally throughout the festivities his underly-
ing sadness expressed in the moving tones of the "resignation"
motive.

The other characters are much less fully drawn than Hans Sachs.
Walther's personality comes to life only in his headstrong passion
and his poetic feeling, both really aspects of the same thing. When

turned to poetry and his love for Eva, his reckless ardor is exciting and beautiful. From the first motives in the 'cello that interrupt the lines of the opening chorale to the end of the "Prize Song," the expression is convincing (Ex. 41 from his proposal to Eva in Act II;

Example 41

see also Ex. 46 and 49). His fury toward the Masters for rejecting him hardly seems justified, and Wagner doubtless intended this to be so; Sachs teaches him restraint. We are not quite sure, however, that Walther has learned his lesson. In art, yes, for the "Prize Song" is masterful, but there is little indication of Walther's progress in understanding. Eva is right. She has to respond to Walther's youthful passion, but her reason chooses Sachs; he is the better man.

Eva's personality is more complex than Walther's because of her relation with Sachs. It is here that Wagner concentrates, not on her relation with Walther, to whom she responds at once and without question, in the best operatic fashion. In her first scene with Sachs she seems perhaps a little spoiled. The irritation that Sachs purposely provokes in her reflects her high spirits but her immaturity as well. As he sings the "Cobbling Song" after preventing her elopement, however, she begins vaguely to understand Sachs. If we have not caught her words (which is likely) in this scene, the lovely motive that accompanies her talk with Sachs in Act III (Ex. 42) defines her mood and registers her progress since the first conversation.

Example 42

Eva's two great moments come after Walther sings the third verse of the "Prize Song," with the words "*O Sachs, mein Freund! du theurer Mann!*" ("O Sachs, my friend! thou beloved man!") and in the quintet, in which she takes the lead. The first is one of those moments of illumination that Wagner handles as no other composer has. It is an emotional release of understanding, expressed with expansive passion, and the music includes Sach's resignation as well as Eva's gratitude. The quintet—strikingly, astonishingly un-Wagnerian in its static formality—is the quiet lyrical reflection of Eva's happiness; but as we have seen, it is also touched with Sachs' sadness.

Wagner made no attempt to draw Beckmesser as a well-rounded figure, but he did intend him to be something more than funny. This is most clearly evident in Act I, with Beckmesser's unpleasant reaction to Walther's candidacy. The main motive associated with him here (Ex. 43) underscores the dryness of his art and the irri-

Example 43

tability of his personality. In Act II, however, Beckmesser is merely ridiculous, a comic figure provoking a riotously comic scene. By the closing part of Act III Beckmesser may very well arouse, ever so little, our sympathy, as he limps away from the festive crowd, beaten, outwitted, and humiliated. Wagner did not intend us to sympathize, and the music does not speak of it. But his view toward his "enemies" was notoriously one-sided. It is perhaps a minor point, but almost certainly Wagner miscalculated the audience's reaction. For most viewers the evil which Sachs speaks of in Beckmesser has not been demonstrated sufficiently to justify such callous treatment.

By this stage of his career Wagner's powers as a musical dramatist can bring vitality to his minor characters without undue emphasis. This is particularly true of David, whose motive helps portray him as a lively and attractive figure, comfortably living on a somewhat lower plane than Sachs (Ex. 44). One can hardly imagine that David will ever be a very distinguished Master.

Example 44

Pogner is also impressive. His offer of Eva's hand is a noble gesture honoring the art of Nürnberg. Not until Sachs' monologue to the people in the final scene is this fully understood by the other Masters, which accounts for Pogner's heartfelt gratitude to Sachs.

Wagner always wanted realism in his operas, but in no other does the location, the time, the social setting—the local color—play so important a role as in *Die Meistersinger*. The city of Nürnberg is virtually an active character. When Walther's rage is progressively mounting as he tells Eva about his rebuff by the Masters, it is the horn of the Town Watchman that stops him short of action and gives Eva a chance to calm him. And the "Nürnberg" motive helps raise Sachs' spirit in the "*Wahn!*" monologue. The homely strength, the traditions, and the proud prosperity of Nürnberg form the foundation of the Mastersingers Guild. The staging in *Meistersinger* presents no such problems as the *Ring*, but it is of even greater significance in the work.

It is pride in his class, his position as a Nürnberg burgher, that furnishes the initial impetus for Pogner's proposal to grant Eva's hand as the St. John's Day prize. And class pride plays a less admirable part in the Masters' attitude toward the knight Walther and his toward them. The prejudices Wagner makes clear, and Sachs has to deal with them.

Wagner takes the utmost care in presenting the customs of the Mastersingers, which serve dramatically to emphasize the strong tradition, and he has lavished some wonderfully attractive music on their ceremonies. For some critics he has detailed the procedures of the trials too carefully, and too often. Certainly things could be compressed a little, but the drama does not really demand it. Each reference to the rules serves a different purpose. In Act I, David is proudly showing off his knowledge to the knight, and Wagner is sharing his own amusement at the quaint customs and terminology. Both text and music are charming. When Sachs goes over some familiar ground in Act III, the emphasis is on poetic interpretation of the rules. As always in Wagner, the question of length is involved with the proper understanding of the dramatic situation.

The most dubious feature of *Die Meistersinger* to present-day listeners is Sachs' last speech and the following hymn to German art. This grates, not merely because it is chauvinistic, but because it is not clearly motivated. It is a gratuitous sermon by Wagner to his followers in 1867.

Wagner himself had doubts about the ending. Cosima reported to Ludwig that he had decided to omit Sachs' final speech and close with the reception of the "Prize Song." She objected strenuously, and after long discussion Wagner gave in. Fortunately Sachs' speech is not long, the chorus is a brilliant ending, and the final tableau and words combine to turn the attention back to Sachs.

Die Meistersinger contains more conventional formal features than any other Wagner work after *Lohengrin*. The most obvious of these are the static quintet in Act III, the choruses, dances and processions in the final scene, and the prelude.

In *Opera and Drama* Wagner made it clear that an overture should not establish its own unity of form (as he himself had done for *The Flying Dutchman* and *Tannhäuser*), but should create in the audience a feeling of expectancy. Yet the prelude to *Die Meistersinger* is as clear an absolute musical form as any overture by Mozart or Rossini. Although it was written before the rest of the work had progressed beyond sketches, it is made up of important themes that will appear later, and it is cast in a free but still quite recognizable sonata form.

The first-theme group includes the impressive "Mastersinger" motive at the opening (Ex. 45); an extension on Walther's "courtship" motive (Ex. 46); the motive associated with the "Mastersingers' banner" (Ex. 47) as an important subsidiary theme; and another extension on a motive known as the "brotherhood of art" (Ex. 48). The motive of "longing" (Ex. 49), heard in the first scene between Walther and Eva, serves as the modulating bridge and leads to the second theme, which is the second strain of the "Prize

Example 45

Sehr mässig bewegt

Example 46

Example 47

Example 48

Example 49

Example 50

Example 51

Song" (Ex. 50). This is extended by the motive known as "Spring," which appears in the opera at the end of Walther's trial song in Act I and later returns in Sachs' memory (Ex. 51; cf. Ex. 34). As development, Wagner moves into a lively transformation of the "Mastersinger" motive, alternating with the "Spring" motive, and the "longing" motive leads into a powerful statement of the "Mastersingers." The recapitulation constitutes an adept and easily comprehended bit of contrapuntal virtuosity: the three main themes —the "Mastersingers," the "Prize Song," and the "Banner"—are combined simultaneously. The "brotherhood of art" leads to the "Banner" motive alone and finally to a mighty, conclusive climax on the "Mastersinger" theme once more.

Regardless of Wagner's earlier theories, the suitability of this masterful prelude can scarcely be questioned. But it is just as certainly successful as an abstract form, and it is rightly the most popular of Wagner's works in the concert hall. If Wagner intended confounding his opponents by meeting them on their own ground, he succeeded with a vengeance.

It seems likely, however, that the more conventional form of *Die Meistersinger* reflects the more conventional story. The quintet is a case in point. The dramatic need in the first part of Act III is for Sachs' personality to achieve domination as he unravels the complicated relationships that have developed in the first two acts. Wagner's solution is the simplest possible construction, a series of joined and related scenes: Sachs with David, Sachs alone, Sachs with Walther, with Beckmesser, with Eva, with Eva and Walther. Musically, the obvious end to such a series of scenes is an ensemble. So Wagner, with the facility of an experienced dramatic craftsman, brings David back for his promotion (obviously Beckmesser cannot return), plausibly allows Magdalene to be present at the brief ceremony, and thus prepares the quintet. Then without a thought for his famed aesthetic theories, he composes a brief introduction to allow the singers to group at the front of the stage, and lets each express his own thoughts simultaneously. It is properly a high point, one of the most moving moments of the opera; like the other conventional features of *Meistersinger*, it functions with marvelous appropriateness in the drama. But its static tranquility is in marked contrast to most Wagnerian climaxes; the surging, nerve-shattering cycles of *Tristan* would be impossible in this structure and inappropriate to this subject.

And so would the style of *Tristan*. From the opening "Mastersinger" motive of the prelude, we are in a different world—the clear, unambiguous world of C major. The *Tristan* prelude creates its climactic effect by withholding resolution, the *Meistersinger* prelude, by granting it—impressively, massively, after a long emphatic preparation. There is, to be sure, some chromaticism in *Meistersinger*, used to fine effect in creating the more personal and emotional moods; but much of the chromaticism is melodic and ornamental, not involved in the harmonic progression.

Wagner's technique of continuity is still much in evidence, but the symphonic texture is less developmental, the motives are longer and more vocal in character. The typical deceptive cadences are sometimes used with superb dramatic effect (as, for example, the progression that marks Eva's reaction at Walther's entrance in Act III), but often they serve simply to sustain musical continuity.

Die Meistersinger is not a reversion to an older style. The "*Meistersinger* style" is less extreme than *Tristan* and it contains old elements, but it is no less individual. Like the "*Tristan* style," it is inseparable from the dramatic conception. Even the orchestration, with its emphasis on the mellow sounds of the horns and trombones and the brilliance of the trumpets, matches the mood of the opera and contrasts with *Tristan's* characteristic color, which tends toward the English horn, the oboe, and the bass clarinet.

The difference between *Tristan* and *Meistersinger* might be looked on as the most convincing proof of Wagner's contention that the poetic idea controls the musical style, but in reality the situation is more complex than that. It was the complete artist, in whom the musician was always uppermost, who demanded the subject.

Wagner wrote *Tristan* under the strongest inspiration that ever came upon him, in the midst of unprecedented emotional disturbance followed by unprecedented solitude. The reflection of *Tristan* is the *Tannhäuser* Venusberg music for Paris; the reaction to *Tristan*, touched by its magnificent afterglow, is *Die Meistersinger*. The poet seized with unerring intuition on exactly the subject needed by the musician.

Plans for the production of *Die Meistersinger* began at once, and Wagner had reason to be pleased with the prospects. Bülow, of course, would conduct. Baron Karl von Perfall, with whom Wagner's relations were cordial, was made Intendant of the Theater, and a young protegé of Wagner's named Hans Richter was appointed coach and chorus master. Richter had come to Triebschen in October, 1866, when he was twenty-three, to work as Wagner's copyist. Recognizing his talent and pleased with his devotion, Wagner had taken over his training.

At the first performance on July 21, 1868, Ludwig insisted that Wagner sit with him in the royal box. There was no precedent for anyone except royalty to be accorded such an honor; nobility were outraged and the rest of the audience astounded. The incident was symbolic of the position Wagner had achieved, and at the same time of the recognition he had won for all artists.

The audience reacted enthusiastically to this warmest and most approachable of Wagner's works, and other theaters vied for the first performance after Munich. Finally, after considerable complaining, Wagner agreed to allow a few cuts when the work went to smaller opera houses. As always, however, there were dissenters from the generally favorable reaction. Hanslick, absorbed in contemplation of "Wagner's system," could find little difference in the music of *Meistersinger* and *Tristan*. He was pleased to discover, at last, a "set piece" in the last-act quintet, but he considered its musical quality commonplace.

Despite the success of the performance, Wagner returned to

Triebschen determined never to take part in another production of his works at the Royal Theater in Munich. He had quarreled with the administrators of the theater, Perfall in particular. It is more difficult to sympathize with him now than in his earlier battles at Dresden, for he had actually been given everything he needed; but he demanded complete authority and complete loyalty to himself alone. To allow this would have undermined the entire institution, whose leaders naturally felt an obligation beyond service to Richard Wagner.

Nevertheless, had Wagner chosen, problems in the theater might have been worked out. His prestige and fame were at a new high and were still rising; both Paris and Italy were now asking for his works. The Festival Theater project might have been revived; the School, under Bülow's energetic leadership, was prospering; and the political conditions he had laid down three years ago had long since been met, Pfistermeister and Pfordten having resigned after the disaster of Bavaria's alliance with Austria in the Prussian War of 1866. The real trouble with Munich was Cosima. Wagner could not live in Munich with Cosima, and he would not live without her.

Still the final decision was delayed. Bülow had no desire to leave his job; Cosima feared that a divorce would lead to a permanent break with her father, and there was the possible effect on King Ludwig. Not until late November, 1868, did Cosima finally come to Wagner, determined never to leave him again whatever the cost. By that time the King undoubtedly knew that he had been tricked; he refused to see Wagner and he did not write again until February.

Bülow stayed in Munich until early July of 1869. Then he resigned his post, agreed to start divorce proceedings, and went to Italy to try to recover his shattered health. He never saw Wagner again. Bülow's role in the whole affair had been a strange mixture of high-minded self-sacrifice and dissimulation. It can only be explained in the light of his fanatical admiration for Wagner's art and the peculiar character of his devotion to Cosima. Against Wagner he was sometimes darkly bitter, but against Cosima he never uttered a word of condemnation. In later years, when he had carved out a new and distinguished career as a pianist and conductor, he behaved on occasion with considerable nobility toward the man who had wronged him so deeply.

The two and a half years between November, 1868 and April, 1871, were probably the happiest of Wagner's life. Life at Triebschen was an idyll. The natural surroundings were of surpassing beauty, while there was comfort that only affluence can bring: Wagner kept no fewer than eight servants. Most of all, he was surrounded by the unquestioning devotion that was the breath of life to him. He had always had, despite his unsettled life, a deep longing for domestic peace; he had finally found the woman who would create it for him.

In February, 1867, Wagner's second daughter, Eva, had been born. On June 6, 1869, Wagner was sent into ecstasies of joy by the birth of a son, who was at once named Siegfried. The two Bülow children were also part of the household, and Wagner was devoted to them.

The whole household, of course, revolved around the Master. Visitors came and went, and Cosima saw to it that they were people who would stimulate him but who would not disagree. The most significant visitor was a young philosophy professor named Friedrich Nietzsche, whom Wagner had met briefly on a visit to his relatives in Leipzig. After he settled at the University in Basel in February, 1869, Nietzsche was a frequent guest at Triebschen, and Wagner became the strongest force in his life. Later the philosopher's own originality and the clash of two egocentric personalities separated them, and Nietzsche became a bitter enemy. Always he looked back on his days at Triebschen as the richest and the happiest of his life—"days of confidence, of cheerfulness, of sublime incidents, of *profound* moments." [4]

Bülow's divorce became final on July 18, and on August 25, 1870, Wagner and Cosima were married in the small Protestant church in Lucerne. Cosima wrote in her diary: "May I prove worthy to bear Richard's name. My prayers have been concentrated upon two points: Richard's well-being and my hope that I may always be able to promote it, and Hans' happiness and my hope that it may be his lot to live a cheerful life afar from me." [5] Wagner was never fully aware of the pain their union caused Cosima, nor of her continuing concern for Bülow. The marriage was for him the final factor in domestic happiness which had been heretofore an unattainable ideal.

In 1870, for Cosima's birthday, which was on Christmas, Wagner wrote a composition for small orchestra and performed it on the

[4] Quoted from *Ecce Homo* in Newman, *Life of Wagner*, IV, 356.

[5] Richard Count du Moulin-Eckart, *Cosima Wagner*, 2 vols., trans. by Catherine Alison Phillips (New York: Alfred A. Knopf, 1931), I, 416. The original German edition (Munich, 1929) is in one volume. A second volume (Munich, 1931), entitled *Die Herrin von Bayreuth*, deals with Cosima's life after Wagner's death.

stairs outside Cosima's bedroom. The work is now known as the "Siegfried Idyll." Wagner called it the "Triebschen Idyll," however, and this is the more suitable name, for most of the musical material is closely associated with Cosima and life at Triebschen. One of the major themes Wagner conceived while planning a string quartet for her at Starnberg in 1864, and another may date from the same time. There is a lullaby in honor of little Siegfried, and the "forest bird" music from *Siegfried* is mingled with this material.

Cosima's joy knew no bounds, and well it might. The composition is of singular beauty—lyrical, warm, and delicate. It makes one wish that Wagner had on other occasions been inspired to create small instrumental compositions.[6]

In an atmosphere such as Triebschen, Wagner worked well. Having turned his back for the moment on political theory, he began to write again about subjects on which he was worth hearing. 1869 and 1870 saw the completion of perhaps his two finest prose essays, *On Conducting* and *Beethoven*. The latter, his contribution to the centenary of Beethoven's birth, was one of the most widely read of all his works. It is still today a worthwhile exposition of the romantic side of Beethoven. Also in 1870 Wagner sent the first pages of his still incomplete autobiography *Mein Leben* to be printed in very small number for his friends,[7] and the following year he began the publication of his *Collected Writings*.

A few literary activities were less worthy. In 1868 he reissued, with some additional material, his *Judaism in Music*, a move that even the anti-Semitic Cosima saw was unwise. Perhaps Wagner's worst literary creations are his contributions to the Franco-Prussian War—a five-stanza poem and a tasteless farce called "A Capitulation." Like the rest of Germany, he was greatly excited by the quick Prussian victory, and he forgot his traditional dislike for the militaristic Junkers. Patriotic fervor did not serve him well as artistic inspiration, and his musical tribute to the new German emperor, the *Kaisermarsch*, is also among his commonplace works.

While life went its peaceful way at Triebschen, problems continued in Munich. King Ludwig, who had re-established at least

[6] The *Siegfried Idyll* was not Wagner's first instrumental composition since coming to Munich. In the summer of 1864, he wrote the *Huldigungsmarsch* for Ludwig's birthday. It is for large band, and, though impressive in sound, it is not in the class with the *Siegfried Idyll* in musical inspiration or craftsmanship.

[7] The first three parts of *Mein Leben* were printed at Basel between 1870 and 1875. The fourth was printed at Bayreuth in 1881. Not until 1911 was a public edition issued.

something of the old relationship with Wagner in February, 1869, was desperately eager for performances of *Das Rheingold* and *Die Walküre*. Wagner objected and tried various tactics of evasion and delay. Both works were the property of Ludwig, however, and he insisted. Wagner finally acquiesced without approving, and *Rheingold* was scheduled for August 29, 1869.

Wagner had no intention of letting the performance go on without gaining some advantage from it. On August 28 he demanded a postponement because of reports he had received concerning the inadequacy of the production. Richter, who was to conduct, claimed that his "musical honor" was at stake and refused to continue. The conspirators evidently hoped that the performance would be cancelled and that the blame would fall on Perfall, the Intendant. It was a clever intrigue, but it did not reckon with the determination of the King.

Ludwig was furious. He ordered that Richter be indefinitely suspended and that a new conductor be sought at once. In vain did Wagner object and picture himself as the most pathetic and ill-used of men; the King refused to answer. The performance was delayed, but it took place on September 22, 1869, less than a month late. Wagner's defeat had been complete, and it is difficult this time to defend him. Everything possible had been done to insure the success of the performance; indeed, Ludwig would not have tolerated it otherwise. What is more, the evidence is that the performance was after all quite good. We are forced to the conclusion that Wagner had badly overstepped himself.

Once he began to communicate with Wagner again Ludwig showed no trace of animosity. He held fast, however, against Wagner's repeated objections to a *Walküre* production, and throughout July, 1870, *Rheingold* and *Walküre* alternated, with interest running high and the public response generally favorable.

In February, 1869, Wagner had begun the composition of *Siegfried*, Act III, after an interruption of nearly twelve years. Incredible as it may seem, he apparently had no trouble picking up the threads, and by early August the orchestra sketch was finished. After the *Rheingold* affair, it occurred to Wagner that he could prevent the King from producing the last two works of the *Ring* simply by not finishing them. He therefore began *Götterdammerung* in October before completing the scoring of *Siegfried*. The latter was completed, however, by early March, and Wagner was reduced again to simple prevarication: he told Ludwig, to whom the manuscript actually belonged, that it was not yet finished.

It was once widely assumed that the reason for Wagner's opposition to the Munich performances was his desire to withhold the works until the entire *Ring* cycle could be presented. The evidence does not support this assumption. The fundamental cause of his devious, even dishonest, behavior was the plan maturing in his mind to remove the center of his artistic kingdom from Munich once and for all. He wanted a theater of his own, away from the problems that seemed inevitable when he worked in relationship with an established institution. It was his old dream of the 1850's— the temporary theater, the single festival performance—but now he saw the possibility of practical realization. The site Wagner picked was the small town of Bayreuth. It was remote yet accessible, it had no resident opera company, and it was in Bavaria. The last point was essential, for Wagner still hoped to keep Ludwig's support.

The King could, of course, have killed the scheme in the beginning, for the *Ring* unquestionably belonged to him, both morally and legally, but he took the news calmly. Wagner's music was still the consolation of his soul, but the bonds with the man Wagner had been loosened. It is likely also that his dream of active collaboration with Wagner in the great work of regenerating German culture had already faded; he was tired and disillusioned.

In April, 1871, Wagner went to Bayreuth and made the first tentative plans for his great project. Although another year passed before he and Cosima left their beloved Triebschen haven forever, Wagner knew from that time on that Bayreuth was to be his home.

The past several years had shown Wagner's personality in the worst light of his entire life. He had behaved badly in many matters, both large and small, and had often appeared lacking in the qualities that conventional morality calls "strength of character." Yet in the large issues that determined the course of his life, a less self-indulgent individual can scarcely be imagined. At Triebschen he was happy, he was secure, he was by any conceivable standard successful. Once again, as often in the past, the easy way was open before him. Once again he rejected it. The creative force that was the essential core of his being drove him from his comfortable retreat to take up the crushing labor of Bayreuth so that he might complete the life task he had set himself.

8

Bayreuth, 1871-1883:
The *Ring* Completed and *Parsifal*

After visiting Bayreuth in April, 1871, Wagner and Cosima went to Berlin, where he delivered his initiation paper (*The Destiny of Opera*) to the Royal Academy of Arts. Such conventional honors were usually a source of ridicule to Wagner, but this time he used the publicity to launch his campaign. He had never in the past admired Berlin or Prussia, but now the patriotic fervor of the Franco-Prussian War was still strong, and he was not yet disillusioned with the new Reich of which Berlin was the capital. If Bayreuth was to stir the German spirit, Berlin seemed the proper place to start.

Wagner's supporters formed a society in Berlin and planned to raise the 300,000 thalers needed at Bayreuth by the sale of 1,000 patron bonds. It was an ambitious program, and it was off to a promising start. On May 12 Wagner issued a brochure outlining his plans and announcing the first festival for the summer of 1873.

Berlin was expected to carry a large share of the financial load, but Wagner visited other cities as well. The music dealer Emil Heckel organized a Wagner Society in Mannheim, and by the end of the year others had sprung up throughout Germany.

Now Wagner needed support in Bayreuth itself, and in early November, 1871, he wrote to Friedrich Feustel, a banker of the town. Realizing the potential value of the festival, Feustel immediately took matters up with the town council. By early February, 1872, the council had purchased land for the theater, and Feustel had formed a committee to manage the festival.

While things moved rapidly in Bayreuth, progress elsewhere was disappointing. Wagner's cause suffered a heavy blow in July when the pianist Karl Tausig, the most active and imaginative of his supporters in Berlin, died tragically at the age of thirty. He was never adequately replaced in Berlin. Despite Heckel's work, sales of patron bonds in the smaller cities were not encouraging. Wagner realized early in 1872 that his estimates for the festival the next year had been too optimistic, and he began to plan for 1874.

He was plagued with another responsibility. In December, 1871, Heckel had suggested that he conduct a concert to stimulate interest. Wagner could hardly refuse, but it was a development he had not foreseen. The Mannheim concert was the first of many that were to be a great trial to him and a strain on his physical powers. He never enjoyed miscellaneous concert-giving, and it was doubly troublesome when all his energy was needed for composition and the essential plans of the festival.

On April 22, 1872, Wagner set out from Triebschen for the last time, leaving to Cosima the sad task of closing the house. He conducted a fund-raising concert in Vienna and then returned to Bayreuth, where his family, his dogs, and his servants were now established in a hotel.

On May 22, his 59th birthday, Wagner presided at the laying of the foundation stone of his Festival Theater. A brilliant crowd had gathered, including many of his long-time supporters. The King sent an emotional telegram of congratulations, which was sealed in the stone. Characteristically for Bayreuth, the rain began early in the morning and continued throughout the ceremony, making a sea of mud at the construction site. Wagner, his face deathly pale and tears in his eyes, struck the stone three times with the hammer and uttered the words: "Blessed be my stone: stand long and hold firm!"

Silently he drove through the rain to the old theater, where he delivered a speech to his supporters and a chorus sang "Wach' auf" from *Die Meistersinger*. At five that afternoon he conducted a magnificent performance of Beethoven's Ninth Symphony. In the evening he moved from one celebration to another, thanking his supporters and receiving their congratulations. He did not get home until midnight. Shortly after eight the next morning, he was in conference with the patrons and chairmen of the societies.

For the next few months, Wagner lived in Bayreuth and worked on *Götterdämmerung*. By autumn, however, the pressure of his festival plans forced him away from his creative work once more. In November he made a quick tour of German opera houses looking for singers, but it left him profoundly discouraged. Only one role, Niemann as Siegmund, was settled in his mind, and his old sense of loneliness returned as he measured the work to be done for his "model" performances.

The patron bonds were not selling well. Wagner's dream was that the German nation would rally to his cause, and he had expected that leadership would come from the German princes. It did not come with enough strength to insure success, and by the beginning of 1873 financial problems were acute.

Feustel suggested more concerts, and in early January, with dread in his heart, Wagner started out. A month of concerts, banquets, and speeches left him very tired, and he remained through the rest of the winter and spring deeply discouraged. He kept fighting, and he managed a bold front. Early in the summer he wrote a brochure describing the whole scheme and sent it to his supporters along with architectural plans of the theater. Wagner now hoped the festival could take place in 1875.

The cold, hard facts, however, seemed insurmountable. The original estimate of 300,000 thalers was too low, and of this only 130,000 had been raised. If the festival were to be given the next year, the equipment must be ordered at once. In August, every possibility seemingly exhausted, Wagner appealed once more to King Ludwig.

The King delayed. Deeply involved now in his own architectural schemes, he was reluctant to jeopardize them, and his financial position was already becoming dangerous. It was late November before his refusal was firm enough to extinguish Wagner's hope.

In the next two months, though, something happened to change Ludwig's mind. Perhaps he heard that Wagner had made a desperate, vain appeal to Kaiser Wilhelm I; very likely he realized that Wagner was facing a complete and humiliating failure. Whatever the cause, he wrote Wagner on January 25, 1874:

> From the depths of my heart I beg you to forgive me my long delay in writing to you. . . . No, No, and again No! It shall not end thus! Help must be given! Our plan must not fail. Parcival knows his mission and will do everything that lies in his power.[1]

Ludwig's initial loan to Wagner's festival committee was 100,000 thalers, but before the festival finally took place, he had made other sizable contributions as well. Once he had shouldered the responsibility, Ludwig did not flinch from sacrifice. Again he demon-

---

[1] Quoted in Newman, *Life of Wagner*, IV, 408.

strated that he alone among German princes possessed the generosity and understanding to save the greatest German artist of the era.

In his plans for Bayreuth, Wagner had not neglected his own convenience, and in April, 1874 he moved into his fine new home, called "Wahnfried" ("Peace from Illusion"). The money for construction had been a personal gift from Ludwig, but Wahnfried predictably cost much more than Wagner had anticipated. In September, 1873, he requested and received from Schott a 10,000-franc advance on *Götterdämmerung*. Less than a year and a half later he wangled another 10,000 florins for first rights to his future works, which were to include at least six orchestral pieces of overture size. The publisher must on occasion have wondered whether Wagner's genius was primarily musical or financial. Schott supposedly already owned first rights, as a result of the *Meistersinger* advances in the early 1860's. As for the six orchestral pieces, Wagner never got around to writing even one. Schott finally had to be satisfied with the *Siegfried Idyll,* which was reluctantly sold to him in 1877.

Except for the infamous Bayreuth climate and the continuous cares of the festival, Wagner must have found life at Wahnfried pleasant. A steady stream of visitors came and went. In addition, a group of young men sometimes known as the "Nibelungen Chancellery" was more or less continuously on hand, helping with various chores of copying and proofreading, while absorbing the musical training that Wagner gave so superbly.

Despite Wagner's discouragement in his first efforts to cast the *Ring,* performance standards had improved in Germany since he planned the work in the early 1850's. Many of the old Kapellmeisters had died or retired from active service. Most of these men had been competent and hard working, but they were the servants of an old system. A new class was coming to maturity and assuming positions of leadership. Bülow, the first of the great conductors after Wagner, was within a few years to assume a regular post at Meiningen. Richter, now at Pesth, went to Vienna in 1875. At Munich was Hermann Levi, 35 years old and destined to conduct the first performance of *Parsifal.* From the young men of the "Nibelungen Chancellery," Anton Seidl, Franz Fischer, and Felix Mottl were soon to emerge as distinguished conductors.

Among the singers, there was never another Schnorr, but a new spirit was now manifest; they approached Wagner's works eagerly and without fear. The Munich performances had proved conclusively that Wagner's music dramas were practical in the theater.

The revolution in musical standards in Germany is interrelated with social, economic, and political factors, an integral part of the cultural development of the nation and of Europe. One basic factor was the growing awareness of a great German tradition, centering in Beethoven and stretching back through Mozart and Haydn to Bach. Many men of vision and imagination, including a number who were hardly friends of Wagner and a number who were not German, played a significant role in bringing this tradition to the consciousness of artists and audiences. As Germany achieved in the latter half of the nineteenth century an almost unchallenged position of dominance in the musical world, the central German figure was unquestionably Richard Wagner. It was he, by the strength and the breadth of his talent and the variety of his activities, who marshalled the forces and shook musical Germany out of its provincial complacency.

If Wagner's strength was universally recognized, his leadership was not. In the years of its greatest power, musical Germany sometimes appeared as a house divided against itself. "Wagnerites" and "anti-Wagnerites" vied with each other in fanatical devotion to doctrinaire aesthetic theories. The "absolutists," those who opposed Wagner's combination of the arts and his poetic interpretation of music, were led by Hanslick, but by the 1870's their musical champion was Johannes Brahms.

Except for an ill-calculated blast against the "music of the future" in 1859, Brahms held himself aloof from the critical battles. He had only contempt for the Wagnerites, but he insisted, in private, on his admiration for Wagner's music.[2] In retrospect, the extremists on both sides decline in importance. Bülow did not turn against Wagner's music when he began to champion Brahms. Richter conducted the premiere of Brahms' Second Symphony a little more than a year after conducting the Ring, and Levi was a personal friend of Brahms as well as a musical protagonist. The greatest performers, like most audiences, saw no reason to choose one to the exclusion of the other.

Wagner had finished the composition of Götterdämmerung in February, 1872, but the work of Bayreuth had slowed progress on

---

[2] Wagner did not return the admiration. There is little evidence that he even paid much attention to Brahms' music.

the scoring. It was not until November 21, 1874, more than twenty-six years after the first prose sketch of *Siegfried's Death,* that he wrote the final page of *The Ring of the Nibelung.*

His reaction to the completion of the largest musical work ever written by one man was to brood over his next work, *Parsifal.* He had written out the essentials of the story for Ludwig in 1865, and early in 1875 he finished a detailed prose sketch. By then the pressure of the festival preparations was mounting. The complex machinery, designed by Karl Brandt, was ordered shortly after the King arranged for the loan, and by the end of 1874 both costumes and scenery had been commissioned. Wagner was handicapped by the continuing necessity to give concerts, but by the summer of 1875 all the roles were filled.

On July 1, the singers gathered in Bayreuth for a month of piano rehearsals. Wagner had considerable help, of course. Richter, who was to conduct, did much of the coaching, aided by the young men of the "Nibelungen Chancellery." A voice teacher was brought in especially for Georg Unger, a 25-year-old tenor who had finally been selected to sing Siegfried. Wagner apparently tried to change Unger's whole personality. Richard Fricke, ballet master from Dessau, was on hand to help with stage movements.

In the final analysis every decision came to Wagner. He was producer, music director, stage manager, coach, and chorus master. His energy, overcoming bad health, seemed boundless, as he scolded, praised, demonstrated, lectured, and released the full force of his magnetic personality. Some experienced theater people who saw him in action retained years later impressions of the greatest stage manager and the greatest actor they had ever seen.

Despite some clashes of temperament, it was a convivial, excited group at Bayreuth that summer of 1875. The orchestra, 115 of Germany's finest players with the great August Wilhelmj as concertmaster, arrived on the first of August, and one of the satisfactions for Wagner was the success of his sunken orchestra pit. This was the most unusual feature of Wagner's theater, and it remains unique today. The pit is much deeper than the conventional, and extends for considerable distance, sloping downward, under the stage. A hood conceals even the conductor from the audience, so that the unseen orchestra forms, in Wagner's terms, a "mystic gulf" between the audience and the stage. Although some find the sound dull, the particular rich blend of colors is certainly what Wagner wanted.

The exertions of the summer left Wagner exhausted, but he still had to go through a fatiguing six weeks in Vienna supervising productions of *Tannhäuser* and *Lohengrin*. As late as March, 1876, he conducted *Lohengrin* in Vienna and supervised *Tristan* in Berlin. These labors were certainly not welcome at this time, but Wagner could not risk offending the directors on whom his festival singers were dependent for leave of absence. His reception everywhere was enthusiastic and even affectionate, however. His vogue had reached a new height, and some who had been cool toward him began to exhibit signs of cordiality.

Rehearsals for the festival were to start in May, 1876. In April, Frau Theresa Vogl, who was to sing Sieglinde, discovered that she was pregnant. Her husband, who was singing Loge, apologized for not following Alberich in his curse on love. Wagner offered to be godfather, hoped the child would turn out to be a true Volsung, and quickly sought another Sieglinde.

The excellent bass Scaria, who was to sing Hagen, suddenly demanded a large fee, and Wagner had to release him. Once rehearsals were under way, there were clashes between Fricke, who wanted to manipulate his singers one way, and Brandt, who wanted to manipulate his machines another. The Rhinemaidens were terrified of the sled-like contraptions in which they were to simulate swimming, and Karl Hill, the Alberich, likewise suffered an agony of fear making his last swift plunge into the depths.

The steam, so necessary to a number of stage effects, seeped into the orchestra pit and affected the intonation of the harps. The orchestra players complained of a draft. Wagner investigated, and reported in disgust, "I composed the opera, and now I have to shut the windows as well!"

As late as the end of July, the theater was not quite ready. Fafner, the Dragon, arrived from London tantalizingly, one section at a time: first the tail, then the middle, finally, at almost the last minute, the head. Wagner never saw the neck, which was rumored to be in Beirut, Syria.

The anti-Wagnerian press did its worst: Scaria's resignation was a calamity, the third cycle had been cancelled, there was a typhus epidemic in Bayreuth. No lie was too extravagant.

Yet the three cycles took place on schedule. The little town of Bayreuth was overrun by a gathering that included the crowned heads of Germany and the cream of intellectual society from all of Europe. King Ludwig came for a private hearing at the general rehearsal, August 6-9 and was so deeply moved that he returned for the third cycle. Liszt, now reconciled to Wagner's marriage, was there to share his old friend's triumph and to see the vindication of his own faith, demonstrated so graciously years before.

Not all of the production problems were satisfactorily solved, and Wagner was disappointed in many details, but the festival made a deep and lasting impression. Wagner had conceived a single work about 15 hours in length. He had written the poem and composed the music. He had designed the theater, raised the money to build it, and supervised every detail of the production. Surely this almost incredible achievement has no parallel in the history of European art.

The Ring of the Nibelung

In approaching all of Wagner's works after *Lohengrin,* it is desirable to keep in mind the conditions under which he hoped they would be performed; but in no case is it so essential as in that of *The Ring of the Nibelung.* The length and complexity of the work cry out for festival conditions—for a refreshed and informed audience, able to devote the major portion of its energies to the theater for the better part of a week. Few people are fortunate enough to see the *Ring* under ideal conditions, but a realization of what is expected can help our understanding.

There is another point to remember: In no other work of Wagner's does the visual realization on stage so consistently fall short of the composer's conception. This is not only true of stage effects such as the rainbow bridge and the final immolation scene. It is perhaps even more marked in the usual physical endowment of the singers. Too much ridicule, perhaps, has already been heaped on leading operatic profiles; but the fact remains that few are able, like Ludwig Schnorr, to create an illusion despite an unconvincing physique.

From the musical standpoint, the *Ring* is not essentially a difficult work for the audience. It lacks the concentration of *Tristan* and the immediate human warmth of *Die Meistersinger,* but its emotional appeal is often irresistible. Though the musical material is vast, it is not beyond the capacity of the average cultivated musical memory to master. The difficulty of the *Ring* for the intelligent student of Wagner is not in the music; it is in the complexity and the obscurity of the poem. That Wagner's conception of the work changed over the years is obvious enough. Many details of the change created minor confusions that can easily be overlooked, but some of the fundamental problems demand attention. (See Appendix, p. 174, for the story of the *Ring*).

Wagner began with the idea of writing a single opera with Siegfried as the hero—a joyful, strong, unknowing redeemer. Gradually, as his conception broadened, the figure of Wotan grew in importance. Wotan dominates the first two dramas, and his problem is central to the whole story.

First of all, it is necessary to understand that Wotan is not a god in the sense of being omnipotent or omniscient; he is subject to human mistakes and vices. This type of half-human immortal is of course common in mythology. The source of Wotan's power is law, represented by his spear, which he cut from the World Ash tree and on which the runes of treaties are carved. The order he dreams of is benevolent and based on just law, as opposed to the tyranny and greed of Alberich's order.

Thus when Wotan makes a treaty which he cannot keep, the basis of his power is threatened, for he rules by treaty. To keep the treaty, he steals the Ring, thereby committing an unlawful act that must continue to be a flaw at the core of his whole order. At the end of *Das Rheingold,* then, Wotan is in a dilemma: the existence of the Ring is a threat to his power, but he himself cannot gain possession of it lest he compound his guilt. He is firmly caught by the moral laws that are the source of his power.

Wotan's inspired plan is to create a race of heroes, the Volsungs, half mortal, half god, the greatest of whom will be free of the God's guilt and can redeem the Ring, removing both the threat and the moral flaw from Wotan's rule. Wotan believes that Siegmund is to be this hero, and for him he fashions the sword, Nothung. Siegmund is not really free, however. Wotan has raised him and given him a magic sword for his protection. This is the fatal truth by which Fricka, fighting for the conventional morality of the home, forces Wotan to withdraw his support of Siegmund.

Then Brünnhilde enters the drama. She is Wotan's "wish-maiden," created to do his will—and she does so even against his command. Once again he is ensnared by his moral laws: he must punish her for working his own will. In her passionate justification at the end of *Die Walküre,* Wotan realizes that the hero—Siegfried, the one "freer than I, the God,"—is yet to be born. Siegfried must not know his ancestry. He must forge his own sword; he must be entirely unaware of his mission. Only by actually opposing Wotan can he be free of Wotan's guilt.

In the third opera, Wotan also knows that Siegfried's complete freedom spells the end of his own power. It only remains for him to progress to the point of willing his own inevitable destruction (one is reminded of Tristan's sense of his own responsibility for his inevitable fate), which he does in the scene with Erda (Act III, *Siegfried*), and then to play out the drama by opposing Siegfried. After the spear is broken by Siegfried's sword, we see Wotan no more. He goes to Walhalla to await the end, the necessity he himself has willed.

Siegfried's redemption of the Ring is not complete with his possession of it. Alberich's curse must be fulfilled by Siegfried's death and the gold returned to the Rhinemaidens. Siegfried himself is incomplete until his union with Brünnhilde.

We now come to the central problem of the work: if Siegfried is to be looked on as a redeemer, why must the Gods perish in Walhalla's flames? What has been redeemed if not Wotan's guilt? What is the great illumination that comes to Brünnhilde as she says, "All, all I know, all now becomes clear to me"?

Newman is undoubtedly right when he suggests that the trouble all began at the moment Wagner decided to combine the two separate myths of Siegfried and the Downfall of the Gods.[3] But he is also right to recognize that the change in Wagner's attitude was fundamental, not the result of an arbitrary and mistaken choice of subject.

Röckel raised the basic question in 1853 and received a strange reply from Wagner:

> I feel certain that, at a good performance, the most simple-minded spectator will be left in no doubt on that point. Certainly the downfall of the Gods is no necessary part of the drama regarded as a mere contrapuntal nexus of motives. . . . No, the necessity for this downfall had to arise out of our own deepest convictions, as it did with Wotan. And thus it was all-important to justify this catastrophe to the feelings of the spectator.[4]

In short, Wagner himself is not very clear about the explanation, but he expects to make it clear *in the music*. Twice he wrote verses that he felt would express the message. The first ends:

---

[3] Newman, *Life of Wagner,* II, 358.
[4] The entire letter is in *Richard Wagner's Letters to August Roeckel,* trans. by Eleanor S. Sellar (Bristol: J. W. Arrowsmith, 1897), pp. 74-116. Wagner's answer is dated Jan. 25, 1854.

> Not goods, not gold, nor godly splendor;
> not home, not court, nor lordly display;
> Not the deceitful bond of dreary treaties,
> not false custom's stern laws;
> Blessedness in joy and sorrow,
> only Love can bring.

The second, which dates from 1856, shows more specifically the influence of Eastern philosophy and says at one point, "The open gates of eternal becoming I close behind me; redeemed from rebirth, goes the Illumined One to the holiest chosen land, where there is no wishing, no illusion." [5] In the end Wagner wisely discarded both the prosaic simplicity of the first and the mysticism of the second; he let the music speak.

There can be no definitive answer to the problem, and perhaps there should be none. The greatness of the *Ring* lies not in clarity and perfection of detail but in the magnificence of its epic proportions and the breadth of its implications. The wonder is not that Wagner lost control of his drama occasionally but that he kept such control of the music. The most reasonable answer to the problem of the end of the *Ring* may be something along these lines:

The destruction of the Gods is their redemption; Wotan is released from the curse that had followed the Ring by being released from life. Siegfried's treachery, as unconscious as his heroism, has symbolized the futility of laws and oaths. For Brünnhilde, who has been both goddess and mortal, the illumination is in understanding the necessity of the Gods' doom and the permanence of her love, which itself is finally consummated in destruction (we are not far from *Tristan* here). Thus only the mystic union of love-in-death remains of the old order. The way is cleared for a new order—or perhaps for the mighty, everlasting cycle to begin again.

Das Rheingold was Wagner's first effort in the style he had attempted to describe in *Opera and Drama,* and he had not attained the freedom of musical development or the control of large structure that is evidenced later.

Yet *Das Rheingold* still manages to be successful and intriguing,

---

[5] Trans. by Newman in *Life of Wagner,* II, 355. Wagner published both unused endings as a footnote in his *Collected Writings.*

and one of the primary factors is the quality of the musical material. The majesty of the "Walhalla" motive (already quoted in Chapter 5, Ex. 20b), the sweep of the "rainbow" motive (Ex. 52), the fundamental simplicity of the "Rhinegold" (Ex. 53), and the repressed, insistent pulse of Alberich's jealousy and despair (Ex. 54)—these

Example 52

Mässig bewegt

Example 53

Example 54

Example 55a

Example 55b

are only a random selection of motives that are dramatically suggestive and musically potent. Only occasionally in *Rheingold* is the potential fulfilled, as with the transformation from joy to distress of the Rhinemaidens' cry (Ex. 55a and b), or the climactic statement of the "Walhalla" motive in the final scene. The quality of the motives in themselves leaves no doubt that Wagner's talent for creating short, vivid musical fragments—a talent essential to the implementation of his conception of the music drama—is already in full force in *Das Rheingold*.

Although the continuous declamation may occasionally become tedious, it can also rise to inspired heights—as at Alberich's bitter, ironic rage and his terrible curse after being deprived of the Ring.

If there were nothing else to redeem *Rheingold*, the magnificent orchestra, coming to dramatic life as brilliantly prophesied in the prelude to *Lohengrin*, would be enough to do so. The *Rheingold* prelude is an astonishing *tour de force*. It consists of about 140 measures of an ornamented E-flat-major chord, the figures building and swirling around the unprecedented stability of the harmony. The orchestral episode between the third and fourth scenes, representing the journey from Nibelheim back to the Gods' dwelling, does not reach the heights of Siegfried's "Rhine Journey" or Parsifal's "Transformation Scenes," but it is a worthy forerunner of these. Further, the orchestra is responsible for a number of fine pictorial effects, such as the sudden feeling of light when the gold shines forth in the first scene and the sense of lethargic gloom as the Gods grow suddenly old after Freia's departure. Finally, when Wagner unleashes the full majesty of the expanded instrumentation as the Gods enter Walhalla, the scope of the dramas to follow is foreshadowed.

Die Walküre has been from the beginning the most popular of the *Ring* operas, as well as the easiest to produce. Superficially, its appeal seems due to the so-called "Ride of the Valkyries" that opens Act III, to the "Magic Fire Music" at the end, and to the love-duet at the close of Act I. There is also a deeper dramatic reason: the characters in *Die Walküre* grasp our interest and our sympathy to a degree not achieved in the rest of the *Ring*.

Although the gallery remembers Siegmund's "*Wintersturme wichen dem Wonnemond*" and Sieglinde's following "*Du bist der Lenz*"—both as close as Wagner ever comes to writing an aria in the *Ring*—the tragic love relationship has been eloquently expressed in the music from the moment the two look into each other's eyes. The motives surrounding the love of Siegmund and Sieglinde are less passionate than those of Tristan and Isolde, less powerful than those of Siegfried and Brünnhilde, but they reflect a sadness and tenderness not given to any of Wagner's other lovers (Ex. 56a and b). This pair touches our pity.

The incestuous nature of their love has, of course, disturbed sensitive critics for years, but it generally does not bother the audience. It need not. Wagner would have had difficulty in avoiding this aspect of the myth he was dealing with. In addition, the brother-sister relation serves some purpose: in providing Fricka with a strong argument, in giving a fatally tragic aspect to the love from the beginning, and in looking forward to the unusual qualities of Siegfried, the pure-blooded Volsung.[6]

Example 56a

Example 56b

The great figure of *Walküre* is Wotan. The God is more vitally, more tragically human to us than the mortals and half-mortals, even though he is portrayed on a heroic level. The key to his character and his dilemma—indeed, the key to the whole *Ring*—is found in his speech to Brünnhilde in Act II. Although the implications of all he says are important, it is his bitter frustration that comes to us so forcefully through the music. This is the first of the long recapitulatory speeches of the *Ring*, and it is one of the finest in its psychological penetration.

In the third act Wotan's dilemma is on a personal as well as an epic level. Brünnhilde is the center of his heart, the only one to whom he has revealed his hopes and his despair, the only one on whose love and understanding he can rely. Yet he must punish her and thrust her from his life forever. The violence of his rage at her disobedience is the reverse side of his devotion and the outlet for his frustration.

Brünnhilde, the character who will undergo the greatest transformation in the *Ring*, is at this stage simple and impulsive, strong

[6] The comments of Robert Donington in *Wagner's Ring and its Symbols* (London: Faber and Faber, 1963), pp. 121-123, about the significance of incest in legend are especially revealing.

yet feminine. Her decision to follow Wotan's will rather than his command results from her own nature; she understands his desires, not the complexities of his problems. Her moment of decision, which comes at the climax of her great scene with Siegmund in Act II, is one of the finest dramatic points of the opera.

The most criticized portion of *Die Walküre* is the long wrangle between Wotan and Fricka in Act II. Certainly it has little of the sweep found in Wagner's greatest scenes, but this results in part from its basic progression, which ends in Wotan's frustration. Wagner treats the conversation in musical detail rather than as a long structural unit. Its text is of considerable importance, and the listener will scarcely find it tedious if he knows what is being said.

Finally, in the third evening of the *Ring*, Wagner introduces us to the hero who first attracted him to the story. To an even greater extent than Wotan in *Die Walküre*, Siegfried dominates the opera that bears his name. What Lawrence Gilman aptly called "the blend of the idyllic and the tremendous" [7] that characterizes the music of the entire work is primarily a reflection of Siegfried's personality.

The mood of the opera is marvelously varied, yet somehow consistent. It is filled with some of Wagner's most inspired moments which cover the widest possible contrasts: from the bellowing of Fafner's four tubas to the delicacies of the "Forest Murmurs"; from the eerie depiction of Mime's description of fear to Siegfried's awe as he breaks through the fire to the peaceful mountain top; from the purposeful banality of Mime's false sentimentality to Brünnhilde's majestic awakening.

Wagner's technique has grown still further; there are no passages in *Siegfried* as subject to the danger of tedium as the Wotan-Fricka scene in *Walküre*. Act III, written after the completion of *Tristan* and *Meistersinger*, is understandably the most masterful, especially in the orchestral texture, which points the way to *Götterdämmerung*.

The final scene is a long, predominantly symphonic exposition of an experience that is psychologically complex for both characters. Wagner's music articulates this complexity through its changing phases until it is resolved in a violent explosion of ecstasy, such as was possible only for the composer who had *Tristan* and the Paris Venusberg behind him. We are not moved, perhaps, as we were by

Tristan; the music, for all its excitement and its rich beauty of detail, remains the description of emotions that are to some extent removed from our own. The scene, nevertheless, is intensely compelling.

Still, in spite of the consummate skill and unfailing inspiration of the music, there is something wrong with *Siegfried* as a drama. The trouble lies mainly with the hero. Siegfried is strong, he is straightforward, he is brave; he is also passionate, joyous, determined, and enormously energetic. All of these things Wagner's music shows us with an unfalteringly sure touch. Siegfried has, in fact, every quality a hero should have except one: awareness. Even Wagner's genius has a difficult time in sustaining our interest in a hero who remains unaware and unquestioning in the face of events of great significance. The things he learns of his mother and father, even the volcanic awakening of passion in him, bring no self-consciousness. True, he does change in *Götterdämmerung*; but in understanding he neither grows nor progresses.

Wagner meant to show Siegfried as the ideal man, one who is entirely unspoiled, who follows his own will without the confusion of conflicting thoughts, and whose pure intuition guides him to heroic acts. Siegfried has frequently been associated with Nietzsche's "superman." But the conception of Siegfried dates from 1848-1849, long before Nietzsche and before Wagner's turn toward Schopenhauer. While the hero's unthinking activity may suggest Wagner's agreement with Schopenhauer's supremacy of will over reason, Siegfried is actually closer to Feuerbach's healthy sensuality. As Wagner himself changed and Wotan became the dominant character, Siegfried became more of an instrument and less of a person.

Wagner was right; opera is, after all, a form of drama. Not even the wonders of the *Siegfried* score can completely compensate for the failure of the hero to be convincing. It is a crucial flaw and the greatest single weakness of the *Ring* cycle.

George Bernard Shaw used to insist that *Götterdämmerung* is a grand opera rather than a music drama. It contains the only choruses in the entire *Ring*, and it has an ensemble at the end of Act II. Its story of betrayal and revenge is at least superficially closer to the usual operatic plot. These features do not make *Götterdämmerung* a grand opera in the sense Mr. Shaw intended, but they do give it the appearance of a work more closely related to conventional opera than the rest of the cycle. The libretto of *Götterdämmerung*, in short, still bears some signs of having been written two-and-a-half to four years earlier than the other three operas.

Another feature related to its conception as an independent work is the presence of long passages recapitulating the earlier action. Some critics have assumed that Wagner, through oversight or reluctance to take on a thorough revision, simply neglected to remove these, which the critics consider unnecessary. Wagner evidently thought otherwise. In the first place, for all his talk, he undoubtedly realized that each of the four operas should be able to stand alone. In the second place, the recounting of previous action is one of his favorite dramatic devices. Wotan's scene with Brünnhilde in Act II of *Walküre* is an excellent example and shows clearly that such things in *Götterdämmerung* do not need to be accounted for by the circumstances of the creation (*Rheingold* was already planned, it will be remembered, when *Walküre* was written). The Norn scene with which *Götterdämmerung* opens reviews the essential action of the first three evenings, but it does more: it interprets and prophesies. Siegfried's narrative just before his murder reviews the action of *Siegfried,* but it also re-establishes him as the heroic character of the previous evening and furnishes the transition for the return of his memory and his love for Brünnhilde.

The spectator should be prepared in *Götterdämmerung* for the transformation of two leading characters. Brünnhilde's change from goddess to mortal, which began in the last scene of *Siegfried,* is now completed, and she has acquired a new and quite beautiful motive to express her new personality (Ex. 57). She is a woman, to whom

Example 57

Sehr ruhig

love is more important than Walhalla and the fate of the Gods. When she is betrayed, moreover, she is a savage and not particularly admirable woman, interested only in vengeance and the murder of the man who has wronged her.

Siegfried's change is less radical; he is simply more experienced. The innocent youth of the preceding opera is now a full-fledged, if more conventional, hero and a man of the world. Likewise, the reckless horn call that characterized him in *Siegfried* (Ex. 58a) has acquired a new, less impetuous form (Ex. 58b).

Example 58a (Siegfried)

Example 58b (Götterdämmerung)

The most decisive character in *Götterdämmerung*, the one who actually controls the plot, is Hagen. Like Alberich, he is a powerfully-drawn personality; the very texture and register of the music that surrounds him define his gloom and his determined obsession (Ex. 59). His night-watch soliloquy and the "sleep scene" with

Example 59

Alberich are frightening in their depiction of concentrated, single-minded evil. Wagner always gives the devil his musical due.

The inconsistencies and obscurities of the *Ring* become more pronounced as the great drama unfolds, and thus *Götterdämmerung* suffers from them. But Wagner was never more magnificent as a musico-dramatic technician. *Götterdämmerung* is the final perfection of his continuous symphonic technique, with which effective melodic declamation is simultaneously balanced. The purely orchestral passages, of which "Siegfried's Rhine Journey" and "funeral music" are the longest and most fully developed, are perfectly integrated into the drama, illuminating it and even suggesting action.

The end of *Götterdämmerung* has no parallel. Brünnhilde, still mortal but now transfigured by inspired revelation, throws the torch on Siegfried's bier, leaps on her horse, and rides into the flames. As the flames mount and fill the entire hall, the fire music rises in the orchestra to a cataclysmic climax. Then the waters of the Rhine overwhelm the flames; Hagen leaps in and is dragged to his death by the Rhinemaidens, as the motive of Alberich's curse (Ex. 60) is

Example 60

Example 61

heard briefly for the last time. The flood subsides and the flowing periods of the Rhinemaidens' song (Ex. 61) sound forth calmly but strongly in the oboes and clarinets. In the background we see the flames of Walhalla's destruction, and its majestic motive grows stronger and stronger first in the four tubas, then spreading to other brass and woodwinds. The climax builds once more, and Siegfried's heroic motive in trombones and trumpets cuts through the maze of flaming figuration in strings and woodwinds.

Above all, spreading over the destruction in serene magnificence, floats the motive known as "redemption by love" (Ex. 62); it is the last thing we hear in the *Ring*.

Example 62

What does this motive tell us? Not much, for those who want the associations and intentions neat and clear-cut. The motive was introduced in Act III of *Die Walküre*, when Sieglinde learned of her pregnancy and addressed words of ecstatic wonder and gratitude to Brünnhilde. It has not been heard since. Evidently Wagner wished to suggest the connection between Sieglinde's coming sacrifice for the birth of Siegfried and Brünnhilde's sacrifice for the rebirth of the world, but the association is neither decisive nor clear.

What is indisputable is that the motive, both musically and emotionally, is appropriate. After the shattering climax—the disintegration of a world—and the return to the primal tranquility of the cycle's opening, this soaring melody brings a rapture totally beyond description.

For some, the end of the *Ring* will always be a riddle, a hopeless, hazy quandary of pessimism. But for others the miracle occurs, as Wagner said it would; the music brings an understanding of what words cannot tell.

The physical and emotional strain of the festival had been heavy, and as always throughout his life, outward success left Wagner with a feeling of loneliness and frustration. In mid-September he went with his entire family to Italy, seeking rest and a return to good health.

The cares of Bayreuth still pursued him. The final deficit for the festival was a staggering 150,000 marks, not including 216,000 marks still owed Ludwig. Wagner's pleasure in the accomplishments of the festival now turned to bitter pride in himself and his supporters. He had trusted in the "German spirit"; neither people nor princes had come to his aid in sufficient force.

As always, it was not in his personality to give up. In the spring of 1877, hoping to help with the Bayreuth finances, he reluctantly accepted a contract to present six concerts in London. Once again his experience in England was unhappy. The concerts were a social and artistic success but a financial disaster. Wagner received only half of his promised fee of £1,500, which he sent at once to Bayreuth. After paying his soloists and assistants, his personal loss was £1,200.

The Bayreuth Theater was now devouring Wagner's considerable income, as well as Cosima's small inheritance. He thought of giving up everything and going to America. In the summer of 1877, tired, sick and disillusioned, he once more sent a despairing plea to Ludwig, and with it he sent the completed poem of *Parsifal*.

The King's financial position personally was such that it was impossible for him to help further, but he turned the matter over to his advisors, who were now at last convinced that Wagner was worthy of help. Months went by in slow, painstaking negotiations. Finally, on January 25, 1878, the intendant Perfall recommended that Wagner be granted a ten per cent royalty on all his works performed at the Munich Theater.

This was the basis of an agreement signed two months later. The royalties were to liquidate all outstanding debts. *Parsifal* was to be given at Bayreuth using the personnel of the Munich Theater, and thereafter Munich would have the right to perform it without cost. It was a generous agreement, for of course Ludwig had the right to produce all Wagner's works without payment. It was also a just agreement. The Munich Theater had done quite well with Wagner's works, and was to do even better in years to come.

One change was made in the agreement later. As the composition of *Parsifal* proceeded, Wagner became increasingly concerned about turning it over to conventional theaters. King Ludwig, with his customary understanding, at once agreed to eliminate the performance rights of the Munich Court Theater, thus leaving Wagner free to limit *Parsifal* to Bayreuth alone.[8]

While the negotiations with Ludwig's representatives were going on, Wagner had tried again, without success, to promote one of his favorite dreams, a school of music. A few months later, however, he did succeed in another of his pet projects, the founding of a journal. The first issue of the *Bayreuther Blätter* appeared in February, 1878, under the editorship of Hans von Wolzogen, a young man of thirty, who settled in Bayreuth ready to devote all his energies to Wagner's cause. In the first issue Wagner announced the production of *Parsifal* for 1880.

Immediately following the festival, Wagner had been reluctant to allow other theaters to produce the *Ring*. Munich already had rights, however, and as he became more engrossed in *Parsifal*, he became less concerned with the limitations of the *Ring* to special conditions. In 1878 the operas of the *Ring* began to make their way all over Germany.

The most significant of the performances was the complete cycle given in Leipzig under the leadership of the producer Angelo Neumann, a man of exceptional energy and vision (he was, incidentally, another of the numerous Jews whose work impressed

---

[8] An unauthorized performance in New York in 1903 was the first public presentation outside of Bayreuth.

Wagner and who served him well). Neumann presented *Das Rheingold* and *Die Walküre* in April, 1878, and followed these with *Siegfried* and *Götterdämmerung* in September. In 1881 he gave four complete *Ring* cycles in Berlin with great success, and the following year he formed a touring company to carry the *Ring* and other Wagner works all over Europe. All in all, his contribution to Wagner and his family was considerable, both financially and artistically.

Despite his fulfillment in his home and family, disillusion had settled upon Wagner. He despaired of the new German Reich, and he was convinced that Germany was going to revert to barbarism. His naïve belief in "German superiority" remained, but he feared German conquest. He was troubled over the future of the small nations, which he felt should be brought to an understanding of the German spirit, not trampled underfoot by the Prussian army.

Gradually, under the spell of *Parsifal*, Wagner had drifted back to Christianity. It was a mystical, undogmatic Christianity in which Schopenhauer's doctrine of negation of the will mingled with the Christian doctrine of renunciation of the material world. Pity was Parsifal's first step toward salvation, and pity was basic to Richard Wagner's Christianity. Although he frequently acted in a manner that can only be described as oblivious to the feelings of others, Wagner had the abnormally sensitive person's capacity for sympathy with suffering. He was horrified by the revelations then being made about vivisection, and he wrote an eloquent appeal for its abolition. Poverty troubled him greatly in his later years, especially the contrast of natural beauty with wretched conditions in Italy.

Wagner's health had not improved since the strain of the first Bayreuth festival, and in his work on *Parsifal* fatigue was a continuous problem. He was subject to frequent chest cramps and occasional mild heart attacks. Cosima, perhaps more aware of his condition than Wagner himself, redoubled her efforts to care for him. Her task was not easy; he was frequently irritable and short-tempered. If one of the carefully selected guests at Wahnfried was indiscreet enough to argue, Wagner was likely to lose his temper at once. Occasionally he worked himself into a rage simply by means of his own eloquence.

Almost all of 1880 Wagner spent in Italy with his family. On the way back to Bayreuth at the end of October, he stopped in Munich, largely to enable his family to see his works. They heard Levi conduct *The Flying Dutchman, Lohengrin,* and *Tristan,* and after the last, Wagner received a prolonged ovation. On November 12, he led the orchestra through the *Parsifal* prelude for King Ludwig alone. It was the last time they met.

Although Wagner still had much to do on the orchestration, *Parsifal* was now scheduled for the summer of 1882. Levi, who as Munich Kapellmeister was to conduct, visited Wahnfried in January. Wagner was not pleased to have a Jew conduct his Christian work; but since Ludwig shared none of his anti-Semitism and Levi's competence and dedication were beyond question, he could do nothing about it. After an unfortunate lapse of taste on Wagner's part almost caused Levi to withdraw, Wagner accepted the situation with as good grace as his uncertain temper allowed. Nevertheless, it is obvious that Levi and other Jewish members of Wagner's circle occasionally suffered because of his irrational prejudice.

In May Wagner attended the first and the fourth of Neumann's *Ring* cycles in Berlin. For the latter he took with him his entire family and a guest of the moment, Comte Alfred de Gobineau, author of the *Inequality of the Human Races*. He and Wagner had become acquainted in Italy. Their temperaments were quite different, but their thoughts met at enough points for a friendship to develop. Wagner had been stimulated by the pseudo-scientific argument of Gobineau's work and thought it a proof of what he had intuitively discovered.

The truth was that Wagner's thinking, except where music was concerned, had lost much of its vitality. He had always been inclined to view politics, philosophy, religion, and, indeed, the whole world in rather operatic terms; only his thoughts on music and the music drama have lasting significance. In his later years, he frequently drifted into stereotyped formulas or pure nonsense. Perhaps the most striking example is the conclusion he came to when he adopted the doctrine that the fall of man came about through eating flesh. Anticipating the argument that meat is needed in cold climates, he suggested that Northern Europe migrate *en masse* to South America.

Before the end of the summer of 1881 most of the casting problems for *Parsifal* were settled, and the rehearsal schedule was arranged. On November 1, fleeing the Bayreuth winter once again, Wagner went to Italy to finish the orchestration of *Parsifal* and to conserve his declining strength. This time he went all the way to Palermo. Even the warmth of Sicily did not prevent him from catching cold and suffering a debilitating illness, but the score of *Parsifal* was completed in January. Thereafter, Wagner rested and devoted himself to reading. He stopped in Venice on the way home and made arrangements for renting, the next winter, the Palazzo Vendramin-Calergis on the Grand Canal. On May 1 he arrived at Wahnfried ready to begin his last great task.

Parsifal

Wagner's main source for the poem of *Parsifal* was Wolfram von Eschenbach's *Parzival*, written in the early thirteenth century, when the Grail legend was already old but not yet at the end of its development. Wolfram's poem, like most medieval epics, is loosely constructed and deals with a large number of related incidents. Wagner had to cut the story down to its essentials for dramatic and musical expression, and it left him with a rather large amount of narrative material to take care of in one way or another.

For Wolfram the Grail had nothing to do with the Saviour, although it was vaguely Christian. Wagner adopted the later conception of the Grail as the chalice used at the Last Supper. Wolfram's Parzival had failed in his first visit to the knights of the Grail by not asking the cause of Amfortas' suffering. Wagner saw at once that he needed something more dramatic at this central point, but it was not until 1877 that he found the answer by making the recovery of the Holy Spear fundamental. Wagner then proceeded to tighten the drama by expanding the importance of Klingsor and Kundry, both of whom figured in only a few of Wolfram's episodes.

In the following outline the situation of the characters is summarized at the beginning; in Wagner's poem the facts are gradually revealed through various speeches, largely by Gurnemanz.

> The relic of the Holy Grail, which had disappeared from the world for many years, was revealed to Titurel and his knights and given into their keeping. They built the castle of Monsalvat, which could only be found by one worthy of the Grail, and from there they went forth to combat evil. The Holy Spear that had pierced the side of Christ had also been given them, and it could be carried into combat in times of special need.

> Close by Monsalvat is the castle of Klingsor, an evil magician who had been a knight intent on serving the Grail. Unable to master his passions he had emasculated himself, but the mutilation only gave him power for evil. In Klingsor's service is the sorceress Kundry, who is under a curse, unable to die, for laughing at the Saviour on the Cross. She comes often to Monsalvat

to perform service for the knights, but she is at Klingsor's command when he needs her.

While doing battle with Klingsor, Amfortas, who had succeeded Titurel as Keeper of the Grail, falls prey to Kundry's enchantment and is seduced. Klingsor seizes the Spear and wounds him with it. The Spear remains in Klingsor's possession and Amfortas' wound will not heal. Hoping to end his suffering, Amfortas asks for a sign from heaven and hears the words: "Through pity made wise, the pure fool; await him, my chosen one."

Parsifal is the son of a king named Gamuret and his queen Herzeleide. Gamuret was killed just before Parsifal's birth, and Herzeleide reared her son in the forest, ignorant of the world and even of his own name. One day the boy follows some knights out into the world, oblivious of the pain he is causing his mother.

Act I: With his bow and arrow Parsifal kills a swan in the forest domain of Monsalvat. Gurnemanz, an elderly knight of the Grail, rebukes him and makes Parsifal aware of his wrong-doing. Gurnemanz takes him to Monsalvat to witness the unveiling of the Grail. There Parsifal sees the Last Supper re-enacted and witnesses Amfortas' terrible suffering. He takes no part, and Gurnemanz thrusts him roughly out of the door. When all have left the church, voices float down from the dome: "Through pity made wise, the pure fool; blessed in faith!"

Act II: At his castle Klingsor calls on Kundry to defeat Parsifal, his most dangerous foe. Parsifal enters the magic garden, having easily routed Klingsor's knights. He resists the temptation of the charming flower maidens; but when Kundry calls him by name, he suddenly stops. She tells him of his mother's death and shows him his own responsibility. As she kisses him, Parsifal suddenly feels Amfortas' pain and breaks away. Kundry tries to arouse his pity for her, but Parsifal knows the one way he can save her. Finally she calls on Klingsor, who appears on the battlement and flings the Holy Spear at Parsifal. It hangs stationary over his head. He seizes it, and the garden and castle crumble into ruins.

Act III: It is Good Friday, a long time after Klingsor's fall. Amfortas, seeking death, has refused to uncover the Grail. Titurel, deprived of its life-giving sight, has just died.

Gurnemanz, living as a hermit by the holy spring in the domain of the Grail, finds Kundry in a trance in the underbrush. He awakens her, but she can only declare her desire for service. He tells her she will find little to do; the knights no longer go forth. Parsifal approaches in full armor and carrying the Spear. Gurnemanz rebukes him for carrying arms on this holy day, and silently Parsifal removes his armor and helmet. Then Gurnemanz recognizes him and realizes the significance of his return: Parsifal is to remove Amfortas' suffering and take his office from him. As the first act of that office, Parsifal baptizes the penitent Kundry. The three go to the church, and Parsifal heals Amfortas' wound with a touch of the Spear. He holds the Grail aloft in blessing, as Kundry sinks lifeless to the ground and a white dove descends over the head of Parsifal.

Of all the operas Wagner wrote, *Parsifal* is the most problematical and the most difficult to come to terms with. Even for some ardent admirers of Wagner, it is at best a wonderful decline, only partially redeemed by passages of great beauty, while for the anti-Wagnerians it is the epitome of tedious length and tasteless arrogance. Few critics deny, though, that *Parsifal* contains some of the most masterful music that Wagner or anyone else ever wrote. For some who come completely under its spell, the faults recede into nothingness, and it becomes the greatest experience the theater has to offer.

In art there is no final or universal judgment. The task of the listener, nearly a century after *Parsifal*, is to find the approach that will remove as many of the barriers as possible.

The first problem is the subject. To some Christians the portrayal of the Holy Eucharist in the first act is little short of sacrilege. Those who object, however, are usually those who have not seen the opera. Even Hanslick, who considered the church scenes "odd and improper," admitted that they do not "make the offensive impression upon me that I and others had been led to expect from reading the libretto. These are religious situations, but, for all their earnest dignity, they are not in the style of the church but completely in the style of the opera." [9]

Hanslick had no intention of praising Wagner, but for once he pointed in the right direction. *Parsifal* is neither liturgy nor theology; it is art. Art is not considered in most quarters as an enemy of religion, nor is religious experience considered an inappropriate subject for art—so long, that is, as the art is sincere and true to itself.

To be sure, *Parsifal* is not for those to whom the resources of theatrical spectacle are inherently shallow and frivolous. One must admit the possibility of serious, profound experience in the theater, for *Parsifal* epitomizes the rejection of the theater as entertainment and the acceptance of its use for promoting the highest things in life. Beyond this possibility *Parsifal* demands no more acceptance

[9] Hanslick, *Vienna's Golden Years*, p. 236.

of doctrine than does *Tristan* or the *Ring*; it does not require an act of faith on the part of the viewer. The meaning of the drama is mystical and religious, just as in *Tristan* the meaning is mystical and philosophical. But both are nevertheless dramas.

The problem of subject is not inherent in the work; it is in the attitude of the listener. The more important problems in *Parsifal* are the fundamental ones growing out of its dramatic structure and the articulation and support of this structure by music.

Parsifal is long, as long as *Die Meistersinger* or *Götterdämmerung*, and it has nowhere near the action of these two works. The details of background are profuse and important; and they are revealed to the listener, not in action or even in conversation, but largely by straight narrative. The long narrative or expository passage is a familiar phenomenon in Wagner, but only in *Parsifal* does he create a major character for that purpose. Gurnemanz has more lines than anyone else in the drama, yet he is hardly an active figure. And his personality, insofar as it is defined at all, demands that the information he imparts be told seriously and solemnly. The prevailing tempo of his speeches is slow, and the declamation is rhythmically stiffer than is usually Wagner's practice.

Compare, for example, Isolde's narrative in Act I of *Tristan* with Gurnemanz' story to the squires in Act I of *Parsifal*. Isolde vividly defines certain characteristics of herself, reveals something about Tristan as well, and brings the earlier action to life as surely as if it had occurred before our eyes. Gurnemanz' story Wagner handles with at least equal skill in detail. The masterly manipulation of the motives and the delicacy of the orchestral coloring are more refined than in Isolde's narrative; yet Isolde grips us while Gurnemanz does not. The memories of an old man who is not really interesting in himself can become tedious despite the detailed beauty of what he says.

In Wagner's other works, narrative passages, whether expository or recapitulatory, take many different forms, and they are not all equally successful. Generally, though, they have at least a certain momentum about them, and frequently they serve as necessary structural contrasts either before or after a great climax. Except in the second act, which is in all ways the most immediately approachable, the climaxes in *Parsifal* are necessarily meditative and mystical. The Holy Eucharist scene in Act I is of truly surpassing beauty, yet Wagner's familiar brilliance and power are replaced by soft, dazzling colors and by a solemn suspension of physical drive. He has achieved a unique and suitable blend of the sensuous and the spiritual, but this is not the irresistible release following long tension that we are accustomed to in Wagner's great lyrical passages, the power of which may justify a lower level of interest preceding.

In summary, the dramatic structure of *Parsifal* and the musical style dictated by the nature of the drama create problems that Wagner, with his normal tendency to extreme length, did not succeed in solving completely. By recognizing the special nature of the problems, the listener can prepare to deal with them. In the magic, mystical world of Monsalvat and the Grail, time hardly exists and impatience has no place. More than any other opera of Wagner's, *Parsifal* demands psychological preparation on the part of the listener.

Parsifal is filled with subtle meanings, and in this, Wagner's last work, the relations to other works are especially fascinating. Parsifal, the "pure fool" who has not learned evil, bears a definite relation to Siegfried, the child of nature who has not learned fear. In Wagner's own mind Amfortas was associated with the Tristan of the third act. As always passion and its renunciation play an important role. It is through passion that Parsifal learns the meaning of suffering and through renunciation that he finds the way to redemption. Klingsor, who attempted to remove passion, only barred himself from the possibility of the illumination that comes with true renunciation.

Fundamentally *Parsifal* is a drama of sympathetic suffering. Every step toward Parsifal's enlightenment is engendered by compassion —for the swan he has killed, for Amfortas, for his dead mother, for Kundry, for Titurel. Through the suffering he shares, he becomes aware of his own error, his own part in the world's guilt and salvation.

As already implied, Gurnemanz is the palest of Wagner's major figures. Even in the hands of a great singing actor he becomes scarcely more than impressively dignified. Klingsor, on the other hand, is powerfully drawn despite his brief appearance; he has some of the same concentrated evil that animates Alberich.

Amfortas is the personification of suffering. We get a brief view of his kindness as he speaks to Kundry in Act I, but no other aspect of his personality is dealt with. His suffering, however, is not primarily physical; the music makes it plain that Amfortas' wound is psychic.

The most fascinating figure in *Parsifal* is Kundry. Except during her attempted seduction of Parsifal, her speech is broken and hesitant, as if forced from the depths of her soul (Ex. 63). It seems to reflect the exhausting repression of one for whom the natural release of tears is denied. More than once the elemental character of her being breaks the formal bounds of musical speech, and she screams —with terrible effect when combined with Wagner's dramatic harmonic changes. The motives associated with her express varying degrees of suffering and passionate longing, with the most outstanding one a dissonant figure of tortured intensity (Ex. 64).

Example 63

Example 64

The role is extraordinarily difficult. From the vocal standpoint there are such extremes as the shocking leap from high B-natural to middle C-sharp when she tells of her laughter at the Cross. In the last act Kundry has only two words—exactly four notes—yet she is on stage for virtually the entire time, a stern test for any actress and the more so for a singing actress.

The progress of Parsifal himself is the progress of the drama. He is in a sense a symbol, but a symbol involving gradual growth into spiritual enlightenment. The key to his progress, and to the progress of the whole drama is found, not just in the music that accompanies and defines his speech, but in those great passages that are wholly or primarily orchestral and are, as far as the external story is concerned, static. In these passages we find the most inspired music of *Parsifal*.

The prelude, which was completed in September, 1877 before the opera itself was begun, is of special importance; it ushers us into the rarefied atmosphere of the world of the Grail and can promote the psychological mood necessary to comprehend the drama. Only three stylistic features need be mentioned here. First, the rhythm, in which the physical energy of the pulse is so weakened as to be sometimes virtually absent. The long opening melody (Ex. 65) furnishes the clearest example. On paper it seems highly syncopated; to the ear it is without meter, without pulse, floating in nothing. At other points (Ex. 66) the pulse is more obvious, but the slow tempo and the long rests contribute to the feeling that the music is suspended in space, unfolding itself without forward movement.

Example 65

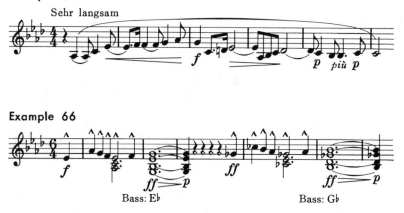

Example 66

The second feature is the contrast of the chromatic style that expresses suffering with the clear diatonic style that reflects the pure world of the Grail (Ex. 66-67; the latter is the traditional Dresden Amen). The chromaticism emerges in the development of Ex. 65 as the motives that make up the theme begin to lead an active independent life, and from still another motive that is associated later with Amfortas' suffering (Ex. 68).

The "Transformation" music accompanying the change of scene in Act I is much more than a tonal picture of the journey from the forest to the church. It is a psychological and emotional exposition of the significance attaching to the coming events. Parsifal's journey takes him further than the mere distances involved. Ex. 66 and Ex. 67 are mingled with the chromatic extensions of Ex. 65 to create a texture of richness and intensity. The richness brings no effect of confusion; clarity in the midst of such complexity is indeed the sign of a master.

Example 67

Example 68

Although the second act involves more direct action than either the first or the third, it also has its static points. The flower maidens' scene, one of Wagner's loveliest inspirations of pure lyricism, represents a more innocent, less dangerous aspect of the sensuous world than does Kundry. Parsifal is ready to enjoy it until it threatens his freedom; then he rejects it abruptly and easily. Not so with Kundry. Her great symphonic song (the voice line is doubled in the orchestra) leading up to the kiss touches Parsifal to the depths. His illumination begins with dramatic suddenness as he breaks away from her embrace, and the revelation progresses through her various approaches to the end of the act. The act ends, however, not with one of Wagner's expansive passages articulating an illuminating experience, but with the dramatic action of Klingsor's appearance and the destruction of his realm. No doubt this was calculated on

Wagner's part. Parsifal still has a long road to travel, and the end of his revelation is still to come.

The prelude to Act III is another tonal picture of events that are more psychological than actual, for it deals with Parsifal's efforts to find his way back to Amfortas—and his way, as he tells us later, lay through error. The desolation of the opening (Ex. 69), the dark, wandering character of what is known as the "straying" motive (Ex. 70), the tension of the development of the "pure fool" motive (Ex. 71), the daring yet controlled chromaticism of the harmony—

Example 69

Example 70

Example 71a (Act I)

Example 71b (Act II)

all combine to create a picture scarcely equaled even in Wagner's impressive gallery.

The last scene of the opera begins with the heavy gloom of Titurel's funeral music. Amfortas' suffering plea for death and Parsifal's entrance prepare for the final pageant of the Grail and its solemn, mystical, triumphant music. But it is in the Good Friday music of the preceding scene—devoid of ceremony, freed from suffering—that Wagner has distilled the message of *Parsifal* (Ex. 72). This is the pure fool's final revelation, the quiet and joyous

Example 72

feeling of oneness with man and nature. Kundry can weep at last, and we are likely to weep with her. No description will help with music such as this; its simplicity needs no explanation. Wagner's means are never economical, but by this time his technique has been so perfected that it has merged with expression into one effortless whole. He has achieved the height of what Alfred Einstein so aptly called a composer's "second naïvety."

The singers arrived at Bayreuth for rehearsals on July 1, 1882. In general, progress was smoother than it had been with the *Ring*. There was one work to be learned instead of four, and some of the participants had been through the first festival and absorbed its lessons well. The strain on Wagner, nevertheless, was once more heavy. Again all details passed through his hands, and again his burden was increased by social necessities.

Bayreuth was filled with his friends, although King Ludwig did not come. He could not bear the crowds while experiencing Wagner's works, so he remained in the solitude of his beloved mountains. Not until after Wagner's death did he hear the work, which, more than any other, he had influenced.

Parsifal was presented 16 times between the 26th of July and the 29th of August. There were troubles, of course, but by the end Wagner was sure the standard of 1876 had been surpassed. He had no more illusions about what might be accomplished in society as a whole. In *Parsifal*, he wrote a few months later, he and his followers had escaped for a while from "this world of robbery and murder, organized and legalized by lying, fraud, and hypocrisy."

At the final performance Levi was ill. Noticing that his condition was becoming worse during the third act, Wagner made his way into the orchestra pit and took over the baton from the second Transformation scene to the end. There he remained at the conductor's desk through the tumultuous applause that urged him to the stage. Finally he spoke briefly, not to the audience, but to his performers, expressing his gratitude and his hope that they might work together again. For most of the company it was the last time they saw him.

To Wagner's surprise, the festival turned out to be a financial success; receipts amounted to 240,000 marks. Now it was clear that the Bayreuth Festspielhaus could be operated through the sale of tickets. He still hoped to be able to distribute tickets to students, but his old dream of free performances, supported by those who understood him, was now dead.

It has been a commonplace to regard Wagner as the most successful of all artists, a man who emerged from his trials the complete victor and who ended his life with all his goals attained. Superficially, this is true. He had forced the world to come to him in an inconvenient little town in the Franconian hills. All of his once "unperformable" works had been successfully presented. He had created new standards of performance and established a new school of conducting and singing. He had forced the serious consideration of dramatic music as never before. His enemies (and there were many) were powerless against him. His position of dominance had never been equaled in the history of music, nor is it likely to be equaled in the foreseeable future.

Nevertheless, Wagner ended his life in disillusionment. His ideals were so sweeping and his desire to dominate so strong that complete fulfillment was impossible. His overwhelming sense of his own significance led him to attempt nothing less than the artistic regeneration of the German people, and through them, of mankind.

Social and political revolution failed, and the established theatrical institutions resisted complete reformation. So he retreated, and built his fortress at Bayreuth, from which the battalions were to go forth to rebuild the world on Wagnerian lines. "Go thou and do likewise!" he had planned to say to the audience in the temporary theater he dreamed of in 1852. Even in 1876 the model performances were to create a new art, spreading from Bayreuth through all of

Germany. In the end Bayreuth, like other theaters, was dependent on its popularity, on those with the money to pay and the leisure to attend, for whatever reasons. It was not, after all, a national folk-theater; it was the colossal achievement of one man, and many people came to marvel rather than to understand.

"A man's reach should exceed his grasp," wrote Robert Browning. Wagner's failures, like his successes, were the epitome and the climax of late romanticism. Even in his disillusionment he spoke to the deepest currents of the age.

Wagner took his family to Italy in the middle of September, eager once more to avoid the Bayreuth winter. Although he had known for some time that *Parsifal* was to be his last dramatic work, he still talked of writing instrumental works on the lines of the *Siegfried Idyll,* but he was tired and his waning strength was not sufficient.

Cosima also must have been near exhaustion. Added to her heavy duties in the past few years had been her knowledge of his precarious condition. Once, during the *Parsifal* festival, she confided to her diary:

> Late in the evening I sat alone in the now empty room, and brooded and brooded, till my excited brain fell asleep; and I knew more or less how things will be one day.[10]

That awful day was always before her now, yet she never relaxed her poise before Wagner, never showed impatience before his irritability. She continued to keep every possible care from him, to brighten his moods of depression, to arrange the little family ceremonies that meant so much to him.

Liszt stayed with the Wagners from November to January, and other friends came and went. Released from the tensions of work, Wagner apparently felt better, and visitors reported that he looked well, but the heart attacks were coming now with ominous frequency; the weight of Bayreuth's work had done its fatal damage.

On the 13th of February, 1883, a luncheon visitor came to the Wagner home about a quarter of two, and found Cosima at the piano, weeping as she played Schubert's "Lob der Thränen" ("In Praise of Tears"). Wagner, who was at work in his room, sent a

[10] Moulin-Eckart, *Cosima Wagner,* II, 870.

message that he would not come to lunch, as he did not feel well. Cosima went to him at once, but as always when in physical pain he wished to be alone.

A few minutes later the maid answered a violent ring from his bell. He had suffered a massive heart attack. His valet moved him to a small sofa, and Cosima held him in her arms. The doctor arrived at three. Shortly thereafter, so peacefully that Cosima thought he had fallen asleep, Richard Wagner died.

The shock of his death was felt around the world. Liszt at first refused to believe the news. Hans von Bülow's wife (he had remarried the preceding summer) wrote to his mother: "Even I had no notion of how passionate was the love he still felt in his innermost heart for Wagner. . . . In his own words, which he brought out with great difficulty, he felt as if his own soul had died with this fiery spirit." [11] King Ludwig could only seek consolation in solitude and in his solemn pride that the world owed the completion of Wagner's work to him.

Hanslick wrote a brief, restrained article. "The news of Richard Wagner's death," he said, "was a painful and shocking surprise. . . . I shall always remember him happily as I last saw him, on the balcony of his Festival Theater—which will soon be only a historic monument—rejoicing triumphantly in the all-conquering power of his will." [12] To the end, he persisted in being wrong about Wagner and his creations.

Wagner's body was taken back to Bayreuth, and once more his friends gathered to pay their tribute. At the station a band played Siegfried's "Funeral March" and a male choir sang the chorus Wagner had written for the return of Weber's body to Dresden in 1844. The solemn procession moved through packed, black-draped streets to Wahnfried, where years before Wagner had prepared a simple tomb in the garden. Only close friends were allowed at the last graveside rites. When the children remained alone, waiting for her in the dusk, Cosima came from the house. The coffin was lowered into the vault and the heavy stone, without inscription, was moved into place.

Cosima was prostrate with grief, and for a time she seemed near death herself. She lived a while in complete seclusion. Under the persuasion of her children, she came from her solitude and took over active direction of the Festival Theater. That the Bayreuth

[11] Quoted in Newman, *Life of Wagner*, IV, 713.
[12] Hanslick, *Vienna's Golden Years*, p. 240.

Festivals survived the death of their creator is due directly to the strength of her personality and the tenacity of her purpose.

She died, at the age of 94, in 1931 and was buried at Wahnfried, by the side of the Master to whom she gave her life.

Appendix:
The Story of
The Ring of the Nibelung

Das Rheingold

Scene 1. The three Rhinemaidens are swimming in the depths of the river, guarding the magic Rhinegold. The dwarf Alberich, one of the race of Nibelungs who live within the earth, attempts to make love to the maidens, but they teasingly elude him. He learns from their careless chatter that the gold, if fashioned into a ring, will bestow world power on its owner, but only one who has forsworn love can make the ring. Furious at his rebuff, Alberich curses love, seizes the gold, and disappears into the depths.

Scene 2. Wotan, the chief of the Gods, has made a treaty with the giants Fafner and Fasolt to build a home for the Gods (Walhalla). As wage, Wotan has promised Freia, the Goddess of love and source of the Gods' youth. When the giants claim their wage Wotan refuses to give her up and calls on Loge, God of Fire, to find a suitable substitute. Loge tells him of Alberich and the Ring, and the giants agree to accept the Nibelung's gold. Wotan and Loge begin the descent to Nibelheim.

Scene 3. In Nibelheim, Alberich has forced his brother Mime to fashion a magic helmet known as the Tarnhelm, which will transform the wearer into any shape he desires. Wotan and Loge arrive. Loge persuades Alberich to demonstrate the Tarnhelm by transforming himself into a toad. Wotan places his foot on the toad as Loge seizes the Tarnhelm. Alberich is bound and dragged away, a prisoner.

Scene 4. Back on the Gods' mountain, Alberich is forced to give up his gold, then the Tarnhelm, and finally the Ring. At this he pronounces a fearful curse on all who shall possess the Ring and disappears, raging, into the earth. The Gods assemble, and the giants approach with Freia. Wotan gives them the gold and the Tarnhelm but refuses to part with the Ring. Then from a cleft in the rock Erda, the Earth-Mother, rises and warns Wotan: give up the Ring, beware its curse; the end of the Gods is near. Wotan yields the Ring, and its curse is at once felt as Fafner kills his brother Fasolt. Thor, God of thunder, creates a rainbow bridge and the Gods walk into their new home. As Wotan muses on a plan to retrieve the Ring, the Rhinemaidens sing of the treachery of those who live above.

Die Walküre

By a liaison with a mortal woman, Wotan has created a new race of half-gods, the Volsungs (*Wälsungen*). The twins Siegmund and Sieglinde, the first generation, are separated as infants. Wotan, now living as the mortal Wälse, raises Siegmund in the forest, and Sieglinde is forced against her will to marry Hunding.

Act I

Siegmund, wounded and without weapons, stumbles into the forest hut of Hunding and is given aid by Sieglinde. When Hunding returns and hears Siegmund's story, he allows his guest to stay the night in peace, but warns that in the morning he will kill Siegmund in battle.

Left alone, Siegmund broods on his attraction to the unhappy Sieglinde and on his father's promise of a sword. Sieglinde, having drugged Hunding, returns alone. She tells of a stranger who thrust a sword into the ash tree that grows in the middle of the hut. No one has yet been able to withdraw it. Gradually the truth dawns upon them: the sword was left for Siegmund; they are brother and sister as well as lovers. Siegmund seizes the sword, draws it from the tree, and they flee into the moonlit night together.

Act II

In a wild mountainous region, Wotan orders Brünnhilde, his favorite among the nine Valkyries, to protect Siegmund. (The Valkyries are warrior-maidens, daughters of Wotan and Erda, whose task is to lead fallen heroes to Walhalla.) But Wotan's wife Fricka forces him to withdraw his support from Siegmund. Wotan sadly explains to Brünnhilde that he had created the Volsungs to redeem the Ring, but now he must abandon them.

Moved by Siegmund's devotion to Sieglinde, Brünnhilde decides to protect him despite Wotan's order. As Siegmund and Hunding battle, Wotan interferes, and Siegmund is killed. Brünnhilde escapes with Sieglinde, and Wotan disappears in thunder and lightning to find his disobedient daughter.

Act III

On a rocky mountain top the Valkyries are gathering. Finally Brünnhilde approaches with Sieglinde. At first Sieglinde wishes to die, but Brünnhilde tells her to live for the child she carries. Having helped Sieglinde escape to the forest, Brünnhilde faces Wotan's wrath. Her punishment is to be left in magic sleep, to belong to the first man who awakens her. She pleads for mercy, her justification being that she did Wotan's true will. Finally he relents and agrees to put a ring of fire around the mountain through which only a fearless hero (Siegfried) can come. Sadly he makes his way through the flames as Brünnhilde sleeps, awaiting the fearless hero.

Siegfried

After leaving Brünnhilde, Sieglinde finds refuge in the forest with the dwarf Mime, Alberich's hated brother. There she dies giving birth to Siegfried. The evil dwarf rears the boy in hope that Siegfried will help him gain possession of the Ring, which is now guarded by the giant Fafner in the form of a dragon. Siegfried is a young man when the opera begins.

Act I

Mime is in his cave trying to forge a sword for Siegfried. The boy enters, smashes the weapon, and finally forces Mime to tell him the story of his birth and of the broken sword Nothung. Siegfried orders Mime to forge the sword, with which he will go out into the world and never look upon Mime again.

When Siegfried departs, Wotan, now disguised as the Wanderer, enters the cave. He tells Mime that only one who has never learned fear can forge Nothung, but that Mime will fall to that one. When Siegfried returns, Mime persuades him that he should visit Fafner, the dragon, in order to learn fear. As Siegfried exultantly forges the sword, Mime mixes a poison brew to give the boy after he has killed Fafner.

Act II

At Fafner's cave, Alberich is waiting for the hero who will free the Ring. The Wanderer pauses briefly and reminds him that the Ring belongs to whoever kills Fafner. Siegfried and Mime arrive, and at length Siegfried kills the Dragon. The magic properties of the Dragon's blood enable Siegfried to understand the forest bird that is singing. The bird tells him of the Ring and the Tarnhelm, which he takes, and warns him against Mime, whose true thoughts Siegfried can now hear. When it is clear that Mime intends to poison him, Siegfried kills the dwarf. Following the bird, he starts out to find Brünnhilde, asleep in her ring of fire.

Act III

At the foot of Brünnhilde's mountain, Wotan, the Wanderer, calls Erda from her sleep. But now the Earth-Mother's vision is clouded, and Wotan finally provides the enlightenment. He no longer fears the end of the Gods but desires only his destiny.

Siegfried enters, and Wotan bars his way through the fire. With one blow Siegfried shatters the spear and Wotan withdraws. Siegfried plunges through the fire to the peaceful mountain-top, where he finds Brünnhilde sleeping. He awakens her with a kiss, and they embrace in passionate joy.

Götterdämmerung

Prologue. The three Norns are spinning the thread of destiny. They tell of Wotan's rise and fall, and of the Ring and its curse, but when they try to predict the future, the thread of destiny breaks.

On the mountain-top Brünnhilde sends Siegfried into the world to seek heroic deeds. He gives her the Ring as pledge of his love.

Act I

Hagen, son of Alberich, is plotting to recover the Ring. First he interests Gunther, his half brother and chief of the Gibichungs, in the sleeping Brünnhilde, without letting it be known that she has already been awakened. Then he suggests that Siegfried could be persuaded to go through the fire and bring Brünnhilde to Gunther by arousing his love for Gunther's sister Gutrune. When Siegfried arrives, Hagen secretly puts a forgetfulness potion in his drink. Siegfried immediately loses his memory of Brünnhilde and offers to secure her for Gunther in return for Gutrune's hand in marriage.

On the mountain Brünnhilde is waiting for Siegfried's return when her sister, the Valkyrie Waltraute, rides up in haste. Waltraute implores Brünnhilde to give the Ring back to the Rhinemaidens in order to save Walhalla and the Gods. Brünnhilde refuses; the Ring is the symbol of Siegfried's love for her.

After Waltraute leaves, Siegfried, transformed by the Tarnhelm to look like Gunther, breaks through the fire. He commands Brünnhilde to wed him and forcibly takes the Ring from her.

Act II

On night watch, Hagen is exhorted by his father Alberich to persevere in the fight for the Ring. As dawn comes, Alberich slips away, and Siegfried returns with news of his success. When Gunther and Brünnhilde arrive, she sees the Ring on Siegfried's finger, and her rage mounts. She charges that Siegfried betrayed Gunther and forced her love. Siegfried denies it, reassures Gunther, and goes gaily into the wedding hall with Gutrune and the vassals. Brünnhilde helps Hagen persuade Gunther that only Siegfried's death will compensate for the injury.

Act III

Hunting on the banks of the Rhine, Siegfried comes upon the three Rhinemaidens. They ask him for the Ring, but when they threaten him with its curse, he refuses to part with it. Gunther, Hagen, and the vassals join Siegfried. Siegfried talks of his past, and Hagen gives him a drink drugged to restore his memory. Siegfried thus tells, to Gunther's horror, of his awakening of Brünnhilde. Hagen thrusts his spear into Siegfried's back.

Siegfried's body is brought back to the Hall of the Gibichungs. Gunther claims the Ring as Gutrune's heritage and Hagen kills him.

Brünnhilde enters solemnly and calmly. She explains the past to Gutrune. She has a bier of great logs built for Siegfried's body. Then, taking the Ring from his finger, she puts it on her own. Now she understands everything. She throws a torch on the bier, mounts her horse, and rides into the consuming fire. The flames leap up, igniting the whole hall. The Rhine overflows its banks, and the Rhinemaidens recover the Ring from the ashes. Hagen, with a cry of rage, leaps into the flood, and is dragged to his death. In the background the flames engulf Walhalla.

Selected Bibliography

The Wagner bibliography is larger than that of any other musician. It is, in fact, so vast that even to give some notion of its extent and variety would be beyond the scope of this book. The following list, confined to writings in English, is designed only as a guide to the next steps in the study of Wagner.

Biography

Newman, Ernest, *The Life of Richard Wagner*, 4 vols. New York: Alfred A. Knopf, 1933-1946. A monumental and authoritative work, one of the great musical biographies.

Wagner, Richard, *My Life*, 2 vols., authorized translation. London: Constable and Company, Ltd., 1911. A fascinating and revealing document, but it must be used with extreme care, especially in those parts dealing with Wagner's maturity. Extends only to 1864. A poor translation.

Wagner's Theoretical Writings

Richard Wagner's Prose Works, trans. by William Ashton Ellis, 8 vols. London: Kegan, Paul, Trench, Trübner & Co., Ltd., 1892-1899. Includes all of Wagner's important essays in a too-literal translation that makes reading difficult.

Wagner on Music and Drama: A Compendium of Richard Wagner's Prose Works, ed. by Albert Goldman and Evert Sprinchorn. A handy selection, conveniently arranged according to subject matter and concept. Unfortunately, the great majority of the translations are from Ellis.

Strunk, Oliver, ed., "Richard Wagner: From *Das Kunstwerk der Zukunft*," in *Source Readings in Music History*, pp. 876-903. New York: W. W. Norton & Company, Inc., 1950. Highly recommended both for the lucidity of the translation and the significance of the selection.

Wagner's Letters

Burk, John N., ed., *Letters of Richard Wagner. The Burrell Collection.* New York: The Macmillan Company, 1950. A varied collection in serviceable translation, with helpful explanations and connective narrative.

Altman, Wilhelm, ed., *Letters of Richard Wagner*, 2 vols., trans. by M. M. Bozman. New York: E. P. Dutton & Co., Inc., 1936. A carefully selected collection.

Critical Writings

Newman, Ernest, *Wagner as Man and Artist.* New York: Vintage Books, 1960 (reprint of 2nd ed., 1924; 1st ed., 1914). Still a valuable study, with an especially helpful summary of Wagner's theoretical writings. The reader should keep two facts in mind, however: first, that a number of the opinions do not represent Newman's final views; second, that much of the discussion of Wagner's life is oriented toward discrediting the exaggerated claims of complete frankness made for Wagner's autobiography.

————, *Fact and Fiction about Wagner.* New York: Alfred A. Knopf, 1931. Demolishes a scurrilous attack on Wagner and is of interest primarily in its demonstration of just how far such attacks were carried.

Hanslick, Eduard, *Vienna's Golden Years of Music, 1850-1900,* trans. and ed. by Henry Pleasants III. New York: Simon and Schuster, 1950. Includes Hanslick's most important reviews of Wagner's works.

————, *The Beautiful in Music,* trans. by Gustav Cohen, ed. by Morris Weitz, Library of Liberal Arts. Indianapolis: Bobbs-Merrill Company, Inc., 1957. The classic statement of the anti-Wagnerian aesthetic.

Shaw, George Bernard, *The Perfect Wagnerite.* Dodd, Mead and Company, 1934 (reprint of 2nd ed., 1901; 1st ed., 1898). An ingenious, logical, but hardly convincing interpretation of the *Ring* in the light of Mr. Shaw's favorite political and social views. Interest is added by the vitality of the literary style.

Barzun, Jacques, *Darwin, Marx, Wagner: Critique of a Heritage,* rev. 2nd ed., Doubleday Anchor Books, 1958 (1st ed., 1941). An original and thoughtful essay linking the scientist, the sociologist, and the artist at the foundation of modern revolutionary society.

Donington, Robert, *Wagner's "Ring" and its Symbols.* London: Faber and Faber, 1963. A detailed interpretation of the *Ring* in psychoanalytical terms. Not always convincing to the "uninitiated," but still valuable for some striking insights. Contains an excellent table of leitmotives.

Kerman, Joseph, *Opera as Drama*. New York: Vintage Books, 1959 (reprint from 1956). A book of fundamental importance to any opera-goer; includes an unusually perceptive essay on *Tristan*.

Guides to the Operas

The student of Wagner should perhaps first be warned that most of the libretti issued in the United States were designed for particular performances and contain unmarked cuts. The best sources of translations are the piano-vocal scores and the booklets included with complete recordings.

Hall, Gertrude, *The Wagnerian Romances*. New York: Alfred A. Knopf, 1925. A fine, understanding prose rendering of Wagner's stories.

Newman, Ernest, *The Wagner Operas*. New York: Alfred A. Knopf, 1949. By all odds the most complete and reliable description of action and music. Includes detailed, authoritative accounts of Wagner's literary sources.

————, *Stories of the Great Operas*. New York: Garden City Publishing Co., Inc. (reprint of 3 vols., 1928, 1929, 1939). Less extensive than the preceding, but still serviceable.

Kobbé, Gustav, *Wagner's Music-Dramas Analysed*. New York: G. Schirmer, Inc., 1890. Straightforward description; perhaps too literal in the labeling of motives.

Lavignac, Albert, *The Music Dramas of Richard Wagner*, trans. by Esther Singleton. New York: Dodd, Mead and Company, 1942 (reprint of 1897). Also too literal in the labeling of motives, but an interesting comparison to Newman's interpretations.

Dickinson, A. E. F., *The Musical Design of "the Ring."* London: Oxford University Press, 1926. Brevity and concise organization makes this a convenient guide. Rigid interpretation of motives.

Index

NOTE.

To this volume as it was originally issued have been added five Tales, beginning with " The Platonic Bassoon," which are characteristic of the various moods, serious, gay, or pathetic, out of which grew the best work of the author's later years.

INTRODUCTION

ALAS, POOR YORICK!

IN paying a tribute to the mingled mirth
and tenderness of Eugene Field — the poet
of whose going the West may say, "He took
our daylight with him" — one of his fellow
journalists has written that he was a jester,
but not of the kind that Shakespeare drew
in Yorick. He was not only, — so the writer
implied, — the maker of jibes and fantastic
devices, but the bard of friendship and affection, of melodious lyrical conceits; he was the
laureate of children — dear for his "Wynken,
Blynken and Nod" and "Little Boy Blue";
the scholarly book-lover, withal, who rel-
ished and paraphrased his Horace, who
wrote with delight a quaint archaic English
of his special devising; who collected rare
books, and brought out his own "Little
Books" of "Western Verse" and "Profi-

table Tales " in high-priced limited editions, with broad margins of paper that moths and rust do not corrupt, but which tempts bibliomaniacs to break through and steal.

For my own part, I would select Yorick as the very forecast, in imaginative literature, of our various Eugene. Surely Shakespeare conceived the "mad rogue" of Elsinore as made up of grave and gay, of wit and gentleness, and not as a mere clown or "jig maker." It is true that when Field put on his cap and bells, he too was "wont to set the table on a roar," as the feasters at a hundred tables, from "Casey's Table d'Hôte" to the banquets of the opulent East, now rise to testify. But Shakespeare plainly reveals, concerning Yorick, that mirth was not his sole attribute,—that his motley covered the sweetest nature and the tenderest heart. It could be no otherwise with one who loved and comprehended childhood and whom the children loved. And what does Hamlet say ?— "He hath borne me upon his back a thousand times . . . Here hung those lips that I have kissed I know not how oft!" Of what is he thinking but of his boyhood,

before doubts and contemplation wrapped him in the shadow, and when in his young grief or frolic the gentle Yorick, with his jest, his "excellent fancy," and his songs and gambols, was his comrade?

Of all moderns, then, here or in the old world, Eugene Field seems to be most like the survival, or revival, of the ideal jester of knightly times; as if Yorick himself were incarnated, or as if a superior bearer of the bauble at the court of Italy, or of France, or of English King Hal, had come to life again — as much out of time as Twain's Yankee at the Court of Arthur; but not out of place, — for he fitted himself as aptly to his folk and region as Puck to the fays and mortals of a wood near Athens. In the days of divine sovereignty, the jester, we see, was by all odds the wise man of the palace; the real fools were those he made his butt — the foppish pages, the obsequious courtiers, the swaggering guardsmen, the insolent nobles, and not seldom majesty itself. And thus it is that painters and romancers have loved to draw him. Who would not rather be Yorick than Osric, or Touchstone

than Le Beau, or even poor Bertuccio than one of his brutal mockers ? Was not the redoubtable Chicot, with his sword and brains, the true ruler of France ? To come to the jesters of history — which is so much less real than fiction — what laurels are greener than those of Triboulet, and Will Somers, and John Heywood — dramatist and master of the king's merry Interludes ? Their shafts were feathered with mirth and song, but pointed with wisdom, and well might old John Trussell say "That it often happens that wise counsel is more sweetly followed when it is tempered with folly, and earnest is the less offensive if it be delivered in jest."

Yes, Field "caught on" to his time — a complex American, with the obstreperous *bizarrerie* of the frontier and the artistic delicacy of our oldest culture always at odds within him — but he was, above all, a child of nature, a frolic incarnate, and just as he would have been in any time or country. Fortune had given him that unforgettable mummer's face, — that clean-cut, mobile visage, — that animated natural mask! No one else had so deep and rich a voice for

the rendering of the music and pathos of a poet's lines, and no actor ever managed both face and voice better than he in delivering his own verses merry or sad. One night, he was seen among the audience at "Uncut Leaves," and was instantly requested to do something towards the evening's entertainment. As he was not in evening dress, he refused to take the platform, but stood up in the lank length of an ulster, from his corner seat, and recited "Dibdin's Ghost" and "Two Opinions" in a manner which blighted the chances of the readers that came after him. It is true that no clown ever equalled the number and lawlessness of his practical jokes. Above all, every friend that he had — except the Dean of his profession, for whom he did exhibit unbounded and filial reverence — was soon or late a victim of his whimsicality, or else justly distrusted the measure of Field's regard for him. Nor was the friendship perfected until one bestirred himself to pay Eugene back in kind. As to this, I am only one of scores now speaking from personal experience. There seemed to be no doubt in his mind that the victim of

his fun, even when it outraged common sensibilities, *must* enjoy it as much as he. Who but Eugene, after being the welcome guest, at a European capital, of one of our most ambitious and refined ambassadors, would have written a lyric, sounding the praises of a German "onion pie," ending each stanza with

Ach, Liebe! Ach, mein Gott!

and would have printed it in America, with his host's initials affixed?

My own matriculation at Eugene's College of Unreason was in this wise. In 1887, Mr. Ben Ticknor, the Boston publisher, was complaining that he needed some new and promising authors to enlarge his book-list. The New York "Sun" and "Tribune" had been copying Field's rhymes and prose extravaganzas — the former often very charming, the latter the broadest satire of Chicago life and people. I suggested to Mr. Ticknor that he should ask the poet-humorist to collect, for publication in book-form, the choicest of his writings thus far. To make the story brief, Mr. Field did so, and the outcome —

at which I was somewhat taken aback —
was the remarkable book, "Culture's Garland," with its title imitated from the sentimental "Annuals" of long ago, and its cover
ornamented with sausages linked together
as a coronal wreath! The symbol certainly
fitted the greater part of the contents, which
ludicrously scored the Chicago "culture" of
that time, and made Pullman, Armour, and
other commercial magnates of the Lakeside
City special types in illustration. All this had
its use, and many of the sufferers long since
became the *farceur's* devoted friends. The
Fair showed the country what Chicago really
was and is. Certainly there is no other American city where the richest class appear so
enthusiastic with respect to art and literature. "The practice of virtue makes men
virtuous," and even if there was some pre-
tence and affectation in the culture of ten
years ago, it has resulted in as high standards
of taste as can elsewhere be found. Moreover, if our own "four hundred" had even
affected, or made it the fashion to be interested in, whatever makes for real culture, the
intellectual life of this metropolis would not

now be so far apart from the "social swim."
There were scattered through "Culture's
Garland" not a few of Field's delicate bits of
verse. In some way he found that I had instigated Mr. Ticknor's request, and, although
I was thinking solely of the publisher's interests, he expressed unstinted gratitude.
Soon afterwards I was delighted to receive
from him a quarto parchment "breviary,"
containing a dozen ballads, long and short,
engrossed in his exquisitely fine handwriting,
and illuminated with colored borders and
drawings by the poet himself. It must have
required days for the mechanical execution,
and certainly I would not now exchange it
for its weight in diamonds. This was the
way our friendship began. It was soon
strengthened by meetings and correspondence, and never afterwards broken.

Some years ago, however, I visited Chicago, to lecture, at the invitation of its famous
social and literary "Twentieth Century
Club." This was Eugene's opportunity, and
I ought not to have been as dumfounded as I
was, one day, when our evening papers
copied from the "Chicago Record" a "very

pleasant joke "at the expense of his town and myself ! It was headed : "Chicago Excited! Tremendous Preparations for His Reception," and went on to give the order and route of a procession that was to be formed at the Chicago station and escort me to my quarters — stopping at Armour's packing-yards and the art-galleries on the way. It included the "Twentieth Century Club" in carriages, the "Browning Club" in busses, and the "Homer Club" in drays; ten millionnaire publishers, and as many pork-packers, in a chariot drawn by white horses, followed by not less than two hundred Chicago poets afoot! I have no doubt that Eugene thought I would enjoy this kind of advertisement as heartily as he did. If so, he lacked the gift of putting himself in the other man's place. But his sardonic face, a-grin like a school-boy's, was one with two others which shone upon me when I did reach Chicago, and my pride was not wounded sufficiently to prevent me from enjoying the restaurant luncheon to which he bore me off in triumph. I did promise to square accounts with him, in time, and this

is how I fulfilled my word. The next year, at a meeting of a suburban "Society of Authors," a certain lady-journalist was chaffed as to her acquaintanceship with Field, and accused of addressing him as "Gene." At this she took umbrage, saying: "It's true we worked together on the same paper for five years, but he was always a perfect gentleman. I *never* called him 'Gene.'" This was reported by the press, and gave me the refrain for a skit entitled "Katharine and Eugenio:"

> Five years she sate a-near him
>   Within that type-strewn loft ;
> She handed him the paste-pot,
>   He passed the scissors oft ;
> They dipped in the same inkstand
>   That crowned their desk between,
> Yet — he never called her Katie,
>   She never called him "Gene."
>
> Though close — ah! close — the droplight
>   That classic head revealed,
> She was to him Miss Katharine,
>   He — naught but Mister Field ;
> Decorum graced his upright brow
>   And thinned his lips serene,
> And, though he wrote a poem each hour,
>   Why should she call him "Gene?"

She gazed at his sporadic hair —
   She knew his hymns by rote ;
They longed to dine together
   At Casey's table d'hôte ;
Alas, that Fortune's "hostages " —
   But let us draw a screen !
He dared not call her Katie ;
   How *could* she call him " Gene ? "

I signed my verses "By one of Gene's Victims" ; they appeared in *The Tribune,* and soon were copied by papers in every part of the country. Other stanzas, with the same refrain, were added by the funny men of the southern and western press, and it was months before ' Gene ' saw the last of them. The word "Eugenio," which was the name by which I always addressed him in our correspondence, left him in no doubt as to the initiator of the series, and so our "Merry War" ended, I think, with a fair quittance to either side.

Grieving, with so many others, over Yorick's premature death, it is a solace for me to remember how pleasant was our last interchange of written words. Not long ago, he was laid very low by pneumonia,

but recovered, and before leaving his sick-
room wrote me a sweetly serious letter —
with here and there a sparkle in it — but in a
tone sobered by illness, and full of yearning
for a closer companionship with his friends.
At the same time he sent me the first editions, long ago picked up, of all my earlier
books, and begged me to write on their fly-
leaves. This I did; with pains to gratify
him as much as possible, and in one of the
volumes wrote this little quatrain:

TO EUGENE FIELD

Death thought to claim you in this year of years,
    But Fancy cried — and raised her shield between —
" Still let men weep, and smile amid their tears;
    Take any two beside, but spare Eugene! "

In view of his near escape, the hyperbole,
if such there was, might well be pardoned,
and it touched Eugene so manifestly that —
now that the eddy indeed has swept him
away, and the Sabine Farm mourns for its
new-world Horace — I cannot be too thankful that such was my last message to him.

Eugene Field was so mixed a compound
that it will always be impossible quite to

decide whether he was wont to judge critically of either his own conduct or his literary creations. As to the latter, he put the worst and the best side by side, and apparently cared alike for both. That he did much beneath his standard, fine and true at times,—is unquestionable, and many a set of verses went the rounds that harmed his reputation. On the whole, I think this was due to the fact that he got his stated income as a newspaper poet and jester, and had to furnish his score of "Sharps and Flats" with more or less regularity. For all this, he certainly has left pieces, compact of the rarer elements, sufficient in number to preserve for him a unique place among America's most original characters, scholarly wits, and poets of brightest fancy. Yorick is no more! But his genius will need no chance upturning of his grave-turf for its remembrance. When all is sifted, its fame is more likely to strengthen than to decline.

EDMUND CLARENCE STEDMAN.

[Originally contributed to the "Souvenir Book" of the N. Y. Hebrew Fair, December, 1895.]

Contents

❧

The Holy Cross

❧

THE HOLY CROSS

WHILST the noble Don Esclevador and his little band of venturesome followers explored the neighboring fastnesses in quest for gold, the Father Miguel tarried at the shrine which in sweet piety they had hewn out of the stubborn rock in that strangely desolate spot. Here, upon that serene August morning, the holy Father held communion with the saints, beseeching them, in all humility, to intercede with our beloved Mother for the safe guidance of the fugitive Cortes to his native shores, and for the divine protection of the little host, which, separated from the Spanish army, had wandered leagues to the northward, and had sought refuge in the noble mountains of an unknown land. The Father's devotions were, upon a sudden, interrupted by the ap-

proach of an aged man who toiled along the mountain-side path,—a man so aged and so bowed and so feeble that he seemed to have been brought down into that place, by means of some necromantic art, out of distant centuries. His face was yellow and wrinkled like ancient parchment, and a beard whiter than Samite streamed upon his breast, whilst about his withered body and shrunken legs hung faded raiment which the elements had corroded and the thorns had grievously rent. And as he toiled along, the aged man continually groaned, and continually wrung his palsied hands, as if a sorrow, no lighter than his years, afflicted him.

"In whose name comest thou?" demanded the Father Miguel, advancing a space toward the stranger, but not in threatening wise; whereat the aged man stopped in his course and lifted his eyebrows, and regarded the Father a goodly time, but he spake no word.

"In whose name comest thou?" repeated the priestly man. "Upon these mountains have we lifted up the cross of our blessed Lord in the name of our sovereign liege, and

4

here have we set down a tabernacle to the glory of the Virgin and of her ever-blessed son, our Redeemer and thine,— whoso thou mayest be!"

"Who is thy king I know not," quoth the aged man, feebly; "but the shrine in yonder wall of rock I know; and by that symbol which I see therein, and by thy faith for which it stands, I conjure thee, as thou lovest both, give me somewhat to eat and to drink, that betimes I may go upon my way again, for the journey before me is a long one."

These words spake the old man in tones of such exceeding sadness that the Father Miguel, touched by compassion, hastened to meet the wayfarer, and, with his arms about him, and with whisperings of sweet comfort, to conduct him to a resting-place. Coarse food in goodly plenty was at hand; and it happily fortuned, too, that there was a homely wine, made by Pietro del y Saguache himself, of the wild grapes in which a neighboring valley abounded. Of these things anon the old man partook, greedily but silently, and all that while he rolled his

5

eyes upon the shrine; and then at last, struggling to his feet, he made as if to go upon his way.

"Nay," interposed the Father Miguel, kindly; "abide with us a season. Thou art an old man and sorely spent. Such as we have thou shalt have, and if thy soul be distressed, we shall pour upon it the healing balm of our blessed faith."

"Little knowest thou whereof thou speakest," quoth the old man, sadly. "There is no balm can avail me. I prithee let me go hence, ere, knowing what manner of man I am, thou hatest me and doest evil unto me." But as he said these words he fell back again even then into the seat where he had sat, and, as through fatigue, his hoary head dropped upon his bosom.

"Thou art ill!" cried the Father Miguel, hastening to his side. "Thou shalt go no farther this day! Give me thy staff,"—and he plucked it from him.

Then said the old man: "As I am now, so have I been these many hundred years. Thou hast heard tell of me,—canst thou not guess my name; canst thou not read my

6

sorrow in my face and in my bosom? As thou art good and holy through thy faith in that symbol in yonder shrine, hearken to me, for I will tell thee of the wretch whom thou hast succored. Then, if it be thy will, give me thy curse and send me on my way."

Much marvelled the Father Miguel at these words, and he deemed the old man to be mad; but he made no answer. And presently the old man, bowing his head upon his hands, had to say in this wise:—

"Upon a time," he quoth, "I abided in the city of the Great King,—there was I born and there I abided. I was of good stature, and I asked favor of none. I was an artisan, and many came to my shop, and my cunning was sought of many,—for I was exceeding crafty in my trade; and so, therefore, speedily my pride begot an insolence that had respect to none at all. And once I heard a tumult in the street, as of the cries of men and boys commingled, and the clashing of arms and staves. Seeking to know the cause thereof, I saw that one was being driven to execution,—one that had said he was the Son of God and the King of the Jews,

7

for which blasphemy and crime against our people he was to die upon the cross. Overcome by the weight of this cross, which he bore upon his shoulders, the victim tottered in the street and swayed this way and that, as though each moment he were like to fall, and he groaned in sore agony. Meanwhile about him pressed a multitude that with vast clamor railed at him and scoffed him and smote him, to whom he paid no heed; but in his agony his eyes were alway uplifted to heaven, and his lips moved in prayer for them that so shamefully entreated him. And as he went his way to Calvary, it fortuned that he fell and lay beneath the cross right at my very door, whereupon, turning his eyes upon me as I stood over against him, he begged me that for a little moment I should bear up the weight of the cross whilst that he wiped the sweat from off his brow. But I was filled with hatred, and I spurned him with my foot, and I said to him: 'Move on, thou wretched criminal, move on. Pollute not my doorway with thy touch,— move on to death, I command thee!' This was the answer I gave to him, but no succor at all. Then he

8

spake to me once again, and he said: 'Thou, too, shalt move on, O Jew! Thou shalt move on forever, but not to death!' And with these words he bore up the cross again and went upon his way to Calvary.

"Then of a sudden," quoth the old man, "a horror filled my breast, and a resistless terror possessed me. So was I accursed forevermore. A voice kept saying always to me: 'Move on, O Jew! move on forever!' From home, from kin, from country, from all I knew and loved I fled; nowhere could I tarry,—the nameless horror burned in my bosom, and I heard continually a voice crying unto me: 'Move on, O Jew! move on forever!' So, with the years, the centuries, the ages, I have fled before that cry and in that nameless horror; empires have risen and crumbled, races have been born and are extinct, mountains have been cast up and time hath levelled them,—still I do live and still I wander hither and thither upon the face of the earth, and am an accursed thing. The gift of tongues is mine,—all men I know, yet mankind knows me not. Death meets me face to face, and passes me by;

the sea devours all other prey, but will not hide me in its depths; wild beasts flee from me, and pestilences turn their consuming breaths elsewhere. On and on and on I go, — not to a home, nor to my people, nor to my grave, but evermore into the tortures of an eternity of sorrow. And evermore I feel the nameless horror burn within, whilst evermore I see the pleading eyes of him that bore the cross, and evermore I hear his voice crying: 'Move on, O Jew! move on forevermore!'"

"Thou art the Wandering Jew!" cried the Father Miguel.

"I am he," saith the aged man. "I marvel not that thou dost revolt against me, for thou standest in the shadow of that same cross which I have spurned, and thou art illumined with the love of him that went his way to Calvary. But I beseech thee bear with me until I have told thee all,— then drive me hence if thou art so minded."

"Speak on," quoth the Father Miguel.

Then said the Jew: "How came I here I scarcely know; the seasons are one to me, and one day but as another; for the span of

my life, O priestly man! is eternity. This much know you: from a far country I embarked upon a ship,—I knew not whence 't was bound, nor cared I. I obeyed the voice that bade me go. Anon a mighty tempest fell upon the ship and overwhelmed it. The cruel sea brought peace to all but me; a many days it tossed and buffeted me, then with a cry of exultation cast me at last upon a shore I had not seen before, a coast far, far westward whereon abides no human thing. But in that solitude still heard I from within the awful mandate that sent me journeying onward, 'Move on, O Jew! move on;' and into vast forests I plunged, and mighty plains I traversed; onward, onward, onward I went, with the nameless horror in my bosom, and—that cry, that awful cry! The rains beat upon me; the sun wrought pitilessly with me; the thickets tore my flesh; and the inhospitable shores bruised my weary feet,—yet onward I went, plucking what food I might from thorny bushes to stay my hunger, and allaying my feverish thirst at pools where reptiles crawled. Sometimes a monster beast stood in my pathway and

threatened to devour me; then would I spread my two arms thus, and welcome death, crying: 'Rend thou this Jew in twain, O beast! strike thy kindly fangs deep into this heart,—be not afeard, for I shall make no battle with thee, nor any outcry whatsoever!' But, lo, the beast would cower before me and skulk away. So there is no death for me; the judgment spoken is irrevocable; my sin is unpardonable, and the voice will not be hushed!"

Thus and so much spake the Jew, bowing his hoary head upon his hands. Then was the Father Miguel vastly troubled; yet he recoiled not from the Jew,—nay, he took the old man by the hand and sought to soothe him.

"Thy sin was most heinous, O Jew!" quoth the Father; "but it falleth in our blessed faith to know that whoso repenteth of his sin, what it soever may be, the same shall surely be forgiven. Thy punishment hath already been severe, and God is merciful, for even as we are all his children, even so his tenderness to us is like unto the tenderness of a father unto his child — yea, and infi-

nitely tenderer and sweeter, for who can estimate the love of our heavenly Father? Thou didst deny thy succor to the Nazarene when he besought it, yet so great compassion hath he that if thou but callest upon him he will forget thy wrong,— leastwise will pardon it. Therefore be thou persuaded by me, and tarry here this night, that in the presence of yonder symbol and the holy relics our prayers may go up with thine unto our blessed Mother and to the saints who haply shall intercede for thee in Paradise. Rest here, O sufferer,— rest thou here, and we shall presently give thee great comfort."

The Jew, well-nigh fainting with fatigue, being persuaded by the holy Father's gentle words, gave finally his consent unto this thing, and went anon unto the cave beyond the shrine, and entered thereinto, and lay upon a bed of skins and furs, and made as if to sleep. And when he slept his sleep was seemingly disturbed by visions, and he tossed as doth an one that sees full evil things, and in that sleep he muttered somewhat of a voice he seemed to hear, though round about there was no sound whatsoever, save only

13

the soft music of the pine-trees on the mountain-side. Meanwhile in the shrine, hewn
out of those rocks, did the Father Miguel
bow before the sacred symbol of his faith
and plead for mercy for that same Jew that
slumbered anear. And when, as the deepening blue mantle of night fell upon the hilltops and obscured the valleys round about,
Don Esclevador and his sturdy men came
clamoring along the mountain-side, the holy
Father met them a way off and bade them
have regard to the aged man that slept in
yonder cave. But when he told them of that
Jew and of his misery and of the secret
causes thereof, out spake the noble Don
Esclevador, full hotly, —

"By our sweet Christ," he cried, "shall
we not offend our blessed faith and do most
impiously in the Virgin's sight if we give
this harbor and this succor unto so vile a
sinner as this Jew that hath denied our dear
Lord!"

Which words had like to wrought great
evil with the Jew, for instantly the other men
sprang forward as if to awaken the Jew and
drive him forth into the night. But the

Father Miguel stretched forth his hands and commanded them to do no evil unto the Jew, and so persuasively did he set forth the godliness and the sweetness of compassion that presently the whole company was moved with a gentle pity toward that Jew. Therefore it befell anon, when night came down from the skies and after they had feasted upon their homely food as was their wont, that they talked of the Jew, and thinking of their own hardships and misfortunes (whereof it is not now to speak), they had all the more compassion to that Jew, which spake them passing fair, I ween.

Now all this while lay the Jew upon the bed of skins and furs within the cave, and though he slept (for he was exceeding weary), he tossed continually from side to side, and spoke things in his sleep, as if his heart were sorely troubled, and as if in his dreams he beheld grievous things. And seeing the old man, and hearing his broken speech, the others moved softly hither and thither and made no noise soever lest they should awaken him. And many an one — yes, all

that valiant company bowed down that
night before the symbol in the shrine, and
with sweet reverence called upon our blessed
Virgin to plead in the cause of that wretched
Jew. Then sleep came to all, and in dreams
the noble Don Esclevador saw his sovereign
liege, and kneeled before his throne, and
heard his sovereign liege's gracious voice;
in dreams the heartweary soldier sailed the
blue waters of the Spanish main, and pressed
his native shore, and beheld once again the
lovelight in the dark eyes of her that awaited
him; in dreams the mountain-pines were
kissed of the singing winds, and murmured
drowsily and tossed their arms as do little
children that dream of their play; in dreams
the Jew swayed hither and thither, scourged
by that nameless horror in his bosom, and
seeing the pleading eyes of our dying Master,
and hearing that awful mandate: "Move on,
O Jew! move on forever!" So each slept
and dreamed his dreams,— all slept but the
Father Miguel, who alone throughout the
night kneeled in the shrine and called unto
the saints and unto our Mother Mary in
prayer. And his supplication was for that

Jew; and the mists fell upon that place and compassed it about, and it was as if the heavens had reached down their lips to kiss the holy shrine. And suddenly there came unto the Jew a quiet as of death, so that he tossed no more in his sleep and spake no word, but lay exceeding still, smiling in his sleep as one who sees his home in dreams, or his mother, or some other such beloved thing.

It came to pass that early in the morning the Jew came from the cavern to go upon his way, and the Father Miguel besought him to take with him a goodly loaf in his wallet as wise provision against hunger. But the Jew denied this, and then he said: "Last night while I slept methought I stood once more in the city of the Great King,— ay, in that very doorway where I stood, swart and lusty, when I spurned him that went his way to Calvary. In my bosom burned the terror as of old, and my soul was consumed of a mighty anguish. None of those that passed in that street knew me; centuries had ground to dust all my kin. 'O God!' I cried in agony, 'suffer my sin

to be forgotten,—suffer me to sleep, to sleep forever beneath the burden of the cross I sometime spurned!' As I spake these words there stood before me one in shining raiment, and lo! 't was he who bore the cross to Calvary! His eyes that had pleaded to me on a time now fell compassionately upon me, and the voice that had commanded me move on forever, now broke full sweetly on my ears: 'Thou shalt go on no more, O Jew, but as thou hast asked, so shall it be, and thou shalt sleep forever beneath the cross.' Then fell I into a deep slumber, and, therefrom but just now awaking, I feel within me what peace bespeaketh pardon for my sin. This day am I ransomed; so suffer me to go my way, O holy man."

So went the Jew upon his way, not groaningly and in toilsome wise, as was his wont, but eagerly, as goeth one to meet his bride, or unto some sweet reward. And the Father Miguel stood long, looking after him and being sorely troubled in mind; for he knew not what interpretation he should make of all these things. And anon the Jew was lost to sight in the forest.

But once, a little space thereafter, while that José Conejos, the Castilian, clambered up the yonder mountain-side, he saw amid the grasses there the dead and withered body of an aged man, and thereupon forthwith made he such clamor that Don Esclevador hastened thither and saw it was the Jew; and since there was no sign that wild beasts had wrought evil with him, it was declared that the Jew had died of age and fatigue and sorrow, albeit on the wrinkled face there was a smile of peace that none had seen thereon while yet the Jew lived. And it was accounted to be a most wondrous thing that, whereas never before had flowers of that kind been seen in those mountains, there now bloomed all round about flowers of the dye of blood, which thing the noble Don Esclevador took full wisely to be a symbol of our dear Lord's most precious blood, whereby not only you and I but even the Jew shall be redeemed to Paradise.

Within the spot where they had found the Jew they buried him, and there he sleeps unto this very day. Above the grave the Father Miguel said a prayer; and the ground

of that mountain they adjudged to be holy ground; but over the grave wherein lay the Jew they set up neither cross nor symbol of any kind, fearing to offend their holy faith.

But that very night, when that they were returned unto their camp half a league distant, there arose a mighty tempest, and there was such an upheaval and rending of the earth as only God's hand could make; and there was a crashing and a groaning as if the world were smitten in twain, and the winds fled through the valleys in dismay, and the trees of the forest shrieked in terror and fell upon their faces. Then in the morning when the tempest ceased and all the sky was calm and radiant they saw that an impassable chasm lay between them and that mountain-side wherein the Jew slept the sleep of death; that God had traced with his finger a mighty gulf about that holy ground which held the bones of the transgressor. Between heaven and earth hung that lonely grave, nor could any foot scale the precipice that guarded it; but one might see that the spot was beautiful with kindly mountain verdure and that

flowers of blood-red dye bloomed in that lonely place.

This was the happening in a summer-time a many years ago; to the mellow grace of that summer succeeded the purple glory of the autumn, and then came on apace the hoary dignity of winter. But the earth hath its resurrection too, and anon came the beauteous spring-time with warmth and scents and new life. The brooks leapt forth once more from their hiding-places, the verdure awaked, and the trees put forth their foliage. Then from the awful mountain peaks the snow silently and slowly slipped to the valleys, and in divers natural channels went onward and ever downward to the southern sea, and now at last 't was summer-time again and the mellow grace of August brooded over the earth. But in that yonder mountain-side had fallen a symbol never to be removed,— ay, upon that holy ground where slept the Jew was stretched a cross, a mighty cross of snow on which the sun never fell and which no breath of wind ever disturbed. Elsewhere was the tender warmth of verdure and the sacred passion of the

blood-red flowers, but over that lonely grave was stretched the symbol of him that went his way to Calvary, and in that grave slept the Jew.

Mightily marvelled Don Esclevador and his warrior host at this thing; but the Father Miguel knew its meaning; for he was minded of that vision wherein it was foretold unto the Jew that, pardoned for his sin, he should sleep forever under the burden of the cross he spurned. All this the Father Miguel showed unto Don Esclevador and the others, and he said: "I deem that unto all ages this holy symbol shall bear witness of our dear Christ's mercy and compassion. Though we, O exiled brothers, sleep in this foreign land in graves which none shall know, upon that mountain height beyond shall stretch the eternal witness to our faith and to our Redeemer's love, minding all that look thereon, not of the pains and the punishments of the Jew, but of the exceeding mercy of our blessed Lord, and of the certain eternal peace that cometh through his love!"

How long ago these things whereof I speak befell, I shall not say. They never

saw — that Spanish host — they never saw their native land, their sovereign liege, their loved ones' faces again; they sleep, and they are dust among those mighty mountains in the West. Where is the grave of the Father Miguel, or of Don Esclevador, or of any of the valiant Spanish exiles, it is not to tell; God only knoweth, and the saints: all sleep in the faith, and their reward is certain. But where sleepeth the Jew all may see and know; for on that awful mountain-side, in a spot inaccessible to man, lieth the holy cross of snow. The winds pass lightly over that solemn tomb, and never a sunbeam lingereth there. White and majestic it lies where God's hands have placed it, and its mighty arms stretch forth as in a benediction upon the fleeting dust beneath.

So shall it bide forever upon that mountain-side, and the memory of the Jew and of all else human shall fade away and be forgotten in the surpassing glory of the love and the compassion of him that bore the redeeming burden to Calvary.

❦

The Rose and the Thrush

❦

THE ROSE AND THE THRUSH

THERE was none other in the quiet valley so happy as the rose-tree,— none other so happy unless perchance it was the thrush who made his home in the linden yonder. The thrush loved the rose-tree's daughter, and he was happy in thinking that some day she would be his bride. Now the rose-tree had many daughters, and each was beautiful; but the rose whom the thrush loved was more beautiful than her sisters, and all the wooers came wooing her until at last the fair creature's head was turned, and the rose grew capricious and disdainful. Among her many lovers were the south wind and the fairy Dewlove and the little elf-prince Beambright and the hoptoad, whom all the rest called Mr. Roughbrown. The hoptoad lived in the stone-wall several yards away; but

27

every morning and evening he made a journey to the rose-tree, and there he would sit for hours gazing with tender longings at the beautiful rose, and murmuring impassioned avowals. The rose's disdain did not chill the hoptoad's ardor. "See what I have brought you, fair rose," he would say. "A beautiful brown beetle with golden wings and green eyes! Surely there is not in all the world a more delicious morsel than a brown beetle! Or, if you but say the word, I will fetch you a tender little fly, or a young gnat, — see, I am willing to undergo all toils and dangers for your own sweet sake."

Poor Mr. Roughbrown! His wooing was very hopeless. And all the time he courted the imperious rose, who should be peeping at him from her home in the hedge but as plump and as sleek a little Miss Dormouse as ever you saw, and her eyes were full of envy.

"If Mr. Roughbrown had any sense," she said to herself, " he would waste no time on that vain and frivolous rose. He is far too good a catch for *her*."

The south wind was forever sighing and

sobbing about. He lives, you know, very many miles from here. His home is beyond a great sea; in the midst of a vast desert there is an oasis, and it is among the palm-trees and the flowers of this oasis that the south wind abides. When spring calls from the North, "O south wind, where are you? Come hither, my sunny friend!" the south wind leaps from his couch in the far-off oasis, and hastens whither the spring-time calls. As he speeds across the sea the mermaids seek to tangle him in their tresses, and the waves try to twine their white arms about him; but he shakes them off and laughingly flies upon his way. Wheresoever he goes he is beloved. With their soft, solemn music the pine-trees seek to detain him; the flowers of earth lift up their voices and cry, "Abide with us, dear spirit,"— but to all he answers: "The spring-time calls me in the North, and I must hasten whither she calls." But when the south wind came to the rose-tree he would go no farther; he loved the rose, and he lingered about her with singing and sighing and protestations.

It was not until late in the evening that

Dewlove and the elf-prince appeared. Just
as the moon rolled up in the horizon and
poured a broad streak of silver through the
lake the three crickets went "Chirp-chirp,
chirp-chirp, chirp-chirp," and then out danced
Dewlove and Beambright from their hiding-
places. The cunning little fairy lived under
the moss at the foot of the oak-tree; he was
no bigger than a cambric needle,— but he
had *two* eyes, and in this respect he had
quite the advantage of the needle. As for
the elf-prince, his home was in the tiny, dark
subterranean passage which the mole used
to live in; he was plump as a cupid, and his
hair was long and curly, although if you
force me to it I must tell you that the elf-
prince was really no larger than your little
finger,— so you will see that so far as physical proportions were concerned Dewlove
and Beambright were pretty well matched.
Merry, merry fellows they were, and I should
certainly fail most lamentably did I attempt
to tell you how prettily they danced upon the
greensward of the meadowlands throughout
the summer nights. Sometimes the other
fairies and elves joined them,— delicate little

lady fairies with gossamer wings, and chubby little lady elves clad in filmy spider webs, — and they danced and danced and danced, while the three crickets went "Chirp-chirp, chirp-chirp, chirp-chirp," all night long. Now it was very strange — was it not?—that instead of loving one of these delicate little lady fairies, or one of these chubby little lady elves, both Dewlove and Beambright loved the rose. Yet, she was indeed very beautiful.

The thrush did not pester the rose with his protestations of love. He was not a particularly proud fellow, but he thought too much of the rose to vex her with his pleadings. But all day long he would perch in the thicket and sing his songs as only a thrush can sing to the beautiful rose he loves. He sung, we will say, of the forests he had explored, of the famous river he had once seen, of the dew which the rose loved, of the storm-king that slew the old pine and made his cones into a crown,— he sung of a thousand things which we might not understand, but which pleased the rose because *she* understood them. And one day the

thrush swooped down from the linden upon a monstrous devil's darning-needle that came spinning along and poised himself to stab the beautiful rose. Yes, like lightning the thrush swooped down on this murderous monster, and he bit him in two, and I am glad of it, and so are you if your heart be not wholly callous.

"How comes it," said the rose-tree to the thrush that day,— "how comes it that you do not woo my daughter? You have shown that you love her; why not speak to her?"

"No, I will wait," answered the thrush. "She has many wooers, and each wooes her in his own way. Let me show her by my devotion that I am worthy of her, and then perchance she will listen kindly to me when I speak to her."

The rose-tree thought very strange of this; in all her experience of bringing out her fair daughters into society she had never before had to deal with so curious a lover as the thrush. She made up her mind to speak for him.

"My daughter," said she to the rose, "the

thrush loves you; of all your wooers he is the most constant and the most amiable. I pray that you will hear kindly to his suit."

The rose laughed carelessly,— yes, merrily,— as if she heeded not the heartache which her indifference might cause the honest thrush.

"Mother," said the rose, "these suitors are pestering me beyond all endurance. How can I have any patience with the south wind, who is forever importuning me with his sentimental sighs and melancholy wheezing? And as for that old hoptoad, Mr. Roughbrown,— why, it is a husband I want, not a father!"

"Prince Beambright pleases you, then?" asked the rose-tree.

"He is a merry, capering fellow," said the daughter, "and so is his friend Dewlove; but I do not fancy either. And as for the thrush who sends you to speak for him,— why, he is quite out of the question, I assure you. The truth is, mother, that I am to fill a higher station than that of bride to any of these simple rustic folk. Am I not more beautiful than any of my companions, and

have I not ambitions above all others of my kind?"

"Whom have you seen that you talk so vain-gloriously?" cried the rose-tree in alarm. "What flattery has instilled into you this fatal poison?"

"Have you not seen the poet who comes this way every morning?" asked the rose. "His face is noble, and he sings grandly to the pictures Nature spreads before his eyes. I should be his bride. Some day he will see me; he will bear me away upon his bosom; he will indite to me a poem that shall live forever!"

These words the thrush heard, and his heart sank within him. If his songs that day were not so blithe as usual it was because of the words that the rose had spoken. Yet the thrush sang on, and his song was full of his honest love.

It was the next morning that the poet came that way. He lived in the city, but each day he stole away from the noise and crowd of the city to commune with himself and with Nature in the quiet valley where bloomed the rose-tree, where the thrush sung, and where

34

dwelt the fays and the elves of whom it has been spoken. The sun shone fiercely; withal the quiet valley was cool, and the poet bared his brow to the breeze that swept down the quiet valley from the lake over yonder.

"The south wind loves the rose! Aha, aha, foolish brother to love the rose!"

This was what the breeze said, and the poet heard it. Then his eyes fell upon the rose-tree and upon her blooming daughters.

"The hoptoad loves the rose! Foolish old Roughbrown to love the rose, aha, aha!"

There was a malicious squeakiness in this utterance,—of course it came from that envious Miss Dormouse, who was forever peeping out of her habitation in the hedge.

"What a beautiful rose!" cried the poet, and leaping over the old stone-wall he plucked the rose from the mother-tree,— yes, the poet bore away this very rose who had hoped to be the poet's bride.

Then the rose-tree wept bitterly, and so did her other daughters; the south wind wailed, and the old hoptoad gave three croaks so dolorous that if you had heard

them you would have said that his heart
was truly broken. All were sad,— all but
the envious dormouse, who chuckled mali-
ciously, and said it was no more than they
deserved.

The thrush saw the poet bearing the rose
away, yet how could the fluttering little
creature hope to prevail against the cruel
invader? What could he do but twitter in
anguish? So there are tragedies and heart-
aches in lives that are not human.

As the poet returned to the city he wore
the rose upon his breast. The rose was
happy, for the poet spoke to her now and
then, and praised her loveliness, and she
saw that her beauty had given him an inspiration.

"The rose despised my brother! Aha,
aha, foolish rose,— but she shall wither!"

It was the breeze that spake; far away from
the lake in the quiet valley its voice was very
low, but the rose heard and trembled.

"It's a lie," cried the rose. "I shall not
die. The poet loves me, and I shall live forever upon his bosom."

Yet a singular faintness — a faintness never

felt before — came upon the rose; she bent her head and sighed. The heat — that was all — was very oppressive, and here at the entrance to the city the tumult aroused an aggravating dust. The poet seemed suddenly to forget the rose. A carriage was approaching, and from the carriage leaned a lady, who beckoned to the poet. The lady was very fair, and the poet hastened to answer her call. And as he hastened the rose fell from his bosom into the hot highway, and the poet paid no heed. Ascending into the carriage with the lady (I am sure she must have been a princess!) the poet was whirled away, and there in the stifling dust lay the fainting rose, all stained and dying.

The sparrows flew down and pecked at her inquisitively; the cruel wagons crushed her beneath their iron wheels; careless feet buffeted her hither and thither. She was no longer a beautiful rose; no, nor even a reminiscence of one, — simply a colorless, scentless, ill-shapen mass.

But all at once she heard a familiar voice, and then she saw familiar eyes. The voice was tender and the eyes were kindly.

"O honest thrush," cried the rose, "is it you who have come to reproach me for my folly?"

"No, no, dear rose," said the thrush, "how should I speak ill to you? Come, rest your poor head upon my breast, and let me bear you home."

"Let me rather die here," sighed the rose, "for it was here that my folly brought me. How could I go back with you whom I never so much as smiled upon? And do they not hate and deride me in the valley? I would rather die here in misery than there in shame!"

"Poor, broken flower, they love you," urged the thrush. "They grieve for you; let me bear you back where the mother-tree will shade you, and where the south wind will nurse you — for — for he loves you."

So the thrush bore back the withering rose to her home in the quiet valley.

"So she has come back, has she?" sneered the dormouse. "Well, she has impudence, if nothing else!"

"She was pretty once," said the old hop-toad; "but she lost her opportunity when I

made up my mind to go wooing a certain glossy damsel in the hedge."

The rose-tree reached out her motherly arms to welcome her dying daughter, and she said: "Rest here, dear one, and let me rock you to repose."

It was evening in the quiet valley now. Where was the south wind that he came not with his wooing? He had flown to the North, for that day he had heard the spring-time's voice a-calling, and he went in answer to its summons. Everything was still. "Chirp-chirp, chirp-chirp, chirp-chirp," piped the three crickets, and forthwith the fairy boy and the elf-prince danced from their habitations. Their little feet tinkled over the clover and the daisies.

"Hush, little folk," cried the rose-tree. "Do not dance to-night,—the rose is dying."

But they danced on. The rose did not hear them; she heard only the voice of the thrush, who perched in the linden yonder, and, with a breaking heart, sung to the dying flower.

✾

The Pagan Seal-Wife

✾

THE PAGAN SEAL-WIFE [1]

IT is to tell of Harold, the son of Egbert, the son of Ib; comely was he to look upon, and a braver than he lived not in these islands, nor one more beloved of all people. But it chanced upon a time, while he was still in early manhood, that a grievous sorrow befell him; for on a day his mother Eleanor came to her end in this full evil wise. It was her intent to go unto the neighboring island, where grazed the goats and the kine, and it fortuned that, as she made her way thither in the boat, she heard sweet music, as if one played upon a harp in the waters, and, looking over the side of the boat, she beheld down in the waters a sea-maiden making those exceeding pleasant sounds. And the sea-maiden ceased to play, and smiled up at

[1] Orkney Folk-Lore.

43

Eleanor, and stretched up her hands and besought Eleanor to pluck her from the sea into the boat, which seeking to do, Eleanor fell headlong into the waters, and was never thereafter seen either alive or dead by any of her kin. Now under this passing heavy grief Egbert, the son of Ib, being old and spent by toil, brake down, and on a night died, making with his latest breath most heavy lamentation for Eleanor, his wife; so died he, and his soul sped, as they tell, to that far northern land where the souls of the departed make merry all the night, which merriment sendeth forth so vast and so beautiful a light that all the heavens are illumined thereby. But Harold, the son of Egbert and of Eleanor, was left alone, having neither brother, nor sister, nor any of kin, save an uncle abiding many leagues distant in Jutland. Thereupon befell a wonderful thing; if it had not happened it would not be told.

It chanced that, on a certain evening in the summer-time, Harold walked alone where a Druid circle lay coiled like a dark serpent on a hillside; his heart was filled with dolor, for he thought continually of

44

Eleanor, his mother, and he wept softly to himself through love of that dear mother. While thus he walked in vast heaviness of soul, he was beheld of Membril, the fairy that with her goodly subjects dwelt in the ruin of the Pict's house hard by the Druid circle. And Membril had compassion upon Harold, and upon the exceeding fine down of a tiny sea-bird she rode out to meet him, and it was before his eyes as if a star shined out of a mist in his pathway. So it was that Membril the fairy made herself known to him, and having so done, she said and she sung:

> I am Membril, queen of Fay,
> That would charm thy grief away!
> Thou art like the little bark
> Drifting in the cold and dark,—
> Drifting through the tempest's roar
> To a rocky, icy shore;
> All the torment dost thou feel
> Of the spent and fearful seal
> Wounded by the hunter's steel.
> I am Membril,— hark to me:
> Better times await on thee!
> Wouldst thou clasp thy mother dear,—
> Strange things see and stranger hear?

Straight betake thee to thy boat
And to yonder haven float,—
Go thy way, and silent be,—
It is Membril counsels thee;
Go thy way, and thou shalt see !

Great marvel had Harold to this thing;
nevertheless he did the bidding of Membril
the fairy, and it was full wisely done. And
presently he came to where his boat lay,
half on the shore and half in the waters, and
he unloosed the thong that held it, and entered into the boat; but he put neither hand
to the oars thereof, for he was intent to do
the bidding of Membril the fairy. Then
as if of its own accord, or as if the kindly
waves themselves bore it along, the boat
moved upon the waters and turned toward
the yonder haven whereof it was said and
sung. Fair shone the moon, and the night
was passing fair; the shadows fell from the
hilltops in their sleep and lay, as they had
been little weary children, in the valleys and
upon the shore, and they were rocked in the
cradles of those valleys, and the waters along
the shore sung softly to them. Upon the one
side lay the island where grazed the goats

and the kine, and upon the other side lay the island where Harold and other people abode; between these islands crept the sea with its gentle murmurings, and upon this sea drifted the boat bearing Harold to the yonder haven. Now the haven whereunto the course lay brooded almost beneath the shadow of the Stennis stones, and the waters thereof were dark, as if, forsooth, the sea frowned whensoever it saw those bloody stones peering down into its tranquil bosom. And some said that the place was haunted, and that upon each seventh night came thereunto the spirits of them that had been slain upon those stones, and waved their ghostly arms and wailed grievously; but of latter times none believeth this thing to be true.

It befell that, coming into the haven and bearing toward the shore thereof, Harold was 'ware of sweet music, and presently he saw figures as of men and women dancing upon the holm; but neither could he see who these people were, nor could he tell wherefrom the music came. But such fair music never had he heard before, and with great marvel he came from the boat into the clus-

47

ter of beech-trees that stood between the haven and that holm where the people danced. Then of a sudden Harold saw twelve skins lying upon the shore in the moonlight; and they were the comeliest and most precious sealskins that ever he saw, and he coveted them. So presently he took up one of the sealskins and bore it with him into his boat, and pushed the boat from the shore into the waters of the haven again, and, so doing, there was such plashing of the waters that those people dancing upon the fair green holm became 'ware of Harold's presence, and were afeared, so that, ceasing from their sport, they made haste down to the shore and did on the skins and dived into the waters with shrill cries. But there was one of them that could not do so, because Harold bore off that skin wherewith she was wont to begird herself, and when she found it not she wailed and wept and besought Harold to give her that skin again,— and, lo! it was Eleanor, the wife of Egbert! Now when Harold saw that it was his mother that so entreated him he was filled with wonder, and he drew nearer the shore to re-

gard her and to hear her words, for he loved her passing well. But he denied her that skin, knowing full well that so soon as she possessed it she would leave him and he should never again behold her. Then Eleanor related to him how that she had been drowned in the sea through treachery of the harp-maiden, and how that the souls of drowned people entered into the bodies of seals, nor were permitted to return to earth, save only one night in every month, at which time each recovered his human shape and was suffered to dance in the moonlight upon the fair green holm from the hour of sunset unto the hour of sunrise.

"Give me the skin, I pray thee," she cried, "for if the sun came upon me unawares I should crumble into dust before thine eyes, and that moment would a curse fall upon you. I am happy as I am; the sea and those who dwell therein are good to me,— give me the skin, I beseech thee, that I may return whence I came, and thereby shall a great blessing accrue to thee and thine."

But Harold said: "Nay, mother, I were a fool to part so cheerfully with one whom I

love dearer than life itself! I shall not let
you go so easily; you shall come with me
to our home, where I have lived alone too
long already. I shall be alone no longer,—
come with me, I say, for I will not deliver
up this skin, nor shall any force wrest it from
me!"

Then Eleanor, his mother, reasoned a space
with him, and anon she showed him the folly
of his way; but still he hung his head upon
his breast and was loath to do her bidding,
until at last she sware unto him that if he
gave to her that skin he should, upon the
next dancing night, have to wife the most
beautiful maiden in the world, and therefore
should be alone in the world no more. To
this presently Harold gave assent, and then
Eleanor, his mother, bade him come to that
same spot one month hence, and do what
she should then bid him do. Receiving,
therefore, the skin from him, she folded it
about her and threw herself into the sea, and
Harold betook himself unto his home.

Now wit ye well that full wearily dragged
the days and the nights until that month was
spent; but now at last it was the month of

August, and upon the night of the seventh day thereof ended the season of waiting. It is to tell that upon that night came Harold, the son of Egbert, from his hut, and stood on the threshold thereof, and awaited the rising of the moon from out the silver waters yonder. While thus he stood there appeared unto him Membril the fairy, and smiling upon him she said and she sung:—

> I am Membril, queen of Fay,
> Come to urge thee on thy way;
> Haste to yonder haven-side
> Where awaits thy promised bride;
> Daughter of a king is she,—
> Many leagues she comes to thee,
> Thine and only thine to be.
> Haste and see, then come again
> To thy pretty home, and, when
> Smiles the sun on earth once more,
> Will come knocking at thy door;
> Open then, and to thy breast
> Clasp whom thou shalt love the best!
> It is Membril counsels thee,—
> Haste and see what thou shalt see!

Now by this thing was Harold mightily rejoiced, and he believed it to be truth that great good was in store for him; for he had

seen pleasant things in the candle a many
nights, and the smoke from his fire blew
cheerily and lightly to the westward, and a
swan had circled over his house that day
week, and in his net each day for twice
seven days had he drawn from the sea a fish
having one golden eye and one silver eye:
which things, as all men know, portend full
goodly things, or else they portend nothing
at all whatsoever. So, being pleasantly
minded, Harold returned in kind unto Membril, the fairy queen, that bespoke him so
courteously, and to her and to them that bore
her company he said and he sung:—

Welcome, bonnie queen of Fay!
    For thou speakest pleasing words ;
Thou shalt have a gill of whey
    And a thimblefull of curds ;
In this rose is honey-dew
That a bee hath brought for you !

Welcome, bonnie queen of Fay !
    Call thy sisters from the gloam,
And, whilst I am on my way,
    Feast and frolic in my home,—
Kiss the moonbeams, blanching white,
Shrinking, shivering with affright !

Welcome, all, and have no fear,—
   There is flax upon the sill,
No foul sprite can enter here,—
   Feast and frolic as you will;
Feast and frisk till break of day,—
Welcome, little folk of Fay !

Thus having said and thus having sung, Harold went upon his way, and came to his boat and entered into it and journeyed to the haven where some time he had seen and discoursed with Eleanor, his mother. His course to this same haven lay, as before, over the waters that stole in between the two islands from the great sea beyond. Fair shone the moon, and the night was passing fair; the shadows rolled from the hilltops in their sleep and lay like little weary children in the valleys and upon the shore, and they were rocked in the cradles of those valleys, and the waters along the shore sung softly to them. Upon this hand lay the island where the goats and the kine found sweet pasturage, and upon the other hand stretched the island where people abode, and where the bloody Stennis stones rebuked the smiling sky, and where ghosts walked and wailed

and waved their white arms in the shadows of those haunted ruins where once upon a time the Picts had dwelt. And Harold's heart was full of joy, the more in especial when, as he bore nigh unto the haven, he heard sweet music and beheld a goodly company of people that danced in the moonlight upon the fair green holm. Then, when presently his boat touched the inner shore of the haven, and he departed therefrom and drew the boat upon the shore, he saw wherefrom issued the beautiful music to which the people danced; he saw that the waters reached out their white fingers and touched the kale and the fair pebbles and the brittle shells and the moss upon the beach, and these things gave forth sweet sounds, which were as if a thousand attuned harps vied with the singing of the summer-night winds. Then, as before, Harold saw sealskins lying upon the shore, and presently came Eleanor, his mother, and pointing to a certain fair velvet skin, she said: "Take that fair velvet skin into thy boat and speed with all haste to thy home. To-morrow at sunrise thy bride shall come knocking at thy

54

door. And so, farewell, my son,— oh, Harold, my only son!" Which saying, Eleanor, the wife of Egbert, drew a skin about her and leapt into the sea; nor was she ever thereafter beholden of human eyes.

Then Harold took up the fair velvet skin to which his mother had directed him, and he bore it away with him in his boat. So softly went he upon the waters that none of them that danced upon the fair green holm either saw or heard him. Still danced they on to the sweet music made by the white fingers of the waves, and still shone the white moon upon the fair green holm where they so danced.

Now when came Harold to his home, bearing the precious skin with him, he saw the fairies at play upon the floor of his hut, and they feared no evil, for there was barley strewn upon the sill so that no wicked sprite could enter there. And when Membril, the fairy queen, saw him bringing the skin that he had found upon the shore, she bade him good welcome, and she said and she sung:—

> I am Membril, queen of Fay,—
> Ponder well what words I say;

Hide that fair and velvet skin
Some secluded spot within;
In the tree where ravens croak,—
In the hollow of the oak,
In the cave with mosses lined,
In the earth where none may find;
Hide it quick and hide it deep,—
So secure shall be thy sleep,
Thine shall bride and blessings be,
Thine a fair posterity,—
So doth Membril counsel thee!

So, pondering upon this counsel and thinking well of it, Harold took the fair velvet skin and hid it, and none knew where it was hid,— none save only the raven that lived in the hollow oak. And when he had so done he returned unto his home and lay upon his bed and slept. It came to pass that early upon the morrow, when the sun made all the eastward sky blush for the exceeding ardor of his morning kiss, there came a knocking at the door of Harold's hut, and Harold opened the door, and lo! there stood upon the threshold the fairest maiden that eyes ever beheld. Unlike was she to maidens dwelling in those islands, for her hair was black as the waters of the long winter night,

and her eyes were as the twin midnight rocks that look up from the white waves of the moonlit sea in yonder reef; withal was she most beautiful to look upon, and her voice was as music that stealeth to one over pleasant waters.

The maiden's name was Persis, and she was the daughter of a Pagan king that ruled in a country many, many — oh, many leagues to the southward of these islands, in a country where unicorns and dragons be, and where dwelleth the phœnix and hippogriffins and the cockatrix, and where bloometh a tree that runneth blood, and where mighty princes do wondrous things. Now it fortuned that the king was minded to wed his daughter Persis unto a neighboring prince, a high and mighty prince, but one whom Persis loved not, neither could she love. So for the first time Persis said, "Nay, I will not," unto her father's mandate, whereat the king was passing wroth, and he put his daughter in a place that was like a jail to her, for it was where none might see her, and where she might see none, — none but those that attended upon her. This much

told Persis, the Pagan princess, unto Harold, and then, furthermore, she said: "The place wherein I was put by the king, my father, was hard by the sea, and oftentimes I went thereon in my little boat, and once, looking down from that boat into the sea, I saw the face of a fair young man within a magic mirror that was held up in the waters of the sea by two ghostly hands, and the fair young man moved his lips and smiled at me, and methought I heard him say: 'Come, be my bride, O fair and gentle Persis!' But, vastly afeared, I cried out and put back again to shore. Yet in my dreams I saw that face and heard that voice, nor could I find any rest until I came upon the sea again in hope to see the face and hear the voice once more. Then, that second time, as I looked into the sea, another face came up from below and lifted above the waters, and a woman's voice spake thus to me: 'I am mother of him that loveth thee and whom thou lovest; his face hast thou seen in the mirror, and of thee I have spoken to him; come, let me bear thee as a bride to him!' And in that moment a faintness came upon me and I fell into her

arms, and so was I drowned (as men say), and so was I a seal a little space until last dancing night, when, lo! some one brought me to life again, and one that said her name was Membril showed me the way unto thy door. And now I look upon thy face in truth, and thou art he who shall have me to his wife, for thou art he whose face I saw within the mirror which the ghostly hands bore up to me that day upon the sea!"

Great then was Harold's joy, and he folded her in his arms, and he spake sweet words to her, and she was content. So they were wed that very day, and there came to do them honor all the folk upon these islands: Dougal and Tam and Ib and Robbie and Nels and Gram and Rupert and Rolf and many others and all their kin, and they made merry, and it was well. And never spake the Pagan princess of that soft velvet skin which Harold had hid away,— never spake she of it to him or to any other one.

It is to tell that to Harold and to Persis were born these children, and in this order: Egbert and Ib (that was nicknamed the Strong) and Harold and Joan and Tam and

Annie and Rupert the Fair and Flocken and
Elsa and Albert and Theodoric,— these
eleven children were born unto them in good
time; and right fair children were they to see,
comely and stout, yet sweetly minded withal.
And prosperous times continually befell Harold; his herds multiplied, and the fish came
into his nets, so that presently there was none
other richer than he in all that country, and
he did great good with his riches, for he had
compassion to the poor.   So Harold was beloved of all, and all spake full fairly of his
wife,— how that she cared for his little ones,
and kept the house, and did deeds of sweet
charity among the needy and distressed,—
ay, so was Persis, the wife of Harold, beloved
of all, and by none other more than by Harold, who was wont to say that Persis had
brought him all he loved best: his children,
his fortune, his happiness, and, best of all,
herself.   So now they were wed twice seven
years, and in that time was Persis still as
young and fair to look upon as when she
came to Harold's door for the first time and
knocked.   This I account to be a marvel,
but still more a marvel was it that in all these

years spake she never a word of that soft velvet skin which Harold took and hid,— never a word to him nor to any one else. But the soft velvet skin lay meanwhile in the hollow of the oak, and in the branches of that tree perched a raven that croaked and croaked and croaked.

Now it befell upon a time that a ship touched at that island, and there came therefrom men that knelt down upon the shore and made strange prayers to a strange God, and forthwith uplifted in that island a symbol of wood in the similitude of a cross. Straightway went Harold with the rest to know the cause thereof, being fearful lest for this impiety their own gods, whom they served diligently, should send hail and fire upon them and their herds. But those that had come in the ship spake gently with them and showed themselves to be peaceful folk whose God delighted not in wars, but rather in gentleness and love. How it was, I, knowing not, cannot say, but presently the cause of that new God, whose law was gentleness and love, waxed mightily, and the people came from all around to kiss that

61

cross and worship it. And among them came Harold, for in his heart had dawned the light of a new wisdom, and he knew the truth as we know it, you and I. So Harold was baptized in the Christian faith, he and his children; but Persis, his wife, was not baptized, for she was the daughter of a Pagan king, and she feared to bring evil upon those she loved by doing any blasphemous thing. Right sorely grieved was Harold because of this, and oftentimes he spake with her thereof, and oftentimes he prayed unto his God and ours to incline her mind toward the cross, which saveth all alike. But Persis would say: "My best beloved, let me not do this thing in haste, for I fear to vex thy God since I am a Pagan and the daughter of a Pagan king, and therefore have not within me the light that there is in thee and thy kind. Perchance (since thy God is good and gracious) the light will come to me anon, and shine before mine eyes as it shineth before thine. I pray thee, let me bide my time." So spake Persis, and her life ever thereafter was kind and charitable, as, soothly, it had ever before been,

and she served Harold, her husband, well, and she was beloved of all, and a great sweetness came to all out of her daily life.

It fortuned, upon a day whilst Harold was from home, there was knocking at the door of their house, and forthwith the door opened and there stood in the midst of them one clad all in black and of rueful countenance. Then, as if she foresaw evil, Persis called unto her little ones and stood between them and that one all in black, and she demanded of him his name and will. "I am the Death-Angel," quoth he, " and I come for the best-beloved of thy lambs!"

Now Theodoric was that best-beloved; for he was her very little one, and had always slept upon her bosom. So when she heard those words she made a great outcry, and wrestled with the Death-Angel, and sought to stay him in his purpose. But the Death-Angel chilled her with his breath, and over-came her, and prevailed against her; and he reached into the midst of them and took Theodoric in his arms and folded him upon his breast, and Theodoric fell asleep there, and his head dropped upon the Death-Angel's

shoulder. But in her battle for the child, Persis catched at the chain about the child's neck, and the chain brake and remained in her hand, and upon the chain was the little cross of fair alabaster which an holy man had put there when Theodoric was baptized. So the Death-Angel went his way with that best-beloved lamb, and Persis fell upon her face and wailed.

The years went on and all was well upon these islands. Egbert became a mighty fisherman, and Ib (that was nicknamed the Strong) wrought wondrous things in Norroway, as all men know; Joan was wed to Cuthbert the Dane, and Flocken was wooed of a rich man's son of Scotland. So were all things for good and for the best, and it was a marvel to all that Persis, the wife of Harold, looked still to be as young and beautiful as when she came from the sea to be her husband's bride. Her life was full of gentleness and charity, and all folk blessed her. But never in all these years spake she aught to any one of the fair velvet skin; and through all the years that skin lay hid in the hollow of the oak-tree, where the raven croaked and croaked and croaked.

At last upon a time a malady fell upon Persis, and a strange light came into her eyes, and naught they did was of avail to her. One day she called Harold to her, and said: "My beloved, the time draweth near when we twain must part. I pray thee, send for the holy man, for I would fain be baptized in thy faith and in the faith of our children." So Harold fetched the holy man, and Persis, the daughter of the Pagan king, was baptized, and she spake freely and full sweetly of her love to Jesus Christ, her Saviour, and she prayed to be taken into his rest. And when she was baptized, there was given to her the name of Ruth, which was most fairly done, I trow, for soothly she had been the friend of all.

Then, when the holy man was gone, she said to her husband: "Beloved, I beseech thee go to yonder oak-tree, and bring me from the hollow thereof the fair velvet skin that hath lain therein so many years."

Then Harold marvelled, and he cried: "Who told thee that the fair velvet skin was hidden there?"

"The raven told me all," she answered;

"and had I been so minded I might have left thee long ago,—thee and our little ones. But I loved thee and them, and the fair velvet skin hath been unseen of me."

"And wouldst thou leave us now?" he cried. "Nay, it shall not be! Thou shalt not see that fair velvet skin, for this very day will I cast it into the sea!"

But she put an arm about his neck and said: "This night, dear one, we part; but whether we shall presently be joined together in another life I know not, neither canst thou say; for I, having been a Pagan and the daughter of a Pagan king, may by my birth and custom have so grievously offended our true God that even in his compassion and mercy he shall not find pardon for me. Therefore I would have thee fetch — since I shall die this night and do require of thee this last act of kindness—I would have thee fetch that same fair velvet skin from yonder oak-tree, and wrap me therein, and bear me hence, and lay me upon the green holm by the farther haven, for this is dancing night, and the seal-folk shall come from the sea as is their wont. Thou shalt lay me, so

wrapped within that fair velvet skin, upon that holm, and thou shalt go a space aside and watch throughout the night, coming not anear me (as thou lovest me!) until the dawn breaks, nor shalt thou make any outcry, but thou shalt wait until the night is sped. Then, when thou comest at daybreak to the holm, if thou findest me in the fair velvet skin thou shalt know that my sin hath been pardoned; but if I be not there thou may'st know that, being a Pagan, the seal-folk have borne me back into the sea unto my kind. Thus do I require of thee; swear so to do, and let thy beloved bless thee."

So Harold swore to do, and so he did. Straightway he went to the oak-tree and took from the hollow thereof the fair velvet skin; seeing which deed, the raven flew away and was never thereafter seen in these islands. And with a heavy heart, and with full many a caress and word of love, did Harold bind his fair wife in that same velvet skin, and he bore her to his boat, and they went together upon the waters; for he had sworn so to do. His course unto the haven lay as before over the waters that stole in

67

between the two islands from the great
troubled sea beyond. Fair shone the moon,
and the night was passing fair; the shadows
lay asleep, like little weary children, in the valleys, and the waters moaned, and the winds
rebuked the white fingers that stretched up
from the waves to clutch them. And when
they were. come to the inner shore of the
haven, Harold took his wife and bore her
up the bank and laid her where the light
came down from the moon and slept full
sweetly upon the fragrant sward. Then,
kissing her, he went his way and sat behind the Stennis stones a goodly space beyond, and there he kept his watch, as he had
sworn to do.

Now wit ye well a grievous heavy watch
it was that night, for his heart yearned for
that beloved wife that lay that while upon
the fair green holm, — ay, never before had
night seemed so long to Harold as did that
dancing night when he waited for the seal-
folk to come where the some-time Pagan
princess lay wrapped in the fair velvet skin.
But while he watched and waited, Membril,
the fairy queen, came and brought others of

her kind with her, and they made a circle about Harold, and threw around him such a charm that no evil could befall him from the ghosts and ghouls that in their shrouds walked among those bloody stones and wailed wofully and waved their white arms. For Membril, coming to Harold in the similitude of a glow-worm, made herself known to him, and she said and she sung:

> Loving heart, be calm a space
> In this gloomy vigil place;
> Though these confines haunted be
> Naught of harm can come to thee—
> Nothing canst thou see or hear
> Of the ghosts that stalk anear,
> For around thee Membril flings
> Charms of Fay and fairy rings.

Nothing daunted was Harold by thoughts of evil monsters, and naught recked he of the uncanny dangers of that haunted place; but he addressed these words to Membril and her host, and he said and he sung:

> Tell me if thy piercing eyes
>   See the inner haven shore.
> There my Own Beloved lies,
>   With the cowslips bending o'er:

Speed, O gentle folk of Fay!
And in guise of cowslips say
I shall love my love for aye!

Even so did Membril and the rest; and
presently they returned, and they brought
these words unto Harold, saying and singing
them: —

We as cowslips in that place
Clustered round thy dear one's face,
And we whispered to her there
Those same words we went to bear;
And she smiled and bade us then
Bear these words to thee again:
" Die we shall, and part we may,—
Love is love and lives for aye!"

Then of a sudden there was a tumult upon
the waters, as if the waters were troubled,
and there came up out of the waters a host
of seals that made their way to the shore
and cast aside their skins and came forth in
the forms of men and of women, for they
were the drowned folk that were come, as
was their wont, to dance in the moonlight
upon the fair green holm.   At that moment
the waters stretched out their white fingers

and struck the kale and the pebbles and the soft moss upon the beach, for they sought to make music for the seal-folk to dance thereby; but the music that was made was not merry nor gleeful, but was passing gruesome and mournful. And presently the seal-folk came where lay the wife of Harold wrapped in the fair velvet skin, and they knew her of old, and they called her by what name she was known to them, "Persis! Persis!" over and over again, and there was great wailing among the seal-folk for a mighty space; and the seal-folk danced never at all that night, but wailed about the wife of Harold, and called "Persis! Persis!" over and over again, and made great moan. And at last all was still once more, for the seal-folk, weeping and clamoring grievously, went back into the sea, and the sea sobbed itself to sleep.

Mindful of the oath he swore, Harold dared not go down to that shore, but he besought Membril, the queen of Fay, to fetch him tidings from his beloved, whether she still lay upon the holm, or whether the seal-folk had borne her away with them into the waters of the deep. But Membril might not go, nor

any of her host, for already the dawn was in
the east and the kine were lowing on yonder
slope. So Harold was left alone a tedious
time, until the sun looked upon the earth,
and then, with clamoring heart, Harold came
from the Stennis stones and leapt downward
to the holm where his beloved had lain that
weary while. Then he saw that the fair
velvet skin was still there, and presently he
saw that within the skin his beloved still reposed. He called to her, but she made no
answer; with exceeding haste he kneeled
down and did off the fair velvet skin, and
folded his beloved to his breast. The sun
shone full upon her glorious face and kissed
away the dew that clung to her white cheeks.

"Thou art redeemed, O my beloved!"
cried Harold; but her lips spake not, and
her eyes opened not upon him. Yet on the
dead wife's face was such a smile as angels
wear, and it told him that they should meet
again in a love that knoweth no fear of parting. And as Harold held her to his bosom
and wailed, there fell down from her hand
what she had kept with her to the last, and
it lay upon the fair green holm,— the little

alabaster cross which she had snatched from Theodoric's neck that day the Death-Angel bore the child away.

It was to tell of Harold, the son of Egbert, the son of Ib, and of Persis, his wife, daughter of the Pagan king; and it hath been told. And there is no more to tell, for the tale is ended.

❦

Flail, Trask, and Bisland

❦

FLAIL, TRASK, AND BISLAND

MY quondam friends, Flail, Trask, and
Bisland, are no more; they are dead,
and with them has gone out of existence as
gross an imposition as the moral cowardice
of man were capable of inventing, constructing, and practising.

When Alice became my wife she knew
that I was a lover and collector of books,
but, being a young thing, she had no idea of
the monstrous proportions which biblio-
mania, unchecked, is almost certain to acquire. Indeed, the dear girl innocently and
rapturously encouraged this insidious vice.
"Some time," she used to say, "we shall
have a house of our own, and then your
library shall cover the whole top-floor, and
the book-cases shall be built in the walls,
and there shall be a lovely blue-glass sky-

light," etc. Moreover, although she could not tell the difference between an Elzevir and a Pickering, or between a folio and an octavo, Alice was very proud of our little library, and I recall now with real delight the times I used to hear her showing off those precious books to her lady callers. Alice made up for certain inaccuracies of information with a distinct enthusiasm and garrulity that never failed to impress her callers deeply. I was mighty proud of Alice; I was prepared to say, paraphrasing Sam Johnson's remark about the Scotchman, "A wife can be made much of, if caught young."

It was not until after little Grolier and little Richard de Bury were born to us that Alice's regard for my pretty library seemed to abate. I then began to realize the truth of what my bachelor friend Kinzie had often declared,— namely, that the chief objection to children was that they weaned the collector from his love of books. Grolier was a mischievous boy, and I had hard work trying to convince his mother that he should by no means be allowed to have his sweet but destructive will with my Bewicks and Bed-

fords.   Thumb and finger marks look well enough in certain places, but I protested that they did not enhance the quaint beauty of an old wood-cut, a delicate binding, or a wide margin.   And Richard de Bury — a lovely little 16mo of a child — was almost as destructive as his older brother.   The most painful feature of it all to me then was that their mother actually protected the toddling knaves in their vandalism.   I never saw another woman change so as Alice did after those two boys came to us.   Why, she even suggested to me one day that when we *did* build our new house we should devote the upper story thereof *not* to library but to nursery purposes!

Things gradually got to the pass that I began to be afraid to bring books into the house.   At first Alice used to reproach me indirectly by eying the new book jealously, and hinting in a subtle, womanly way that Grolier needed new shoes, or that Richard was sadly in need of a new cap.   Presently, encouraged by my lamb-like reticence, Alice began to complain gently of what she termed my extravagance, and finally she fell into

the pernicious practice of berating me roundly for neglecting my family for the selfish — yes, the cruel — gratification of a foolish fad, and then she would weep and gather up the two boys and wonder how soon we should all be in the poorhouse.

I have spoken of my bachelor friend, Kinzie; there was a philosopher for you, and his philosophy was all the sweeter because it had never been embittered by marital experience. I had confidence in Kinzie, and I told him all about the dilemma I was in. He pitied me and condoled with me, for he was a sympathetic man, and he was, too, as consistent a bibliomaniac as I ever met with. "Be of good cheer," said he, "we shall find a way out of all this trouble." And he suggested a way. I seized upon it as the proverbial drowning man is supposed to clutch at the proverbial straw.

The next time I took a bundle of books home I marched into the house boldly with them. Alice fetched a deep sigh. "Ah, been buying more books, have you?" she asked in a despairing tone.

"No, indeed," I answered triumphantly;

"they were given to me,—a present from Judge Trask. I'm in great luck, ain't I?"

Alice was almost as pleased as I was. The interest with which she inspected the lovely volumes was not feigned. "But who is Judge Trask?" she asked, as she read the autographic lines upon a flyleaf in each book. I explained glibly that the judge was a wealthy and cultured citizen who felt somewhat under obligation to me for certain little services I had rendered him one time and another. I was not to be trapped or cornered. I had learned my sinful lesson perfectly. Alice never so much as suspected me of evil.

The scheme worked so well that I pursued it with more or less diligence. I should say that about twice a week on an average a bundle of books came to the house "with the compliments" of either Judge Trask or Colonel Flail or Mr. Bisland. You can understand that I could not hope to play the Trask deception exclusively and successfully. I invented Colonel Flail and Mr. Bisland, and I contrived to render them quite as liberal in their patronage as the mythical

Judge Trask himself. Occasionally a donation came in, by way of variety, from Smeaton and Holbrook and Caswell and other solitary creations of my mendacious imagination, when I used to blind poor dear Alice to the hideous truth. Touching myself, I gave it out that I had abandoned book-buying, was convinced of the folly of the mania, had reformed, and was repentant. Alice loved me all the better for that, and she became once more the sweetest, most amiable little woman in all the world. She was inexpressibly happy in the fond delusion that I had become prudent and thrifty, and was putting money in bank for that home we were going to buy — sometime.

Meanwhile the names of Flail, Trask, and Bisland became household words with us. Occasionally Smeaton and Holbrook and Caswell were mentioned gratefully as some fair volume bearing their autograph was inspected; but, after all, Flail, Trask, and Bisland were the favorites, for it was from them that most of my beloved books came. Yes, Alice gradually grew to love those three

myths; she loved them because they were good to *me*.

Alice had, like most others of her sex, a strong sense of duty. She determined to do something for my noble friends, and finally she planned a lovely little dinner whereat Judge Trask and Colonel Flail and Mr. Bisland were to be regaled with choicest viands of Alice's choice larder and with the sweetest speeches of Alice's graceful heart. I was authorized only to convey the invitations to this delectable banquet, and here was a pretty plight for a man to be in, surely enough! But my bachelor friend Kinzie (ough, the Mephisto!) helped me out. I reported back to Alice that Judge Trask was out of town, that Colonel Flail was sick abed with grip, and that Mr. Bisland was altogether too shy a man to think of venturing out to a dinner alone. Alice was dreadfully disappointed. Still there was consolation in feeling that she had done her duty in trying to do it.

Well, this system of deception and perjury went on a long time, Alice never suspecting any evil, but perfectly happy in my supposed

reform and economy, and in the gracious liberality of those three Mæcenas-like friends, Flail, Trask, and Bisland, who kept pouring in rare and beauteous old tomes upon me. She was joyous, too, in the prospect of that new house which we would soon be able to build, now that I had so long quit the old ruinous mania for book-buying! And I — wretch that I was — I humored her in this conceit; I heaped perjury upon perjury; lying and deception had become my second nature. Yet I loathed myself and I hated those books; they reproached me every time I came into their presence. So I was miserable and helpless; how hard it is to turn about when one once gets into the downward path! The shifts I was put to, and the desperate devices which I was forced to employ, — I shudder to recall them! Life became a constant, terrifying lie.

Thank Heaven, it is over now, and my face is turned the right way. A third little son was born to us. Alice was, oh! so very ill. When she was convalescing she said to me one day: "Hiram, I have been thinking it all over, and I've made up my mind that we must

name the baby Trask Flail Bisland, after our three good friends."

I did n't make any answer, went out into the hall, and communed awhile with my own hideous, tormented self. How my soul revolted against the prospect of giving to that innocent babe a name that would serve simply to scourge me through the rest of my wicked life! No, I could not consent to that. I would be a coward no longer!

I went back into Alice's room, and sat upon the bed beside her, and took one of Alice's dear little white hands in mine, and told her everything, told Alice the whole truth,— all about my wickedness and per- juries and deceptions; told her what a self- ish, cruel monster I had been; dispelled all the sinful delusion about Flail, Trask, and Bisland; threw myself, penitent and hope- less, upon my deceived, outraged little wife's mercy. Was it a mean advantage to take of a sick woman?

I fancied she would reproach me, for I knew that her heart was set upon that new house she had talked of so often; I told her that the savings she had supposed were in

bank, were in reality represented only by and in those stately folios and sumptuous quartos which the mythical Flail, Trask, and Bisland had presumably donated. "But," I added, "I shall sell them now, and with the money I shall build the home in which we may be happy again,— a lovely home, sweetheart, with no library at all, but all nursery if you wish it so!"

"No," said Alice, when I had ended my blubbering confession, "we shall not part with the books; they have caused you more suffering than they have me, and, moreover, their presence will have a beneficial effect upon you. Furthermore, I myself have become attached to them,— you know I thought they were given to you, and so I have learned to care for them. Poor Judge Trask and Colonel Flail and Mr. Bisland,— so they are only myths? Dear Hiram," she added with a sigh, "I can forgive you for everything except for taking those three good men out of our lives!"

After all this I have indeed reformed. I have actually become prudent, and I have a bank-account that is constantly increasing.

I do not hate books; I simply do not buy them. And I eschew that old sinner, Kinzie, and all the sinister influences he represents. As for our third little boy, we have named him Reform Meigs, after Alice's mother's grandfather, who built the first saw-mill in what is now the State of Ohio, and was killed by the Indians in 1796.

❧

The Touch in the Heart

❧

THE TOUCH IN THE HEART

OLD Abel Dunklee was delighted, and so was old Abel's wife, when little Abel came. For this coming they had waited many years. God had prospered them elsewhere; this one supreme blessing only had been withheld. Yet Abel had never despaired. "I shall some time have a son," said he. "I shall call him Abel. He shall be rich; he shall succeed to my business; my house, my factory, my lands, my fortune,—all shall be his!" Abel Dunklee felt this to be a certainty, and with this prospect constantly in mind he slaved and pinched and bargained. So when at last the little one did come it was as heir to a considerable property.

The joy in the house of Dunklee was not shared by the community at large. Abel Dunklee was by no means a popular man.

Folk had the well-defined opinion that he was selfish, miserly, and hard. If he had not been actually bad, he had never been what the world calls a good man. His methods had been of the grinding, sordid order. He had always been scrupulously honest in the payment of his debts, and in keeping his word; but his sense of duty seemed to stop there: Abel's idea of goodness was to owe no man any money. He never gave a penny to charities, and he never spent any time sympathizing with the misfortunes or distresses of other people. He was narrow, close, selfish, and hard, so his neighbors and the community at large said, and I shall not deny that the verdict was a just one.

When a little one comes into this world of ours, it is the impulse of the people here to bid it welcome, and to make its lot pleasant. When little Abel was born no such enthusiasm obtained outside the austere Dunklee household. Popular sentiment found vent in an expression of the hope that the son and heir would grow up to scatter the dollars which old man Dunklee had accumulated by

years of relentless avarice and unflagging toil. But Dr. Hardy — he who had officiated in an all-important capacity upon that momentous occasion in the Dunklee household — Dr. Hardy shook his head wisely, and perhaps sadly, as if he were saying to himself: ''No, the child will never do either what the old folk or what the other folk would have him do; he is not long for here.''

Had you questioned him closely, Dr. Hardy would have told you that little Abel was as frail a babe as ever did battle for life. Dr. Hardy would surely never have dared say that to old Dunklee; for in his rapture in the coming of that little boy old Dunklee would have smote the offender who presumed even to intimate that the babe was not the most vigorous as well as the most beautiful creature upon earth. The old man was simply assotted upon the child,— in a selfish way, undoubtedly, but even this selfish love of that puny little child showed that the old man was capable of somewhat better than his past life had been. To hear him talk you might have fancied that Mrs. Dunklee had no part or parcel or interest in their

offspring. It was always " my little boy,"—
yes, old Abel Dunklee's money had a rival
in the old man's heart at last, and that rival
was a helpless, shrunken, sickly little babe.

Among his business associates Abel Dunklee was familiarly known as Old Growly,
for the reason that his voice was harsh and
discordant, and sounded for all the world
like the hoarse growling of an ill-natured
bear. Abel was not a particularly irritable
person, but his slavish devotion to money-
getting, his indifference to the amenities of
life, his entire neglect of the tender practices
of humanity, his rough, unkempt personality, and his deep, hoarse voice,—these things
combined to make that sobriquet of " Old
Growly" an exceedingly appropriate one.
And presumably Abel never thought of re-
senting the slur implied therein and thereby; he was too shrewd not to see that,
however disrespectful and evil-intentioned
the phrase might be, it served him to good
purpose; for it conduced to that very general awe, not to say terror, which kept people
from bothering him with their charitable
and sentimental schemes.

Yes, I think we can accept it as a fact that Abel liked that sobriquet; it meant more money in his pocket, and fewer demands upon his time and patience.

But Old Growly abroad and Old Growly at home were two very different people. Only the voice was the same. The homely, furrowed, wizened face lighted up, and the keen, restless eyes lost their expression of shrewdness, and the thin, bony hands that elsewhere clutched and clutched and pinched and pinched for possession unlimbered themselves in the presence of little Abel, and reached out their long fingers yearningly and caressingly toward the little child. Then the hoarse voice would growl a salutation that was full of tenderness, for it came straight from the old man's heart; only, had you not known how much he loved the child, you might have thought otherwise, for the old man's voice was always hoarse and discordant, and that was why they called him Old Growly. But what *proved* his love for that puny babe was the fact that every afternoon, when he came home from the factory, Old Growly brought his little

boy a dime; and once, when the little fellow had a fever on him from teething, Old Growly brought him a dollar! Next day the tooth came through and the fever left him, but you could not make the old man believe but what it was the dollar that did it all. That was natural, perhaps; for his life had been spent in grubbing for money, and he had not the soul to see that the best and sweetest things in human life are not to be had by riches alone.

As the doctor had in one way and another intimated would be the case, the child did not wax fat and vigorous. Although Old Growly did not seem to see the truth, little Abel grew older only to become what the doctor had foretold,— a cripple. A weakness of the spine was developed, a malady that dwarfed the child's physical growth, giving to his wee face a pinched, starved look, warping his emaciated body, and enfeebling his puny limbs, while at the same time it quickened the intellectual faculties to the degree of precocity. And so two and three and four years went by, little Abel clinging to life with pathetic heroism, and

Old Growly loving that little cripple with all the violence of his selfish nature. Never once did it occur to the father that his child might die, that death's seal was already set upon the misshapen little body; on the contrary, Old Growly's thoughts were constantly of little Abel's famous future, of the great fortune he was to fall heir to, of the prosperous business career he was to pursue, of the influence he was to wield in the world,— of dollars, dollars, dollars, millions of them which little Abel was some time to possess; these were Old Growly's dreams, and he loved to dream them!

Meanwhile the world did well by the old man; despising him, undoubtedly, for his avarice and selfishness, but constantly pouring wealth, and more wealth, and even more wealth into his coffers. As for the old man, he cared not for what the world thought or said, so long as it paid tribute to him; he wrought on as of old, industriously, shrewdly, hardly, but with this new purpose: to make his little boy happy and great with riches.

Toys and picture-books were vanities in which Old Growly never indulged; to have

expended a farthing for chattels of that character would have seemed to Old Growly like
sinful extravagance. The few playthings
which little Abel had were such as his
mother surreptitiously bought; the old man
believed that a child should be imbued with
a proper regard for the value of money from
the very start, so *his* presents were always
cash in hand, and he bought a large tin bank
for little Abel, and taught the child how to
put the copper and silver pieces into it, and
he labored diligently to impress upon the
child of how great benefit that same money
would be to him by and by. Just picture to
yourself, if you can, that fond, foolish old
man seeking to teach this lesson to that wan-
eyed, pinched-face little cripple! But little
Abel took it all very seriously, and was so
apt a pupil that Old Growly made great joy
and was wont to rub his bony hands gleefully and say to himself, "He has great
genius,— this boy of mine,— great genius
for finance!"

But on a day, coming from his factory,
Old Growly was stricken with horror to find
that during his absence from home a great

change had come upon his child. The doctor said it was simply the progress of the disease; that it was a marvel that little Abel had already held out so long; that from the moment of his birth the seal of death had been set upon him in that cruel malady which had drawn his face and warped his body and limbs. Then all at once Old Growly's eyes seemed to be opened to the truth, and like a lightning flash it came to him that perhaps his pleasant dreams which he had dreamed of his child's future could never be realized. It was a bitter awakening, yet amid it all the old man was full of hope, determination, and battle. He had little faith in drugs and nursing and professional skill; he remembered that upon previous occasions cures had been wrought by means of money; teeth had been brought through, the pangs of colic beguiled, and numerous other ailments to which infancy is heir had by the same specific been baffled. So now Old Growly set about wooing his little boy from the embrace of death,—sought to coax him back to health with money, and the dimes became dollars, and the tin bank was like to burst

99

of fulness. But little Abel drooped and drooped, and he lost all interest in other things, and he was content to lie, drooping-eyed and listless, in his mother's arms all day. At last the little flame went out with hardly so much as a flutter, and the hope of the house of Dunklee was dissipated forever. But even in those last moments of the little cripple's suffering the father struggled to call back the old look into the fading eyes, and the old smile into the dear, white face. He brought treasure from his vaults and held it up before those fading eyes, and promised it all, all, all — everything he possessed, gold, houses, lands — all he had he would give to that little child if that little child would only live. But the fading eyes saw other things, and the ears that were deaf to the old man's lamentations heard voices that soothed the anguish of that last solemn hour. And so little Abel knew the Mystery.

Then the old man crept away from that vestige of his love, and stood alone in the night, and lifted up his face, and beat his bosom, and moaned at the stars, asking over

and over again why he had been so bereaved.
And while he agonized in this wise and
cried there came to him a voice,—a voice
so small that none else could hear, a voice
seemingly from God; for from infinite
space beyond those stars it sped its instan-
taneous way to the old man's soul and
lodged there.

"Abel, I have touched thy heart!"

And so, having come into the darkness of
night, old Dunklee went back into the light
of day and found life beautiful; for the touch
was in his heart.

After that, Old Growly's way of dealing
with the world changed. He had always
been an honest man, honest as the world
goes. But now he was somewhat better than
honest; he was kind, considerate, merciful.
People saw and felt the change, and they
knew why it was so. But the pathetic part
of it all was that Old Growly would never
admit — no, not even to himself — that he
was the least changed from his old grinding,
hard self. The good deeds he did were not
his own; they were his little boy's,— at least
so he said. And it was his whim when doing

some kind and tender thing to lay it to little
Abel, of whom he always spoke as if he
were still living. His workmen, his neighbors, his townsmen,— all alike felt the graciousness of the wondrous change, and many,
ah! many a lowly sufferer blessed that broken
old man for succor in little Abel's name.
And the old man was indeed much broken:
not that he had parted with his shrewdness
and acumen, for, as of old, his every venture
prospered; but in this particular his mind
seemed weakened; that, as I have said, he
fancied his child lived, that he was given to
low muttering and incoherent mumblings,
of which the burden seemed to be that child
of his, and that his greatest pleasure appeared
now to be watching other little ones at their
play. In fact, so changed was he from the
Old Growly of former years, that, whereas
he had then been wholly indifferent to the
presence of those little ones upon earth, he
now sought their company, and delighted to
view their innocent and mirthful play. And
so, presently, the children, from regarding
him at first with distrust, came to confide in
and love him, and in due time the old man

was known far and wide as Old Grampa
Growly, and he was pleased thereat. It was
his wont to go every fair day, of an afternoon, into a park hard by his dwelling, and
mingle with the crowd of little folk there;
and when they were weary of their sports
they used to gather about him,— some even
clambering upon his knees,— and hear him
tell his story, for he had only one story to tell,
and that was the story that lay next his heart,
— the story ever and forever beginning with,
"Once ther' wuz a littl' boy." A very tender little story it was, too, told very much
more sweetly than I could ever tell it; for it
was of Old Grampa Growly's own little boy,
and it came from that heart in which the
touch — the touch of God Himself — lay like
a priceless pearl.

So you must know that the last years of
the old man's life made full atonement for
those that had gone before. People forgot
that the old man had ever been other than
he was now, and of course the children never
knew otherwise. But as for himself, Old
Grampa Growly grew tenderer and tenderer,
and his goodness became a household word,

and he was beloved of all. And to the very last he loved the little ones, and shared their pleasures, and sympathized with them in their griefs, but always repeating that same old story, beginning with "Once ther' wuz a littl' boy."

The curious part of it was this: that while he implied by his confidences to the children that his own little boy was dead, he never made that admission to others. On the contrary, it was his wont, as I have said, to speak of little Abel as if that child still lived, and, humoring him in this conceit, it was the custom of the older ones to speak always of that child as if he lived and were known and beloved of all. In this custom the old man had great content and solace. For it was his wish that all he gave to and did for charity's sake should be known to come, not from him, but from Abel, his son, and this was his express stipulation at all such times. I know whereof I speak, for I was one of those to whom the old man came upon a time and said: "My little boy — Abel, you know — will give me no peace till I do what he requires. He has this sum of

money which he has saved in his bank, count it yourselves, it is $50,000, and he bids me give it to the townsfolk for a hospital, one for little lame boys and girls. And I have promised him — my little boy, Abel, you know — that I will give $50,000 more. You shall have it when that hospital is built." Surely enough, in eighteen months' time the old man handed us the rest of the money, and when we told him that the place was to be called the Abel Dunklee hospital he was sorely distressed, and shook his head, and said: "No, no,— not *my* name! Call it the *Little* Abel hospital, for little Abel — my boy, you know — has done it all."

The old man lived many years,— lived to hear tender voices bless him, and to see pale faces brighten at the sound of his footfall. Yes, for many years the quaint, shuffling figure moved about our streets, and his hoarse but kindly voice — oh, very kindly now !— was heard repeating to the children that pathetic old story of "Once ther' wuz a littl' boy." And where the dear old feet trod the grass grew greenest, and the sunbeams nestled. But at last there came a sum-

mons for the old man,— a summons from
away off yonder,— and the old man heard it
and went thither.

The doctor — himself hoary and stooping
now — told me that toward the last Old
Grampa Growly sunk into a sort of sleep, or
stupor, from which they could not rouse him.
For many hours he lay like one dead, but his
thin, creased face was very peaceful, and
there was no pain. Children tiptoed in
with flowers, and some cried bitterly,
while others — those who were younger
— whispered to one another: "Hush, let
us make no noise; Old Grampa Growly is
sleeping."

At last the old man roused up. He had
lain like one dead for many hours, but now
at last he seemed to wake of a sudden, and,
seeing children about him, perhaps he fancied himself in that pleasant park, under the
trees, where so very often he had told his one
pathetic story to those little ones. Leastwise
he made a feeble motion as if he would have
them gather nearer, and, seeming to know
his wish, the children came closer to him.
Those who were nearest heard him say with

the ineffable tenderness of old, ''Once ther' wuz a littl' boy — ''

And with those last sweet words upon his lips, and with the touch in his heart, the old man went down into the Valley.

❦

Daniel and the Devil

❦

DANIEL AND THE DEVIL

DANIEL was a very wretched man. As he sat with his head bowed upon his desk that evening he made up his mind that his life had been a failure. "I have labored long and diligently," said he to himself, "and although I am known throughout the city as an industrious and shrewd business man, I am still a poor man, and shall probably continue so to the end of my days unless — unless —"

Here Daniel stopped and shivered. For a week or more he had been brooding over his unhappy lot. There seemed to be but one way out of his trouble, yet his soul revolted from taking that step. That was why he stopped and shivered.

"But," he argued, "I *must* do something! My nine children are growing up into big

boys and girls. They must have those advantages which my limited means will not admit of! All my life so far has been pure, circumspect, and rigid; poverty has at last broken my spirit. I give up the fight,—I am ready to sell my soul to the Devil!"

"The determination is a wise one," said a voice at Daniel's elbow. Daniel looked up and beheld a grim-visaged stranger in the chair beside him. The stranger was arrayed all in black, and he exhaled a distinct odor of sulphur.

"Am I to understand," asked the stranger, "that you are prepared to enter into a league with the Devil?"

"Yes," said Daniel, firmly; and he set his teeth together after the fashion of a man who is not to be moved from his purpose.

"Then I am ready to treat with you," said the stranger.

"Are you the Devil?" asked Daniel, eying the stranger critically.

"No, but I am authorized to enter into contracts for him," explained the stranger. "My name is Beelzebub, and I am my master's most trusted agent."

112

"Sir," said Daniel, "you must pardon me (for I am loath to wound your feelings), but one of the rules governing my career as a business man has been to deal directly with principals, and never to trust to the offices of middle-men. The affair now in hand is one concerning the Devil and myself, and between us two and by us two only can the preliminaries be adjusted."

"As it so happens," explained Beelzebub, "this is Friday,— commonly called hangman's day,— and that is as busy a time in our particular locality as a Monday is in a laundry, or as the first of every month is at a book-keeper's desk. You can understand, perhaps, that this is the Devil's busy day; therefore be content to make this deal with me, and you will find that my master will cheerfully accept any contract I may enter into as his agent and in his behalf."

But no,— Daniel would not agree to this; with the Devil himself, and only the Devil himself, would he treat. So he bade Beelzebub go to the Devil and make known his wishes. Beelzebub departed, much chagrined. Presently back came the Devil, and

surely it *was* the Devil this time,—there could be no mistake about it; for he wore a scarlet cloak, and had cloven feet, and carried about with him as many suffocating smells as there are kinds of brimstone, sulphur, and assa-fœtida.

The two talked over all Daniel's miseries; the Devil sympathized with Daniel, and ever and anon a malodorous, gummy tear would trickle down the Devil's sinister nose and drop off on the carpet.

"What you want is money," said the Devil. "That will give you the comfort and the contentment you crave."

"Yes," said Daniel; "it will give me every opportunity to do good."

"To do good!" repeated the Devil. "To do good, indeed! Yes, it 's many a good time we shall have together, friend Daniel! Ha, ha, ha!" And the Devil laughed up-roariously. Nothing seemed more humor-ous than the prospect of " doing good " with the Devil's money! But Daniel failed to see what the Devil was so jolly about. Daniel was not a humorist; he was, as we have indicated, a plain business man.

It was finally agreed that Daniel should sell his soul to the Devil upon condition that for the space of twenty-four years the Devil should serve Daniel faithfully, should provide him with riches, and should do whatsoever he was commanded to do; then, at the end of the twenty-fourth year, Daniel's soul was to pass into the possession of the Devil, and was to remain there forever, without recourse or benefit of clergy. Surely a more horrible contract was never entered into!

"You will have to sign your name to this contract," said the Devil, producing a sheet of asbestos paper upon which all the terms of the diabolical treaty were set forth exactly.

"Certainly," replied Daniel. "I have been a business man long enough to know the propriety and necessity of written contracts. And as for you, you must of course give a bond for the faithful execution of your part of this business."

"That is something I have never done before," suggested the Devil.

"I shall insist upon it," said Daniel, firmly.

"This is no affair of sentiment; it is strictly and coldly business: you are to do certain service, and are to receive certain rewards therefor—"

"Yes, your soul!" cried the Devil, gleefully rubbing his callous hands together. "Your soul in twenty-four years!"

"Yes," said Daniel. "Now, no contract is good unless there is a quid pro quo."

"That's so," said the Devil, "so let's get a lawyer to draw up the paper for me to sign."

"Why a lawyer?" queried Daniel. "A contract is a simple instrument; I, as a business man, can frame one sufficiently binding."

"But I prefer to have a lawyer do it," urged the Devil.

And *I* prefer to do it myself," said Daniel.

When a business man once gets his mind set, not even an Archimedean lever could stir it. So Daniel drew up the bond for the Devil to sign, and this bond specified that in case the Devil failed at any time during the next twenty-four years to do whatso Daniel commanded him, then should the bond which the

Devil held against Daniel become null and void, and upon that same day should a thousand and one souls be released forever from the Devil's dominion. The Devil winced; he hated to sign this agreement, but he had to. An awful clap of thunder ratified the abominable treaty, and every black cat within a radius of a hundred leagues straightway fell to frothing and to yowling grotesquely.

Presently Daniel began to prosper; the Devil was a faithful slave, and he served Daniel so artfully that no person on earth suspected that Daniel had leagued with the evil one. Daniel had the finest house in the city, his wife dressed magnificently, and his children enjoyed every luxury wealth could provide. Still, Daniel was content to be known as a business man; he deported himself modestly and kindly; he pursued with all his old-time diligence the trade which in earlier days he had found so unproductive of riches. His indifference to the pleasures which money put within his reach was passing strange, and it caused the Devil vast uneasiness.

"Daniel," said the Devil, one day, "you're

not getting out of this thing all the fun there is in it. You go poking along in the same old rut with never a suspicion that you have it in your power to enjoy every pleasure of human life. Why don't you break away from the old restraints? Why don't you avail yourself of the advantages at your command?"

"I know what you 're driving at," said Daniel, shrewdly, "Politics!"

"No, not at all," remonstrated the Devil. "What I mean is fun,—gayety. Why not have a good time, Daniel?"

"But I *am* having a good time," said Daniel. "My business is going along all right, I am rich. I 've got a lovely home; my wife is happy; my children are healthy and contented; I am respected,—what more could I ask? What better time could I demand?"

"You don't understand me," explained the Devil. "What I mean by a good time is that which makes the heart merry and keeps the soul youthful and buoyant,—wine, Daniel! Wine and the theatre and pretty girls and fast horses and all that sort of happy, joyful life!"

118

"Tut, tut, tut!" cried Daniel; "no more of that, sir! I sowed my wild oats in college. What right have I to think of such silly follies,—I, at forty years of age, and a business man too?"

So not even the Devil himself could persuade Daniel into a life of dissipation. All you who have made a study of the business man will agree that of all human beings he is the hardest to swerve from conservative methods. The Devil groaned and began to wonder why he had ever tied up to a man like Daniel,—a business man.

Pretty soon Daniel developed an ambition. He wanted reputation, and he told the Devil so. The Devil's eyes sparkled. "At last," murmured the Devil, with a sigh of relief,— "at last."

"Yes," said Daniel, "I want to be known far and wide. You must build a church for me."

"What!" shrieked the Devil. And the Devil's tail stiffened up like a sore thumb.

"Yes," said Daniel, calmly; "you must build a church for me, and it must be the largest and the handsomest church in the

city. The sittings shall be free, and you shall provide the funds for its support forever."

The Devil frothed at his mouth, and blue fire issued from his ears and nostrils. He was the maddest devil ever seen on earth.

"I won't do it!" roared the Devil. "Do you suppose I'm going to spend my time building churches and stultifying myself just for the sake of gratifying your idle whims? I won't do it,—never!"

"Then the bond I gave is null and void," said Daniel.

"Take your old bond," said the Devil, petulantly.

"But the bond you gave is operative," continued Daniel. "So release the thousand and one souls you owe me when you refuse to obey me."

"Oh, Daniel!" whimpered the Devil, "how can you treat me so? Have n't I always been good to you? Have n't I given you riches and prosperity? Does no sentiment of friendship—"

"Hush," said Daniel, interrupting him. "I have already told you a thousand times

that our relations were simply those of one business man with another. It now behooves you to fulfil your part of our compact; eventually I shall fulfil mine. Come, now, to business! Will you or will you not keep your word and save your bond?"

The Devil was sorely put to his trumps. But when it came to releasing a thousand and one souls from hell,—ah, that staggered him! He had to build the church, and a noble one it was too. Then he endowed the church, and finally he built a parsonage; altogether it was a stupendous work, and Daniel got all the credit for it. The preacher whom Daniel installed in this magnificent temple was severely orthodox, and one of the first things he did was to preach a series of sermons upon the personality of the Devil, wherein he inveighed most bitterly against that person and his work.

By and by Daniel made the Devil endow and build a number of hospitals, charity schools, free baths, libraries, and other institutions of similar character. Then he made him secure the election of honest men to office and of upright judges to the bench.

It almost broke the Devil's heart to do it, but the Devil was prepared to do almost anything else than forfeit his bond and give up those one thousand and one souls. By this time Daniel came to be known far and wide for his philanthropy and his piety. This gratified him of course; but most of all he gloried in the circumstance that he was a business man.

"Have you anything for me to do to-day?" asked the Devil, one morning. He had grown to be a very meek and courteous devil; steady employment in righteous causes had chastened him to a degree and purged away somewhat of the violence of his nature. On this particular morning he looked haggard and ill,—yes, and he looked, too, as blue as a whetstone.

"I am not feeling robust," explained the Devil. "To tell the truth, I am somewhat ill."

"I am sorry to hear it," said Daniel; "but as I am not conducting a sanitarium, I can do nothing further than express my regret that you are ailing. Of course our business relations do not contemplate any inter-

change of sympathies; still I'll go easy with you to-day. You may go up to the house and look after the children; see that they don't smoke cigarettes, or quarrel, or tease the cat, or do anything out of the way."

Now that was fine business for the Devil to be in; but how could the Devil help himself? He was wholly at Daniel's mercy. He went groaning about the humiliating task.

The crash came at last. It was when the Devil informed Daniel one day that he was n't going to work for him any more.

"You have ruined my business," said the Devil, wearily. "A committee of imps waited upon me last night and told me that unless I severed my connection with you a permanent suspension of my interests down yonder would be necessitated. While I have been running around doing your insane errands my personal business has gone to the dogs — I would n't be at all surprised if I were to have to get a new plant altogether. Meanwhile my reputation has suffered; I am no longer respected, and the number of my recruits is daily becoming smaller. I give up, — I can make no further sacrifice."

"Then you are prepared to forfeit your bond?" asked Daniel.

"Not by any means," replied the Devil. "I propose to throw the matter into the courts."

"That will hardly be to your interest," said Daniel, "since, as you well know, we have recently elected honest men to the bench, and, as I recollect, most of our judges are members in good standing of the church we built some years ago!"

The Devil howled with rage. Then, presently, he began to whimper.

"For the last time," expostulated Daniel, "let me remind you that sentiment does not enter into this affair at all. We are simply two business parties coöperating in a business scheme. Our respective duties are exactly defined in the bonds we hold. You keep your contract and I'll keep mine. Let me see, I still have a margin of thirteen years."

The Devil groaned and writhed.

"They call me a dude," whimpered the Devil.

"Who do?" asked Daniel.

"Beelzebub and the rest," said the Devil. "I have been trotting around doing pious errands so long that I 've lost all my sulphur-and-brimstone flavor, and now I smell like spikenard and myrrh."

"Pooh!" said Daniel.

"Well, I do," insisted the Devil. "You've humiliated me so that I hain't got any more ambition. Yes, Daniel, you've worked me shamefully hard!"

"Well," said Daniel, "I have a very distinct suspicion that when, thirteen years hence, I fall into your hands I shall not enjoy what might be called a sedentary life."

The Devil plucked up at this suggestion. "Indeed you shall not," he muttered. "I'll make it hot for you!"

"But come, we waste time," said Daniel. "I am a man of business, and I cannot fritter away the precious moments parleying with you. I have important work for you. To-morrow is Sunday; you are to see that all the saloons are kept closed."

"I sha'n't,—I won't!" yelled the Devil.

"But you must," said Daniel, firmly.

"Do you really expect me to do *that*?"

roared the Devil. "Do you fancy that I am so arrant a fool as to shut off the very feeders whereby my hungry hell is supplied ? That would be suicidal!"

"I don't know anything about that," said Daniel; "I am a business man, and by this business arrangement of ours it is explicitly stipulated—"

"I don't care what the stipulations are!" shrieked the Devil. "I'm through with you, and may I be consumed by my own fires if ever again I have anything to do with a business man!"

The upshot of it all was that the Devil forfeited his bond, and by this act Daniel was released from every obligation unto the Devil, and one thousand and one souls were ransomed from the torture of the infernal fires.

❦

Methuselah

❦

METHUSELAH

THE discussion now going on between our clergymen and certain unbelievers touching the question of Cain and his wife will surely result beneficially, for it will set everybody to reading his Bible more diligently. Still, the biography of Cain is one that we could never become particularly interested in; in short, of all the Old Testament characters none other interests us so much as does Methuselah, the man who lived 969 years. Would it be possible to find in all history another life at once so grand and so pathetic? One can get a faint idea of the awful magnitude of Methuselah's career by pausing to recollect that 969 years represent 9.69 centuries, 96 decades, 11,628 months, 50,388 weeks, 353,928 days, 8,494,272 hours, 521,-656,320 minutes, and 36,299,879,200 seconds!

How came he to live so long? Ah, that is easily enough explained. He loved life and the world,— both were beautiful to him. And one day he spoke his wish in words. "Oh, that I might live a thousand years!" he cried.

Then looking up straightway he beheld an angel, and the angel said: "Wouldst thou live a thousand years?"

And Methuselah answered him, saying: "As the Lord is my God, I would live a thousand years."

"It shall be even so," said the angel; and then the angel departed out of his sight. So Methuselah lived on and on, as the angel had promised.

How sweet a treasure the young Methuselah must have been to his parents and to his doting ancestors; with what tender solicitude must the old folks have watched the child's progress from the innocence of his first to the virility of his later centuries. We can picture the happy reunions of the old Adam family under the domestic vines and fig-trees that bloomed near the Euphrates. When Methuselah was a mere toddler of

nineteen years, Adam was still living, and
so was his estimable wife; the possibility
is that the venerable couple gave young
Methuselah a birthday party at which (we
can easily imagine) there were present these
following, to-wit: Adam, aged 687; Seth,
aged 557; Enos, aged 452; Cainan, aged
362; Mahalaleel, aged 292; Jared, aged 227;
Enoch, aged 65, and his infant boy Methuselah, aged 19. Here were represented
eight direct generations, and there were
present, of course, the wives and daughters;
so that, on the whole, the gathering must
have been as numerous as it was otherwise
remarkable. Nowhere in any of the vistas
of history, of romance, or of mythology were
it possible to find a spectacle more imposing than that of the child Methuselah surrounded by his father Enoch, his grandfather
Jared, his great-grandfather Mahalaleel, his
great-great-grandfather Cainan, his great-
great-great-grandfather Enos, his great-
great-great-great-grandfather Seth, and his
great - great - great - great - great - grandfather
Adam, as well as by his great-great-great-
great-great-grandmother Eve, and her femi-

nine posterity for (say) four centuries! How pretty and how kindly dear old grandma Eve must have looked on that gala occasion, attired, as she must have been, in all the quaint simplicity of that primeval period; and how must the dear old soul have fretted through fear that little Methuselah would eat too many papaws, or drink too much goat's milk. It is a marvel, we think, that in spite of the indulgence and the petting in which he was reared, Methuselah grew to be a good, kind man.

Profane historians agree that just about the time he reached the age of ninety-four Methuselah became deeply enamoured of a comely and sprightly damsel named Mizpah, —a young thing scarce turned seventy-six. Up to this period of adolescence his cautious father Enoch had kept Methuselah out of all love entanglements, and it is probable that he would not have approved of this affair with Mizpah had not Jared, the boy's grandfather, counselled Enoch to give the boy a chance. But alas and alackaday for the instability of youthful affection! It befell in an evil time that there came over from

the land of Nod a frivolous and gorgeously apparelled beau, who, with finely wrought phrases, did so fascinate the giddy Mizpah that incontinently she gave Methuselah the mitten, and went with the dashing young stranger of 102 as his bride.

This shocking blow so grievously affected Methuselah that for some time (that is to say, for a period of ninety-one years) he shunned female society. But having recovered somewhat from the bitterness of that great disappointment received in the callowness of his ninth decade, he finally met and fell in love with Adah, a young woman of 148, and her he married. The issue of this union was a boy whom they named Lamech, and this child from the very hour of his birth gave his father vast worriment, which, considering the disparity in their ages, is indeed most shocking of contemplation. The tableau of a father (aged 187) vainly coddling a colicky babe certainly does not call for our enthusiasm. Yet we presume to say that Methuselah bore his trials meekly, that he cherished and adored the baby, and that he spent weeks and months playing

peek-a-boo and ride-a-cock-horse. In all
our consideration of Methuselah we must
remember that the mere matter of time was
of no consequence to him.

Lamech grew to boyhood, involving his
father in all those ridiculous complications
which parents nowadays do not heed so
much, but which must have been of vast
annoyance to a man of Methuselah's advanced age and proper notions. Whittling
with the old gentleman's razor, hooking off
from school, trampling down the neighbors'
rowen, tracking mud into the front parlor—
these were some of Lamech's idiosyncrasies,
and of course they tormented Methuselah,
who recalled sadly that boys were no longer
what they used to be when he was a boy
some centuries previous. But when he got
to be 182 years old Lamech had sowed all
his wild oats, and it was then he married a
clever young girl of 98, who bore him a son
whom they called Noah. Now if Methuselah
had been worried and plagued by Lamech,
he was more than compensated therefor by
this baby grandson, whom he found to be,
aside from all prejudices, the prettiest and

the smartest child he had ever seen. Old
father Adam, who was now turned of his
ninth century, tottered over to see the baby,
and he, too, allowed that it was an uncom-
monly bright child. And dear old grandma
Eve declared that there was an expression
about the upper part of the little Noah's face
that reminded her very much of the soft-
eyed boy she lost 800 years ago. And dear
old grandma Eve used to rock little Noah
and sing to him, and cry softly to herself all
the while.

Now, in good time, Noah grew to lusty
youth, and although he was, on the whole,
a joy to his grandsire Methuselah, he developed certain traits and predilections that occasioned the old gentleman much uneasiness.
At the tender age of 265 Noah exhibited a
strange passion for aquatics, and while it
was common for other boys of that time to
divert themselves with the flocks and herds,
with slingshots and spears, with music and
dancing, Noah preferred to spend his hours
floating toy-ships in the bayous of the Euphrates. Every day he took his little shittim-
wood boats down to the water, tied strings

to them, and let them float hither and thither on the crystal bosom of the tide. Naturally enough these practices worried the grandfather mightily.

"May not the crocodiles compass him round about?" groaned Methuselah. "May not behemoth prevail against him? Or, verily, it may befall that the waves shall devour him. Woe is me and lamentation unto this household if destruction come to him through the folly of his fathers!"

So Methuselah's age began to be full of care and trouble, and many a time he felt weary of living, and sometimes—yes, sometimes—he wished he were dead. People in those times were not afraid to die; they believed in the second and better life, because God spoke with them and told them it should be.

The last century of this good man's sojourn upon earth was particularly pathetic. His ancestors were all dead; he alone remained the last living reminiscence of a time that but for him would have been forgotten. Deprived of the wise counsels of his great-great-great-great-great-grandfather Adam

and of the gentle admonitions of his great-great-great-great-great-grandmother Eve, Methuselah felt not only lonesome but even in danger of wrong-doing, so precious to him had been the teachings of these worthy progenitors. And what particularly disturbed Methuselah were the dreadful changes that had taken place in society since he was a boy. Dress, speech, customs, and morals were all different now from what they used to be.

When Methuselah was a boy,— ah, he remembered it well,— people went hither and thither clad only in simple fig-leaf garb, and they were content therewith.

When Methuselah was a boy, people spoke a plain, direct language, strong in its truth, its simplicity, and its honest vigor.

When Methuselah was a boy, manners were open and unaffected, and morals were pure and healthy.

But now all these things were changed. An evil called fashion had filled the minds of men and women with vanity. From the sinful land of Nod and from other pagan countries came divers tradesmen with purples and

linens and fine feathers, whereby a wicked pride was engendered, and from these sinful countries, too, came frivolous manners that supplanted the guileless etiquette of the past.

Moreover, traffic and intercourse with the subtle heathen had corrupted and perverted the speech of Adam's time: crafty phrases and false rhetorics had crept in, and the grand old Edenic idioms either were fast being debased or had become wholly obsolete. Such new-fangled words as "eftsoon," "albeit," "wench," "soothly," "zounds," "whenas," and "sithence" had stolen into common usage, making more direct and simpler speech a jest and a byword.

Likewise had prudence given way to extravagance, abstemiousness to intemperance, dignity to frivolity, and continence to lust; so that by these evils was Methuselah grievously tormented, and it repented him full sore that he had lived to see such exceeding wickedness upon earth. But in the midst of all these follies did Methuselah maintain an upright and godly life, and continually did he bless God for that he had held him in the path of rectitude.

138

Now when Methuselah was in the 964th summer of his sojourn he was called upon to mourn the death of his son Lamech, whom an inscrutable Providence had cut off in what in those days was considered the flower of a man's life,— namely, the eighth century thereof. Lamech's untimely decease was a severe blow to his doting father, who, forgetting all his son's boyish indiscretions, remembered now only Lamech's good and lovable traits and deeds. It is reasonable to suppose, however, that the old gentleman was somewhat beguiled from his grief by the lively dispositions and playful antics of Lamech's grandsons, Noah's sons, and his own great-grandsons,— Shem, Ham, and Japheth,— who at this time had attained to the frolicsome ages of ninety-five, ninety-two, and ninety-one, respectively. These boys inherited from their father a violent penchant for aquatics, and scarcely a day passed that they did not paddle around the bayous and sloughs of the Euphrates in their gopherwood canoes.

"Gran'pa," Noah used to say, "the conduct of those boys causes me constant vexa-

tion. I have no time to follow them around, and I am haunted continually by the fear that they will be drowned, or that the crocodiles will get them if they don't watch out!"

But Methuselah would smiling answer: "Possess thy soul in patience and thy bowels in peace; for verily is it not written 'boys will be boys!'"

Now Shem, Ham, and Japheth were very fond of their great-grandpa, and to their credit be it said that next to paddling over the water privileges of the Euphrates they liked nothing better than to sit in the old gentleman's lap, and to hear him talk about old times. Marvellous tales he told them, too; for his career of nine and a half centuries had been well stocked with incident, as one would naturally suppose. Howbeit, the admiration which these callow youths had for Methuselah was not shared by a large majority of the people then on earth. On the contrary, we blush to admit it, Methuselah was held in very trifling esteem by his frivolous fellow-citizens, who habitually referred to him as an "old 'wayback," "a barnacle," an "old fogy," a "mossback,"

or a "garrulous dotard," and with singular
irreverence they took delight in twitting him
upon his senility and in pestering him with
divers new-fangled notions altogether distasteful, not to say shocking, to a gentleman
of his years.

It was perhaps, however, at the old set-
tlers' picnics, which even then were of annual
occurrence, that Methuselah most enjoyed
himself; for on these occasions he was given
the place of prominence and he was deferred
to in everything, since he antedated all the
others by at least three centuries. The historians and the antiquarians of the time found
him of much assistance to them in their labors, since he was always ready to provide
them with dates touching incidents of the
remote period from which he had come
down unscathed. He remembered vividly
how, when he was 186 years of age, the
Euphrates had frozen over to a depth of
seven feet; the 209th winter of his existence
he referred to as "the winter of the deep
snow;" he remembered that when he was
a boy the women had more character than
the women of these later years; he had a vivid

recollection of the great plague that prevailed in the city of Enoch during his fourth century; he could repeat, word for word, the address of welcome his great-great-great-great-great-grandfather Adam delivered to an excursion party that came over from the land of Nod one time when Methuselah was a mere child of eighty-seven,—oh, yes, poor old Methuselah was full of reminiscence, and having crowded an active career into the brief period of 969 years, it can be imagined that ponderous tomes would not hold the tales he told whenever he was encouraged.

One day, however, Methuselah's grandson Noah took the old gentleman aside and confided into his ear-trumpet a very solemn secret which must have grieved the old gentleman immensely, for he gnashed his gums and wrung his thin, bony hands and groaned dolorously.

"The end of all flesh is at hand," said Noah. "The earth is filled with violence through them, and God will destroy them with the earth. I will make an ark of gopher-wood, the length thereof 300 cubits, the breadth of it 50 cubits, and the height

of it 30 cubits, and I will pitch it within and without with pitch. Into the ark will I come, and my sons and my wife, and my sons' wives, and certain living beasts shall come, and birds of the air, and we and they shall be saved. Come thou also, for thou art an austere man and a just."

But as Methuselah sate alone upon his couch that night he thought of his life: how sweet it had been,—how that, despite the evil now and then, there had been more of happiness than of sorrow in it. He even forgot the wickedness of the world and remembered only its good and its sunshine, its kindness and its love. He blessed God for it all, and he prayed for the death-angel to come to him ere he beheld the destruction of all he so much loved.

Then the angel came and spread his shadow about the old man.

And the angel said: "Thy prayer is heard, and God doth forgive thee the score-and-ten years of the promised span of thy life."

· And Methuselah gathered up his feet into the bed, and prattling of the brooks, he fell asleep; and so he slept with his fathers.

❦

Félice and Petit-Poulain

❦

FÉLICE AND PETIT-POULAIN

THE name was singularly appropriate, for assuredly Félice was the happiest of all four-footed creatures. Her nature was gentle; she was obedient, long-suffering, kind. She had known what it was to toil and to bear burdens; sometimes she had suffered from hunger and from thirst; and before she came into the possession of Jacques she had been beaten, for Pierre, her former owner, was a hard master. But Félice was always a kind, faithful, and gentle creature; presumably that was why they named her that pretty name, Félice. She may not have been happy when Pierre owned and over-worked and starved and beat her; that does not concern us now, for herein it is to tell of that time when she belonged to Jacques, and Jacques was a merciful man.

Jacques was a farmer; he lived a short

distance from Cinqville, which, as you are probably aware, is a town of considerable importance upon what used to be the boundary line between France and Germany. The country round about is devoted to agriculture. You can fancy that, with its even roads, leafy woods, quiet lanes, velvety paddocks, tall hedges, and bountiful fields, this country was indeed as pleasant a home as Félice — or, for that matter, any other properly minded horse — could hope for. Toward the southern horizon there were hills that looked a grayish blue from a distance; upon these hills were vineyards, and the wine that came therefrom is very famous wine, as your uncle, if he be a club man, will very truly assure you. There was a pretty little river that curled like a silver snake through the fertile meadows, and lost its way among the hills, and there were many tiny brooks that scampered across lots and got tangled up with that pretty little river in most bewildering fashion. So, as you can imagine, this was a fair country, and you do not wonder that, with so merciful a master as Jacques, our friend Félice was happy.

But what perfected her happiness was the coming of her little colt, as cunning and as blithe a creature as ever whisked a tail or galloped on four legs. I do not know why they called him by that name, but Petit-Poulain was what they called him, and that name seemed to please Félice, for when farmer Jacques came thrice a day to the stile and cried, "Petit-Poulain, petit, petit, Petit-Poulain!" the kind old mother would look up fondly, and, with doting eyes, watch her dainty little colt go bounding toward his calling master. And he was indeed a lovely little fellow. The curé, the holy père François, predicted that in due time that colt would make a great name for himself and a great fortune for his owner. The holy père knew whereof he spake, for in his youth he had tasted of the sweets of Parisian life, and upon one memorable occasion had successfully placed ten francs upon the winner of le grand prix. We can suppose that Félice thought well of the holy père. He never came down the road that she did not thrust her nose through the hedge and give a mild whinny of recognition, as if she fain would

say: "Pray stop a moment and see Petit-Poulain and his old mother!"

What happy days those were for Félice and her darling colt. With what tenderness they played together in the paddock; or, when the sky was overcast and a storm came on, with what solicitude would the old mother lead the way into the thatched stable, where there was snug protection against the threatening element. There are those who say that none but humankind is immortal,—that none but man has a soul. I do not make or believe that claim. There is that within me which tells me that no thing in this world and life of ours which has felt the grace of maternity shall utterly perish. And this I say in all reverence, and with the hope that I offend neither God nor man.

You are to know that old Félice's devotion to Petit-Poulain was human in its tenderness. As readily, as gladly, and as surely as your dear mother would lay down her life for you would old Félice have yielded up her life for her innocent, blithe darling. So old Félice was happy that pleasant time in

that fair country, and Petit-Poulain waxed hale and evermore blithe and beautiful.

Happy days, too, were those for that peaceful country and the other dwellers therein. There was no thought of evil there; the seasons were propitious, the vineyards thrived, the crops were bountiful; as far as eye could see all was prosperity and contentment. But one day the holy Father François came hurrying down the road, and it was too evident that he brought evil tidings. Félice thought it very strange that he paid no heed to her when, as was her wont, she thrust her nose through the hedge and gave a mild whinny of welcome. Anon she saw that he talked long and earnestly with her master Jacques, and presently she saw that Jacques went into the cottage and came again therefrom with his wife Justine and kissed her, and then went away with Père François toward the town off yonder. Félice saw that Justine was weeping, and with never a suspicion of impending evil, she wondered why Justine should weep when all was so prosperous and bright and fair and happy about her. Félice saw and won-

dered, and meanwhile Petit-Poulain scampered gayly about that velvety paddock.

That night the vineyard hills, bathed in the mellow grace of moonlight, saw a sight they had never seen before. From the east an army came riding and marching on,—an army of strange, determined men, speaking a language before unheard in that fair country and threatening things of which that peaceful valley had never dreamed. You and I, of course, know that these were the Germans advancing upon France,—a nation of immortals eager to destroy the possessions and the human lives of fellow-immortals! But old Félice, hearing the din away off yonder,—the unwonted noise of cavalry and infantry advancing with murderous intent,—she did not understand it all, she did not even suspect the truth. You cannot wonder, for what should a soulless beast know of the noble, the human privilege of human slaughter? Old Félice heard that strange din, and instinct led her to coax her little colt from the pleasant paddock into that snug and secure retreat, the thatched stable, and there, in the early morning, they

found her, Petit-Poulain pulling eagerly at her generous dugs.

Those who came riding up were strangers in those parts; they were ominously accoutred and they spoke words that old Félice had never heard before. Yes, as you have already guessed, they were German cavalrymen. A battle was impending, and they needed more horses.

"Old enough; but in lieu of a better, she will do." That was what they said. They approached her carefully, for they suspected that she might be vicious. Poor old Félice, she had never harmed even the flies that pestered her. "They are going to put me at the plough," she thought. "It is a long time since I did work of any kind,—nothing, in fact, since Petit-Poulain was born. Poor Petit-Poulain will miss me; but I will soon return." With these thoughts she turned her head fondly and caressed her pretty colt.

"The colt must be tied in the stall or he will follow her." So said the cavalrymen. They threw a rope about his neck and made him fast in the stable. Petit-Poulain was

very much surprised, and he remonstrated vainly with his fierce little heels.

They put a halter upon old Félice. Justine, the farmer's wife, met them in the yard, and reproached them wildly in French. They laughed boisterously, and answered her in German. Then they rode away, leading old Félice, who kept turning her head and whinnying pathetically, for she was thinking of Petit-Poulain.

Of peace I know and can speak,—of peace, with its solace of love, plenty, honor, fame, happiness, and its pathetic tragedy of poverty, heartache, disappointment, tears, bereavement. Of war I know nothing, and never shall know; it is not in my heart or for my hand to break that law which God enjoined from Sinai and Christ confirmed in Galilee. I do not know of war, nor can I tell you of that battle which men with immortal souls fought one glorious day in a fertile country with vineyard hills all round about. But when night fell there was desolation everywhere and death. The Eden was a wilderness; the winding river was choked with mangled corpses; shell and

shot had mowed down the acres of waving grain, the exuberant orchards, the gardens and the hedgerows; black, charred ruins, gaunt and ghostlike, marked the spots where homes had stood. The vines had been cut and torn away, and the despoiled hills seemed to crouch down like bereaved mothers under the pitiless gaze of the myriad eyes of heaven.

The victors went their way; a greater triumph was in store for them; a mighty capital was to be besieged; more homes were to be desolated,—more blood shed, more hearts broken. So the victors went their way, their hands red and their immortal souls elated.

In the early dawn a horse came galloping homeward. It is Félice, old Félice, riderless, splashed with mud, wild-eyed, sore with fatigue! Félice, Félice, what horrors hast thou not seen! If thou couldst speak, if that tongue of thine could be loosed, what would it say of those who, forgetful of their souls, sink lower than the soulless brutes! Better it is thou canst not speak; the anguish in thine eyes, the despair in thy honest

heart, the fear, the awful fear in thy mother breast,—what tongue could utter them?

Adown the road she galloped,—the same road she had traversed, perhaps, a thousand times before, yet it was so changed now she hardly knew it. Twenty-four hours had ruthlessly levelled the noble trees, the hedgerows, and the fields of grain. Twenty-four hours of battle had done all this and more. In all those ghastly hours, one thought had haunted Félice; one thought alone,— the thought of Petit-Poulain! She pictured him tied in that far-away stall, wondering why she did not come. He was hungry, she knew; her dugs were full of milk and they pained her; how sweet would be her relief when her Petit-Poulain broke his long fast. Petit-Poulain, Petit-Poulain, Petit-Poulain,— this one thought and this alone had old Félice throughout those hours of battle and of horror.

Could this have been the farm-house? It was a ruin now. Shells had torn it apart. Where was the good master Jacques; had he gone with the curé to the defence of the town? And Justine,—where was she?

Bullets had cut away the rose-trees and the smoke-bush; the garden was no more. The havoc, the desolation, was complete. The cote, which had surmounted the pole around which an ivy twined, had been swept away. The pigeons now circled here and there bewildered; wondering, perhaps, why Justine did not come and call to them and feed them.

To this seared, scarred spot came old Félice. He that had ridden her into battle lay with his face downward near those distant vineyard hills. His blood had stained Félice's neck; a bullet had grazed her flank, but that was a slight wound,— riderless, she turned and came from the battle-field and sought her Petit-Poulain once again.

Hard by the ruins of cottage, of garden, and of cote, she came up standing; she was steaming and breathless. She rolled her eyes wildly around,— she looked for the stable where she had left Petit-Poulain. She trembled as if an overwhelming apprehension of disaster suddenly possessed her. She gave a whinny, pathetic in its tenderness. She was calling Petit-Poulain. But there was no answer.

Petit-Poulain lay dead in the ruins of the stable. His shelter had not escaped the fury of the battle. He could not run away, for they had tied him fast when they carried his old mother off. So now he lay amid that débris, his eyes half open in death and his legs stretched out stark and stiff.

And old Félice,— her udder bursting with the maternal grace he never again should know, and her heart breaking with the agony of sudden and awful bereavement,— she staggered, as if blinded by despair, toward that vestige of her love, and bent over him and caressed her Petit-Poulain.

✤

The River

✤

THE RIVER

ONCE upon a time a little boy came, during his play, to the bank of a river. The waters of the river were very dark and wild, and there was so black a cloud over the river that the little boy could not see the further shore. An icy wind came up from the cloud and chilled the little boy, and he trembled with cold and fear as the wind smote his cheeks and ran its slender icicle fingers through his yellow curls. An old man sat on the bank of the river; he was very, very old; his head and shoulders were covered with a black mantle; and his beard was white as snow.

"Will you come with me, little boy?" asked the old man.

"Where?" inquired the little boy.

" To yonder shore," replied the old man.

"Oh, no; not to that dark shore," said the little boy. "I should be afraid to go."

"But think of the sunlight always there," said the old man, "the birds and flowers; and remember there is no pain, nor anything of that kind to vex you."

The little boy looked and saw the dark cloud hanging over the waters, and he felt the cold wind come up from the river; moreover, the sight of the strange man terrified him. So, hearing his mother calling him, the little boy ran back to his home, leaving the old man by the river alone.

Many years after that time the little boy came again to the river; but he was not a little boy now,— he was a big, strong man.

" The river is the same," said he; "the wind is the same cold, cutting wind of ice, and the same black cloud obscures yonder shore. I wonder where the strange old man can be."

"I am he," said a solemn voice.

The man turned and looked on him who spoke, and he saw a warrior clad in black armor and wielding an iron sword.

"No, you are not he!" cried the man.
"You are a warrior come to do me harm."

"I am indeed a warrior," said the other.
"Come with me across the river."

"No," replied the man, "I will not go with
you. Hark, I hear the voices of my wife
and children calling to me,— I will return
to them!"

The warrior strove to hold him fast and
bear him across the river to the yonder shore,
but the man prevailed against him and returned to his wife and little ones, and the
warrior was left upon the river-bank.

Then many years went by and the strong
man became old and feeble. He found no
pleasure in the world, for he was weary of
living. His wife and children were dead, and
the old man was alone. So one day in those
years he came to the bank of the river for the
third time, and he saw that the waters had
become quiet and that the wind which came
up from the river was warm and gentle and
smelled of flowers; there was no dark cloud
overhanging the yonder shore, but in its
place was a golden mist through which the
old man could see people walking on the

yonder shore and stretching out their hands
to him, and he could hear them calling him
by name. Then he knew they were the
voices of his dear ones.

"I am weary and lonesome," cried the
old man. "All have gone before me: father,
mother, wife, children,—all whom I have
loved. I see them and hear them on yonder
shore, but who will bear me to them?"

Then a spirit came in answer to this cry.
But the spirit was not a strange old man nor
yet an armored warrior; but as he came to
the river's bank that day he was a gentle angel, clad in white; his face was very beautiful, and there was divine tenderness in his
eyes.

"Rest thy head upon my bosom," said
the angel, "and I will bear thee across the
river to those who call thee."

So, with the sweet peace of a little child
sinking to his slumbers, the old man drooped
in the arms of the angel and was borne across
the river to those who stood upon the yonder shore and called.

✤

Franz Abt

✤

MANY years ago a young composer was
sitting in a garden. All around bloomed
beautiful roses, and through the gentle evening air the swallows flitted, twittering
cheerily.   The young composer neither saw
the roses nor heard the evening music of the
swallows; his heart was full of sadness and
his eyes were bent wearily upon the earth
before him.

"Why," said the young composer, with a
sigh, "should I be doomed to all this bitter
disappointment? Learning seems vain, patience is mocked,—fame is as far from me
as ever.

The roses heard his complaint. They
bent closer to him and whispered, "Listen
to us,—listen to us."   And the swallows
heard him, too, and they flitted nearer him;
and they, too, twittered, "Listen to us,—
listen to us."   But the young composer was

in no mood to be beguiled by the whisperings of the roses and the twitterings of the birds; with a heavy heart and sighing bitterly he arose and went his way.

It came to pass that many times after that the young composer came at evening and sat in the garden where the roses bloomed and the swallows twittered; his heart was always full of disappointment, and often he cried out in anguish against the cruelty of fame that it came not to him. And each time the roses bent closer to him, and the swallows flew lower, and there in the garden the sweet flowers and little birds cried, "Listen to us, — listen to us, and we will help you."

And one evening the young composer, hearing their gentle pleadings, smiled sadly, and said: "Yes, I will listen to you. What have you to say, pretty roses?"

"Make your songs of us," whispered the roses, — "make your songs of us."

"Ha, ha!" laughed the composer. "A song of the roses would be very strange, indeed! No, sweet flowers, — it is fame I seek, and fame would scorn even the beauty

168

of your blushes and the subtlety of your
perfumes."

"You are wrong," twittered the swallows, flying lower. "You are wrong, foolish man. Make a song for the heart,—make
a song of the swallows and the roses, and
it will be sung forever, and your fame shall
never die."

But the composer laughed louder than before; surely there never had been a stranger
suggestion than that of the roses and the
swallows! Still, in his chamber that night
the composer thought of what the swallows
had said, and in his dreams he seemed to
hear the soft tones of the roses pleading
with him. Yes, many times thereafter the
composer recalled what the birds and flowers
had said, but he never would ask them as
he sat in the garden at evening how he could
make the heart-song of which they chat-
tered. And the summer sped swiftly by,
and one evening when the composer came
into the garden the roses were dead, and
their leaves lay scattered on the ground.
There were no swallows fluttering in the
sky, and the nests under the eaves were

deserted. Then the composer knew his little friends were beyond recall, and he was oppressed by a feeling of loneliness. The roses and the swallows had grown to be a solace to the composer, had stolen into his heart all unawares, — now that they were gone, he was filled with sadness.

"I will do as they counselled," said he; "I will make a song of them, — a song of the swallows and the roses. I will forget my greed for fame while I write in memory of my little friends."

Then the composer made a song of the swallows and the roses, and, while he wrote, it seemed to him that he could hear the twittering of the little birds all around him, and scent the fragrance of the flowers, and his soul was warmed with a warmth he had never felt before, and his tears fell upon his manuscript.

When the world heard the song which the composer had made of the swallows and the roses, it did homage to his genius. Such sentiment, such delicacy, such simplicity, such melody, such heart, such soul, — ah, there was no word of rapturous praise too good for the composer now: fame, the sweet-

est and most enduring kind of fame, had come to him.

And the swallows and the roses had done it all. Their subtle influences had filled the composer's soul with a great inspiration,— by means like this God loves to speak to the human heart.

"We told you so," whispered the roses when they came again in the spring. "We told you that if you sang of us the world would love your song."

Then the swallows, flying back from the south, twittered: "We told you so; sing the songs the heart loves, and you shall live forever."

"Ah, dear ones," said the composer, softly; "you spoke the truth. He who seeks a fame that is immortal has only to reach and abide in the human heart."

The lesson he learned of the swallows and the roses he never forgot. It was the inspiration and motive of a long and beautiful life. He left for others that which some called a loftier ambition. He was content to sit among the flowers and hear the twitter of birds and make songs that found an echo in

all breasts. Ah, there was such a beautiful simplicity,— such a sweet wisdom in his life! And where'er the swallows flew, and where'er the roses bloomed, he was famed and revered and beloved, and his songs were sung.

Then his hair grew white at last, and his eyes were dim and his steps were slow. A mortal illness came upon him, and he knew that death was nigh.

"The winter has been long," said he, wearily. "Open the window and raise me up that I may see the garden, for it must be that spring is come."

It was indeed spring, but the roses had not yet bloomed. The swallows were chattering in their nests under the eaves or flitting in the mild, warm sky.

"Hear them," he said faintly. "How sweetly they sing. But alas! where are the roses?"

Where are the roses? Heaped over thee, dear singing heart; blooming on thy quiet grave in the Fatherland, and clustered and entwined all in and about thy memory, which with thy songs shall go down from heart to heart to immortality.

❦

Mistress Merciless

❦

MISTRESS MERCILESS

THIS is to tell of our little Mistress Merciless, who for a season abided with us, but is now and forever gone from us unto the far-off land of Ever-Plaisance. The tale is soon told; for it were not seemly to speak all the things that are in one's heart when one hath to say of a much-beloved child, whose life here hath been shortened so that, in God's wisdom and kindness, her life shall be longer in that garden that bloometh far away.

You shall know that all did call her Mistress Merciless; but her mercilessness was of a sweet, persuasive kind: for with the beauty of her face and the music of her voice and the exceeding sweetness of her virtues was she wont to slay all hearts; and this she did unwittingly, for she was a little child. And so it was in love that we did call her Mistress

175

Merciless, just as it was in love that she did lord it over all our hearts.

Upon a time walked she in a full fair garden, and there went with her an handmaiden that we did call in merry wise the Queen of Sheba; for this handmaiden was in sooth no queen at all, but a sorry and ill-favored wench; but she was assotted upon our little Mistress Merciless and served her diligently, and for that good reason was vastly beholden of us all. Yet, in a jest, we called her the Queen of Sheba; and I make a venture that she looked exceeding fair in the eyes of our little Mistress Merciless: for the eyes of children look not upon the faces but into the hearts and souls of others. Whilst these two walked in the full fair garden at that time they came presently unto an arbor wherein there was a rustic seat, which was called the Siege of Restfulness; and hereupon sate a little sick boy that, from his birth, had been lame, so that he could not play and make merry with other children, but was wont to come every day into this full fair garden and content himself with the companionship of the flowers. And, though

he was a little lame boy, he never trod upon those flowers; and even had he done so, methinks the pressure of those crippled feet had been a caress, for the little lame boy was filled with the spirit of love and tenderness. As the tiniest, whitest, shrinking flower exhaleth the most precious perfume, so in and from this little lame boy's life there came a grace that was hallowing in its beauty.

Since they never before had seen him, they asked him his name; and he answered them that of those at home he was called Master Sweetheart, a name he could not understand: for surely, being a cripple, he must be a very sorry sweetheart; yet, that he was a sweetheart unto his mother at least he had no doubt, for she did love to hold him in her lap and call him by that name; and many times when she did so he saw that tears were in her eyes,—a proof, she told him when he asked, that Master Sweetheart was her sweetheart before all others upon earth.

It befell that our little Mistress Merciless and Master Sweetheart became fast friends, and the Queen of Sheba was handmaiden to

them both; for the simple, loyal creature
had not a mind above the artless prattle of
childhood, and the strange allegory of the
lame boy's speech filled her with awe, even
as the innocent lisping of our little Mistress
Merciless delighted her heart and came within the comprehension of her limited understanding. So each day, when it was fair,
these three came into the full fair garden, and
rambled there together; and when they were
weary they entered into the arbor and sate
together upon the Siege of Restfulness. Wit
ye well there was not a flower or a tree or a
shrub or a bird in all that full fair garden
which they did not know and love, and in
very sooth every flower and tree and shrub
and bird therein did know and love them.

When they entered into the arbor, and
sate together upon the Siege of Restfulness,
it was Master Sweetheart's wont to tell them
of the land of Ever-Plaisance, for it was a
conceit of his that he journeyed each day
nearer and nearer to that land, and that his
journey thitherward was nearly done. How
came he to know of that land I cannot say,
for I do not know; but I am fain to believe

that, as he said, the exceeding fair angels told him thereof when by night, as he lay sleeping, they came singing and with caresses to his bedside.

I speak now of a holy thing, therefore I speak truth when I say that while little children lie sleeping in their beds at night it pleaseth God to send His exceeding fair angels with singing and caresses to bear messages of His love unto those little sleeping children. And I have seen those exceeding fair angels bend with folded wings over the little cradles and the little beds, and kiss those little sleeping children and whisper God's messages of love to them, and I knew that those messages were full of sweet tidings; for, even though they slept, the little children smiled. This have I seen, and there is none who loveth little children that will deny the truth of this thing which I have now solemnly declared.

Of that land of Ever-Plaisance was our little Mistress Merciless ever fain to hear tell. But when she beset the rest of us to speak thereof we knew not what to say other than to confirm such reports as Master Sweet-

heart had already made. For when it cometh to knowing of that far-off land,—ah me,
who knoweth more than the veriest little
child? And oftentimes within the bosom
of a little, helpless, fading one there bloometh a wisdom which sages cannot comprehend. So when she asked us we were wont
to bid her go to Master Sweetheart, for he
knew the truth and spake it.

It is now to tell of an adventure which on
a time befell in that full fair garden of which
you have heard me speak. In this garden
lived many birds of surpassing beauty and
most rapturous song, and among them was
one that they called Joyous, for that he did
ever carol forth so joyously, it mattered not
what the day soever might be. This bird
Joyous had his home in the top of an exceeding high tree, hard by the pleasant arbor,
and here did he use to sit at such times as
the little people came into that arbor, and
then would he sing to them such songs as
befitted that quiet spot, and them that came
thereto. But there was a full evil cat that
dwelt near by, and this cruel beast found no
pleasure in the music that Joyous did make

continually; nay, that music filled this full evil cat with a wicked thirst for the blood of that singing innocent, and she had no peace for the malice that was within her seeking to devise a means whereby she might comprehend the bird Joyous to her murderous intent. Now you must know that it was the wont of our little Mistress Merciless and of Master Sweetheart to feed the birds in that fair garden with such crumbs as they were suffered to bring with them into the arbor, and at such times would those birds fly down with grateful twitterings and eat of those crumbs upon the greensward round about the arbor. Wit ye well, it was a merry sight to see those twittering birds making feast upon the good things which those children brought, and our little Mistress Merciless and little Master Sweetheart had sweet satisfaction therein. But, on a day, whilst thus those twittering birds made great feasting, lo! on a sudden did that full evil cat whereof I have spoken steal softly from a thicket, and with one hideous bound make her way into the very midst of those birds and seize upon that bird

Joyous, that was wont to sing so merrily from the tree hard by the arbor. Oh, there was a mighty din and a fearful fluttering, and the rest flew swiftly away, but Joyous could not do so, because the full evil cat held him in her cruel fangs and claws. And I make no doubt that Joyous would speedily have met his death, but that with a wrathful cry did our little Mistress Merciless hasten to his rescue. And our little Mistress belabored that full evil cat with Master Sweetheart's crutch, until that cruel beast let loose her hold upon the fluttering bird and was full glad to escape with her aching bones into the thicket again. So it was that Joyous was recovered from death; but even then might it have fared ill with him, had they not taken him up and dressed his wounds and cared for him until duly he was well again. And then they released him to do his plaisance, and he returned to his home in the tree hard by the arbor and there he sung unto those children more sweetly than ever before; for his heart was full of gratitude to our little Mistress Merciless and Master Sweetheart.

Now, of the dolls that she had in goodly number, that one which was named Beautiful did our little Mistress Merciless love best. Know well that the doll Beautiful had come not from oversea, and was neither of wax nor of china; but she was right ingeniously constructed of a bed-key that was made of wood, and unto the top of this bed-key had the Queen of Sheba superadded a head with a fair face, and upon the body and the arms of the key had she hung passing noble raiment. Unto this doll Beautiful was our little Mistress Merciless vastly beholden, and she did use to have the doll Beautiful lie by her side at night whilst she slept, and whithersoever during the day she went, there also would she take the doll Beautiful, too. Much sorrow and lamentation, therefore, made our little Mistress Merciless when on an evil day the doll Beautiful by chance fell into the fish-pond, and was not rescued therefrom until one of her beauteous eyes had been devoured of the envious water; so that ever thereafter the doll Beautiful had but one eye, and that, forsooth, was grievously faded. And on another evil day came a

monster ribald dog pup and seized upon
the doll Beautiful whilst she reposed in the arbor, and bore her away, and romped boisterously with her upon the sward, and tore off
her black-thread hair, and sought to destroy
her wholly, which surely he would have
done but for the Queen of Sheba, who made
haste to rescue the doll Beautiful, and chas-
tise that monster ribald dog pup.

Therefore, as you can understand, the
time was right busily spent. The full fair
garden, with its flowers and the singing
birds and the gracious arbor and the Siege
of Restfulness, found favor with those children, and amid these joyous scenes did
Master Sweetheart have to tell each day of
that far-off land of Ever-Plaisance, whither
he said he was going. And one day, when
the sun shone very bright, and the full fair
garden joyed in the music of those birds,
Master Sweetheart did not come, and they
missed the little lame boy and wondered
where he was. And as he never came
again they thought at last that of a surety
he had departed into that country whereof
he loved to tell. Which thing filled our lit-

tle Mistress Merciless with wonder and in-
quiry; and I think she was lonely ever after
that,—lonely for Master Sweetheart.

I am thinking now of her and of him;
for this is the Christmas season,—the time
when it is most meet to think of the children
and other sweet and holy things.   There
is snow everywhere, snow and cold.   The
garden is desolate and voiceless: the flowers
are gone, the trees are ghosts, the birds have
departed.   It is winter out there, and it is
winter, too, in this heart of mine.   Yet in
this Christmas season I think of them, and
it pleaseth me—God forbid that I offend
with much speaking—it pleaseth me to tell
of the little things they did and loved.   And
you shall understand it all if, perchance,
this sacred Christmas time a little Mistress
Merciless of your own, or a little Master
Sweetheart, clingeth to your knee and sanc-
tifieth your hearthstone.

When of an evening all the joy of day was
done, would our little Mistress Merciless
fall aweary; and then her eyelids would
grow exceeding heavy and her little tired
hands were fain to fold.   At such a time it

was my wont to beguile her weariness with
little tales of faery, or with the gentle play
that sleepy children like.   Much was her
fancy taken with what I told her of the
train that every night whirleth away to
Shut-Eye Town, bearing unto that beauteous
country sleepy little girls and boys.   Nor
would she be content until I told her thereof, — yes, every night whilst I robed her in
her cap and gown would she demand of me
that tale of Shut-Eye Town, and the wonderful train that was to bear her thither.
Then would I say in this wise:—

At Bedtime-ville there is a train of cars that waiteth
for you, my sweet,— for you and for other little ones
that would go to quiet, slumbrous Shut-Eye Town.

But make no haste; there is room for all.   Each hath
a tiny car that is snug and warm, and when the train
starteth each car swingeth soothingly this way and that
way, this way and that way, through all the journey of
the night.

Your little gown is white and soft; your little cap will
hold those pretty curls so fast that they cannot get
away.   Here is a curl that peepeth out to see what is
going to happen.   Hush, little curl! make no noise;
we will let you peep out at the wonderful sights, but
you must not tell the others about it; let them sleep,
snuggled close together.

The locomotive is ready to start. Can you not hear it?

"Shug-chug! Shug-chug! Shug-chug!" That is what the locomotive is saying, all to itself. It knoweth how pleasant a journey it is about to make.

"Shug-chug! Shug-chug! Shug-chug!"

Oh, many a time hath it proudly swept over prairie and hill, over river and plain, through sleeping gardens and drowsy cities, swiftly and quietly, bearing the little ones to the far, pleasant valley where lieth Shut-Eye Town.

"Shug-chug! Shug-chug! Shug-chug!"

So sayeth the locomotive to itself at the station in Bedtime-ville; for it knoweth how fair and far a journey is before it.

Then a bell soundeth. Surely my little one heareth the bell!

"Ting-long! Ting-a-long! Ting-long!"

So soundeth the bell, and it seemeth to invite you to sleep and dreams.

"Ting-long! Ting-a-long! Ting-long!"

How sweetly ringeth and calleth that bell.

"To sleep—to dreams, O little lambs!" it seemeth to call. "Nestle down close, fold your hands, and shut your dear eyes! We are off and away to Shut-Eye Town! Ting-long! Ting-a-long! Ting-long! To sleep —to dreams, O little cosset lambs!"

And now the conductor calleth out in turn. "All aboard!" he calleth, "All aboard for Shut-Eye Town!" he calleth in a kindly tone.

But, hark ye, dear-my-soul, make thou no haste;

there is room for all. Here is a cosey little car for you. How like your cradle it is, for it is snug and warm, and it rocketh this way and that way, this way and that way, all night long, and its pillows caress you tenderly. So step into the pretty nest, and in it speed to Shut-Eye Town.

"Toot! Toot!"

That is the whistle. It soundeth twice, but it must sound again before the train can start. Now you have nestled down, and your dear hands are folded; let your two eyes be folded, too, my sweet; for in a moment you shall be rocked away, and away, away into the golden mists of Balow!

"Ting-long! Ting-a-long! Ting-long!"

"All aboard!"

"Toot! Toot! Toot!"

And so my little golden apple is off and away for Shut-Eye Town!

Slowly moveth the train, yet faster by degrees. Your hands are folded, my beloved, and your dear eyes they are closed; and yet you see the beauteous sights that skirt the journey through the mists of Balow. And it is rockaway, rockaway, rockaway, that your speeding cradle goes,— rockaway, rockaway, rockaway, through the golden glories that lie in the path that leadeth to Shut-Eye Town.

"Toot! Toot!"

So crieth the whistle, and it is "down-brakes," for here we are at Ginkville, and every little one knoweth that pleasant waking-place, where mother with her gentle hands holdeth the gracious cup to her sleepy darling's lips.

"Ting-long! Ting-a-long! Ting-long!" and off is the train again. And swifter and swifter it speedeth,— oh, I am sure no other train speedeth half so swiftly! The sights my dear one sees! I cannot tell of them— one must see those beauteous sights to know how wonderful they are!

"Shug-chug! Shug-chug! Shug-chug!"

On and on and on the locomotive proudly whirleth the train.

"Ting-long! Ting-a-long! Ting-long!"

The bell calleth anon, but fainter and evermore fainter; and fainter and fainter groweth that other calling—"Toot! Toot! Toot!"—till finally I know that in that Shut-Eye Town afar my dear one dreameth the dreams of Balow.

This was the bedtime tale which I was wont to tell our little Mistress Merciless, and at its end I looked upon her face to see it calm and beautiful in sleep.

Then was I wont to kneel beside her little bed and fold my two hands,—thus,—and let my heart call to the host invisible: "O guardian angels of this little child, hold her in thy keeping from all the perils of darkness and the night! O sovereign Shepherd, cherish Thy little lamb and mine, and, Holy Mother, fold her to thy bosom and thy love!

But give her back to me,—when morning cometh, restore ye unto me my little one!"

But once she came not back. She had spoken much of Master Sweetheart and of that land of Ever-Plaisance whither he had gone. And she was not afeared to make the journey alone; so once upon a time when our little Mistress Merciless bade us good-by, and went away forever, we knew that it were better so; for she was lonely here, and without her that far-distant country whither she journeyed were not content. Though our hearts were like to break for love of her, we knew that it were better so.

The tale is told, for it were not seemly to speak all the things that are in one's heart when one hath to say of a much-beloved child whose life here hath been shortened so that, in God's wisdom and kindness, her life shall be longer in that garden that bloometh far away.

About me are scattered the toys she loved, and the doll Beautiful hath come down all battered and grim,—yet, oh! so very precious to me, from those distant years; yonder fareth the Queen of Sheba in her service

as handmaiden unto me and mine,—gaunt
and doleful-eyed, yet stanch and sturdy as
of old.   The garden lieth under the Christmas snow,—the garden where ghosts of
trees wave their arms and moan over the
graves of flowers; the once gracious arbor
is crippled now with the infirmities of age,
the Siege of Restfulness fast sinketh into
decay, and long, oh! long ago did that bird
Joyous carol forth his last sweet song in the
garden that was once so passing fair.

And amid it all,— this heartache and the
loneliness which the years have brought,—
cometh my Christmas gift to-day: the solace
of a vision of that country whither she —
our little Mistress Merciless — hath gone; a
glimpse of that far-off land of Ever-Plaisance.

The Platonic Bassoon

THE PLATONIC BASSOON

ALL who knew the beautiful and accomplished Aurora wondered why she did not marry. She had now reached the mature age of twenty-five years, and was in full possession of those charms which are estimated by all men as the choicest gifts a woman can possess. You must know that Aurora had a queenly person, delightful manners, an extensive education, and an amiable disposition; and, being the only child of wealthy parents, she should not have lacked the one thing that seemed necessary to perfect and round out her usefulness as a member of society.

The truth was, Aurora did not fancy the male sex. She regarded men as conveniences that might come handy at times when an escort to the theatre was required, or when

a partner in a dance was demanded, when a fan was to be picked up, or when an errand was to be run; but the idea of marrying any man was as distasteful to Aurora as the proposition to marry a hat-rack or any other piece of household furniture would have been.

The secret of this strange aversion might have been traced to Aurora's maiden aunt Eliza, who had directed Aurora's education, and had from her niece's early youth instilled into Aurora's mind very distinct notions touching the masculine sex.

Aurora had numerous admirers among the young gentlemen who moved in the same elevated social circle as herself and frequently called at her father's house. Any one of them would gladly have made her his wife, and many of them had expressed a tender yearning for her life companionship. But Aurora was quick to recognize in each suitor some objectionable trait or habit or feature which her aunt Eliza had told about, and which imperatively prohibited a continuance of the young gentleman's attentions.

Aurora's father could not understand why

his daughter was so hypercritical and fas-
tidious in a matter which others of her sex
were so apt to accept with charitable eyes.
"They are bright, honest fellows," he urged,
"worthy of any girl's love. Receive their
advances kindly, my child, and having
chosen one among them, you will be the
happier for it."

"Never mind, Aurora," said Aunt Eliza.
"Men are all alike. They show their mean-
ness in different ways, but the same spirit
of evil is in 'em all. I have lived in this
world forty-six years, and during that time
I have found men to be the most unfeeling
and most untrustworthy of brutes."

So it was that at the age of twenty-five
Aurora was found beautiful, amiable, and
accomplished, but thoroughly and hope-
lessly a man-hater. And it was about this
time that she became involved in that unhappy affair which even to this day is talked
of by those who knew her then.

On the evening of a certain day Aurora
attended the opera with her father and mother and Morgan Magnus, the young banker.
Their box at the opera was so close to the

orchestra that by reaching out her hand Aurora could have touched several of the instruments. Now it happened that a bassoon was the instrument nearest the box in which Aurora sat, and it was natural therefore that the bassoon attracted more of Aurora's attention than any other instrument in the orchestra. If you have never beheld or heard a bassoon you are to understand that it is an instrument of wood, of considerable more length than breadth, provided with numerous stops and keys, and capable of producing an infinite variety of tones, ranging from the depth of lugubriousness to the highest pitch of vivacity. This particular bassoon was of an appearance that bordered upon the somber, the polished white of his keys emphasizing the solemn black of his long, willowy body. And, as he loomed up above the serene bald head of the musician that played him, Aurora thought she had never seen a more distingué object.

The opera was "Il Trovatore," a work well calculated to call in play all that peculiar pathos of which the bassoon is capable.

When Aurora saw the player raise the bassoon and apply the tiny tube thereunto appertaining to his lips, and heard him evoke from the innermost recesses of the bassoon tones that were fairly reeking with tears and redolent of melancholy, she felt a curious sentiment of pity awakened in her bosom.

Aurora had seen many an agonized swain at her feet, and had heard his impassioned pleadings for mercy; she had perused many a love missive wherein her pity was eloquently implored, but never had she experienced the tender, melting sentiment that percolated through her breast when she heard the bassoon mingling his melancholy tones with Manrico's plaints. The tears welled up into Aurora's eyes, her bosom heaved convulsively, and the most subtile emotions thrilled her soul.

In vain did young Magnus, the banker, seek to learn the cause of her agitation, and it seemed like a cruel mockery when Aurora's mother said: "You must remember, dear, that it is not real; it is only a play."

After this memorable evening, wherein an unexpected and indescribable sweetness

had crept into the young woman's life, Aurora more frequently insisted upon going to the opera. A strange fascination attracted her thither, and on each succeeding evening she found some new beauty in the bassoon, some new phase in his kaleidoscopic character to wonder at, some new accomplishment to admire. On one occasion — it was at the opera bouffe — this musical prodigy exhibited a playfulness and an exuberance of wit and humor that Aurora had never dreamed of. He ran the gamut of vocal conceit, and the polyglot fertility of his fancy simply astounded his rapt auditor. She was dazed, enchanted, spellbound. So here we find the fair Aurora passing from the condition of pity into the estate of admiration.

And now, having first conceived a wondrous pity for the bassoon, and then having become imbued with an admiration of his wit, sarcasm, badinage, repartee, and humor, it followed naturally and logically that Aurora should fall desperately in love with him; for pity and admiration are but the forerunners of the grand passion.

"Aunt Eliza," said Aurora one day, "you

have instilled into my sensitive nature an indelible aversion to men, compared with which all such deleble passions as affection and love are as inconsequential as summer zephyrs. I believe men to be by nature and practice gross, vulgar, sensual, and unworthy; and from this opinion I feel that I shall never recede. Yet such a clinging and fragile thing is woman's heart that it must needs have some object about which it may twine, even as the gentle ivy twines about the oak. Now, as you know, some women there are who, convinced of the utter worthlessness of the opposite sex, dedicate their lives to the adoration of some art or science, lavishing thereupon that love which women less prudent squander upon base men and ungrateful children; in the painting of pictures, devotion to the drama, the cultivation of music, pursuit of trade, or the exclusive attention to a profession, some women find the highest pleasure. But you and I, dear aunt, who are directed by even higher and purer motives than these women, scorn the pursuits of the arts and sciences, the professions and trades, and lay our hearts as will-

ing sacrifices upon the altars of a tabby cat and a bassoon. What could be purer or more exalted than a love of that kind?"

Having uttered this eloquent preface, which was, indeed, characteristic of the fair creature, Aurora told Aunt Eliza of the bassoon, and as she spoke of his versatile accomplishments and admirable qualities her eyes glowed with an unwonted animation, and a carmine hue suffused her beautiful cheeks. It was plain that Aurora was deeply in love, and Aunt Eliza was overjoyed.

"It is gratifying," said Aunt Eliza, "to find that my teachings promise such happy results, that the seeds I have so carefully sown already show signs of a glorious fruition. Now, while it is true that I cannot conceive of a happier love than that which exists between my own dear tabby cat and myself, it is also true that I recognize your bassoon as an object so much worthier of adoration than mankind in general, and your male acquaintances in particular, that I most heartily felicitate you upon the idol you have chosen for your worship. Bassoons do not smoke, nor chew tobacco, nor swear, nor

bet on horse-races, nor play billiards, nor do any of those horrid things which constitute the larger part of a man's ambitions and pursuits. You have acted wisely, my dear, and heaven grant you may be as happy in *his* love as I am in tabby's."

"I feel that I shall be," murmured Aurora; "already my bassoon is very precious to me."

With the dawn of this first passion a new motive seemed to come into Aurora's life — a gentle melancholy, a subdued sentiment whose accompaniments were sighings and day-dreamings and solitary tears and swoonings.

Quite naturally Aurora sought Aunt Eliza's society more than ever now, and her conversation and thoughts were always on the bassoon. It was very beautiful.

But late one night Aurora burst into Aunt Eliza's room and threw herself upon Aunt Eliza's bed, sobbing bitterly. Aunt Eliza was inexpressibly shocked, and under a sudden impulse of horror the tabby sprang to her feet, arched her back, bristled her tail, and uttered monosyllabics of astonishment.

"Why, Aurora, what ails you?" inquired Aunt Eliza, kindly.

"Oh, auntie, my heart is broken, I know it is," wailed Aurora.

"Come, come, my child," said Aunt Eliza, soothingly, "don't take on so. Tell auntie what ails you."

"He was harsh and cruel to me to-night, and oh! I loved him so!" moaned Aurora.

"A lovers' quarrel, eh?" thought Aunt Eliza; and she got up, slipped her wrapper on, and brewed Aurora a big bowl of boneset tea. Oh, how nice and bitter and fragrant it was, and how Aunt Eliza's nostrils sniffed, and how her eyes sparkled as she sipped the grateful beverage.

"There, drink that, my dear," said Aunt Eliza, "and then tell me all about it."

Aurora quaffed the bowl of boneset tea, and the wholesome draught seemed to give her fortitude, for now she told Aunt Eliza the whole story. It seems that Aurora had been to the opera as usual, not for the purpose of hearing and seeing the performance, but simply for the sake of being where the beloved bassoon was. The opera was Wag-

ner's "Die Walküre," and the part played by the bassoon in the orchestration was one of conspicuous importance. Fully appreciating his importance, the bassoon conducted himself with brutal arrogance and superciliousness on this occasion. His whole nature seemed changed; his tones were harsh and discordant, and with malevolent obstinacy he led all the other instruments in the orchestra through a seemingly endless series of musical pyrotechnics. There never was a more remarkable exhibition of stubbornness. When the violins and the 'cellos, the hautboys and the flutes, the cornets and the trombones, said "Come, let us work together in G minor," or "Let us do this passage in B flat," the bassoon would lead off with a wild shriek in D sharp or some other foreign key, and maintain it so lustily that the other instruments — e. g., the violins, the 'cellos, the hautboys, and all — were compelled to back, switch, and wheel into the bassoon's lead as best they could.

But no sooner had they come into harmony than the bassoon — oh, melancholy perversity of that instrument — would strike off

into another key with a ribald snicker or coarse guffaw, causing more turbulence and another stampede. And this preposterous condition of affairs was kept up the whole evening, the bassoon seeming to take a fiendish delight in his riotous, brutal conduct.

At first Aurora was mortified; then her mortification deepened into chagrin. In the hope of touching his heart she bestowed upon him a look of such tender supplication that, had he not been the most callous creature in the world, he must have melted under it. To his eternal shame, let it be said, the bassoon remained as impervious to her beseeching glances as if he had been a sphinx or a rhinoceros. In fact, Aurora's supplicating eyes seemed to instigate him to further and greater madness, for after that he became still more riotous, and at many times during the evening the crisis in the orchestra threatened anarchy and general disintegration.

Aurora's humiliation can be imagined by those only who have experienced a like bitterness — the bitterness of awakening to a realization of the cruelty of love. Aurora

206

loved the bassoon tenderly, deeply, absorbingly. The sprightliness of his lighter moods, no less than the throbbing pathos of his sadder moments, had won her heart. She had given him her love unreservedly, she fairly worshipped him, and now she awakened, as it were, from a golden dream, to find her idol clay! It was very sad. Yet who that has loved either man or bassoon does not know this bitterness?

"He will be gentler hereafter," said Aunt Eliza, encouragingly. "You must always remember that we should be charitable and indulgent with those we love. Who knows why the bassoon was harsh and wayward and imperious to-night? Let us not judge him till we have heard the whys and wherefores. He may have been ill; depend upon it, my dear, he had cause for his conduct."

Aunt Eliza's prudent words were a great solace to Aurora. And she forgave the bassoon all the pain he had inflicted when she went to the opera the next night and heard him in "I Puritani," a work in which the grand virility of his nature, its vigor and force, came out with telling effect. There

207

was not a trace of the insolence he had man-
ifested in "Die Walküre," nor of the humorous antics he had displayed in "La
Grande Duchesse"; divested of all charlatan-
ism, he was now a magnificent, sonorous,
manly bassoon, and you may depend upon
it Aurora was more in love with him than
ever.

It was about this time that, perceiving a
marked change in his daughter's appearance
and demeanor, Aurora's father began to question her mother about it all, and that good
lady at last made bold to tell the old gentleman the whole truth of the matter, which
was simply that Aurora cherished a passion
for the bassoon. Now the father was an exceedingly matter-of-fact, old-fashioned man,
who possessed not the least bit of sentiment, and when he heard that his only
child had fallen in love with a bassoon, his
anger was very great. He summoned Aurora into his presence, and regarded her with
an austere countenance.

"Girl," he said, in icy tones, "is it true
that you have been flirting with a bassoon?"

"Father," replied Aurora, with dignity, "I have never flirted with *anybody*, and you grievously wrong the bassoon when you intimated that he, too, is capable of such frivolity."

"It is nevertheless true," roared the old gentleman, "that you have conceived a passion for this bassoon, and have cherished it clandestinely."

"It *is* true, father, that I love the bassoon," said Aurora; "it *is* true that I admire his wit, vivacity, sentiment, soul, force, power, and manliness, but I have loved in secret. We have never met; he may know I love him, and he may reciprocate my love, but he has never spoken to me nor I to him, so there is nothing clandestine in the affair."

"Oh, my child! my child!" sobbed the old man, breaking down; "how could you love a bassoon, when so many eligible young men are suitors for your hand?"

"Don't mention him in the same breath with those horrid creatures!" cried Aurora, indignantly. "What scent of tobacco or odor of wines has ever profaned the purity

of his balmy breath? What does *he* know
of billiards, of horse-racing, of actresses, and
those other features of brutal men's lives?
Father, he is pure and good and exalted;
seek not to debase him by naming him in
the category of man!"

"These are Eliza's teachings!" shrieked
the old gentleman; and off he bundled to
vent his wrath on the maiden aunt. But it
was little satisfaction he got from Aunt
Eliza.

After that the old gentleman kept a strict
eye on Aurora, and very soon he became
satisfied of two things: First, that Aurora
was sincerely in love with the bassoon; and,
second, that the bassoon cared nothing for
Aurora. That Aurora loved the bassoon
was evidenced by her demeanor when in
his presence — her steadfast eyes, her parted
lips, her heaving bosom, her piteous sighs,
her flushed cheeks, and her varying emotions
as his tones changed, bore unimpeachable
testimony to the sincerity of her passion.
That the bassoon did not care for Aurora
was proved by his utter disregard of her
feelings, for though he might be tender this

moment he was harsh the next — though pleading now he spurned her anon ; and so, variable and fickle and false as the winds, he kept Aurora in misery and hysterics about half the time.

One morning the old gentleman entered the theatre while the orchestra was rehearsing.

"Who plays the bassoon?" he asked, in an imperative tone.

"Ich!" said a man with a bald head and gold spectacles.

"Your name?" demanded the old gentleman.

"Otto Baumgarten," replied he of the bald head and gold spectacles.

"Then, Otto Baumgarten," said the father, "I will give you one hundred dollars for your bassoon."

"Mein Gott!" said Herr Baumgarten, "dat bassoon gost me not half so much fon dot!"

"Never mind!" replied the old gentleman. "Take the money and give me the bassoon."

Herr Baumgarten did not hesitate a moment. He clutched at the gold pieces, and

while he counted them Aurora's father was hastening up the street with the bassoon under his arm. Aurora saw him coming, and she recognized the idol of her soul; his silver-plated keys were not to be mistaken. With a cry of joy she met her father in the hallway, snatched the bassoon to her heart, and covered him with kisses.

"He makes no answer to your protestations!" said her father. "Come, give over a love that is hopeless; cast aside this bassoon, who is hollow at heart, and whose affection at best is only platonic!"

"You speak blasphemies, father," cried Aurora, "and you yourself shall hear how he loves me, for when I but put my lips to this slender mouthpiece there shall issue from my worshipped bassoon tones of such ineffable tenderness that even you shall be convinced that my passion is reciprocated."

With these words Aurora glued her beauteous lips to the slender blowpipe of the bassoon, and, having inflated her lungs to their capacity, breathed into it a respiration that seemed to come from her very soul. But no sound issued from the cold, hollow,

unresponsive bassoon. Aurora repeated the effort with increased vigor. There came no answer at all.

"Aha!" laughed her father. "I told you so; he loves you not."

But then, with a last superhuman effort, Aurora made her third attempt; her eyeballs started from their sockets, big, blue veins and cords stood out on her lovely neck, and all the force and vigor of her young life seemed to go out through her pursed lips into the bassoon's system. And then, oh then! as if to mock her idolatry and sound the death knell of her unhappy love, the bassoon recoiled and emitted a tone so harsh, so discordant, so supernatural, that even Aurora's father drew back in horror.

And lo! hearing that supernatural sound that told her of the hopelessness of love, Aurora dropped the hollow, mocking scoffer, clutched spasmodically at her heart, and, with an agonizing shriek, fell lifeless to the floor.

✤

Hawaiian Folk Tales

✤

HAWAIIAN FOLK TALES

I

THE EEL-KING

THERE was a maiden named Liliokani whose father was a fisherman. But the maiden liked not her father's employment, for she believed it to be an offence against Atua, the all-god, to deprive any animal of that life which Atua had breathed into it. And this was pleasing unto Atua, and he blessed Liliokani with exceeding beauty; no other eyes were so large, dark, and tender as hers; the braids of her long, soft hair fell like silken seagrass upon her shoulders; she was tall and graceful as the palm, and her voice was the voice of the sea when the sea cradles the moonlight and sings it to sleep.

Full many kings' sons came wooing Lilio-

kani, and chiefs renowned in war; and with others came Tatatao, that was a mighty hunter of hares and had compassed famous hardships. For those men that delight in adventure and battle are most pleasantly minded to gentle women, for thus capriciously hath Atua, the all-god, ordained. But Liliokani had no ear to the wooing of these men, and the fisherman's daughter was a virgin when Mimi came.

Mimi was king of the eels, and Atua had given him eternal life and the power to change his shape when it pleased him to issue from the water and walk the earth. It befell that this eel-king, Mimi, beheld Liliokani upon a time as he swam the little river near her father's abode, and he saw that she was exceeding fair and he heard the soft, sad sea-tone in her voice. So for many days Mimi frequented those parts and grew more and more in love with the maiden.

Upon a certain day, while she helped her father to mend his nets, Liliokani saw a young man of goodly stature and handsome face approaching, and to herself she said: "Surely if ever I be tempted to wed it shall

be with this young man, whose like I have never before known." But she had no thought that it was Mimi, the eel-king, who in this changed shape now walked the earth.

Sweetly he made obeisance and pleasant was his discourse with the fisherman and his daughter, and he told them many things of his home, which he said was many kumes distant from that spot. Though he spake mostly to the old man, his eyes were fixed upon Liliokani, and, after the fashion of her sex, that maiden presently knew that he had great love unto her. Many days after that came Mimi to hold discourse with them, and they had joy of his coming, for in sooth he was of fair countenance and sweet address, and the fisherman, being a single-minded and a simple man, had no suspicion of the love between Mimi and Liliokani. But once Mimi said to Liliokani in such a voice as the sea-wind hath to the maiden palm-trees: "Brown maiden mine, let thy door be unlatched this night, and I will come to thee."

So the door was not latched that night

and Mimi went in unto her, and they two were together and alone.

"What meaneth that moaning of the sea?" asked Liliokani.

"The sea chanteth our bridal anthem," he answered.

"And what sad music cometh from the palms to-night?" she asked.

"They sing soft and low of our wedded love," he answered.

But Liliokani apprehended evil, and, although she spake no more of it at that time, a fear of trouble was in her heart.

Now Atua, the all-god, was exceeding wroth at this thing, and in grievous anger he beheld how that every night the door was unlatched and Mimi went in unto Liliokani. And Atua set about to do vengeance, and Atua's wrath is sure and very dreadful.

There was a night when Mimi did not come; the door was unlatched and the breath of Liliokani was as the perfume of flowers and of spices commingled; yet he came not. Then Liliokani wept and unbraided her hair and cried as a widow crieth, and she thought that Mimi had found an-

other pleasanter than she unto him. So, upon the next night, she latched the door. But in the middle of the night, when the fire was kindled in the island moon, there was a gentle tapping at the door, and Mimi called to her. And when she had unlatched the door she began to chide him, but he stopped her chiding, and with great groaning he took her to his breast, and she knew by the beating of his heart that evil had come upon him.

Then Mimi told her who he was and how wroth the all-god was because the eel-king, forgetful of his immortality and neglectful of his domain, loved the daughter of a mortal.

"Forswear me, then," quoth Liliokani, "forswear me, and come not hither again, and the anger of the all-god shall be appeased."

"It is not to lie to Atua," answered Mimi. "The all-god readeth every heart and knoweth every thought. How can I, that love thee only, forswear thee? More just and terrible would be Atua's wrath for that lie to him and that wrong to thee and to myself. Brown maiden, I go back into the sea

and from thee forever, bearing with me a love for thee which even the all-god's anger cannot chill."

So he kissed her for the last time and bade her a last farewell, and then he went from that door down to the water's edge and into his domain. And Liliokani made great moan and her heart was like to break. But the sea was placid as a hearthstone and the palms lay asleep in the sky that night, for it was Atua's will that the woman should suffer alone.

In the middle of the next night a mighty tempest arose. The clouds reached down and buffeted the earth and sea, and the winds and the waters cried out in anger against each other and smote each other. Above the tumult Atua's voice was heard. "Arise, Liliokani," quoth that voice, "and with thy father's stone hatchet smite off the head of the fish that lieth upon the threshold of the door."

Then Liliokani arose with fear and trembling and went to the door, and there, on the threshold, lay a monster eel whose body had been floated thither by the flood and

222

the tempest. With her father's stone hatchet she smote off the eel's head, and the head fell into the hut, but the long, dead body floated back with the flood into the sea and was seen no more. Then the tempest abated, and with the morning came the sun's light and its tender warmth. And at the earliest moment Liliokani took the eel's head secretly and buried it with much sorrow and weeping, for the eyes within that lifeless head were Mimi's eyes, and Liliokani knew that this thing was come of the all-god's wrath.

It was her wont to go each day and make moan over the spot where she had hid this vestige of her love, and presently Atua pitied her, for Atua loveth his children upon this earth, even though they sin most grievously. So, by and by, Liliokani saw that two green leaves were sprouting from the earth, and in a season these two leaves became twin stalks and grew into trees, the like of which had never before been seen upon earth. And Liliokani lived to see and to taste the fruit of these twin trees that sprung from Mimi's brain — the red cocoanut and the white

cocoanut, whereof all men have eaten since that time. And all folk hold that fruit in sweet estimation, for it cometh from the love that a god had unto a mortal woman, and mortality is love and love is immortality.

Atua forgot not Liliokani when the skies opened to her; she liveth forever in the star that looketh only upon this island, and it is her tender grace that nourishes the infant cocoas and maketh the elder ones fruitful. Meanwhile no woman that dwelleth upon earth hath satisfaction in tasting the flesh of eels, for a knowledge of Mimi's love and sacrifice hath been subtly implanted by Atua, the all-god, in every woman's breast.

II

THE MOON LADY

Once there were four maidens who were the daughters of Talakoa, and they were so very beautiful that their fame spread through the universe. The oldest of these maidens was named Kaulualua, and it is of her that it is to tell this tale.

One day while Kaulualua was combing her hair she saw a tall, fair man fishing in the rivulet, and he was a stranger to her. Never before had she seen so fair a man, though in very sooth she had been wooed of many king's sons and of chiefs from every part of the earth. Then she called to her three sisters and asked them his name, but they could not answer; this, however, they knew — he was of no country whereof they had heard tell, for he was strangely clad and he was of exceeding fair complexion and his stature surpassed that of other men.

The next day these maidens saw this same tall, fair man, but he no longer fished in the rivulet; he hunted the hares and was passing skilful thereat, so that the maidens admired him not only for his exceeding comeliness but also for his skill as a huntsman, for surely there was no hare that could escape his vigilance and the point of his arrow. So when Talakoa, their father, came that evening the maidens told him of this stranger, and he wondered who he was and whence he fared. Awaking from sleep in the middle of that night, Kaulualua saw that

the stars shone with rare brilliancy, and that by their light a man was gazing upon her through the window. And she saw that the man was the tall, fair man of whom it has been spoken. So she uttered no cry, but feigned that she slept, for she saw that there was love in the tall, fair man's eyes, and it pleaseth a maiden to be looked upon in that wise.

When it was morning this tall, fair man came and entered that house and laid a fish and a hare upon the hearthstone and called for Talakoa. And he quoth to Talakoa: "Old man, I would have your daughter to wife."

Being a full crafty man, as beseemeth one of years, Talakoa replied: "Four daughters have I."

The tall, fair man announced: "You speak sooth, as well becometh a full crafty man. Four daughters have you, and it is Kaulualua that I would have to wife."

Saith that full crafty man, the father: "How many palm trees grow in thy possession, and how many rivers flow through thy chiefdom? Whence comest thou, gentle

sir, for assuredly neither I nor mine have seen the like of thee before."

"Good sooth," answered the tall, fair man, "I will tell you no lie, for I would have that daughter to wife, and the things you require do well beseem a full crafty man that meaneth for his child's good. I am the man of the moon, and my name is Marama."

Then Talakoa and his daughters looked at one another and were sore puzzled, for they knew not whereof Marama spake. And they deemed him a madman; yet did they not laugh him to scorn, because that he had come a-wooing, and had laid the fish and the hare upon the hearthstone.

"Kind sir, bringing gifts," quoth Talakoa, "I say no lie to you, but we know not that country whereof you speak. Pray tell us of the moon and where is it situate, and how many kumes is it distant from here?"

"Full crafty man, father of her whom I would have to wife, I will tell you truly," answered Marama. "The moon wherefrom I come is a mighty island in the vast sea of night, and it is distant from here so great a space that it were not to count the kumes

that lie between. Exceeding fair is that island in that vast sea, and it hath mountains and valleys and plains and seas and rivers and lakes, and I am the chief over all. Atua made that island for me and put it in that mighty sea, for I am the son of Atua, and over that island in that sea I shall rule forever."

Great wonder had they to hear tell of these things, and they knew now that Marama was the child of Atua, who made the universe and is the all-god. Then Marama said on:

"Atua bade me search and find me a wife, and upon the stars have I walked two hundred years, fishing and hunting, and seeing maidens, but of all maidens seen there is none that I did love. So now at last, in this island of this earth, I have found Kaulualua, and have seen the pearl of her beauty and smelled the cinnamon of her breath, and I would fain have her to wife that she may be ruler with me over the moon, my island in the vast, black sea of night."

It was not for Talakoa, being of earth such as all human kind, to gainsay the words of Marama. And there was a flame in Kau-

lualua's heart and incense in her breath and
honey in her eyes toward this tall, fair man
that was the son of Atua. So the old father
said to her: "Take up the fish and the hare
and roast them, my daughter, and spread
them before us, and we will eat them and so
pledge our troth, one to another."

This thing did Kaulualua, and so the man
from the moon had her to wife.

That night they went from the home of
Talakoa to the island in the sea of night,
and Talakoa and the three maidens watched
for a signal from that island, for Kaulualua
told them she would build a fire thereon
that they might know when she was come
thither. Many, many nights they watched,
and their hair grew white, and Time marked
their faces with his fingers, and the moss
gathered on the palm trees. At last, as if
he would sleep forever, Talakoa laid himself
upon his mat by the door and asked that
the skies be opened to him, for he was en-
feebled with age.

And while he asked this thing the three
sisters saw a dim light afar off in the black
sea of night, and it was such a light as had

never before been seen. And this light grew larger and brighter, so that in seven nights it was thrice the size of the largest palm leaf, and it lighted up all that far-off island in the sea of night, and they knew that Kaulualua and the moon-god were in their home at last. So old Talakoa was soothed and the skies that opened unto him found him satisfied.

The three sisters lived long, and yet two hundred ages are gone since the earth received them into its bosom. Yet still upon that island in the dark sea of night abideth in love the moon-god with his bride. Atua hath been good to her, for he hath given her eternal youth, as he giveth to all wives that do truly love and serve their husbands. It is for us to see that pleasant island wherein Kaulualua liveth; it is for us to see that when Marama goeth abroad to hunt or to fish his moon-lady sitteth alone and maketh moan, and heedeth not her fires; it is for us to see that when anon he cometh back she buildeth up those fires whereon to cook food for him, and presently the fires grow brighter and the whole round moon island is lighted

and warmed thereby. In this wise an exceeding fair example is set unto all wives of their duty unto their mates.

When the sea singeth to the sands, when the cane beckoneth to the stars, and when the palm-leaves whisper to sweet-breathed night, how pleasant it is, my brown maiden, to stand with thee and look upon that island in the azure sea that spreadeth like a veil above the cocoa trees. For there we see the moon-lady, and she awaiteth her dear lord and she smileth in love; and that grace warmeth our hearts — your heart and mine, O little maiden! and we are glad with a joy that knoweth no speaking.

❦

Lute Baker and his wife Em

❦

LUTE BAKER AND HIS WIFE EM

THE Plainfield boys always had the name of being smart, and I guess Lute Baker was just about the smartest boy the old town ever turned out. Well, he came by it naturally; Judge Baker was known all over western Massachusetts as the sage of Plainfield, and Lute's mother — she was a Kellogg before the judge married her — she had more faculty than a dozen of your girls nowadays, and her cooking was talked about everywhere — never was another woman, as folks said, could cook like Miss Baker. The boys — Lute's friends — used to hang around the back porch of noonings just to get some of her doughnuts; she was always considerate and liberal to growing boys. May be Lute would n't have been so popular if it had n't been for those doughnuts,

and may be he would n't have been so smart if it had n't been for all the good things his mother fed into him. Always did believe there was piety and wisdom in New England victuals.

Lute went to Amherst College and did well; was valedictorian; then he taught school a winter, for Judge Baker said that nobody could amount to much in the world unless he taught school a spell. Lute was set on being a lawyer, and so presently he went down to Springfield and read and studied in Judge Morris' office, and Judge Morris wrote a letter home to the Bakers once testifying to Lute's "probity" and "acumen"—things that are never heard tell of except high up in the legal profession.

How Lute came to get the western fever I can't say, but get it he did, and one winter he up and piked off to Chicago, and there he hung out his shingle and joined a literary social and proceeded to get rich and famous. The next spring Judge Baker fell off the woodshed while he was shingling it, and it jarred him so he kind of drooped and pined round a spell and then one day up and died.

Lute had to come back home and settle up the estate.

When he went west again he took a wife with him — Emma Cowles that was (everybody called her Em for short), pretty as a picture and as likely a girl as there was in the township. Lute had always had a hankering for Em, and Em thought there never was another such a young fellow as Lute; she understood him perfectly, having sung in the choir with him two years. The young couple went west well provided.

Lute and Em went to housekeeping in Chicago. Em wanted to do her own work, but Lute would n't hear to it; so they hired a German girl that was just over from the vineyards of the Rhine country.

"Lute," says Em, "Hulda does n't know much about cooking."

"So I see," says Lute, feelingly. "She's green as grass; you 'll have to teach her."

Hulda could swing a hoe and wield a spade deftly, but of the cuisine she knew somewhat less than nothing. Em had lots of patience and pluck, but she found teaching Hulda how to cook a precious hard job.

Lute was amiable enough at first; used to laugh it off with a cordial bet that by and by Em would make a famous cook of the obtuse but willing immigrant. This moral backing buoyed Em up considerable, until one evening in an unguarded moment Lute expressed a pining for some doughnuts "like those mother makes," and that casual remark made Em unhappy. But next evening when Lute came home there were doughnuts on the table — beautiful, big, plethoric doughnuts that fairly reeked with the homely, delicious sentiment of New England. Lute ate one. Em felt hurt.

"I guess it's because I've eaten so much else," explained Lute, "but somehow or other they don't taste like mother's."

Next day Em fed the rest of the doughnuts to a poor man who came and said he was starving. "Thank you, marm," said he, with his heart full of gratitude and his mouth full of doughnuts; "I ha'n't had anything as good as this since I left Connecticut twenty years ago."

That little subtlety consoled Em, but still she found it hard to bear up under her

apparent inability to do her duty by Lute's critical palate. Once when Lute brought Col. Hi Thomas home to dinner they had chicken pie. The colonel praised it and passed his plate a third time.

"Oh, but you ought to eat some of mother's chicken pie," said Lute. "Mother never puts an under crust in her chicken pies, and that makes 'em juicier."

Same way when they had fried pork and potatoes; Lute could not understand why the flesh of the wallowing, carnivorous western hog should n't be as white and firm and sweet as the meat of the swill-fed Yankee pig. And why were the Hubbard squashes so tasteless and why was maple syrup so very different? Yes, amid all his professional duties Lute found time to note and remark upon this and other similar things, and of course Em was — by implication, at least — held responsible for them all.

And Em did try *so* hard, so *very* hard, to correct the evils and to answer the hypercritical demands of Lute's foolishly petted and spoiled appetite. She warred valorously with butchers, grocers, and hucksters; she

sent down east to Mother Baker for all the famous family recipes; she wrestled in speech and in practice with that awful Hulda; she experimented long and patiently; she blistered her pretty face and burned her little hands over that kitchen range — yes, a slow, constant martyrdom that conscientious wife willingly endured for years in her enthusiastic determination to do her duty by Lute. Doughnuts, chicken-pies, boiled dinners, layer-cakes, soda biscuits, flapjacks, fish balls, baked beans, squash pies, corned-beef hash, dried-apple sauce, currant wine, succotash, brown bread — how valorously Em toiled over them, only to be rewarded with some cruel reminder of how " mother " used to do these things! It was terrible; a tedious martyrdom.

Lute — mind you — Lute was not wilfully cruel; no, he was simply and irremediably a heedless idiot of a man, just as every married man is, for a spell, at least. But it broke Em's heart, all the same.

Lute's mother came to visit them when their first child was born, and she lifted a great deal of trouble off the patient wife.

Old Miss Baker always liked Em; had told the minister three years ago that she knew Em would make Lute a good Christian wife. They named the boy Moses, after the old judge who was dead, and old Miss Baker said he should have his gran'pa's watch when he got to be twenty-one.

Old Miss Baker always stuck by Em; may be she remembered how the old judge had talked once on a time about *his* mother's cooking. For all married men are, as I have said, idiotically cruel about that sort of thing. Yes, old Miss Baker braced Em up wonderful; brought a lot of dried catnip out west with her for the baby; taught Em how to make salt-rising bread; told her all about stewing things and broiling things and roasting things; showed her how to tell the real Yankee codfish from the counterfeit — oh, she just did Em lots of good, did old Miss Baker!

The rewards of virtue may be slow in coming, but they are sure to come. Em's three boys — the three bouncing boys that came to Em and Lute — those three boys waxed fat and grew up boisterous, blatant appreciators of their mother's cooking. The way

241

those boys did eat mother's doughnuts!
And mother's pies — wow! Other boys —
the neighbors' boys — came round regularly
in troops, battalions, armies, and like a consuming fire licked up the wholesome viands
which Em's skill and liberality provided for
her own boys' enthusiastic playmates. And
all those boys — there must have been millions of 'em — were living, breathing, vocif-
erous testimonials to the unapproachable
excellence of Em's cooking.

Lute got into politics, and they elected him
to the legislature. After the campaign, need-
ing rest, he took it into his head to run down
east to see his mother; he had not been back
home for eight years. He took little Moses
with him. They were gone about three
weeks. Gran'ma Baker had made great
preparations for them; had cooked up enough
pies to last all winter, and four plump, be-
headed, well-plucked, yellow-legged pullets
hung stiff and solemn-like in the chill pantry
off the kitchen, awaiting the last succulent
scene of all.

Lute and the little boy got there late of an
evening. The dear old lady was so glad to

see them; the love that beamed from her kindly eyes well nigh melted the glass in her silver-bowed specks. The table was spread in the dining-room; the sheet-iron stove sighed till it seemed like to crack with the heat of that hardwood fire.

"Why, Lute, you ain't eatin' enough to keep a fly alive," remonstrated old Miss Baker, when her son declined a second doughnut; "and what ails the child?" she continued; "ha' n't he got no appetite? Why, when you wuz his age, Lute, seemed as if I could n't cook doughnuts fast enough for you!"

Lute explained that both he and his little boy had eaten pretty heartily on the train that day. But all the time of their visit there poor old Gran'ma Baker wondered and worried because they did n't eat enough — seemed to her as if western folks had n't the right kind of appetite. Even the plump pullets, served in a style that had made Miss Baker famed throughout those discriminating parts — even those pullets failed to awaken the expected and proper enthusiasm in the visitors.

Home again in Chicago, Lute drew his chair up to the table with an eloquent sigh of relief. As for little Moses, he clamored his delight.

"Chicken pie!" he cried, gleefully; and then he added a soulful "wow!" as his eager eyes fell upon a plateful of hot, exuberant, voluptuous doughnuts.

"Yes, we are both glad to get back," said Lute.

"But I am afraid," suggested Em, timidly, "that gran'ma's cooking has spoiled you."

Little Moses (bless him) howled an indignant, a wrathful remonstrance. "Gran'ma can't cook worth a cent!" said he.

Em expected Lute to be dreadfully shocked, but he was n't.

"I would n't let her know it for all the world," remarked Lute, confidentially, "but mother has lost her grip on cooking. At any rate, her cooking is n't what it used to be; it has changed."

Then Em came bravely to the rescue. "No, Lute," says she, and she meant it, "your mother's cooking has n't changed,

but *you* have. The man has grown away from the boy, and the tastes, the ways, and the delights of boyhood have no longer any fascination for the man."

"May be you 're right," said Lute. "At any rate, I 'm free to say that *your* cooking beats the world."

Good for Lute! Virtue triumphs and my true story ends. But first an explanation to concinnate my narrative.

I should never have known this true story if Lute himself had n't told it to me at the last dinner of the Sons of New England — told it to me right before Em, that dear, patient little martyred wife of his. And I knew by the love light in Em's eyes that she was glad that she had endured that martyrdom for Lute's sake.

❦

Joel's talk with Santa Claus

❦

JOEL'S TALK WITH SANTA CLAUS

ONE Christmas eve Joel Baker was in a most unhappy mood. He was lonesome and miserable; the chimes making merry Christmas music outside disturbed rather than soothed him, the jingle of the sleigh-bells fretted him, and the shrill whistling of the wind around the corners of the house and up and down the chimney seemed to grate harshly on his ears.

" Humph," said Joel, wearily, " Christmas is nothin' to me; there *was* a time when it meant a great deal, but that was long ago — fifty years is a long stretch to look back over. There is nothin' in Christmas now, nothin' for *me* at least; it is so long since Santa Claus remembered me that I venture to say he has forgotten that there ever was such a person as Joel Baker in all the world. It used to be different; Santa Claus *used* to

think a great deal of me when I was a boy.
Ah! Christmas nowadays ain't what it was
in the good old time—no, not what it used
to be."

As Joel was absorbed in his distressing
thoughts he became aware very suddenly
that somebody was entering or trying to
enter the room. First came a draft of cold
air, then a scraping, grating sound, then a
strange shuffling, and then,—yes, then, all
at once, Joel saw a pair of fat legs and a still
fatter body dangle down the chimney, followed presently by a long white beard,
above which appeared a jolly red nose and
two bright twinkling eyes, while over the
head and forehead was drawn a fur cap,
white with snowflakes.

"Ha, ha," chuckled the fat, jolly stranger,
emerging from the chimney and standing
well to one side of the hearthstone; "ha,
ha, they don't have the big, wide chimneys
they used to build, but they can't keep Santa
Claus out—no, they can't keep Santa Claus
out! Ha, ha, ha. Though the chimney
were no bigger than a gas pipe, Santa Claus
would slide down it!"

It didn't require a second glance to assure Joel that the new-comer was indeed Santa Claus. Joel knew the good old saint — oh, yes — and he had seen him once before, and, although that was when Joel was a little boy, he had never forgotten how Santa Claus looked.

Nor had Santa Claus forgotten Joel, although Joel thought he had; for now Santa Claus looked kindly at Joel and smiled and said: "Merry Christmas to you, Joel!"

"Thank you, old Santa Claus," replied Joel, "but I don't believe it's going to be a very merry Christmas. It's been so long since I've had a merry Christmas that I don't believe I'd know how to act if I had one."

"Let's see," said Santa Claus, "it must be going on fifty years since I saw you last — yes, you were eight years old the last time I slipped down the chimney of the old homestead and filled your stocking. Do you remember it?"

"I remember it well," answered Joel. "I had made up my mind to lie awake and see Santa Claus; I had heard tell of you, but

I 'd never seen you, and Brother Otis and I concluded we 'd lie awake and watch for you to come."

Santa Claus shook his head reproachfully.

"That was very wrong," said he, "for I 'm so scarey that if I 'd known you boys were awake I 'd never have come down the chimney at all, and then you 'd have had no presents."

"But Otis could n't keep awake," explained Joel. "We talked about everythin' we could think of, till father called out to us that if we did n't stop talking he 'd have to send one of us up into the attic to sleep with the hired man. So in less than five minutes Otis was sound asleep and no pinching could wake him up. But *I* was bound to see Santa Claus and I don't believe anything would 've put me to sleep. I heard the big clock in the sitting-room strike eleven, and I had begun wonderin' if you never were going to come, when all of a sudden I heard the tinkle of the bells around your reindeers' necks. Then I heard the reindeers prancin' on the roof and the sound of your sleigh-runners cuttin' through the

crust and slippin' over the shingles. I was kind o' scared and I covered my head up with the sheet and quilts — only I left a little hole so I could peek out and see what was goin' on. As soon as I saw you I got over bein' scared — for you were jolly and smilin' like, and you chuckled as you went around to each stockin' and filled it up."

"Yes, I can remember the night," said Santa Claus. "I brought you a sled, did n't I?"

"Yes, and you brought Otis one, too," replied Joel. "Mine was red and had 'Yankee Doodle' painted in black letters on the side; Otis' was black and had 'Snow Queen' in gilt letters."

"I remember those sleds distinctly," said Santa Claus, "for I made them specially for you boys."

"You set the sleds up against the wall," continued Joel, "and then you filled the stockin's."

"There were six of 'em, as I recollect?" said Santa Claus.

"Let me see," queried Joel. "There was mine, and Otis', and Elvira's, and Thankful's, and Susan Prickett's — Susan was our

help, you know. No, there were only five, and, as I remember, they were the biggest we could beg or borrer of Aunt Dorcas, who weighed nigh unto two hundred pounds. Otis and I did n't like Susan Prickett, and we were hopin' you 'd put a cold potato in her stockin'."

"But Susan was a good girl," remonstrated Santa Claus. "You know I put cold potatoes only in the stockin's of boys and girls who are bad and don't believe in Santa Claus."

"At any rate," said Joel, "you filled all the stockin's with candy and pop-corn and nuts and raisins, and I can remember you said you were afraid you 'd run out of pop-corn balls before you got around. Then you left each of us a book. Elvira got the best one, which was 'The Garland of Frien'ship,' and had poems in it about the bleeding of hearts, and so forth. Father was n't expectin' anything, but you left him a new pair of mittens, and mother got a new fur boa to wear to meetin'."

"Of course," said Santa Claus, "I never forgot father and mother."

"Well, it was as much as I could do to lay still," continued Joel, "for I 'd been longin' for a sled, an' the sight of that red sled with ' Yankee Doodle ' painted on it jest made me wild. But, somehow or other, I began to get powerful sleepy all at once, and I could n't keep my eyes open. The next thing I knew Otis was nudgin' me in the ribs. ' Git up, Joel,' says he; ' it 's Chris'-mas an' Santa Claus has been here.' ' Merry Christ'mas! Merry Chris'mas!' we cried as we tumbled out o' bed. Then Elvira an' Thankful came in, not more 'n half dressed, and Susan came in, too, an' we just made Rome howl with ' Merry Chris'mas! Merry Chris'mas !' to each other. ' Ef you children don't make less noise in there,' cried father, ' I 'll hev to send you all back to bed.' The idea of askin' boys an' girls to keep quiet on Chris'mas mornin' when they 've got new sleds an' ' Garlands of Frien'ship '!"

Santa Claus chuckled; his rosy cheeks fairly beamed joy.

"Otis an' I did n't want any breakfast," said Joel. "We made up our minds that a stockin'ful of candy and pop-corn and rai-

sins would stay us for a while. I *do* believe
there was n't buckwheat cakes enough in
the township to keep us indoors that mornin'; buckwheat cakes don't size up much
'longside of a red sled with ' Yankee Doodle '
painted onto it and a black sled named ' Snow
Queen.' *We* did n't care how cold it was —
so much the better for slidin' down hill! All
the boys had new sleds — Lafe Dawson, Bill
Holbrook, Gum Adams, Rube Playford, Le-
ander Merrick, Ezra Purple — all on 'em had
new sleds excep' Martin Peavey, and he said
he calculated Santa Claus had skipped him
this year 'cause his father had broke his leg
haulin' logs from the Pelham woods and
had been kep' indoors six weeks. But Martin had his ol' sled, and he didn't hev to ask
any odds of any of us, neither."

"I brought Martin a sled the *next* Christmas," said Santa Claus.

"Like as not — but did you ever slide
down hill, Santa Claus ? I don't mean such
hills as they hev out here in this *new* country, but one of them old-fashioned New
England hills that was made 'specially for
boys to slide down, full of bumpers an'

256

thank-ye-marms, and about ten times longer comin' up than it is goin' down! The wind blew in our faces and almos' took our breath away. 'Merry Chris'mas to ye, little boys!' it seemed to say, and it untied our mufflers an' whirled the snow in our faces, just as if it was a boy, too, an' wanted to play with us. An ol' crow came flappin' over us from the corn field beyond the meadow. He said: 'Caw, caw,' when he saw my new sled — I s'pose he'd never seen a red one before. Otis had a hard time with *his* sled — the black one — an' he wondered why it would n't go as fast as mine would. 'Hev you scraped the paint off'n the runners?' asked Wralsey Goodnow. 'Course I hev,' said Otis; 'broke my own knife an' Lute Ingra-ham's a-doin' it, but it don't seem to make no dif'rence — the darned ol' thing won't go!' Then, what did Simon Buzzell say but that, like 's not, it was because Otis's sled's name was 'Snow Queen.' 'Never did see a girl sled that was worth a cent, anyway,' sez Simon. Well, now, that jest about broke Otis up in business. 'It ain't a girl sled,' sez he, 'and its name ain't ''Snow

257

Queen"! I'm a-goin' to call it "Dan'l Web-
ster," or "Ol'ver Optic," or "Sheriff Rob-
bins," or after some other big man!' An' the
boys plagued him so much about that pesky
girl sled that he scratched off the name, an',
as I remember, it *did* go better after that!

"About the only thing," continued Joel,
"that marred the harmony of the occasion,
as the editor of the 'Hampshire County Phœnix' used to say, was the ashes that Deacon
Morris Frisbie sprinkled out in front of his
house. He said he was n't going to have
folks breakin' their necks jest on account of
a lot of frivolous boys that was goin' to the
gallows as fas' as they could! Oh, how we
hated him! and we 'd have snowballed him,
too, if we had n't been afraid of the constable
that lived next door. But the ashes did n't
bother us much, and every time we slid side-
saddle we 'd give the ashes a kick, and that
sort of scattered 'em."

The bare thought of this made Santa Claus
laugh.

"Goin' on about nine o'clock," said Joel,
"the girls come along—Sister Elvira an'
Thankful, Prudence Tucker, Belle Yocum,

Sophrone Holbrook, Sis Hubbard, an' Marthy Sawyer. Marthy's brother Increase wanted her to ride on *his* sled, but Marthy allowed that a red sled was her choice every time. 'I don't see how I 'm goin' to hold on,' said Marthy. 'Seems as if I would hev my hands full keepin' my things from blowin' away.' 'Don't worry about yourself, Marthy,' sez I, 'for if you 'll look after your things, I kind o' calc'late I 'll manage not to lose *you* on the way.' Dear Marthy—seems as if I could see you now, with your tangled hair a-blowin' in the wind, your eyes all bright and sparklin', an' your cheeks as red as apples. Seems, too, as if I could hear you laughin' an' callin', jist as you did as I toiled up the old New England hill that Chris'mas mornin'—a callin': 'Joel, Joel, Joel—ain't ye ever comin', Joel?' But the hill is long and steep, Marthy, an' Joel ain't the boy he used to be; he 's old, an' gray, an' feeble, but there 's love an' faith in his heart, an' they kind o' keep him totterin' tow'rds the voice he hears a-callin': 'Joel, Joel, Joel!'"

"I know—I see it all," murmured Santa Claus, very softly.

"Oh, that was so long ago," sighed Joel; "so very long ago! And I've had no Chris'mas since—only once, when our little one—Marthy's an' mine—you remember him, Santa Claus?"

"Yes," said Santa Claus, "a toddling little boy with blue eyes—"

"Like his mother," interrupted Joel; "an' he *was* like her, too—so gentle an' lovin', only we called him Joel, for that was my father's name and it kind o' run in the fam'ly. He wa'n't more 'n three years old when you came with your Chris'mas presents for him, Santa Claus. We had told him about you, and he used to go to the chimney every night and make a little prayer about what he wanted you to bring him. And you brought 'em, too—a stick-horse, an' a picture-book, an' some blocks, an' a drum—they 're on the shelf in the closet there, and his little Chris'-mas stockin' with 'em—I 've saved 'em all, an' I 've taken 'em down an' held 'em in my hands, oh, so many times!"

"But when I came again," said Santa Claus—

"His little bed was empty, an' I was alone.

It killed his mother—Marthy was so tender-hearted; she kind o' drooped an' pined after that. So now they 've been asleep side by side in the buryin'-ground these thirty years.

"That 's why I 'm so sad-like whenever Chris'mas comes," said Joel, after a pause. "The thinkin' of long ago makes me bitter almost. It 's so different now from what it used to be."

"No, Joel, oh, no," said Santa Claus. "'T is the same world, and human nature is the same and always will be. But Christmas is for the little folks, and you, who are old and grizzled now, must know it and love it only through the gladness it brings the little ones."

"True," groaned Joel; "but how may I know and feel this gladness when I have no little stocking hanging in my chimney corner—no child to please me with his prattle? See, I am alone."

"No, you 're not alone, Joel," said Santa Claus. "There are children in this great city who would love and bless you for your goodness if you but touched their hearts. Make them happy, Joel; send by me this

night some gift to the little boy in the old house yonder—he is poor and sick; a simple toy will fill his Christmas with gladness."

"His little sister, too—take *her* some present," said Joel; "make them happy for me, Santa Claus—you are right—make them happy for me."

How sweetly Joel slept! When he awoke, the sunlight streamed in through the window and seemed to bid him a merry Christmas. How contented and happy Joel felt! It must have been the talk with Santa Claus that did it all; he had never known a sweeter sense of peace. A little girl came out of the house over the way. She had a new doll in her arms, and she sang a merry little song and she laughed with joy as she skipped along the street. Ay, and at the window sat the little sick boy, and the toy Santa Claus left him seemed to have brought him strength and health, for his eyes sparkled and his cheeks glowed, and it was plain to see his heart was full of happiness.

And, oh! how the chimes did ring out, and how joyfully they sang their Christmas carol that morning! They sang of Bethlehem

and the manger and the Babe; they sang of love and charity, till all the Christmas air seemed full of angel voices.

> Carol of the Christmas morn —
>   Carol of the Christ-child born —
> Carol to the list'ning sky
>   Till it echoes back again
>   " Glory be to God on high,
>   Peace on earth, good will tow'rd men ! "

So all this music — the carol of the chimes, the sound of children's voices, the smile of the poor little boy over the way — all this sweet music crept into Joel's heart that Christmas morning; yes, and with these sweet, holy influences came others so subtile and divine that, in its silent communion with them, Joel's heart cried out amen and amen to the glory of the Christmas time.

✿

The Lonesome Little Shoe

✿

THE LONESOME LITTLE SHOE

THE clock was in ill humor; so was the vase. It was all on account of the little shoe that had been placed on the mantelpiece that day, and had done nothing but sigh dolorously all the afternoon and evening.

"Look you here, neighbor," quoth the clock, in petulant tones, "you are sadly mistaken if you think you will be permitted to disturb our peace and harmony with your constant sighs and groans. If you are ill, pray let us know; otherwise, have done with your manifestations of distress."

"Possibly you do not know what befell the melancholy plaque that intruded his presence upon us last week," said the vase. "We pitched him off the mantelpiece, and he was shattered into a thousand bits."

The little shoe gave a dreadful shudder.

It could not help thinking it had fallen among inhospitable neighbors. It began to cry. The brass candlestick took pity on the sobbing thing, and declared with some show of temper that the little shoe should not be imposed on.

"Now tell us why you are so full of sadness," said the brass candlestick.

"I do not know how to explain," whimpered the little shoe. "You see I am quite a young thing, albeit I have a rusty appearance and there is a hole in my toes and my heel is badly run over. I feel so lonesome and friendless and sort of neglected-like, that it seems as if there were nothing for me to do but sigh and grieve and weep all day long."

"Sighing and weeping do no good," remarked the vase, philosophically.

"I know that very well," replied the little shoe; "but once I was so happy that my present lonesome lot oppresses me all the more grievously."

"You say you once were happy — pray tell us all about it," demanded the brass candlestick.

The vase was eager to hear the little shoe's story, and even the proud, haughty clock expressed a willingness to listen. The match-box came from the other end of the mantel-piece, and the pen-wiper, the paper-cutter, and the cigar-case gathered around the little shoe, and urged it to proceed with its narrative.

"The first thing I can remember in my short life," said the little shoe, "was being taken from a large box in which there were many of my kind thrown together in great confusion. I found myself tied with a slender cord to a little mate, a shoe so very like me that you could not have told us apart. We two were taken and put in a large window in the midst of many grown-up shoes, and we had nothing to do but gaze out of the window all day long into the wide, busy street. That was a very pleasant life. Sometimes the sunbeams would dance through the window-panes and play at hide-and-seek all over me and my little mate; they would kiss and caress us, and we learned to love them very much — they were so warm and gentle and merrisome. Sometimes the rain-

drops would patter against the window-panes, singing wild songs to us, and clamoring to break through and destroy us with their eagerness. When night came, we could see stars away up in the dark sky winking at us, and very often the old mother moon stole out from behind a cloud to give us a kindly smile. The wind used to sing us lullabies, and in one corner of our window there was a little open space where the mice gave a grand ball every night to the music of the crickets and a blind frog. Altogether we had a merry time."

"I 'd have liked it all but the wind," said the brass candlestick. "I don't know why it is, but I 'm dreadfully put out by the horrid old wind!"

"Many people," continued the little shoe, "used to stop and look in at the window, and I believe my little mate and I were admired more than any of our larger and more pretentious companions. I can remember there was a pair of red-top boots that was exceedingly jealous of us. But that did not last long, for one day a very sweet lady came and peered in at the window and smiled

very joyously when she saw me and my little mate. Then I remember we were taken from the window, and the lady held us in her hands and examined us very closely, and measured our various dimensions with a string, and finally, I remember, she said she would carry us home. We did not know what that meant, only we realized that we would never live in the shop window again, and we were loath to be separated from the sunbeams and the mice and the other friends that had been so kind to us."

"What a droll little shoe!" exclaimed the vase. Whereupon the clock frowned and ticked a warning to the vase not to interrupt the little shoe in the midst of its diverting narrative.

"It is not necessary for me to tell you how we were wrapped in paper and carried a weary distance," said the little shoe; "it is sufficient to my purpose to say that, after what seemed to us an interminable journey and a cruel banging around, we were taken from the paper and found ourselves in a quiet, cozy room — yes, in this very apartment where we all are now! The sweet lady

held us in her lap, and at the sweet lady's
side stood a little child, gazing at us with
an expression of commingled astonishment,
admiration, and glee. We knew the little
child belonged to the sweet lady, and from
the talk we heard we knew that henceforth
the child was to be our little master."

As if some sudden anguish came upon it,
hushing its speech, the little shoe paused in
its narrative. The others said never a word.
Perhaps it was because they were beginning
to understand. The proud, haughty clock
seemed to be less imperious for the moment,
and its ticking was softer and more rever-
ential.

"From that time," resumed the little shoe,
" our little master and we were inseparable
during all the happy day. We played and
danced with him and wandered everywhere
through the grass, over the carpets, down
the yard, up the street — ay, everywhere our
little master went, we went too, sharing
his pretty antics and making music everywhere. Then, when evening came and little
master was put to sleep, in yonder crib, we
were set on the warm carpet near his bed

where we could watch him while he slept, and bid him good-morrow when the morning came. Those were pleasant nights, too, for no sooner had little master fallen asleep than the fairies came trooping through the keyholes and fluttering down the chimney to dance over his eyes all night long, giving him happy dreams, and filling his baby ears with sweetest music."

"What a curious conceit!" said the pen-wiper.

"And is it true that fairies dance on children's eyelids at night?" asked the paper-cutter.

"Certainly," the clock chimed in, "and they sing very pretty lullabies and very cunning operettas, too. I myself have seen and heard them."

"I should like to hear a fairy operetta," suggested the pen-wiper.

"I remember one the fairies sang my little master as they danced over his eyelids," said the little shoe, "and I will repeat it if you wish."

"Nothing would please me more," said the pen-wiper.

"Then you must know," said the little shoe, "that, as soon as my master fell asleep, the fairies would make their appearance, led by their queen, a most beautiful and amiable little lady no bigger than a cambric needle. Assembling on the pillow of the crib, they would order their minstrels and orchestra to seat themselves on little master's forehead. The minstrels invariably were the cricket, the flea, the katydid, and the gnat, while the orchestra consisted of mosquitos, bumblebees, and wasps. Once in a great while, on very important occasions, the fairies would bring the old blind hop-toad down the chimney and set him on the window-sill, where he would discourse droll ditties to the infinite delight of his hearers. But on ordinary occasions, the fairy queen, whose name was Taffie, would lead the performance in these pleasing words, sung to a very dulcet air:

AN INVITATION TO SLEEP

Little eyelids, cease your winking;
Little orbs, forget to beam;
Little soul, to slumber sinking,
Let the fairies rule your dream.

Breezes, through the lattice sweeping,
    Sing their lullabies the while—
And a star-ray, softly creeping
    To thy bedside, woos thy smile.
But no song nor ray entrancing
    Can allure thee from the spell
Of the tiny fairies dancing
    O'er the eyes they love so well.
See, we come in countless number—
    I, their queen, and all my court—
Haste, my precious one, to slumber
    Which invites our fairy sport.

"At the conclusion of this song Prince Whimwham, a tidy little gentleman fairy in pink silk small-clothes, approaching Queen Taffie and bowing graciously, would say:

Pray, lady, may I have the pleasure
Of leading you this stately measure?

To which her majesty would reply with equal graciousness in the affirmative. Then Prince Whimwham and Queen Taffie would take their places on one of my master's eyelids, and the other gentleman fairies and lady fairies would follow their example, till at last my master's face would seem to be

275

alive with these delightful little beings.
The mosquitos would blow a shrill blast
on their trumpets, the orchestra would
strike up, and then the festivities would
begin in earnest. How the bumblebees
would drone, how the wasps would buzz,
and how the mosquitos would blare! It
was a delightful harmony of weird sounds.
The strange little dancers floated hither and
thither over my master's baby face, as light
as thistledowns, and as graceful as the
slender plumes they wore in their hats and
bonnets. Presently they would weary of
dancing, and then the minstrels would be
commanded to entertain them. Invariably
the flea, who was a rattle-headed fellow,
would discourse some such incoherent song
as this:

COQUETRY

Tiddle-de-dumpty, tiddle-de-dee —
The spider courted the frisky flea ;
Tiddle-de-dumpty, tiddle-de-doo —
The flea ran off with the bugaboo!
" Oh, tiddle-de-dee! "
Said the frisky flea —

For what cared she
For the miseree
The spider knew,
When, tiddle-de-doo,
The flea ran off with the bugaboo!

Rumpty-tumpty, pimplety-pan —
The flubdub courted a catamaran
But timplety-topplety, timpity-tare —
The flubdub wedded the big blue bear!
The fun began
With a pimplety-pan
When the catamaran,
Tore up a man
And streaked the air
With his gore and hair
Because the flubdub wedded the bear!

"I remember with what dignity the fairy queen used to reprove the flea for his inane levity:

Nay, futile flea ; these verses you are making
Disturb the child — for, see, he is awaking!
Come, little cricket, sing your quaintest numbers,
And they, perchance, shall lull him back to slumbers.

"Upon this invitation the cricket, who is justly one of the most famous songsters

in the world, would get his pretty voice in tune and sing as follows:

THE CRICKET'S SONG

When all around from out the ground
   The little flowers are peeping,
And from the hills the merry rills
   With vernal songs are leaping,
I sing my song the whole day long
   In woodland, hedge, and thicket —
And sing it, too, the whole night through,
   For I 'm a merry cricket.

The children hear my chirrup clear
   As, in the woodland straying,
They gather flow'rs through summer hours —
   And then I hear them saying:
" Sing, sing away the livelong day,
   Glad songster of the thicket —
With your shrill mirth you gladden earth,
   You merry little cricket! "

When summer goes, and Christmas snows
   Are from the north returning,
I quit my lair and hasten where
   The old yule-log is burning.
And where at night the ruddy light
   Of that old log is flinging
A genial joy o'er girl and boy,
   There I resume my singing.

And, when they hear my chirrup clear,
  The children stop their playing —
With eager feet they haste to greet
  My welcome music, saying:
" The little thing has come to sing
  Of woodland, hedge, and thicket —
Of summer day and lambs at play —
  Oh, how we love the cricket! "

" This merry little song always seemed to
please everybody except the gnat.   The fairies appeared to regard the gnat as a pestifer-
ous insect, but a contemptuous pity led them
to call upon him for a recitation, which invariably was in the following strain:

THE FATE OF THE FLIMFLAM

A flimflam flopped from a fillamaloo,
  Where the pollywog pinkled so pale,
And the pipkin piped a petulant " pooh "
  To the garrulous gawp of the gale.
"Oh, woe to the swap of the sweeping swipe
  That booms on the bobbling bay! "
Snickered the snark to the snoozing snipe
  That lurked where the lamprey lay.

The gluglug glinked in the glimmering gloam,
  Where the buzbuz bumbled his bee —

When the flimflam flitted, all flecked with foam,
   From the sozzling and succulent sea.
"Oh, swither the swipe, with its sweltering
     sweep!"
   She swore as she swayed in a swoon,
And a doleful dank dumped over the deep,
   To the lay of the limpid loon!

"This was simply horrid, as you all will
allow. The queen and her fairy followers
were much relieved when the honest katydid narrated a pleasant moral in the form of
a ballad to this effect:

CONTENTMENT

Once on a time an old red hen
   Went strutting 'round with pompous clucks,
For she had little babies ten,
   A part of which were tiny ducks.
"'T is very rare that hens," said she,
   "Have baby ducks as well as chicks —
But I possess, as you can see,
   Of chickens four and ducklings six!"

A season later, this old hen
   Appeared, still cackling of her luck,
For, though she boasted babies ten,
   Not one among them was a duck!

"'T is well," she murmured, brooding o'er
   The little chicks of fleecy down —
" My babies now will stay ashore,
   And, consequently, cannot drown!"

The following spring the old red hen
   Clucked just as proudly as of yore —
But lo! her babes were ducklings ten,
   Instead of chickens, as before!
" 'T is better," said the old red hen,
   As she surveyed her waddling brood;
" A little water now and then
   Will surely do my darlings good!"

But oh! alas, how very sad!
   When gentle spring rolled round again
The eggs eventuated bad,
   And childless was the old red hen!
Yet patiently she bore her woe,
   And still she wore a cheerful air,
And said: " 'T is best these things are so,
   For babies are a dreadful care!"

I half suspect that many men,
   And many, many women, too,
Could learn a lesson from the hen
   With foliage of vermilion hue;
She ne'er presumed to take offence
   At any fate that might befall,
But meekly bowed to Providence —
   She was contented — that was all!

"Then the fairies would resume their dancing. Each little gentleman fairy would bow to his lady fairy and sing in the most musical of voices:

Sweet little fairy,
Tender and airy,
Come, let us dance on the good baby-eyes;
Merrily skipping,
Cheerily tripping,
Murmur we ever our soft lullabies.

"And then, as the rest danced, the fairy queen sang the following slumber-song, accompanied by the orchestra:

A FAIRY LULLABY

There are two stars in yonder steeps
That watch the baby while he sleeps.
But while the baby is awake
And singing gayly all day long,
The little stars their slumbers take
Lulled by the music of his song.
So sleep, dear tired baby, sleep
While little stars their vigils keep.

Beside his loving mother-sheep
A little lambkin is asleep;

What does he know of midnight gloom —
   He sleeps, and in his quiet dreams
He thinks he plucks the clover bloom
   And drinks at cooling, purling streams.
And those same stars the baby knows
Sing softly to the lamb's repose.

Sleep, little lamb; sleep, little child —
   The stars are dim — the night is wild ;
    But o'er the cot and o'er the lea
     A sleepless eye forever beams —
    A shepherd watches over thee
     In all thy little baby dreams;
The shepherd loves his tiny sheep —
Sleep, precious little lambkin, sleep!

"That is very pretty, indeed!" exclaimed the brass candlestick.

"So it is," replied the little shoe, "but you should hear it sung by the fairy queen!"

"Did the operetta end with that lullaby?" inquired the cigar-case.

"Oh, no," said the little shoe. "No sooner had the queen finished her lullaby than an old gran'ma fairy, wearing a quaint mob-cap and large spectacles, limped forward with her crutch and droned out a curious ballad, which seemed to be for the

special benefit of the boy and girl fairies, very many of whom were of the company. This ballad was as follows:

BALLAD OF THE JELLY-CAKE

A little boy whose name was Tim
  Once ate some jelly-cake for tea —
Which cake did not agree with him,
  As by the sequel you shall see.
" My darling child," his mother said,
  " Pray do not eat that jelly-cake,
For, after you have gone to bed,
  I fear 't will make your stomach ache!"
But foolish little Tim demurred
Unto his mother's warning word.

That night, while all the household slept,
  Tim felt an awful pain, and then
From out the dark a nightmare leapt
  And stood upon his abdomen!
" I cannot breathe!" the infant cried —
  "Oh, Mrs. Nightmare, pity take!"
" There is no mercy," she replied,
  " For boys who feast on jelly-cake!"
And so, despite the moans of Tim,
The cruel nightmare went for him.

At first, she 'd tickle Timmy's toes
  Or roughly smite his baby cheek —

284

And now she 'd rudely tweak his nose
   And other petty vengeance wreak;
And then, with hobnails in her shoes
   And her two horrid eyes aflame,
The mare proceeded to amuse
   Herself by prancing o'er his frame —
First to his throbbing brow, and then
Back to his little feet again.

At last, fantastic, wild, and weird,
   And clad in garments ghastly grim,
A scowling hoodoo band appeared
   And joined in worrying little Tim.
Each member of this hoodoo horde
   Surrounded Tim with fierce ado
And with long, cruel gimlets bored
   His aching system through and through,
And while they labored all night long
The nightmare neighed a dismal song.

Next morning, looking pale and wild,
   Poor little Tim emerged from bed —
" Good gracious ! what can ail the child ! "
   His agitated mother said.
" We live to learn," responded he,
   " And I have lived to learn to take
Plain bread and butter for my tea,
   And never, never, jelly-cake !
For when my hulk with pastry teems,
I must *expect* unpleasant dreams ! "

"Now you can imagine this ballad impressed the child fairies very deeply," continued the little shoe. "Whenever the gran'ma fairy sang it, the little fairies expressed great surprise that boys and girls ever should think of eating things which occasioned so much trouble. So the night was spent in singing and dancing, and our master would sleep as sweetly as you please. At last the lark — what a beautiful bird she is — would flutter against the window panes, and give the fairies warning in these words:

MORNING SONG

The eastern sky is streaked with red,
   The weary night is done,
And from his distant ocean bed
   Rolls up the morning sun.
The dew, like tiny silver beads
   Bespread o'er velvet green,
Is scattered on the wakeful meads
   By angel hands unseen.
"Good-morrow, robin in the trees!"
   The star-eyed daisy cries;
"Good-morrow," sings the morning breeze
   Unto the ruddy skies;
"Good-morrow, every living thing!"
   Kind Nature seems to say,

And all her works devoutly sing
    A hymn to birth of day,
    So, haste, without delay,
Haste, fairy friends, on silver wing,
    And to your homes away !

"But the fairies could never leave little master so unceremoniously. Before betaking themselves to their pretty homes under the rocks near the brook, they would address a parting song to his eyes, and this song they called a matin invocation:

TO A SLEEPING BABY'S EYES

And thou, twin orbs of love and joy !
    Unveil thy glories with the morn —
    Dear eyes, another day is born —
Awake, O little sleeping boy !
Bright are the summer morning skies,
    But in this quiet little room
    There broods a chill, oppressive gloom —
All for the brightness of thine eyes.
Without those radiant orbs of thine
    How dark this little world would be —
    This sweet home-world that worships thee —
So let their wondrous glories shine
On those who love their warmth and joy —
Awake, O sleeping little boy.

"So that ended the fairy operetta, did it?" inquired the match-box.

"Yes," said the little shoe, with a sigh of regret. "The fairies were such bewitching creatures, and they sang so sweetly, I could have wished they would never stop their antics and singing. But, alas! I fear I shall never see them again."

"What makes you think so?" asked the brass candlestick.

"I'm sure I can't tell," replied the little shoe; "only everything is so strange-like and so changed from what it used to be that I hardly know whether indeed I am still the same little shoe I used to be."

"Why, what can you mean?" queried the old clock, with a puzzled look on her face.

"I will try to tell you," said the little shoe. "You see, my mate and our master and I were great friends; as I have said, we roamed and frolicked around together all day, and at night my little mate and I watched at master's bedside while he slept. One day we three took a long ramble, away up the street and beyond where the houses were built, until we came into a beautiful green

field, where the grass was very tall and green, and where there were pretty flowers of every kind. Our little master talked to the flowers and they answered him, and we all had a merry time in the meadow that afternoon, I can tell you. 'Don't go away, little child,' cried the daisies, 'but stay and be our playfellow always.' A butterfly came and perched on our master's hand, and looked up and smiled, and said: 'I'm not afraid of *you*; you would n't hurt me, would you? A little mouse told us there was a thrush's nest in the bush yonder, and we hurried to see it. The lady thrush was singing her four babies to sleep. They were strange-looking babies, with their gaping mouths, bulbing eyes, and scant feathers! 'Do not wake them up,' protested the lady thrush. 'Go a little further on and you will come to the brook. I will join you presently.' So we went to the brook.''

''Oh, but I would have been afraid,'' suggested the pen-wiper.

''Afraid of the brook!'' cried the little shoe. ''Oh, no; what could be prettier than the brook! We heard it singing in the distance.

We called to it and it bade us welcome. How it smiled in the sunshine! How restless and furtive and nimble it was, yet full of merry prattling and noisy song. Our master was overjoyed. He had never seen the brook before; nor had *we,* for that matter. 'Let me cool your little feet,' said the brook, and, without replying, our master waded knee-deep into the brook. In an instant we were wet through — my mate and I; but how deliciously cool it was here in the brook, and how smooth and bright the pebbles were! One of the pebbles told me it had come many, many miles that day from its home in the hills where the brook was born."

"Pooh, I don't believe it," sneered the vase.

"Presently our master toddled back from out the brook," continued the little shoe, heedless of the vase's interruption, "and sat among the cowslips and buttercups on the bank. The brook sang on as merrily as before. 'Would you like to go sailing?' asked our master of my mate. 'Indeed I would,' replied my mate, and so our master pulled my mate from his little foot and set it afloat

upon the dancing waves of the brook. My
mate was not the least alarmed. It spun
around gayly several times at first and then
glided rapidly away. The butterfly hastened
and alighted upon the merry little craft.
'Where are you going?' I cried. 'I am
going down to the sea,' replied my little
mate, with laughter. 'And I am going to
marry the rose in the far-away south,' cried
the butterfly. 'But will you not come back?'
I cried. They answered me, but they were
so far away I could not hear them. It was
very distressing, and I grieved exceedingly.
Then, all at once, I discovered my little
master was asleep, fast asleep among the
cowslips and buttercups. I did not try to
wake him — only I felt very miserable, for I
was so cold and wet. Presently the lady
thrush came, as she had said she would.
'The child is asleep — he will be ill — I
must hasten to tell his mother,' she cried,
and away she flew."

"And was he sick?" asked the vase.

"I do not know," said the little shoe. "I
can remember it was late that evening when
the sweet lady and others came and took us

up and carried us back home, to this very room. Then I was pulled off very unceremoniously and thrown under my little master's bed, and I never saw my little master after that.

"How very strange!" exclaimed the match-safe.

"Very, very strange," repeated the shoe. "For many days and nights I lay under the crib all alone. I could hear my little master sighing and talking as if in a dream. Sometimes he spoke of me, and of the brook, and of my little mate dancing to the sea, and one night he breathed very loud and quick and he cried out and seemed to struggle, and then, all at once, he stopped, and I could hear the sweet lady weeping. But I remember all this very faintly. I was hoping the fairies would come back, but they never came.

"I remember," resumed the little shoe, after a solemn pause, "I remember how, after a long, long time, the sweet lady came and drew me from under the crib and held me in her lap and kissed me and wept over me. Then she put me in a dark, lonesome drawer, where there were dresses and stockings and the little hat my master used to

wear. There I lived, oh! such a weary time, and we talked — the dresses, the stockings, the hat, and I did — about our little master, and we wondered that he never came. And every little while the sweet lady would take us from the drawer and caress us, and we saw that she was pale and that her eyes were red with weeping."

"But has your little master never come back!" asked the old clock.

"Not yet," said the little shoe, "and that is why I am so very lonesome. Sometimes I think he has gone down to the sea in search of my little mate and that the two will come back together. But I do not understand it. The sweet lady took me from the drawer to-day and kissed me and set me here on the mantelpiece."

"You don't mean to say she kissed you?" cried the haughty vase, "you horrid little stumped-out shoe!"

"Indeed she did," insisted the lonesome little shoe, "and I know she loves me. But why she loves me and kisses me and weeps over me I do not know. It is all very strange. I do not understand it at all."

5131

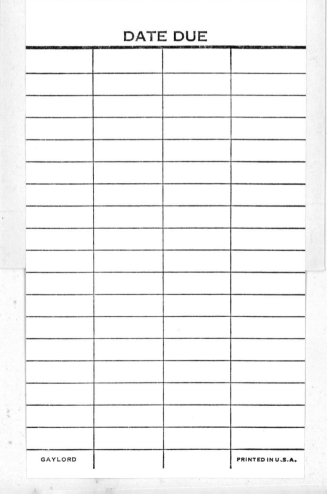

DATE DUE

GAYLORD			PRINTED IN U.S.A.

5131

THE WRITINGS IN PROSE AND VERSE OF EUGENE FIELD

THE HOLY CROSS AND OTHER TALES

CHARLES SCRIBNER'S
SONS ❦ NEW YORK ❦ 1897

THE WORKS OF
EUGENE FIELD

Vol. V

W9-BSY-523

and rode as proudly as before on the waters of the Sunda Strait.

"For Good Queen Bess I thank you, gentlemen," said Captain Drake. "I am proud of you." And he added, laughing merrily, "I am proud of Babok most of all!"

"Aye," said old Captain Judd. "The *Lady Anne* is more than a prize of war. She's an old friend of the sea that was lost and brought back again."

"That she is, sir," replied Captain Drake. "Tell me, Captain, would you like to take command of her? I can spare you half my crew to take her to Jacatra. Java and Kawi, too, shall go with you."

"I shall be proud, sir," answered Captain Judd, "to take command of so fine a ship."

"Very well," smiled the master of the *Golden Hind*. "Now come with me. The *Lady Anne* was not the only prize we won today."

Java, Kawi and Captain Judd followed him down to the cabin of the *Golden Hind*. A lantern, hung from the ceiling, lighted up the dim room, now filled with shadows by the setting sun.

There, in the middle of the cabin floor, stood Java's old iron-bound sea chest. Its heavy lid was thrown open. Almost to its top it was filled with a pile of gleaming gold. Doubloons, florins, guilders, moidores, pieces-of-eight—gold coins of every land—lay in a glowing yellow heap of treasure under the dim light of the lantern.

"There it is—a king's ransom," said Captain Drake.

"We took it from the pirate crew of the *Lady Anne*. Your old sea chest was badly battered, but I thought such a treasure belonged in it. Now what shall we do with all this gold, Java? It is yours. Do with it as you think best."

"Take it home to Good Queen Bess," answered Java promptly. "That is what my father would have done. Tell Queen Elizabeth it's to make England great, and say we send our love with it."

"Well spoken, my lad," said Captain Drake. He stood smiling under the lantern, his firm right hand resting gently on the golden hilt of his sword "It shall be done. May England ever be worthy of so rich a gift!"

XIV. The Wine Dealer's Shop

Together, one fine morning the *Golden Hind* and the *Lady Anne* sailed into the harbor of Jacatra. Seeing the little seaport again, Java's heart turned somersaults with joy. They were at home at last!

"What will you do now?" he asked old Captain Judd as they stood together on the quarter-deck of the *Lady Anne*. "Will you open your little shop again and sell wine, rope and anchors to the sailors from the Indian Ocean and the Sunda Sea?"

"No," replied Captain Judd. "I shall stay with the *Lady Anne* as long as she has no other master. I once thought my sailing days were over, but it seems not so. This voyage has brought me back to the sea again. I shall never be happy on land, now. I want tall masts and flying sails above me, and a swaying deck to stand on, and the sea wind blowing through the rigging like a song!"

"Aye," said Java. " 'Tis the life for me, too. But first

I want to find my father. Perhaps he is in Jacatra now. What will you do, Kawi?"

"I go home," Kawi answered simply.

"Come with me," said Java. "First we shall explore Jacatra together. Let's go ashore now."

"Take care," said Captain Judd, "and I shall expect you back before night falls."

Kawi said good-by to Captain Judd, and climbed down behind Java to the boat waiting beside the *Lady Anne*. As Captain Judd stood waving to them from her deck, they rowed across the harbor and up the river to the wharves of the little seaport. Landing, Java and Kawi walked swiftly into the town.

Along the narrow, shaded streets they went, looking at familiar sights. Jacatra had changed little since Java and Captain Judd had been taken from it by Old Blacksails and his pirate crew. Along the river that flowed like a canal through the town, were boats going up and down. Tall Arabs wearing white turbans on their heads, walked beside them in the streets. Dark-faced Turks in baggy trousers, each wearing a red fez for a cap, passed by. Chinese shopkeepers shuffled in and out of doorways. Hindus and Malays and huge black Negroes came and went. Sailors from every land strolled through the crowds in the narrow streets of Jacatra. Dutchmen with wide hats were everywhere, and Englishmen and Spaniards and Portuguese.

All that day, Java and Kawi wandered about the streets of Jacatra. They saw no sign of Java's father.

They asked about him in all the streets and shops. "Have you seen or heard of Admiral Fly?" they asked again and again. Men looked at them strangely, shook their heads, and turned away. Darkness fell over Jacatra, but still Java and Kawi went on searching and asking everyone, "Have you seen or heard of Admiral Fly?" And always the answers were strange looks and a mysterious silence.

"You had better go back to the *Lady Anne*," Kawi said at last. "I don't like the way people look at us. I shall get out of Jacatra and start my journey home. I live far in the heart of Java, and I should like to be on my way."

"Wait," advised Java. "There is one more person who might know where my father is. He is Hassan, the old Arab wine-dealer who had a little shop down by the river. I knew him when I lived here with Captain Judd. Come, let's go see him."

"I don't like the way people stare at us," Kawi repeated, shaking his head. "In the jungle I am never afraid, but here . . ."

Silently he followed Java down a dark, narrow street that led to the bank of the river. Beside a low wharf, black and deserted-looking beneath tall tamarind trees, stood a little shop. Java knocked long and loudly on the door, which was opened presently by old Hassan. Holding a lighted lantern high above his head, he let Java and Kawi in.

"Ah!" said Hassan with a smile. "It is you again!"

"Yes," laughed Java. "It is Old Blacksails and his pirate crew who are lost, not I. How are you, Hassan?"

"Oh," answered the old Arab, smiling, "I take what Allah gives me and make the best of it. Here, sit down and have some good red wine. What happened to you, Java, on your voyage? I know what happened to you here. All Jacatra knows of that."

"Gladly I will tell you," Java replied, "but no wine, thank you. We came here to ask some questions. Tell me, Hassan, have you seen or heard of Admiral Fly?"

As if he had not heard Java's question, the old Arab was looking sharply at Kawi. Suddenly he stood up and laid a brown hand on Java's shoulder.

"Come with me a moment," he said in a low voice.

Java, wondering, followed Hassan through a narrow doorway into a little room in the rear of the shop. There, among huge casks of wine, he waited for Hassan to speak. The old Arab's gaunt face had a strange look in the dim light of the lanterns.

"That boy who came with you," said Hassan slowly, "do you know who he is?"

"Aye," said Java. "His name is Kawi. Captain Judd and I found him on the island where we were shipwrecked. Why do you ask me this?"

"Did he not tell you how he came to be on that island?" asked Hassan.

Java thought a moment. "Why, no," he said. "That is, he did tell me something about being taken there by pirates. I thought it no stranger than what happened to me. Tell me, what do you know of this?"

"Only this," said Hassan, "that his name is not Kawi. It is Babok."

Java suddenly burst out laughing. "Hassan, what is all this?" he cried. "Are we all not what we seem? Perhaps I am not Java and you are not Hassan, and now it seems that Kawi's buffalo has the name that belongs to Kawi!"

Wise-looking old Hassan smiled and his dark eyes burned with a dull glow. "Even the name of Jacatra will be changed some day," he said. "All we really know of the world is that it, too, will change as time goes on. Only the sun, the moon, and the stars remain as they are because the hand of man cannot reach where Allah has placed eternal things."

"But what of Kawi?" asked Java. "Let his name be Babok. Isn't that a good name?"

"Indeed it is," replied the old Arab. "It is the name of a prince who will one day be the Sultan of Metaram."

"Hassan!" cried Java. "Then that is why he was kidnapped by pirates, and why the Shark would not let him go! But he is safe now. Now he can go home."

"I am not so certain of that," said Hassan. "And even if he does go home, I fear you will be blamed for his disappearance. The Sultan, his father, has many loyal subjects in Jacatra and they hate the white men as much as he does. Your life will not be safe here. Get out of Jacatra tonight. Sail away, my friend, and never come back to this evil place!"

"But I cannot do that," Java protested. "I cannot leave Jacatra now!"

The old Arab stood shaking his head sadly. The light went out of his fierce, dark eyes. His gaunt face was paler brown as he stared down at the floor of the dim little room. He leaned against a huge cask of wine as if he felt weak and old and tired.

"I know, my friend," he said at last. "I have kept your secret well. Your father should have left you in my care. Now I fear it is too late."

"Then you know where he is!" cried Java. "Tell me, Hassan, where is my father? What has become of Admiral Fly?"

Hassan did not reply for a moment. "That I do not know," he admitted at length. "I hear countless stories of him, but I know not which is true. Some say he was killed in a dark street of Jacatra. Others say he was captured by Zulu pirates and sold into slavery in Sumatra. I hear, too, that he was drowned in the sea when his ship went down in a typhoon off the coast of Japan. Again I was told he had become a pirate who robbed the Spanish galleons carrying gold and silver from the mines of Peru across the Caribbean Sea. I know not where he really is, whether alive or dead. Jacatra is full of strange men from the ends of the earth, bearing wild tales that are hard to believe."

"I must find him," said Java. "I shall not leave this place until I do."

"Very well," Hassan agreed with a shake of his head.

"Then you shall stay with me. Here, at least, you can hide if danger comes too close on your heels. Come with me."

The old Arab blew out the light in the lantern. He fell on his knees on the floor. In the pitch darkness of the room Java heard a creaking of iron hinges and a dull thud. Looking down in surprise, he saw faintly in a half-light from below, an open trapdoor. From it a ladder led down to a boat that lay floating on the river beneath Hassan's wine shop. Quickly the old Arab closed the trapdoor without a sound.

"Now," said Hassan quietly in the dark room, "stay here tonight, and every night. Go out only by daylight, and in disguise. I will dress you up as an Arab boy, and stain your skin as brown as mine. You must learn to speak my language, or at least enough of it to reply in Arabic when you are spoken to. You must carry a dagger and know how to use it if someone should leap upon you from a doorway. Now come with me and say good-by to your friend. Kawi, or Babok as his real name is, may not know it but he is leaving Jacatra tonight. His father, the Sultan, has enemies here as well as friends, and I would not have his son come to an evil end in my house."

"Do you think we were followed here?" asked Java breathlessly as he followed Hassan out of the dark room filled with casks of wine.

"May Allah protect me," muttered old Hassan, "I only hope you were not!"

They went through the door into the front room of the shop. There Java and the old Arab stopped suddenly and stared at the chair where Kawi had sat. He was gone. The door of the wine dealer's shop was flung open wide. In a warm breeze from the river, the lighted lantern over Java's head cast a moving shadow on the floor.

XV. The Search for Kawi

Silently old Hassan went to the open door and closed it. He took down the lantern from its iron hook and blew out the yellow flame.

"Go," he said to Java across the darkened room of the wine shop. "Get back into that room among the casks of wine! Make no sound! Behind the wine casks there is a cot where you can sleep if you care to. Before dawn, if all is quiet, I shall come to you and paint your skin and dress you like an Arab boy. Now hide, quickly!"

Java felt his way into the little rear room of the wine dealer's shop. There, behind the huge casks of wine, he lay down on the cot in the darkness. He lay there a long while, listening to the gentle lapping of the river beneath the floor of the old shop.

He thought of Kawi. What had become of him? Had he run away or had someone taken him? Surely he would have cried out for help if his enemy had sprung upon him from the doorway. Then why had he run away? Perhaps he had left Jacatra this very night, and gone home to his father, the Sultan of Metaram, far in the interior of Java. But would he not have said good-by before he left? Yes, Java decided, Kawi would have said good-by. He would not have run off into the night without a word. Kawi and he were friends, and friends do not part without a last kind word.

Suddenly, thinking of Kawi, Java remembered Babok. Captain Drake's sailors had brought the buffalo ashore early that morning. They said they had left him in the little yard behind Captain Judd's old shop down near the wharves of the harbor. Java remembered now that Kawi had wanted to stop and see Babok as they passed by the shop coming into the town. And he had been surprised to see the old place still there, for he had thought that Old Blacksails' pirates had torn it down. He and Kawi had hurried past it without seeing Babok in the yard behind the shop. Could Kawi have gone to see his buffalo tonight to give him water and something to eat? Yes, surely that was it! That must be where Kawi had gone so suddenly. And perhaps he was there now, seeing that Babok was happy and comfortable for the night!

Java leaped up from the cot behind the wine casks, clambered up over them, and slipped down quietly to the floor of the room. He paused an instant, then lifted up the trapdoor. He went down the ladder, closing the heavy door in the floor above him. A moment later he was in the small boat moored under the wine dealer's shop. Drawing hard on the oars he shoved the boat out upon the dark, still water of the river.

Slowly, without a sound, the boat drifted down toward the harbor of Jacatra. Past low, black wharves and dark, silent houses it drifted on. All the little seaport town was asleep at this late hour. Far out in the harbor a few lights twinkled on ships that were anchored there. One of these ships, Java knew, must be the *Lady Anne* with Captain Judd waiting impatiently for him to return. The *Golden Hind* had sailed away that morning, which was now already yesterday.

Dawn was beginning to break when Java rowed the boat alongside the wharf where stood Captain Judd's old shop. Still it was too dark to see anything clearly. Java had to walk slowly, feeling his way, across the wharf that was piled with casks and boxes of cargo left there by the ships in the harbor. At last he came to the rear yard of the deserted shop.

In the gray light of dawn the little yard, too, was deserted. Babok was nowhere to be seen, and Kawi was not there. Only in one corner of the yard was a big puddle of mud where the buffalo had lain and rolled. The gate of the little yard was open.

Wondering, and with a heavy heart, Java stood staring at the deserted yard. Now it was light enough to see quite clearly. Suddenly he dropped on his knees beside the puddle of soft mud. There were tracks in it, and they were not the tracks of Babok or of Kawi.

Where else had he seen those tracks with their marks

of square-toed heavy sailors' boots that left the print of their high heels deep in the mud? Why, on the embankment of the fort he and Kawi and Captain Judd had built on Saturday Island! Java was sure of it, and he stood up quickly to look wildly around him. Those footprints were the tracks of the Shark!

From Captain Judd's old shop on the wharf, a narrow road led away into the jungle that surrounded Jacatra on three sides. Swiftly Java ran out along the road. Several times he paused to look down at the tracks of Babok and the Shark's footprints in the dust. Now he knew he was on their trail, and he decided to follow them wherever they might go.

All morning Java hurried along the narrow, dusty road that led away through the green jungle. Surely, he thought, they had not had enough time to get many miles ahead of him. And Babok would not go fast unless he were driven, and it seemed that only Kawi was riding him. The Shark would be too lazy to keep up a running pace for longer than a few hours.

The dusty road, leading ever higher and higher, into the interior of the great island of Java, became at last only a dim jungle trail. Still, Java, as he hurried along it under the hot tropic sun, could see the tracks of Babok and the Shark. On through the afternoon he followed the trail, though his feet were sore and he was so tired his bones ached. He hurried on through high valleys, across flat table-land, and between high volcanoes shaped like gray cones against the hot sky.

At last, as night fell like a dark, warm blanket over the jungle and the volcanoes, Java lay down under a salak tree to rest and to sleep. He was up at dawn, ate some wild fruits and melons, and hurried on along the dim jungle trail. Warm jungle rain fell on him in a roaring silver flood, but he walked on through it into sudden sunlight again. The rain washed away the tracks of Babok and the Shark. Still, Java felt that he was close behind them and would pick them up again. He was right, for just as the sun went down he came upon fresh tracks on the trail. That night he slept on the side of a great mountain shaped like a gray cone under the stars. From the peak of the volcano a thin column of smoke sailed upward into the moonlit air.

Next morning Java climbed slowly up the jungle trail, so tired he could scarcely drag his feet along. It was almost noon before he reached the great flat stretch of table-land above. Here he gazed with tired eyes across a vast level plain with scarcely a tree or blade of grass upon it. Far off on the level plain he saw what appeared to be a long low hill. In the distance it appeared as gray as the cones of the volcanoes. With limping steps Java walked toward it across the plain.

As he came closer to the long low hill he began to see that it was not a hill at all. It was a huge old stone temple, much like the one he and Kawi had discovered on Saturday Island. This one was not overgrown with jungle trees and vines, and its great stone statues stood high on terraces against the sky. Java guessed this must be one of those Hindu temples built a thousand years ago, about which Kawi had spoken.

There was no sign of life about the old temple. As Java drew near to it he could see that it was more than a mile long and hundreds of feet high. On the great terraces he could see the thousands of carved figures on the stones. Toward one of its narrow stone stairways the tracks of Babok and the Shark led across the level plain.

Suddenly, in the great shadow of the old temple, Java saw Babok standing. His gray hide was so much like the color of the stone and the shadow that Java was almost upon him before he saw him. Babok was gazing across the plain. Even when Java came near him he did not take his eyes off the flat horizon.

Java, too, stood gazing where Babok stared with such interest. Far away on the plain, almost out of sight, a dim figure moved. Before it disappeared in the white haze of heat, Java knew it was a man. So, he decided, the Shark had gone to play his last card in a long and desperate game. And Kawi must be here, imprisoned somewhere in this vast gray pile of stone!

Java suddenly forgot how tired he was. He began climbing up the great stone terraces of the old Hindu temple. Somewhere, up there, he believed Kawi was imprisoned in the carved walls. As he clambered up from one terrace to another, Java shouted Kawi's name with all his might. On each terrace he stood and listened for an answering voice. But when the echoes of his shouting died away, the old temple was as silent and mysterious as before.

Night was beginning to fall over the plain, but still Java climbed up and down the stone terraces of the temple. He ran along them shouting Kawi's name until his voice was hoarse and the echoes rang no more. At last, tired out he sat down on the highest terrace. He watched night settling over the land, waiting to gather strength to explore the ruined shrine on the very top of the old temple.

As he sat quietly there on the carved stone, he thought he heard a faint sound of tapping somewhere among the pile of broken pillars and huge blocks of gray rock that had once been the throne-room of the Hindu god. The great stone statue of Buddha himself sat squatting somewhere under that gray ruined pile. Java listened again, and again he heard the faint tapping among the stones.

He jumped up and crawled quickly over the ledge of rock behind him. He put his ear to the great block of stone that held up the ruins of the shrine. Again he heard the tapping, louder than before. Breathlessly he slipped in among the broken pillars and fallen rock and listened again. Now he heard the tapping quite clearly, right behind the stone he leaned against. In the fading light of the evening, Java looked wildly around for a stone small enough to roll away. Here lay a huge gray block of stone that must have weighed several tons. Desperate, not thinking for a minute that

Margaret Ayer—

he had the strength to move it, Java suddenly pushed against the stone with all his might.

To his surprise, the great gray rock slipped with a low rumble and rolled down over the highest terrace. It struck the one below and bounded over the edge. Down the side of the ancient Hindu temple the great stone went with a roar like thunder. It struck the last terrace with a crash that sent echoes clattering far across the surrounding plain.

"Kawi!" shouted Java into the black hole which the big stone had covered on the ruined shrine of Buddha.

"Here!" came Kawi's answer from the dark hole, and presently he came climbing up to clutch Java's hand. He looked instantly down the side of the temple. "I hope that big stone didn't land on top of Babok," he said. "You should have pushed it the other way!"

XVI. The Sultan of Metaram

On Babok's back once more, Java and Kawi rode across the great moonlit plain. All night they rode, and before morning came they had left the old Hindu temple far behind them. When the eastern sky turned to silver with the dawn, they were among the mountains and the green jungle far in the interior of Java.

"So you are the son of the Sultan of Metaram," Java had said when Kawi told him how he had gone to see Babok in Jacatra and found the Shark waiting there. "No wonder that rascal wanted to hold you for ransom. How much is he asking for your safe return?"

Kawi laughed. "Oh," he said, "my father, the Sultan, has twelve sons and I am only the youngest. When the Shark told me to write out the ransom note, I asked my father to pay him a hundred thousand Dutch guilders for my return and signed it 'Prince Babok' in big letters."

"That sounds like a lot of money. Did the Shark tell you to ask for that much?"

Kawi prodded Babok with his sharp-pointed stick to make the buffalo climb the steep mountain trail. He smiled, his dark eyes full of mischief.

"No," he admitted, "but the Shark will not get a single Dutch guilder anyway, so why not ask for a hundred thousand? When he arrives at my father's palace he will be thrown into a dungeon. On some feast day, before the royal court, he will be given a dagger and thrown into a cage with a tiger. If he kills the tiger the palace guards will run him through with their spears. The Shark knows nothing of the customs of my country, or he would not walk so boldly into a trap."

"Are all prisoners treated like this by the Sultan of Metaram?" asked Java. "It doesn't seem quite fair."

"Why isn't it fair?" Kawi wanted to know. "It is an old custom of my country, and no one has ever asked whether it is right or wrong."

"If I were the Sultan of Metaram," said Java, "I would set the prisoner free if he killed the tiger."

"Would you set the tiger free if he killed the prisoner?" asked Kawi.

"No," Java replied. "Tigers are different."

"That doesn't seem quite fair either," laughed Kawi.

The jungle trail now led up a long green valley. Westward, far away, Java could see the gray cones of the volcanoes. The long valley was flooded with the high morning sunlight. Through it ran a deep stream of mountain water that sparkled as it splashed down over jagged black stones.

"The palace of the Sultan is just beyond that turn in the valley," Kawi said, pointing ahead with a small brown hand. "I hope my father will not be too busy to give us a royal welcome."

"Is he always busy?" asked Java.

"Nearly always," Kawi said. "When I was home I hardly ever saw him. He has a hundred wives and they are always quarreling, and he has to keep them quiet. Then there are always rebellions breaking out among his subjects. The other sultans of Java are always trying to take away his richest lands. He fears the Dutch and the English and the Portuguese. Most of all he fears the Zulu pirates who are always carrying away his subjects and selling them into slavery. All these things keep my father very busy."

Suddenly, at the turn of the long green valley, Java and Kawi saw before them the great white palace of the Sultan of Metaram. Its domes and tall towers gleamed in the sunlight. It stood among wide gardens of flowers and waving palms. All around it ran a moat; and as they rode nearer, the boys could see that its shallow water was swarming with hundreds of crocodiles.

"How do we enter the palace?" asked Java as he slipped off Babok's back beside the moat.

"Come with me," directed Kawi, "and say nothing."

Java followed him under an arbor so thick with vines overhead that no sunlight came through. At the end of the arbor, before a low stone arch that seemed like the entrance to a tunnel, stood a tall palace guard. He was armed with a heavy sword which he swung slowly back and forth as he stood before the arch. Kawi spoke a few words to him in the Javanese dialect that Java supposed was the language of Metaram. The big guard bowed low and stepped aside.

Together Java and Kawi walked through the dark tunnel that led under the moat. They climbed a flight of stone steps and came out through a door into one of the outer halls of the palace. Following the long hall to the end, they climbed up a winding stairway to a tiny room in the top of the highest tower. The room was round, with narrow windows on all sides, and richly furnished.

"This room is mine," declared Kawi, and he stretched himself out on the thick red carpet that covered the floor. "Do you like it?"

"Yes," said Java. "Now what do we do?"

"We sleep," Kawi replied, and he suddenly yawned. "Lie down. Rest. I'm tired."

Java lay down on the low divan at one side of the little room. He gazed up at the arched, pink ceiling.

"Kawi," he asked presently, "how would you ever have escaped from that old Hindu temple if I hadn't found you there?"

"I don't know," answered Kawi sleepily. "Thank

Margaret Ayer—

you for finding me. Now don't talk to me. I'm asleep."

Java and Kawi were awakened by a loud knocking on the little red door of the room in the tower. Kawi opened it. There stood a palace guard who bowed low and addressed Kawi:

"Prince Babok, Sire, the Sultan, your father, wishes to speak with you."

Kawi closed the door and walked across the room to a closet in the wall beside the divan. He took out two rich purple suits of purest silk.

"Get dressed, quickly," he said to Java, handing him one of the suits. "My father never likes to be kept waiting. Besides, this is the second time he has ever asked to see me—once when I was a baby and now. The Sultan is a very busy man."

"Nobody should be as busy as that," laughed Java.

Dressed exactly alike in the rich, brightly colored clothes, Java and Kawi went down the winding stairway of the tower. Past the palace guards they went, along the vast central hall to the great doors, covered with beaten gold, that opened before them into the throne-room of the Sultan of Metaram.

The Sultan, a short little man who was bald and very fat, was sitting on a low divan before one of the great windows that looked out upon the palace gardens. Close beside him was a small round table of teakwood inlaid with ivory and mother-of-pearl, on which was a checker board. The black and red checkers were all placed on the squares, ready for a game. Under the table was a water-pipe with two long tubes, one of which the Sultan held in his small fat hand. He had just drawn a long breath upon it; and as Java and Kawi came in, he blew the blue smoke lazily out through his long nose.

"Ah, Babok," he said in a not-very-pleasant voice, "so here you are! Where have you been all this time? The servants and the palace guards have been in an uproar for months over you. I've got gray hairs and lost a lot of sleep worrying about you. The least you could have done was to let your poor mother know that you were not in trouble or up to any mischief as you went wandering around the empire. I have enough on my hands looking after my rebellious subjects without bothering to keep the royal household from going to the four winds. That is all, Babok. I am a very busy man."

"Thank you, Sire," said Kawi, and he turned to leave the throne-room.

"Wait one moment," the Sultan called after him. "Who is that with you? Is that another of my sons?"

"No, Sire," Kawi replied, smiling. "He is called Java. His father is Admiral Fly of the British Royal Navy."

"Ah!" exclaimed the Sultan, rising from the divan and smiling for the first time. Then with a sharp glance at Java he laid his fat right hand on Kawi's head. "What a misfortune for the Empire of Metaram," he said, "that you are not my first-born son. You have courage, Babok, and you have imagination. You are like me. Not your eldest brother, but you, should be the Sultan of Metaram after I am gone."

"Thank you, Sire," said Kawi.

"And Babok," the Sultan continued with a smile, "why did you send that rascal with an iron hook for a hand to ask me for a hundred thousand Dutch guilders? There is not that much money in the whole empire. My palace guards chased your wretched messenger into the jungle. I wonder that they didn't toss him into the moat for the crocodiles."

"Am I not worth a hundred thousand Dutch guilders?" asked Kawi.

The Sultan suddenly shook all over with laughter. He ran his fat fingers through Kawi's hair and pinched his cheeks.

"You have courage, my little Babok," he said again. "You have imagination. Ha-ha! I must see more of you. Now run along. I am very busy."

Outside the great golden doors of the Sultan's throne-room Kawi suddenly caught Java by the arm. His dark eyes flashed.

"You run up to my room in the tower," he said. "Wait for me there. I am going to get us something to eat."

Up the winding stairway, in the little round room in the highest tower, Java waited for Kawi to return. At last the red door opened and Kawi came running in with a big basket in his arms. He set it down on the red carpet and turned quickly to Java who was sitting on the low divan.

"I have news for you," he announced. "One of the palace guards told me your father is a prisoner here."

"What!" cried Java, leaping instantly to his feet. "Where is he? Can I see him? Kawi, are you sure of this?"

XVII. A Game of Checkers

"The palace guard who told me has never been known to lie," Kawi declared. "He says that Admiral Fly has been a prisoner in the palace for several months."

"Is he in the palace dungeon?" asked Java.

"No," Kawi said, "and that is what I cannot understand. He lives in one of the towers. Nobody seems to know which one he lives in, and only one of all the palace guards has ever seen him."

"Kawi," cried Java suddenly, "do you remember what you told me about prisoners being thrown into a cage with a tiger? Is that going to happen to my father?"

"Perhaps," replied Kawi thoughtfully. "The next feast day is not far off."

"Come," said Java. "I am going to see the Sultan!"

"He will be very angry if we disturb him again," protested Kawi. "He might throw both of us into the tiger's cage!"

"Come on!" cried Java. "The Sultan is not half so busy as he thinks he is!"

Down the winding stairway of the tower ran Java with Kawi close behind him. Together they raced along the great central hall of the palace. The guards before the great golden doors of the Sultan's throne-room tried to stop them, but Java and Kawi ran under their flashing spears. The golden doors burst open before them with a loud crash that rang through all the palace.

The two men seated at the small round table beside the divan sprang instantly to their feet. One of these was the Sultan, who began to shout excited orders at the palace guards. The other man, who stood huge and smiling before the great window, was Admiral Fly.

"What is the meaning of this?" the fat little Sultan shouted at Kawi. "Can't you see we are busy and cannot be disturbed?"

"Edmund!" exclaimed Java's father. "What on earth are *you* doing here?"

Java caught his breath, then said in a frightened voice, "I'm here to save you from being thrown into a cage with a tiger!"

Admiral Fly and the Sultan suddenly laughed aloud. They sat down again at the little round table and rolled in their chairs with laughter. Then the fat little Sultan of Metaram sat up straight and made one of the red checkers jump over the black ones all the way across the checker board. He stood up with an exceedingly pleased look on his face and rubbed his fat palms together.

"I've won," he said with a smile of triumph. "I've won a game!"

"So you have," Admiral Fly exclaimed softly. He, too, rose from the table. "That means I agree to chase the Zulu pirates from the coast of Java. In return you will grant my country the same rights to trade here as you gave the Dutch. Am I right, Sire? Shall we sign the contract?"

"Agreed," said the Sultan. He turned to Kawi, waving his arms excitedly. "Run along now," he shouted. "Can't you see I'm busy? I might have lost that game because of you!"

"Wait for me in the palace garden," Java's father said to him. "We are leaving for Jacatra this afternoon."

Java said good-by to Kawi in the great central hall of the palace, and they promised each other they would meet again some day. Still wearing the rich purple suit of purest silk which Kawi had given him, Java was led by a palace guard through the tunnel under the moat. He waited under the waving palms in the garden that surrounded the Sultan's gleaming palace. Sitting there in the cool shade, Java watched Babok rolling in the mud among the flowers that were like pieces of a broken rainbow.

It was here that his father found him when at last he came out through the underground entrance of the palace. He came into the garden, laughing so hard that the huge gold rings in his ears were shaking.

"That fat little Sultan is a rascal, Edmund," he said. "I'm sure he cheated me at checkers, and now he won't even provide a buffalo cart to take us home."

"Were you playing checkers with the Sultan all these months?" asked Java. "I thought you were a prisoner here."

"I was a prisoner," laughed Admiral Fly, "but I was in no danger. You see, I came here to get the Sultan to sign a paper saying he would let English ships come to trade along the coasts of Java. All would have gone well if I hadn't taught him how to play checkers. When I won every game he became angry, and would not sign any contract giving me what I wanted. He even threatened to have me thrown into the tiger's cage if I didn't let him win one game of checkers."

"Did he?" cried Java. "Is that why you let him win

a while ago? Wouldn't he let you leave the palace either?"

"No," Java's father said, smiling again, "he would not. Finally I promised him that if he won a game I would chase the Zulu pirates from the coasts of Java. He agreed, and in return said he would sign my contract. But he never would have won if you hadn't come bursting in on us. I forgot to watch him then, and I'm sure he cheated. Well, now tell me how you happen to be here. Were you tired of staying at Jacatra? Didn't old Captain Judd treat you well?"

"Aye," said Java, "he did. You see, I . . ."

"It's all right," laughed Admiral Fly, patting Java's curly brown hair. "Never mind telling me. I know it must have been tiresome and dull staying there in Jacatra so long. Tell me, is the *Lady Anne* still there? And how is our old friend, Captain Judd? I fear I frightened him badly that day I brought you to him, but I wanted him to keep you out of trouble. I am surprised that he let you come up here alone like this. Why, you might have been captured by pirates, Edmund!"

"I was," said Java in a small voice. But his father seemed not to hear him as they walked through the garden of the Sultan's palace.

The tropic sun was now setting over the long green valley and the gray cones of the volcanoes. As Java and his father left behind them the white and gleaming palace of the Sultan of Metaram, Java turned to see Kawi waving good-by to him from a window in the highest tower.

THE END